Frommer's®

North[ern] Italy

[...]mily

Published by:
Wiley Publishing, Inc.
111 River St.
Hoboken, NJ 07030-5774

ISBN: 978-0-470-05527-4

UK Publisher: Sally Smith
Executive Project Editor: Martin Tribe (Frommer's UK)
Development Editor: Donald Strachan
Content Editor: Hannah Clement (Frommer's UK)
Cartographer: Tim Lohnes
Photo Research: Jill Emeny (Frommer's UK)
Typesetting: Wiley Indianapolis Composition Services

For information on our other products and services or to obtain technical support, please contact our Customer Care Department within the U.S. at 800/762-2974, outside the U.S. at 317/572-3993 or fax 317/572-4002. Within the UK Tel. 01243 779777; Fax. 01243 775878.

Wiley also publishes its books in a variety of electronic formats. Some content that appears in print may not be available in electronic formats.

Printed and bound by Markono Print Media Pte Ltd

5 4 3 2 1

Contents

5 The Veneto & Friuli 151

6 Milan & Lombardy 193

7 Turin & Piedmont 249

8 Liguria: Genoa & the Italian Riviera 283

9 Appendix: Useful terms and Websites 327

About the authors

Nick Bruno is a freelance travel writer and journalist from North London. He has lived in Naples and Venice and spends lots of time in Italy visiting family and friends. After working as a tour guide, a translator and for an outdoor outfitter, peddling haversacks and breathable base layers to the masses, he swapped life in The Smoke for sunny Dundee and the love of a bad woman. **Shona Main** grew up in Shetland and, after moving to the mainland, spent her most informative years working on magazines for teenagers. Following short-lived and rather un-momentous careers in law and politics, she met Nick and returned to writing. She now lives a double life as social work lobbyist by day and contributor to newspapers and books by night. Both love to get away almost as much as they love to come back.

Acknowledgements

A massive thank-you to our editor Sally for her patience and faith in a couple of rookies. And to the copy editor Helen Heyes and everyone at John Wiley who worked on the book.

Thanks to...

Our Italian pals for their endless patience, never ending plates of pasta and answers to incessant questions. Thanks to all our chums back home for putting up with our moaning and lack of attendance at social events over summer/autumn 2006. Congratulations to Pat and Leanne – sorry for missing your wedding.

A very special thanks to Alan Richardson for being the biggest and best photographer, fellow traveller and new best friend. And as big a thank you to his loved ones – Paola, Laurie and Drew – for lending him to us for a fortnight.

Laurie Presswood, you're a delight! And Lady P and Sir Robin for making her that way. The Grimmond family for one of the best weekends in Venice ever. Steve Bell, Orietta and the baby dingers for their help with Genova. Dave Petrie, scourge of the Italian state and gentleman of Verona. Elena, Claudio and Annalisa for more help than they probably realised. La Marchesa Guerrieri Gonzaga for such kindness. And the APT office in Torino – the best in the country.

Ma Bruno for bailing us out of a sticky spot in Venice. The Eames and the Mains. La famiglia Bruno: Babbo, Anita, Barbara, il nonno Gennaro e la nonna, Anita. Dave and Black Salt.

Daniel Craig: sorry we couldn't hang around and be in your film but we had a book to write. Auto Grill – how you lifted our desperate hearts and filled our stomachs. Morricone and Luciano Bruno for the soundtrack. And finally, to Paul and Tony Baron, and Kinky John.

An additional note

Please be advised that travel information is subject to change at any time and this is especially true of prices. We therefore suggest that you write or call ahead for confirmation when making your travel plans. The authors, editors and publisher cannot be held responsible for experiences of readers while travelling. Your safety is important to us, however, so we encourage you to stay alert and be aware of your surroundings.

Star Ratings, Icons & Abbreviations

Hotels, restaurants and attraction listings in this guide have been ranked for quality, value, service, amenities and special features using a star-rating system. Hotels, restaurants, attractions, shopping and nightlife are rated on a scale of zero stars (recommended) to three (exceptional). In addition to the star rating system, we also use four feature icons that point you to the great deals, in-the-know advice and unique experiences. Throughout the book, look for:

FIND	Special finds – those places only insiders know about
MOMENT	Special moments – those experiences that memories are made of
VALUE	Great values – where to get the best deals
OVERRATED	Places or experiences not worth your time or money

A Note on Prices

Frommer's provides exact prices in each destination's local currency. As this book went to press, the rate of exchange was 1€ = £0.67. Rates of exchange are constantly in flux; for up-to-the minute information, consult a currency-conversion website such as www.oanda.com/convert/classic.

An Invitation to the Reader

In researching this book, we discovered my wonderful places – hotels, restaurants, shops and more. We're sure you'll find others. Please tell us about them, so we can share the information with your fellow travellers in upcoming editions. If you were disappointed with a recommendation, we'd love to know that too. Please write to;

Frommer's Northern Italy with Your Family, 1st Edition
John Wiley & Sons, Ltd
The Atrium
Southern Gate
Chichester
West Sussex, PO19 8SQ

Photo Credits

Front cover: © Nick Bruno; © Nick Bruno; © Alan Richardson Pix-AR.co.uk; © Alan Richardson Pix-AR.co.uk; © Alan Richardson Pix-AR.co.uk. Back cover: © Presswood Martin Kerr. p. i: Nick Bruno; p. iii: © Nick Bruno; p iii: © Alan Richardson Pix-AR.co.uk; p iii: © Alan Richardson Pix-AR.co.uk; p. iii: © Alan Richardson Pix-AR.co.uk; p. iv: Nick Bruno; p. iv: © Alan Richardson Pix-AR.co.uk; p. iv: © Alan Richardson Pix-AR.co.uk; p. iv: © Alan Richardson Pix-AR.co.uk; p. 1: © PCL; p. 4: © Alan Richardson Pix-AR.co.uk; p. 4: © PCL; p. 5: © Alan Richardson Pix-AR.co.uk; p. 6: © PCL; p. 6: © PCL; p. 7: © Alan Richardson Pix-AR.co.uk; p. 8: © Alan Richardson Pix-AR.co.uk; p. 8: © Photographic Archives Regione Piemonte; p. 9: © PCL; p. 11 © Nick Bruno; p. 49 © Nick Bruno; p. 52: © PCL; p. 54: © PCL; p. 55: © PCL; p. 59: © PCL; p. 62: © Alan Richardson Pix-AR.co.uk; p. 64: © Alan Richardson Pix-AR.co.uk; p. 65: © Alan Richardson Pix-AR.co.uk; p. 67: © Alan Richardson Pix-AR.co.uk; p. 71: © PCL; p. 74: © PCL; p. 76: © PCL; p. 78: © PCL; p. 81: © PCL; p. 86: © PCL; p. 88: © Alan Richardson Pix-AR.co.uk; p. 89: © Nick Bruno; p. 91: © Chris Fredriksson / Alamy; p. 95: © PCL; p. 99: © Nick Bruno; p. 102: © Nick Bruno; p. 103: © Nick Bruno; p. 107: © Nick Bruno; p. 119: © Nick Bruno; p. 121: © Nick Bruno; p. 126: © Nick Bruno; p. 127: © Nick Bruno; p. 128: © Nick Bruno; p. 130: © Nick Bruno; p. 132: © PCL; p. 133: © Nick Bruno; p. 137: © Nick Bruno; p. 141: © Nick Bruno; p. 151: © PCL; p. 154: © Alan Richardson Pix-AR.co.uk; p. 158: © PCL; p. 160: © Nick Bruno; p. 163: © PCL; p. 168: © Nick Bruno; p. 169: © Nick Bruno; p. 171: © Alan Richardson Pix-AR.co.uk; p. 174: © PCL; p. 177: © PCL; p. 179: © Nick Bruno; p. 182 © CuboImages srl / Alamy; p. 186: © Nick Bruno; p. 187: © Nick Bruno; p. 190: © Alan Richardson Pix-AR.co.uk; p. 193: © PCL; p. 197: © Alan Richardson Pix-AR.co.uk; p. 201: © Alan Richardson Pix-AR.co.uk; p. 206: © Alan Richardson Pix-AR.co.uk; p. 208: © PCL; p. 211: © PCL; p. 213: © PCL; p. 215: © Alan Richardson Pix-AR.co.uk; p. 217: © PCL; p. 220: © Alan Richardson Pix-AR.co.uk; p. 224: © Nick Bruno; p. 227: © PCL; p. 232: © Brian Hamilton / Alamy; p. 235: © Alan Richardson Pix-AR.co.uk; p. 236: © Alan Richardson Pix-AR.co.uk; p. 238: © Alan Richardson; p. 240: © gkphotography / Alamy; p. 241: © Alan Richardson Pix-AR.co.uk; p. 243: © Lugris / Alamy; p. 244: © Nick Bruno; p. 245: © Nick Bruno; p. 249: © Alan Richardson Pix-AR.co.uk; p. 251: © PCL; p. 254: © PCL; p. 257: © Alan Richardson Pix-AR.co.uk; p. 258: © CIS Archives (CIS - Centro Internazionale di Sindonologia di Torino); p. 262: © Photographic Archivies; p. 208: Musco Nazionale del Cinema; p. 263: © Photographic Archivies; p. 208: Museo Egizio;

p. 265: © Alan Richardson Pix-AR.co.uk; p. 269: © Alan Richardson Pix-AR.co.uk; p. 269: © Alan Richardson Pix-AR.co.uk; p. 275: © Alan Richardson Pix-AR.co.uk; p. 275: © PCL; p. 276: © Alan Richardson Pix-AR.co.uk; p. 283: © PCL; p. 289: © Alan Richardson Pix-AR.co.uk; p. 291: © PCL; p. 293: © PCL; p. 295: © Ray Roberts / Alamy; p. 296: © PCL; p. 298: © PCL; p. 303: © Alan Richardson Pix-AR.co.uk; p. 305: © Alan Richardson; p. Pix-AR.co.uk; p.308: © Alan Richardson Pix-AR.co.uk; p. 308: © TNT MAGAZINE / Alamy; p. 315: © Alan Richardson Pix-AR.co.uk; p. 316: © Fonoteca ENIT; p. 317: © Alan Richardson Pix-AR.co.uk; p. 322: © Fonoteca ENIT; p. 323: © Fonoteca ENIT; p. 327: © Nick Bruno

1 Family Highlights of Northern Italy

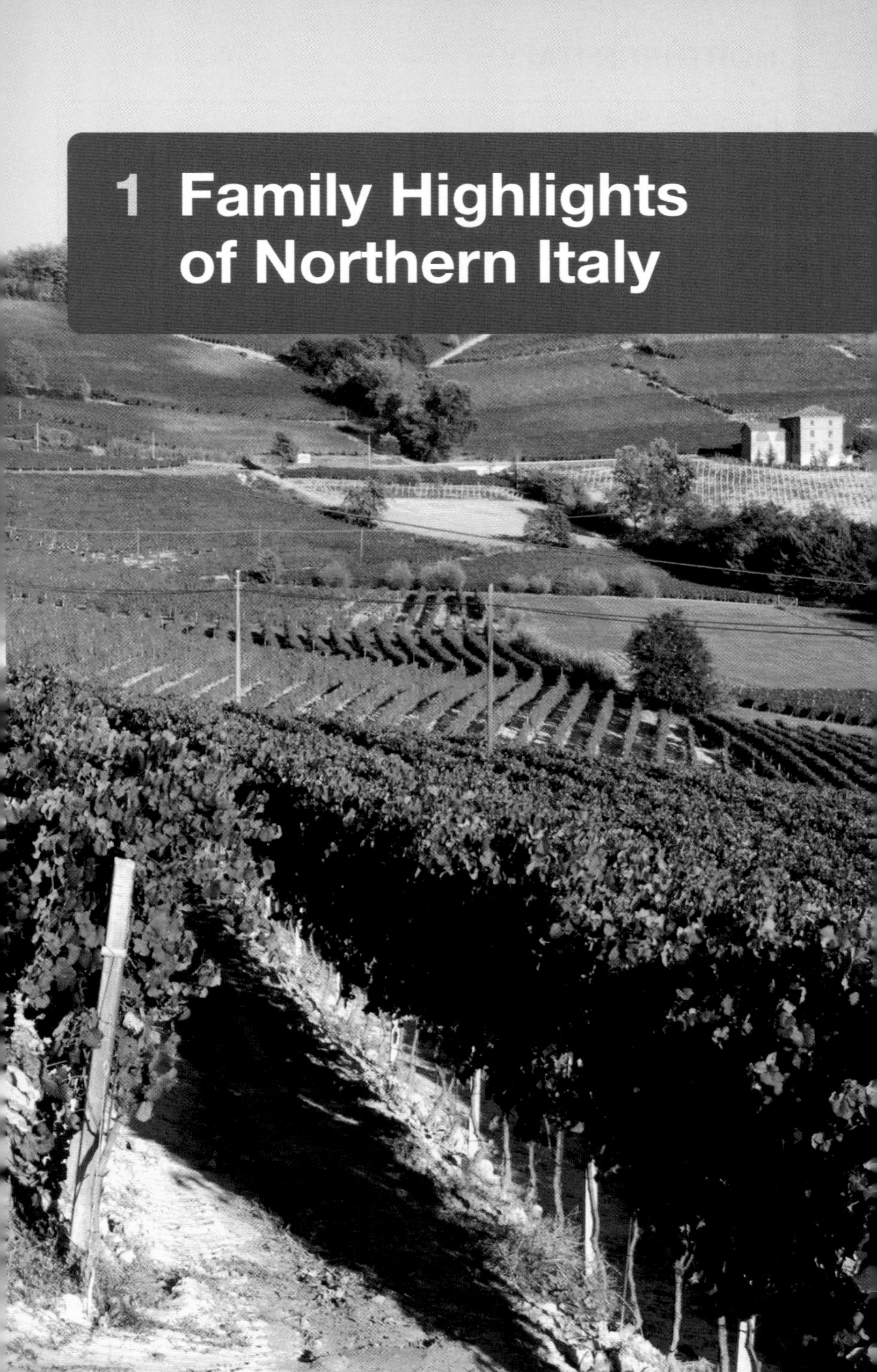

NORTHERN ITALY

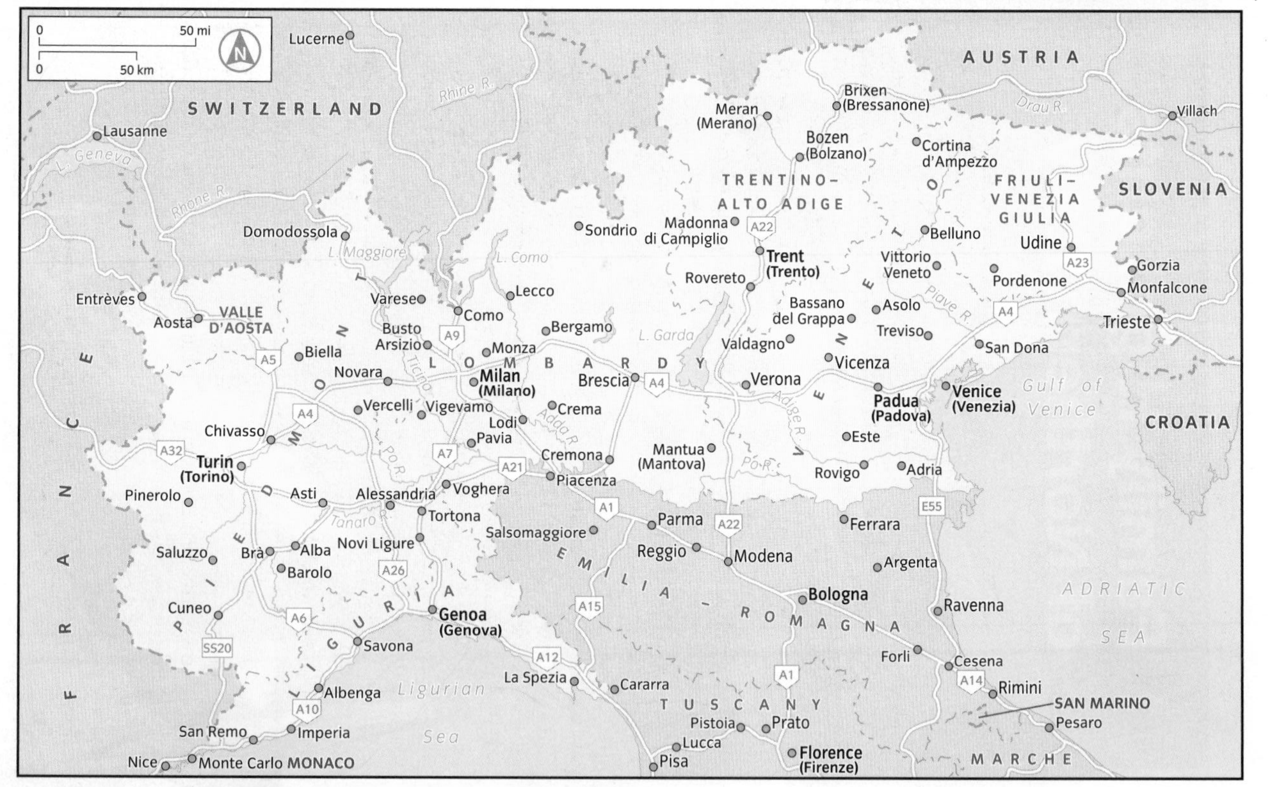

Few places in the world have the allure of Italy. We can't get enough of the food, culture, language or style. The great thing about a trip to Italy with children is that they'll already be won over by the thought of slurping fabulous gelati, saying *ciao* at every turn and wearing shades in all weathers. They'll naturally tune in to the flow of life with more ease than you'll adapt to driving on hair-raising Italian roads. Northerners are not as gregarious and animated as those down South, but they enjoy most of the trappings of *la dolce vita*. Just be prepared for some surprises – northern Italy does border the French, Germanic and Slavonic worlds after all. Accents can be unexpected, and it's not *all* pizza and pasta on the menu.

If you're concerned about the hassles of travelling as a family, don't be. The family remains central to life here. Some things may rile the Anglo Saxon nations (queuing is not the norm, for example) but they love bambini. Your children will feel genuinely welcome and you'll spot jovial youngsters at restaurants and festivals well into the evening. Indeed, travelling with children gives you elevated status – and the smaller they are, the more attention you'll get. That's not to say there are no frustrations for the unprepared, so we've tried to warn you about these along the way to ensure that all the family have a holiday packed with good memories.

As you'd expect in a book about Italy, there's a fair amount of art and architecture, but we've avoided exhaustive descriptions. We've tried to enliven the church and gallery experience for children by adding, hopefully, amusing facts, quizzes and the odd quirky tale. There are child-centred attractions that you won't find in other guidebooks, too. And we haven't forgotten the *al fresco* fun. Once you've escaped the traffic, eating outside is always a joy, so we've pointed out parks and piazzas suited to playing and relaxing, as well as fabulous produce markets and food shops ideal for mixing with locals and stocking up on picnic provisions.

A word of warning: Italy's cultural riches are being revamped constantly, which is a good thing but means that parts of many buildings are out of bounds and museum opening hours can change without notice. I'm afraid this is a country where chaos and caprice are taken to the most exalted levels. To avoid disappointment it's always a good idea to drop into the local tourist office or check their website. What we do know is that Vicenza's Basilica Palladiana is about to undergo long overdue restoration and, as always, some of Venice will be festooned in fancy tarpaulins and bureaucratic jargon detailing ongoing repair works.

Italy isn't just about the past, though. The North is famed for its industry, wealth and creative design: Turin's Olympic makeover continues, Genoa's Old Port has been reinvented (half-successfully), Milan adds annually to its canon of cool hangouts and Trieste is forging yet another new identity alongside its Slavonic neighbours. You won't be short of alternatives anywhere if your favourite church is shut for the summer.

For help in researching this book, we are indebted to our Italian friends who introduced us to some lesser-known parks, zoos, beaches and mountainsides, in some cases a little off the tourist trail but all well worth seeking out. Below we've chosen a few of the best family-friendly attractions in northern Italy to give you a taster. *Buon appetito*!

Una Vespa gialla a Bellagio

BEST FAMILY EXPERIENCES

***Traghetto* ride on the Grand Canal** (Venice) Avoid the overpriced tourist rides and take one of the gondolas that ferry locals across the Canale Grande. It's a bit wobbly at first, but crossing this watery trunk road is a real hoot. See p. 118.

Roman Arena, Verona

Whale Watching off the Ligurian Coast (Genoa) Get splashed by dolphins and whales in the WWF-protected seas aboard a state-of-the-art Whale Watch Liguria boat. See p. 299.

Riding Cable Cars over Mont Blanc (Courmayeur) Rise from Courmayeur in the Valle d'Aosta to 3000 m above the glaciers flanking Europe's tallest peak. It's a dizzying, breathtaking ride. See p. 54.

Opera in the Arena (Verona) As dramatic settings for a spectacular evening of opera go, the Roman Arena is second to none. Sets are colossal; casts are thousands strong. The season spans late June, July and August, and the Arena is open to all except children under 4. See p. 156.

Leonardo Museum, Milan

BEST FAMILY MUSEUMS & GALLERIES

Galleria dell'Accademia (Venice) The good and the great of Venetian painting, including all your Renaissance favourites, line the walls of this revered institution. See p. 122.

Museo Egizio & Galleria Sabauda (Turin) Children of all ages will enjoy being spooked by the Egyptian collection that includes mysterious mummies and statues. See p. 263.

Museo Archeologico dell'Alto Adige (Bolzano) Prepare to be transfixed by Ötzi, the remarkably preserved Stone Age ice-man found high in the Alps, at this high-tech museum. See p. 94.

Leonardo da Vinci National Museum of Science and Technology (Milan) With interactive exhibits based on the inventions of da Vinci and a captivating collection of gadgets, machinery and transport, this sprawling museum is great for children of all ages. See p. 213.

BEST HISTORICAL ATTRACTIONS FOR FAMILIES

Basilica di San Marco and Palazzo Ducale (Venice) The most lavishly adorned church in Europe and the most important

Basilica, San Marco

palace of the Venetian republic next door will blow you away.

Giotto's Scrovegni Chapel (Padua) Giotto's frescoes revolutionized Western art and continue to mesmerize with their vivid colours and emotional intensity. See p. 173.

Duomo (Milan) Preposterously intricate pinnacles on the jaw-dropping exterior and a cavernous interior make this Gothic behemoth one of Italy's most visited cathedrals. See p. 206.

Il Duomo, Milan

Basilica di Aquileia (Aquileia) This 11th century church has an atmospheric crypt with sublime 4th century Roman mosaics that will rock your world. See p. 182.

BEST FESTIVALS & EVENTS FOR FAMILIES

Voga Longa (Venice) This colourful and fun-filled 30-kilometre (19-mile) rowing 'race' from San Marco to Burano and back again, takes place in late May or early June. Grab a spot on the Canal Grande and watch the procession of vessels with hilariously dressed oarsmen. See p. 102

Carnevale (Venice) Buy masks for the children and join in the glammed-up pre-Lent festivities. It's all masked balls, gigs and

Masks for Carnevale

street parades for ten surreal days preceding Shrove Tuesday. See p. 100

Palio (Asti and Alba) The first Sunday in October brings medieval pageantry and a breakneck horse race to Asti's piazza, while Alba spoofs its neighbour with galloping asses in the Palio degli Asini two weeks later. See p. 273 and p. 274.

Calcio! Sample the passion and atmosphere of a *partita di calcio* at one of northern Italy's famous football stadia. As well as top dogs Internazionale, AC Milan and Juventus, there are many smaller clubs with more intimate grounds: try Sampdoria, Genoa, Trieste or Venezia.

BEST ATTRACTIONS FOR TODDLERS

Acquario di Genova (Genoa) Italy's best aquarium has 50 massive tanks with 20,000 sea creatures including seals, penguins and dolphins. See p. 44.

Parco Natura Viva (Lake Garda) Take your vehicle around the safari park to meet giraffes, lions, tigers, chimps, zebras, rhinos and hippos. The adjoining Parco Faunistico can be explored on foot and has Madagascan lemurs, snow leopards and red pandas. See p. 83.

Parco Zoo Punta Verde (Lignano Sabbiadoro) Little ones will enjoy going big game hunting in this lush park with native and exotic animals from alpacas to zebras. See p. 183.

Borgo e Rocca Medievale (Turin) This mock medieval village with artisan workshops, shops, dwellings and churches is a feast for the senses of tottering tots.

Quadrilatero d'Oro, Milan

BEST ATTRACTIONS FOR TEENAGERS

Shopping in Milan Teenage *fashionistas* should check out the designer label shops in the Quadrilatero d'Oro. Alternative types will enjoy the Navgli district's funky shops, cool cafesand flea markets. See p. 224.

Castello di Rivoli, Piedmont

National Film Museum (Turin) The striking Gotham-esque Mole Antonelliana has fabulous technicolour sets from historic blockbusters and a space-age great glass lift which accesses a viewing platform in the sky. See p. 261.

Castello di Rivoli (Piedmont) The skeletal remains of a former hunting lodge have been transformed into Italy's most bizarre and coolest contemporary art gallery. See p. 266.

Biennale d'Arte (Venice) Every two years from June to early November, the art world descends on the grand *giardini*, pavillions and cavernous Arsenale warehouses for an eclectic, edgy and always stimulating celebration of human expression. See p. 102.

Skiing in the Aosta Valley

BEST SPORTING ACTIVITIES FOR FAMILIES

Skiing There are lots of opportunities for winter sports, whether you're a beginner or a powder-hound, from the Valle d'Aosta on the French border to the Dolomites in the east. See p. 50 and p. 91.

Hiking in the National Parks Active families with older children should walk some of the countless hiking trails in northern Italy, especially those among the fishing villages of the Riviera di Levante. See p. 12.

Windsurfing Budding watersports enthusiasts can take to the waves off the Ligurian coast, or on one of the lakes, Garda, Como and Maggiore. See p. 306 and Chapter 3.

Climbing and 'Tarzaning' Older children can go rock climbing in the national parks, while younger adventurers can tackle a few awesome arboreal assault courses. See p. 64, p. 92, p. 96 and p. 305.

BEST WATERY ACTIVITIES

Whether it's on the Mediterranean Ligurian coast, the Adriatic sea beside the Veneto and Friuli, or in the cool waters of one of the lakes, there's aquatic fun aplenty for young and old, from paddling and swimming to windsurfing and inflatable-banana boating.

Boat Trips Take to the oars or let the engine do the work on the lakes or in the waters of the Adriatic or Med: waterborne jaunts off the Ligurian coast and in the Venetian lagoon open your eyes to a whole new marine world. **Be careful though:** go with someone experienced as boating on the seemingly serene lakes can be deadly. See p. 299 and p. 134.

Pools and Slides Bored with your hotel *piscina*? Visit one of the aquatic fun parks, which will keep you busy with twisting water slides, bubbly pools and fun inflatables.

Waterside Eating There's nothing quite like eating *al fresco* next to the ocean or deep lake waters. Grab some picnic snacks and cool refreshments and head to an idyllic spot and drink it all in. Sublime picnic spots include Portofino and the Roman villa at Sirmione. See p. 319 and p. 78.

2 Planning a Trip to Northern Italy

Family trips are always a gamble. It's a tricky job trying to please everyone, but the great thing about northern Italy is that the variety of scenery, attractions and activities gives you options. There are plenty of things to think about when travelling with children: this chapter will give you the essential information for planning an affordable, safe and fun family holiday.

THE REGIONS IN BRIEF

Italy was only unified in the 1860s. Before that it was a collection of regional states, many ruled by foreign dynasties. Regional differences remain strong and are still seen in separate dialects, customs and culinary traditions. Being so close to European neighbours, northern Italy's regions show more French and Germanic influences than in the South. You also won't quite find the warmth and hospitality of southern Italy; that exuberance, passion and playfulness we associate with Italians.

Lakes & Mountains

The roof of Italy cuts a broad arc of spectacular mountains, from the Alps in the Valle d'Aosta to the saw-toothed Dolomites in the east. Outdoor enthusiasts, skiers and nature lovers can enjoy their craggy challenges, winter runs and picnic-perfect meadows. The waters of these mountains empty into three celebrated lakes: Maggiore, Como and Garda.

Venice

The most serene city of canals and architectural wonders defies belief. Its handsome *palazzi* and churches may be threatened by floods and overrun with tourists, but *La Serenissima* is forever a city of dream-like wonders and mysteries. Marooned in its glorious past on muddy islands in a lagoon, it enthrals and frustrates in equal amounts.

The Veneto & Friuli

The flat floodplains of the Veneto are studded with handsome towns: pink-marbled Verona with its *Romeo and Juliet* connections; prosperous Vicenza and its Palladian villas; and Padua's Renaissance art treasures. Friuli-Venezia Giulia, the overlooked north-east corner of Italy, is an intriguing area with Slavonic and Germanic influences. Udine is charming and compact with a Venetian past and a youthful vibe, while the Adriatic port of Trieste has a mixed-up Austro-Hungarian history.

Milan & Lombardy

Lombardy is the industrial and financial powerhouse of Italy and Milan, its cosmopolitan capital, is famed for fashion, football and art. Much of the lakeside shores of Maggiore, Como and Garda are within its territory, as are the mountains in between. Renaissance splendours fill hilltop Bergamo, atmospheric Mantua, underrated Brescia and sweet-toothed Cremona. Towards Emilia-Romagna, the flat and foggy Po valley gives way to wetland nature reserves.

Turin & Piedmont

Piedmont means 'foot of the mountains' and its capital, the baroque city of Turin, is the gateway to the Alps, which rise to the peaks of Monte Bianco and the Matterhorn in the neighbouring region of Valle d'Aosta. The southern provinces of Le Langhe and Monferrato are renowned for gently rolling vine-covered hills, medieval villages and Slow Food.

Liguria & Genoa

The Italian Riviera is a narrow coastal strip backed by mountains, with the city and former maritime republic of Genoa at its centre. Families flock to the beaches of two contrasting coasts on either side of the old capital: the Riviera di Ponente has the largest resorts, while the Riviera di Levante has picturesque fishing villages and hiking trails.

VISITOR INFORMATION

Tourist Offices

A bit of web research before you go will help you to separate the durum wheat from the chaff. ENIT (Ente Nazionale Italiano per il Turismo) (1 Princes Street, London W1B 2AY ☎ Freephone *00800-0048-2542/0207-408-1254* (***www.italiantourism.com***) is a useful starting point. From there, visits to the provincial tourist boards and their websites (APTs: Aziende Provinciale per il Turismo) Liguria: ***www.turismoinliguria.it***

Piedmont: ***www.regione.piemonte.it***

Val d'Aosta: ***www.regione.vda.it***

Lombardy: ***www.regione.lombardia.it***

Trentino: ***www.trentino.to***

Sud Tirol: ***www.suedtirol.info***

Veneto: ***www.turismo.regione.veneto.it***

Friuli Venezia Giulia: ***www.turismo.fvg.it*** will help you get a better feel for what suits your time and circumstances. The local tourist boards have small information offices (Ufficio d'Informazione). These are good for a free local map, flyers and purchasing cumulative tickets, but don't bank on much more than that.

Advice For Family Travel

There are a number of websites giving advice to families travelling with children. For general advice about flying while pregnant, car seats and holiday first aid, try ***www.travelforkids.com; www.family-travel.co.uk; www.babygoes2.com***. For in-depth information on the main cities of northern Italy and a guide to books about Italy for children check out *www.travellingwithchildren.co.uk*.Guardian columnist Dea Birkett has an extremely useful Travelling with Kids Forum on her website, *www.deabirkett.com*. The Italian website *www.bambinopoli.it* has lots of useful listings for parents and even has a list of babysitters.

ENTRY REQUIREMENTS & CUSTOMS

Entry Requirements

EU and EEA (EU plus Iceland, Liechtenstein and Norway) nationals need only produce a valid passport or national identity card to be admitted to Italy. Either is acceptable. No visa is required. All other visitors must have a passport valid at least three months beyond the proposed stay. If you are a US, Canadian, UK, Irish, Australian or New Zealand citizen and, after entering, find you want to stay more than 90 days, you can apply for a permit for an extra 90 days. As a rule, this is granted immediately. Go to the nearest questura (police headquarters) or your home country's consulate. If your passport is lost or stolen, head to your consulate as soon as possible to arrange a replacement.

Obtaining Passports

Babies and children in the UK up to the age of 16 not already on a parent or guardian's passport now need their own child passport to travel abroad. These last for five years.

If your child is already on your passport, they can continue to travel with you in this way until they are 16, your passport runs out, or they get their own.

The Passport Service needs full documentation, including the child's birth certificate; either parent's birth certificate; and, if you and/or the child were born outside the UK or adopted, any naturalisation and registration documentation. The rules are more complicated for fathers applying for a child's passport as this hinges on the issue of parental responsibility. Recent legislation has allowed fathers who were not married to the child's mother at the time of their child's birth, but who jointly registered the birth (after 1/12/2003 in England and Wales; 15/4/2002 in Northern Ireland; and 4/5/2006 In Scotland) to apply for a child passport. Fathers who fall outside the new law must have been awarded parental responsibility by the court or by legal agreement; or the mother must give her formal consent to the passport application. In Ireland, as from 1/10/2004 all children regardless of age must have an individual passport in their own name.

Allow loads of time before your trip to apply – at least 6 weeks in advance of when you need it. It's worth leaving more time during busy periods like spring. Ensure you have completed the form correctly, included the correct documentation and, most importantly, followed the very strict rules relating to photographs. These can, and do, hold up applications.

For more information contact the **United Kingdom Passport Service** (☎ *0870-521-0410*; ***www.ukpa.gov.uk***) or the Irish Passport Office (☎ *00353-1671-1633*; ***www.foreignaffairs.gov.ie/services/passports***). You can pick up an application form for a standard passport at your nearest passport office, major post office or travel agency.

Customs

What You Can Take Into Italy

If you are bringing in tobacco products and alcoholic beverages for genuine personal use, there should be no problem. It might be worth noting that cigarettes and alcohol can both be bought very cheaply in Italian supermarkets – often cheaper than at the airport.

What You Can Bring Home From Italy

Citizens of the UK should contact HM Customs & Excise (☎ *0845-010-9000*; from outside the UK, ☎ *20-8929-0152*), or consult their website (***www.hmce.gov.uk***). The general rule is that all alcohol or tobacco must be for your own use and be transported by you. Irish citizens should contact Irish Customs & Excise (☎ *067-632-23* or the LoCall number ☎ *1890 666 333*; from outside Eire call ☎ *00353-1647-4444* or negotiate their website (***www.revenue.ie***).

MONEY

The currency in Italy is the **euro** (€). Withdrawing euros using your debit or credit card is easy. There are ATMs (*bancomat* in Italian) everywhere. But this is an expensive way to get your hands on your own money: you'll be charged commission plus a handling fee. It's therefore a good idea to take some cash with you. Some banks and travel agencies offer commission-free exchange, but shop around to find the best rates. If you are travelling from the UK the Post Office offers a great service, allowing you to order in person or online and pick up later (☎08457-223-344 (***www.postoffice.uk***).

Euros To The Pound

£1 = 1.48€ or 1€ = £0.67 (though it may have changed by the time you read this).

'Where is the nearest ATM?'

C'è un bancomat qui vicino? (Cheh oon ban-coh-mat, qwee vee-chee-noh)

Hopefully the answer will involve pointing!

TIP Keeping Copies of Everything

Before you go, make copies of your passport, traveller's cheques, credit cards (both sides), itinerary and airline tickets. Carry one copy with you and leave the other and your mobile number with someone back home.

For each of your credit and debit cards, copy down the emergency phone numbers and keep separately.

To convert the price of something in euros into pounds, just multiply by two-thirds. For example, a cappuccino that costs 3€ is roughly £2.

Traveller's Cheques

Less popular these days, but still useful if you want a mix and some extra security. Banks and travel agencies in the UK and Ireland provide them for a small fee. They can be cashed in Italian banks and by bigger hotels. Just remember that dealing with banks in Italy can be slow and bureaucratic. They also close for long lunches.

ATMs

Find out what your bank and credit card provider charge for international withdrawals, and their daily withdrawal limits. Italian banks don't charge for a withdrawal, but your home bank will impose a fee every time you use your card at a different bank's ATM, and that fee can be higher for international transactions. Your bank will also have its own exchange rate, which may be some way off those quoted in the newspapers.

You can also get cash advances on your credit card at an ATM. You will be charged a flat rate for cash withdrawals using your credit card (1%) and again suffer the costs of an unfriendly conversion rate.

Credit & Debit Card Safety & Security

If you intend to use your credit and debit cards abroad, it's wise to let your card providers know before you go. This means they won't become suspicious when they are used in an unusual location, and refuse a withdrawal. If your card is rejected, phone your provider.

It's wise to take more than one card with you. They have been known to get lost, stolen, swallowed up or just not work, so this saves disasters and exorbitant money transfers from home. Most *bancomats* in Italy offer a choice of languages.

It's a good idea to check out that the ATM has not been tampered with before you use your card. Look to see if a device has been placed into the card entry slot of a cash machine to capture card details. And cover your hand when typing your pin number. When using your credit or debit card in shops or restaurants, don't let it out of your sight. As a precaution use cash rather than your card in smaller shops or ones in less desirable neighbourhoods.

What To Do If Your Bag Or Wallet Is Lost Or Stolen

As soon as you discover your wallet is lost or stolen, contact your bank and/or card provider and report your loss at the nearest police station. Your credit card company or insurer may require a police report number. They may be able to send a cash advance immediately or deliver an emergency credit card within a day or two.

Keeping Costs Low

Travellers who remember Italy before the euro will recall a country that was very affordable to visit. However, the new currency's introduction was managed poorly and resulted in huge price rises. These inevitably were passed on to tourists. The north of Italy is as expensive as the UK with the exception of fresh produce, public transport and accommodation in rural areas.

INSIDER TIP

Remember to ask for children's discounts (sconto per bambini), especially in museums and galleries. Under 18s get free admittance to many museums and galleries. Children under a certain height travel free on trams and buses.

There is much you can do to keep costs down. *Supermercati* – supermarkets (Italian high-street favourites are Standa, Billa, Coop, De Spar, Conad, Sigma) – are great places to buy water, meat and cheese, snacks, nappies (avoid pharmacies for these) and anything else you would usually get in Boots. The main piazza or tourist hotspot in any city or town will always have the most expensive cappuccino, *gelato* and *panini*. Have a picnic instead if you're on a budget. The quality of the simplest foods makes it easy to eat well on the go. Fresh fruit and veg is easily bought from a market stall. See the relevant chapters for daily and weekly food markets and recommended delis.

Useful Credit Card Numbers

American Express ☎ 0845-456-6524 and reverse the charges

Barclaycard ☎ *+44 1604-230-230*

MasterCard ☎ *800-870-866* (this is an Italian number and doesn't need a code)

MBNA ☎ *+44 1244-672-111* and reverse the charges

Visa ☎ *800-819-014* (this is an Italian number and doesn't need a code) or reverse the charges to ☎ *+01 410-581-9994*

What Things Cost in Central Milan, Italy	€	(£)
Taxi from Malpensa Airport to city centre hotel	75	(50)
Bus from Malpensa to central station	6	(4)
Tram or bus ride (90 min. travel) – adult or child	1	(0.67)
Panino from café	4	(2.68)
Espresso standing at bar in café	0.8	(0.53)
Caffe latte sitting outside a café	4	(2.68)
500 ml bottle of water (take-away) from café	2	(1.34)
Two scoops of ice cream in a cone	1.50	(1)
Slice of pizza Margherita to take away	2	(1.34)
Pizza Margherita sitting down in pizzeria	6	(4)
Pack of nappies (*pannolini*) at supermarket	7	(4.69)
1 litre of ready mixed infant formula	3	(2)

WHEN TO GO

Italy is a fabulous destination all year – you don't really need good weather to enjoy a visit. However, if you want to see what the country has to offer rather than jostle with the crowds, avoid July and August (*le ferie*, Italians' holiday month). Not only are these months peak season (and so the priciest for hotels), but they are the hottest. Milan in 37 degrees with a couple of toddlers is no fun. Furthermore, many shops and restaurants close in August. Bewildered tourists wandering the streets looking disappointed and hungry isn't an uncommon sight.

The tyranny of school holidays makes you think this is the only time you can go. But is it? It's cheaper, cooler and less packed during Easter, half-term and, for Scottish families, the 'tattie holidays'. It can still be delightfully warm and sunny, but of course you won't have the guarantees that sunbathers want.

If there is any city that should come with a warning, it is Venice. It is unbearably busy and outrageously pricey from June to September. It can be a trial to visit then. February is *Carnevale* month: this can be expensive

Northern Italy's Average Daily Temperatures & Monthly Rainfall

Milan	Jan	Feb	Mar	Apr	May	June	July	Aug	Sept	Oct	Nov	Dec
Temp. (°F)	35	39	47	56	63	72	77	75	69	57	47	37
Temp. (°C)	2	4	8	13	17	22	25	24	21	14	8	3
Rainfall (in.)	0.7	1.2	4.2	0.8	3.3	0.9	3.6	2.8	3.9	7.7	5.6	4.0

Venice	Jan	Feb	Mar	Apr	May	June	July	Aug	Sept	Oct	Nov	Dec
Temp. (°F)	38	41	48	56	64	71	74	74	70	58	48	42
Temp. (°C)	3	5	9	13	18	22	23	23	21	14	9	6
Rainfall (in.)	1.8	1.8	2	1.6	3.2	2.6	2.8	1.7	2.4	3.4	3.1	2.4

and very busy. Throughout November until March it can suffer from aqua alta (high water), when walkways and wellies are the order of the day. This can be miserably wet or surreal fun depending on your point of view.

The winter months across the North can be bitterly cold, particularly in exposed or mountainous areas like Venice, Turin and Udine. But if its the white stuff you are after, the Valle d'Aosta and Dolomites easily compete with the Swiss and Austrian Alps for snowfall and piste action. Outside the ski resorts, a number of hotels close in winter. Check before you go.

CHILDREN'S FAVOURITE ITALIAN EVENTS

For an exhaustive list of events (manifestazioni) check out the Italian website *www.giraitalia.it*.

January

Epiphany Celebrations, nationwide All cities, towns and villages in Italy stage Roman Catholic Epiphany observances and Christmas fairs. From Christmas to 6th January *www.fieradisantorso.it*

Foire de Saint Ours, Aosta, Valle d'Aosta A coming-together of artisans from the mountain valleys to display their wares – often wood, lace, wool and wrought iron. Late January.

February

Carnevale, Venice Venice's Carnival evokes the final theatrical days of the Venetian Republic. The masked balls are by invitation, but cultural events, piazza performances and fireworks (on Shrove Tuesday) are open to everyone. From two Fridays before Shrove Tuesday to Shrove Tuesday. *www.carnivalofvenice.com*

March

Cartoomics, Milan This celebration of comics, cartoons and video games at the Fiera Milano in late March is a perennial hit with the ragazzi.(*02-499-773-79*. *www.fieramilano.com*.

Festival of Italian Popular Song, San Remo A poptastic festival where major artists and up-and-comers perform the latest Italian songs. Cheesy but a hoot. *www.festivalsanremo.com*

April

Good Friday and Easter Week, nationwide Processions and age-old ceremonies – some dating from pagan days, others from the Middle Ages. Beginning on the Thursday or Friday before Easter Sunday.

May

Voga Longa, Venice This 30-kilometre (19-mile) rowing race from San Marco to Burano and back keeps alive the centuries-old heritage of the regatta. The event is colourful and fun, drawing entries from around the world. For details, call ☎ *041-521-0544*; ***(www.vogalonga.com).***One Sunday in mid-May.

June

Regatta of the Great Maritime Republics Every year, the four medieval maritime republics of Italy celebrate their glorious past with a boat race that rotates between Venice, Amalfi, Genoa and Pisa. In 2008 it's Genoa's turn.

Biennale d'Arte, Venice From June to October, this is Europe's most prestigious – and controversial – non-commercial art exposition. It takes place in odd-numbered years only. See ***www.labiennale.org***.

Shakespearean Festival, Verona Ballet, drama and jazz performances of the Bard, with a few performances in English. From June to September. ☎ *045-807-7500* ***www.estateteatraleveronese.it***

July

Arena di Verona (Outdoor Opera Season) Families and culture vultures flock to the open-air, 20,000-seat Roman amphitheatre for perhaps the world's best outdoor operatic event. The season lasts from late June to August, for awesome productions of *Aïda* and others. ***See www.arena.it*** or phone ☎ *045-800-5151*.

Festa del Redentore (Feast of the Redeemer), Venice A bridge of boats from Guidecca's Chiesa del Redentore across to Le Zattere in Dorsoduro marks the 1576 lifting of the plague. It's one big floating *festa* until nightfall brings an awesome half-hour *spettacolo* of fireworks. Third Saturday and Sunday in July.

August

Venice International Film Festival This film extravaganza brings together the movers and shakers in the global industry. Films are shown day and night to an international jury and the public at the Palazzo del Cinema on the Lido and other outdoor venues around the city. Contact the tourist office or the Venice Film Festival ☎ *041 521-8711*; ***www.labiennale.org***. Two weeks in late August and early September.

September

Regata Storica, Grand Canal, Venice The cavalcade of gondolas and *gondolieri* in colourful livery proceeding along the Grand Canal should not be missed. You can buy grandstand tickets through the tourist office or arrive early and park yourselves near the Rialto Bridge for the best seats in town. First Sunday in September.

Calcio! The Football Season

The coolest thing a child can do in Italy is go and see an Italian football game. The season runs from late August to mid-May, with matches played on Sunday afternoons, or occasionally Saturday and Sunday evenings. European games are on Tuesday, Wednesday and Thursday evenings for a select few. The Italian League is split into four divisions: Serie A, B, C1 and C2. Each club has its own arrangements for selling tickets but, generally, it's easier than buying tickets for an English Premiership game. Some UK-based companies will put a footie trip together for you (0208-943-5378; ***www.soccerweekends.co.uk***). See the individual chapters for more information.

October

Sagra del Tartufo, Alba, Piedmont Forage for the world's most coveted fungus in the truffle capital of Italy, with contests, truffle-hound competitions and tastings. Two weeks in mid-October. ***www.fieradeltartufo.org***

Maratona (Marathon), Venice The marathon starts at Villa Pisani on the mainland, runs alongside the Brenta Canal and ends along the Zattere for a finish at the Basilica di Santa Maria della Salute on the tip of Dorsoduro. Usually last Sunday in October. ***www.venicemarathon.it***

November

Festa della Salute, Venice A pontoon bridge is erected across the Grand Canal to connect the churches of La Salute and Santa Maria del Giglio, commemorating Venice's delivery in 1630 from a plague that wiped out a third of the lagoon's population. 21st November.

December

La Scala Opera Season, Teatro alla Scala, Milan At the most famous opera house of them all, the season opens on 7th December, the feast day of Milan's patron St Ambrose, and runs into July. Though close to impossible to get opening-night tickets, it's worth a try. *02-861-778*; ***www.teatroallascala.org***.

Holidays

Offices and shops in Italy are closed on the following dates: **1st January** (New Year's Day), **6th January** (Epiphany or *La Befana*; Italian children's real Christmas Day), **Easter Sunday, Easter Monday, 25th April** (Liberation Day), **1st May** (Labour Day), **15th August** (Assumption of the Virgin, or *ferragosto*) **15th–30th August** (Italy's summer holidays – yes, the whole nation takes a break!), **1st November** (All Saints' Day), **8th December** (Feast of the Immaculate Conception), **25th December** (Christmas Day) and

26th December (Santo Stefano). Italians' Christmas holidays last from 24th December to 6th January.

Closures are also observed in the following cities on feast days honouring patron saints: Venice, **25th April** (St Mark); Genoa and Turin, **24th June** (St John the Baptist); Trieste, **3rd November** (St Just); and Milan, **7th December** (St Ambrose).

WHAT TO PACK

The seasons are fairly reliable in Italy, but if you are travelling at the cusps (April, May, September or October) or near the mountains, bring some cosy socks and jumpers.

If you plan to eat in more salubrious restaurants, men will need to bring a smart shirt and trousers but won't need a jacket (unless you're going for all-out posh). The Italian sun is strong, so hats for children – and anyone with a bald pate! – will save burns and grumbles.

Don't forget to bring travel adapters or you'll be very unpopular with young misses who want to straighten their hair.

A small first-aid kit is useful: bring sterile wipes, plasters, tweezers and tablets for tummy upsets, allergies and headaches. It could save you a lot of money and effort. Sun creams and anti-mosquito bite preparations are also easier to buy in the UK and Ireland.

Plug-in mosquito repellents (with enough tablets or liquid for your stay) are worth their weight in gold. If you're booking more than one room, bring one for each.

A bag with water, juice, snacks, hankies, wet wipes, nappies (if you need them) and sun cream will be invaluable. A collapsible cool-bag will be perfect for picnics.

A small oscillating fan might sound a bit unnecessary, but if you've ever tried to get kids off to sleep in a sweltering room with no air conditioning, this could be the holiday saver. You can pick these up for around 30€ (£20) in Italy or bring your own.

Packing for Planes & Cars

For A Plane Trip

Be sure to check both your children's and your own pockets and hand baggage for those objects which must be put in the hold: boy scouts' pocket knives, your favourite cuticle scissors, crochet hooks, etc. If these are not revealed until going though the security check, you'll never see them again.

When travelling with children, consider packing the following in your carry-on bag:

- The number of nappies your child wears in a day, plus an extra three.
- A changing mat.
- A minimal number of toys – a book, some crayons and a stuffed toy is plenty.

- Bottles for infants, an 'any-way-up cup' and snacks for toddlers

- A bag of tricks, for those moments where you have to pull something out of the bag. Perhaps an iPod, books or someone's favourite dinosaur.

For more advice on flying with children, see 'Getting There', below.

For A Car Trip

If you are hiring a car, enquire about reserving an age-appropriate child safety seat; most major rental agencies have these available for a small fee. (Avis, for example, charges £3 per day for safety or booster seats.)

Long-distance car travel with children presents a completely different packing challenge. Pack the following to help your trip go smoothly:

- Window shades for the sun.

- Talking books or your child's favourite music (your ears will become immune to McFly after the eighth listen, don't worry).

- Other items to consider include a first-aid kit, a box of wet wipes, blankets, plastic bags for motion sickness and a change of clothes. Always have a mobile phone in case of emergencies.

- The RAC website has a whole heap of car games you can download for free. See ***www.rac.co.uk/web/knowhow/going_on_a_journey/games***.

HEALTH, INSURANCE & SAFETY

Travel Insurance

Check your home and/or health insurance policies before you buy travel insurance to cover trip cancellation, lost luggage, medical expenses or car rentals. You may have partial or complete coverage. But if you need some, a simple search with MoneySupermarket (*0845-345-5708*; (***www.moneysupermarket.com***) allows you to compare benefits and prices. The good news is that such is the competition for your business, it's a buyer's market. You can get cover for all the family at a reasonable price. More dangerous activities are likely to be excluded from basic policies, but are you really going to be paragliding with the children? Always, *always* check the small print before you sign; more and more policies have built-in exclusions and restrictions that may leave you out in the cold if something does go awry. Protect yourself further by paying for the insurance with a credit card – by law, consumers can get their money back on goods and services not received if they report the loss within 60 days of their credit card statement.

The European Health Insurance Card (EHIC) (formerly an E111)

UK and Irish residents can obtain free or reduced cost medical treatment when temporarily visiting another EU country such as Italy, but you must have an EHIC to qualify. You can apply for your EHIC by picking up an application form from your local health centre or post office. In the UK, the Post Office charges a fee of £2, and your EHIC will be posted to you within 21 days. For more information see **www.ehic-card.com** or call *090-7707-8370*.

Whilst this covers medical care, it does not cover lost baggage, cancellation, the costs of accidents, repatriation or several other mishaps covered by insurance.

If You Or Your Child Have A Disability

When you book your flight, be sure to let the airline know if you or your child has mobility problems and will require assistance. Long-stay car parks can be a nightmare to negotiate, so it may be worth contacting the airport to see if they have any disabled long-stay spaces available.

All new public buildings in Italy are obliged to be accessible for the disabled. Older buildings may be less easy to get into and around, but you will see real efforts being made in some. More and more hotels are recognising the need to make things easier for customers with mobility problems. Contact them before you book. For help with booking accommodation contact Tourism For All (*0845-124-9971*; (**www.tourismforall.org.uk**).

For information, advice and links see the 'door to door' section of the Disabled Persons Transport Advisory Committee's website (**www.dptac.gov.uk**), the BBC's Ouch (**www.bbc.co.uk/ouch**) and the Disabled Parent's Network (**www.disabledparentsnetwork.org.uk**).

Before You Go

If you have any worries about your health go and see your doctor before you go. Similarly, if you have toothache, sort it out before you get on the plane: trips to a dentist are not conducive to a good holiday.

Find out if you or the children require any vaccinations or boosters before you travel. Pack prescription medicines in your carry-on luggage, and keep them in their original containers, with pharmacy labels. They won't make it through airport security otherwise. Also, bring copies of your prescriptions in case you lose your pills or run out. Italian pharmacies may fill them for you. Don't forget an extra pair of contact lenses or prescription glasses.

It is also a good idea to know the name and location of the hospital with accident and emergency facilities in your destination. These are called *emergenza*. They are easy to locate by Googling '*emergenza*' and the name of the place (using the Italian name, not the English version, i.e. Torino not Turin). When quick action is needed, having this information to hand could be priceless.

At The Farmacia

Most common medicines found in a chemist back home have an equivalent in the Italian *farmacia*. A handy painkiller for minor ailments, containing paracetamol, is *Tachipirina*. For a list of minor ailments in Italian, refer to Appendix A of this book.

What To Do If You Become Ill

If you are staying in a hotel, ask them if they can help you to find a doctor. In most cases, your EHIC will ensure you get treated swiftly. However, this does not exclude you from costs; it will just reduce them.

When you see the doctor, take the EHIC and any travel insurance documents with you. Be sure to ask for a receipt if you make any payment. You can use this receipt to make a claim on your return. If s/he gives you a prescription, ask for directions to the pharmacy.

If your illness, or that of you child, is so severe that you need to go straight to the hospital, again take both the EHIC and your insurance documents. If treatment is not an in–out operation, a call to your insurance company to flag your situation and possible claim will not go amiss.

Emergency Numbers

113 Police

112 Carabinieri (who also deal with crimes)

115 Fire department

118 Medical emergency

There's also a number for child protection, *114*, for children at risk.

Helpful Phrases In An Emergency

Aiuto! **help!** Ayee-oo-toh!

Puo aiutarmi, per favore? **Could you please help me?** Pwo ay-oo-tar-mee, peh-fah-voh-reh

Pronto soccorso **first aid** pron-toh soh-kor-soh

Ambulanza **ambulance** am-boo-lan-dza

Ospedale **hospital** oz-peh-dah-leh

Un medico **doctor** oon meh-dee-ko

Mi fa male qui **It hurts here** mee fah mah-leh kwee

Una ricevuta, per favore? **an invoice/receipt please** oona reech-eh-voo-tah...

C'e una farmacia qui vicino? **Is there a pharmacy near here?** Cheh oona farm-ah-chee-ah kwee vee-chee-noh

Al fuoco! **fire!** Al fwoh-ko

Ferma! Al ladro! **stop! thief!** Fur-mah! Al lah-droh

Staying Safe

Italy is a comparatively safe country. There are, of course, thieves like everywhere, so don't invite them to steal. Don't leave bags unattended in your hire car and take everything out of the boot at night. Exercise good sense when walking around: avoid unlit streets and ensure your wallet isn't easily accessible (or keep it in a money belt). Mobile phones and iPods are obvious targets, so keep these out of sight.

Legal Advice Whilst In Italy

If you find yourself in legal difficulty and need urgent advice relating to a criminal matter, contact your consulate in Milan without delay.

British Consulate at Via San Paolo 7 (☎ *02-230-01*)

Irish Honorary Consul at Piazza San Pietro in Gessate 2 (☎ *02-5518-8848*)

Australian Consulate at Via Borgogna 2 (☎ *02-777-041*)

Canadian Consulate at Via Pisani 19 (☎ *02-675-81*)

New Zealand Consulate at Via Arezzo 6 (☎ *02-4801-2544*)

US Consulate at Via Principe Amadeo 2/10 (☎ *02-290-351*)

If you need advice on a civil matter (breach of contract, personal injury, and so on) the Foreign and Commonwealth Office's website (*www.britishembassy.gov.uk*) has a list of accredited practitioners in Italy.

PLANNING YOUR TRIP ONLINE

Surfing For Airfares

easyJet.com and **Ryanair.com** offer the most extensive range of budget flights to northern Italy. Online travel agencies that sell air tickets are **Lastminute.com, Expedia.co.uk, Travelocity.co.uk** and **Opodo.co.uk**. Each has individual deals with airlines and may offer different fares for the same flights, so shop around. Travel agencies such

TIP Saving Money on Airfares

- **Book well in advance, stay over a Saturday night or fly midweek, to give** you a bigger chance of bagging the lowest fares.
- Gather intelligence on the range of prices offered by the airlines themselves; Internet agents like Travelocity, Expedia and Opodo; and high-street agents.
- Look out for promotional specials or fare wars, when airlines lower prices on their most popular routes. Sometimes newspapers run special offers: it may mean you have to buy a ghastly rag for a week or two to collect the coupons, but it could save you money.

as **Thomsonfly.com** and **ThomasCook.com** also sell cheap flights to the area but have less of a range. Whilst it doesn't sell tickets, **LowFareFlights.co.uk** does comparisons and will direct you to the airline website to book.

Don't forget to check regular airline websites: you can get great deals by side-stepping travel agency commissions. For contact details for airlines that fly to northern Italy, see 'Getting There' in this chapter or in the appendices.

If, for whatever reason, your child between 5 and 14 years old is to travel alone, ask about whether your airline operates an unaccompanied minor service, and what this costs.

Surfing For Hotels

Whether you want to book directly with hotels or through an agency, it is a good idea to spend a bit of time researching hotels and shopping around. Booking directly is often the best bet, although unless you can haggle in Italian, you might not get the best deal this way. However, if things go pear-shaped, it can be easier to sort out if you have a direct relationship with the hotel. It's a good idea to print off the confirmation of the *prenotazione* (booking) to have something to cling to if you're met with blank looks or increased rates when you check in.

If you book over the Internet make sure you get a confirmation number and make a printout of your online booking transaction, which will show how much has been taken from your credit card.

When booking a hotel through a site such as **Lastminute.com**, remember the old Latin maxim, *caveat emptor*: let the buyer beware. Companies like Lastminute act as third parties, selling hotel bookings for partner agencies. This doesn't really matter unless things go wrong. If you arrive and find that the hotel and/or room is mouldy, vibrating with Euro House music or overrun with ants, the chances of being relocated to another, better hotel or getting your money back are thin. If this does happen, your best bet is to keep your cool, complain until every avenue of restitution is exhausted, take photographs and document the problems for future use. If you are very lucky, you will be relocated. If not, write the letter of complaint of your life to the partner agency when you return, in the hope of getting some money back. **HolidayTravelWatch.com** provides invaluable advice on how to complain.

You can reduce – but not eliminate – the risk of booking a dodgy hotel by using websites like **Tripadvisor.com**, **Virtualtourist.com**, **Holidays-uncovered.com** and **HolidayWatchdog.com** These use readers to rate hotels and can offer helpful insights and candid reviews.

Saving Money on Hotel Bookings

With a bit of charm and negotiation you may be able to lower the price of your room:

- **Ask about special rates and other discounts** Dial the hotel directly to ask the price of a room and tell them you're looking for a *sconto* (discount). Ask if children stay free in the room (and clarify at what age they become adults). If not, is there a special rate?
- **Seek deals** See what price the hotel is offering and check if any Internet sites have it cheaper. Many hotels offer Internet-only discounts, or supply rooms to Lastminute or Expedia at rates much lower than those available directly from the hotel.
- **High season means higher prices** Off- or mid-season means lower prices and more room for negotiation.
- **Ask for a long-stay discount** If you're planning a long stay (at least 5 days), you might qualify for a discount. If you don't ask, you won't get it.
- **Avoid excess charges and hidden costs** When you book a room, ask whether the hotel charges for parking. Use your own mobile, pay phones or prepaid phone cards instead of dialling directly from hotel phones, which have rates to make you wince. Eschew the minibar: 3€ (£2) for a tiny bottle of water? Finally, ask about additional charges for the room (balcony, view, cot, air conditioning, etc.). It all adds up.
- **Full- or half-board or B&B?** Many Italian hotels, especially in high season, only offer full- or half-board. Full-board is great if the food is lovely, but can leave you feeling trapped. Is there a choice of places to eat nearby? What is the cost of eating out? If staying half-board, can you choose to have lunch or dinner? Would going out for dinner each night be difficult with a young child?
- **Book an apartment** A room with a kitchenette allows you to shop for groceries and cook your own meals. This is a big money saver, especially for long stays.

What To Look For

The Italian rating system must surely be a desktop exercise as it doesn't appear to be based on fieldwork. Five-star hotels can be wonderful, but some shabbier ones seem to make the grade on the strength of a murky pool alone. Levels of service, the things that make or break a hotel, have no bearing on their grading, which means you can have a 4-star hotel with misery-making, rubbish service and a 2-star that treats you like kings.

An **albergo** is the old name for a hotel. **Locanda** once meant an inn or carriage stop, though it's now sometimes used to refer to a place with charm or delusions of grandeur (used to death in Venice). A **pensione** is a bit like a Blackpool guesthouse. You usually have to share the bathroom, but nylon sheets will be hard to find. They are often the cheapest and most cheerful, and perfect for children. You can now book '**il Bed and Breakfast**' and, in rural parts, an **agriturismo**. This is a broad term for a rustic B&B, sometimes run by farmers trying to diversify. Within this term you will find a group of *agriturismo* purists who only serve locally produced food and drink. There are several websites to help you find an *agriturismo*: try ***www.agriturist.it***; ***www.agriturismo.net***; ***www.agriturismo.com***; ***www. terranostra.it***; ***www.turismoverde.it*** and ***www.bed-and-breakfast-in-italy.com***.

Happy **campers** will find lots of places to pitch up under the stars, with a number of them able to rent you the tent and the gear that goes with it. The Italians are more wholehearted about camping provisions: it's not unusual to find swimming pools, saunas and lush gardens on-site. To find the best campsites in northern Italy, contact the Touring Club Italiano (***www.touringclub.it***) or the Federazione Italiana Campeggiatori (☎ *055-882-391*; ***www.federcampeggio.it***). Useful websites for comparing facilities are ***www.easycamping.it***, ***www.camping.it*** and ***www.campeggi.com***. British-based companies like Eurocamp (☎ *0870-901-9410*; ***www.eurocamp.co.uk***) offer camping packages.

There are a number of cracking **youth hostels**, particularly around the lakes and in the mountains. These vary in size, but are wonderfully economical and a great way to meet other families. Contact the Associazione Italiana Alberghi per la Gioventu (☎ *06-489-077-40* (***www.ostellionline.org***). To obtain an International Youth Hostel Federation membership card call ☎ *0870-770-8868* or go to ***www.yha.org.uk***.

If you like to come and go as you please, it might be an idea to rent your own apartment. There are few really good websites dedicated to renting apartments including ***www.homelidays.com*** and ***www.holiday-rentals.co.uk***. For the best service try those based in a city like ***www.veniceapartments.org***.To weigh up the many options Google your destination, 'appartamento' and 'vacanze', and take your research from there.

Ibis (☎ *0801-606-606* ***www.ibishotel.com***)

Novotel (***www.novotel.com***) (☎ *0870-609 -0962* and **Best Western** (***www.bestwestern.co.uk***) (☎ *08457-737-373* are three major hotel chains where you pretty much know what you're going to get. Let's face it, with children this can be a great help.

Surfing for Rental Cars

Cars from **Hertz, Avis**, **Easy Autos** and **Budget** can all be booked before you go. (For contact details see the appendices.) Make sure you book a car with enough space and – if you plan a lot of driving – doors (some children hate being trapped in a 3-door car), It's wise to book any child seats or boosters in advance. If you decide to hire these when you arrive, they will be more expensive.

As always, check the car before you drive off if you want to avoid paying for someone else's scratch. If you plan doing a lot of miles, there is a chance that the odd carton of juice may be spilt on the upholstery. If you are taking a break from cleaning up horrible messes, contact a car-valeting service. Hotel receptions and petrol stations can find you the nearest one: just ask. Point at the spillages and throw *macchina* and *pulizia* at them, or tell them that you're looking for someone to clean your car: *Cerco qualcuno per pulire la mia macchina per favore.*

INTERNET ACCESS AWAY FROM HOME

Without Your Own Computer

The cities of northern Italy are well furnished with Internet cafés. However, in rural areas you might find it hard to find anywhere to log on. Under Italian anti-terrorism laws, every Internet café must photocopy the passport of non-Italian nationals and log your usage, so come prepared. When registering, many issue you with a card so you can return *senza* passport the next time. An hour's use can cost around 6–8€ (£4–5.35), and there are additional charges for printing and copying.

With Your Own Computer

Wi-Fi (Wireless Fidelity) is increasingly available, especially in Milan, Genoa, Turin and Venice. If it's not available in your hotel, they may have dataports for laptop modems. Failing that, most will have a couple of computers with Internet connection for guests' use. You might find a global Wi-Fi hotspot locator like JiWire (**www.jiwire.com**) useful.

Remember to bring a connection kit with the right power and phone adapters, a spare phone cord and a spare Ethernet cable. The electric current in Italy is 220V, 50HZ. Some older hotels may still use 125V. Italians use power sockets with two or three holes, and these do not have their own switches. Make sure you take plug adapters with you. It's best to buy these before you go.

Using A Mobile Phone

Most UK and Irish mobiles are GSM world-capable multiband (Sony Ericsson, Motorola and Samsung models are), so you can make and receive calls across much of the globe. Call your network provider and ask for 'international roaming' to be activated. Unfortunately, per-minute charges can be high – usually £1–1.50 in mainland Europe.

There is a cheaper (though bureaucratic) way of making mobile calls when you're over there. If you have an 'unlocked' GSM phone, you can take out your Sim card and buy a new Italian one for about 15€ (show your phone to the salesperson; not all phones work on all networks). You will have to display your passport and fill in a form, but your Italian number will have much lower calling charges. To unlock a locked phone, just call your mobile provider and tell them you are going abroad for several months and want to use your phone with a local provider. The main networks in Italy are TIM, Vodafone, Wind and 3. These have stores in most major towns. An alternative is to pick up a Sim card for use in Italy (£30) before you go from providers like ***www.0044.co.uk***.

ESSENTIALS

Getting There

By Plane The main airports in northern Italy are Milan Malpensa, Milan Linate, Bergamo, Brescia, Genoa, Treviso, Trieste, Turin, Verona and Venice Marco Polo. (see the appendices for contact details). Airports outside the area covered that are handily placed are Bologna, Pisa and Rimini. Also worth considering are airports in neighbouring France, Austria, Switzerland and Slovenia like Nice, Innsbruck, Geneva and Ljubljana.

Milan: The gateway to Milan, Lombardy, Piedmont, the lakes and Liguria. easyJet flies to Milan's two airports. **Malpensa** is the newer and bigger, with lots of shops and services. There is an express train that takes you to Cordona station, but to get to the heart of Milan, jump on the shuttle bus. **Linate** is also handy for Como. To get to central Milan, take the shuttle bus or a local bus. There are also direct buses to Como. Once in Milan you can travel anywhere in Italy.

Bergamo: Ryanair flies into **Orio del Serio**, a small airport but very busy in the summer. There's a shuttle bus to Milan or, following a short taxi ride, you can take the train instead; or if you want to head east, to Brescia, to change for Verona and Venice.

Brescia: The airport here is well placed for a visit to Lake Como or Lake Garda, Lombardy and the Veneto. Buses run to Brescia and Verona and, after a taxi ride, there are trains to Milan,Verona, Padua, Vicenza and Venice.

Friuli–Venezia Giulia: **Ronchi dei Legionari** airport is dubbed 'Trieste Airport' by Ryanair, though it's an hour's bus journey away from the port city.

Genoa: **Aeroporto Internazionale di Genova Cristoforo Colombo** is just 6.4 km (4 miles) west of Genoa city centre and is handy for the Italian Riviera.

Treviso: The airport is just 3 km (1.8 miles) from the city centre, within easy reach of Venice, the Veneto, the Dolomites and Friuli.

Turin: **Caselle International Airport**, upgraded for the 2006

Winter Olympics, is ideal for Turin, the Valle d'Aosta, Piedmont and Lake Maggiore. Buses take you straight to the city's main stations in 30 minutes. Better still, there's the new high-speed (19 min) rail link to GTT Dora Railway Station.

Verona: This airport just outside the city is also very handy for Lake Garda and Lake Como, Trentino–Alto Adige, the Veneto and even Venice.

Venice: **Marco Polo Airport,** 30 minutes north-east of Venice, is also ideal for the Veneto (Verona, Padua and Vicenza) and Friuli (Udine and Trieste). All swanky and shiny, it is a dream to land at. There's a good selection of shops and services; buses run to Piazzale Roma and the Alilaguna boat to Venice departs from the jetty outside.

The principal airlines flying to Northern Italy from the UK and Ireland and their relevant routes are: Alitalia (UK *0870-544-8259*/Ireland *01-677-5171*; ***www.alitalia.co.uk***): Dublin/Aberdeen and Edinburgh–Northern Italian airports via Paris; London–Milan; Aer Lingus (Eire *0818 365000*/ UK *0870 876 5000* ***www.fly aerlingus.com***): Dublin–Milan/Turin/Venice. British Airways (*0870-850-9850*; ***www.britishairways.com***): Birmingham/Bristol–Milan; London–Milan/Turin/Verona/Venice. Flybmi (*0870-6070-555*/ *01332-64 –8181* ***www.flybmi.com***): belfast/Dublin/Durham/Glasgow/Bradford/London/Manchester–Venice).

easyJet (*0905-821-0905*. ***www.easyjet.com***): Bristol–Venice; East Midlands–Venice; London–Milan/Venice; Jet2 (UK *0871-226-1737*/ Ireland *0818-200-017*; ***www.jet2.com***): Belfast/Edinburgh/Leeds/Manchester-Milan: Leeds/Manchester-Venice

Ryanair (UK *0871-246-0000*/Ireland *0818-303-030*; ***www.ryanair.com***): Dublin–Bergamo/Treviso/Turin; East Midlands–Bergamo; Glasgow-Bergamo; Liverpool–Bergamo/Treviso; London–Brescia/Genoa/Treviso/Trieste/Turin; Newcastle–Bergamo; Shannon– Bergamo/Treviso

Getting through the airport

The golden rule for happy check-in is 1 hour before a domestic flight and 2 hours before an international one, but, as experience will tell you, it's always better to leave plenty of time when travelling with children. If you are running late, phone the airline (take a note of the local number before leaving). If you turn up late, don't just join a queue: let the airline staff know and give them as great a chance as possible to get you on the plane.

Make one person responsible for keeping the tickets and passports and gathering them together after every security check.

Different airlines offer different check-in arrangements,

Flying with Film & Video

Always take valuables like cameras and camcorders with you as cabin baggage. Unless you have a super-duper travel insurance policy, the single-item recoup is unlikely to cover the cost of replacing most kit.

For those of you who haven't gone digital, don't put **developed or undeveloped film in checked bags**, as the more powerful scanners can fog film. X-ray damage is cumulative: the faster the film, and the more times you put it through a scanner, the more likely the damage, so carry your film in a transparent carrier bag, then you can remove it easily before going through scanners. Some of the busier tourist attractions X-ray visitors' bags, too.

Security scanners will not damage **videotape** in video cameras, but beware of the magnetic fields emitted by the walk-through security gateways and hand-held inspection wands. Put your loaded camcorder on the screening conveyor belt or have it hand-inspected. Be sure your batteries are charged, as you may be required to turn the device on.

particularly for those carrying just hand luggage or with business class tickets, so check to see if these are available and suit your needs.

Make sure you have checked what you can carry on and what you can't. The terrorist threat in the UK has meant that government regulations are liable to change depending on the level of threat. Recent rule changes have involved the carrying of liquids on planes. At the very least, don't pack anything sharp or even thin and made of metal (knitting needles and hair combs have been confiscated at UK airports). It's also worth knowing that Italian security won't let you board with cigarette lighters on the way back.

As for cabin baggage, most airlines have agreed to one bag sized 56 cm x 45 cm x 25 cm and one briefcase, laptop bag or equivalent. However, there may be tougher regulations in force at the time of flying.

Tips for flying with children

If your children have never flown before, or were just babies when they did, it might be an idea to introduce them to things they will come across – such as checking in, going though security, the safety talk and dealing with a bumpy ride – by playing 'let's go to the airport' (***www.TravellingWithChildren.co.uk*** has some other ideas). Use your own methods of persuasion to let them know that they must be on their best behaviour on the plane.

❶ Check with the airline to see if they provide **boosters or car seats** for under-2s. Some also provide special seatbelts.

❷ **Make sure everyone has been to the toilet** just before boarding. Always accompany younger children to the toilet onboard.

❸ **Read the laminated safety card** and know where the exits are. Ditto the lifejackets and oxygen masks.

❹ There are pros (more legroom) and cons (no baggage during take-off and landing) to booking a row where the emergency exits are.

❺ Be sure to pack **water (if allowed by security), snacks and a few toys** for your children in your carry-on luggage. See 'Packing for Planes & Cars', above.

❻ Make sure your child's **seatbelt remains fastened** properly: turbulence can happen at any time.

❼ If your child sits by the window or between two parents, it is harder for him/her to wander off.

❽ When you board, ask a flight attendant if it is possible that your **children are served their meal first**, especially if they are very young or seated at the back of the plane.

❾ Yes, some folk are just grumpy when it comes to young children, but if you have a particularly boisterous or restless child, do bear in mind other passengers' comfort. Watch out for your child constantly kicking the back of someone's seat. Keep international relations cordial by stopping it and apologising.

GETTING AROUND

By Car Italy is best explored by car, but you'll need to be unflappable to cope with Italian driving, some of which is downright dangerous. You only have to look at the number of dented cars to appreciate that the phrase 'safe and courteous driving' is not in the lexicon.

Hiring a car: Remember your driving licence. You must have had a full licence (i.e. passed your driving test) for two years. When booking or picking up you'll also need your passport and a credit card (this will save you making a hefty deposit). Insurance on all vehicles is compulsory, though check the excess and what is not covered.

Driving rules: Italians, of course, drive on the 'wrong' side of the road if you are British – the right. Blame it on Napoleon: everyone drove on the left until the late 18th century. If a car comes up behind you and flashes its lights, that's the signal for you to let it pass. Stay in the right lane on highways; the left is only for passing or those in a hurry.

Autostrade are superhighways, denoted by green signs and a number prefaced with an 'A', like the A1 from Naples to Milan. Those not numbered are called *raccordo,* connecting roads between two cities. On longer stretches, *autostrade* often become toll roads. *Strade statale* are state roads, usually two lanes wide and indicated by blue signs. Their route numbers are prefaced with an SS or an S, but like the *autostrade*, they don't always have numbers; you'll just see blue signs listing destinations by name.

Signage on roads, particularly minor ones, is dismal, with little or no warning for smaller towns. It is also inconsistent, sometimes listing everything within a 50-mile radius, sometimes forgetting to mention a turnoff. Get a good map (the spiral-bound *Michelin Italy Tourist and Motoring Atlas* is good), study it and try to remember all the towns in the direction you want to go. You can plan routes and get a rough idea of journey times using **www.maporama.com**.

The best thing about the *autostrade* is the **Autogrill** service station. If you're expecting an Italian version of stewed tea, all-day-grease-on-a-plate and damp sandwiches, you are about to be stunned. Autogrill is one of the best things about Italy; irrefutable proof that culinary standards need not plunge just because you're beside a motorway. They really are a delight: freshly made pizzas, well-filled *panini* and chunky salads at reasonable prices; shops selling truffle oil, artisan pasta and gourmet chocolate; and toilets that are pleasant to use. Eat well, shop happy, freshen up, then come home and start a campaign to drive up standards in British and Irish service stations.

Driving rules and regulations:

Drink Driving The UK's permitted level of alcohol is 0.8 mg of alcohol per ml; in Italy it's 0.5 mg. Don't risk it: imprisonment is a regular punishment.

Fines Where it's a minor contravention, these are on the spot. Make sure you get a receipt.

Fuel Unleaded petrol is called *benzina*; diesel is called *gasolio*. Make sure you put in the right one. Almost all stations are closed on Sundays, but most have a pump fitted with a machine that accepts bills.

Seat Belts These are **compulsory**. Children under 4 must have a suitable seat or bolster, whilst those between 4 and 12 cannot travel in the front unless suitably restrained (exactly how depends on the size of your child).

Speed Limits Motorway: 80 mph (130 kph)

Dual carriageway: 68 mph (110 kph)

Open space: 56 mph (90 kph)

Town: 31 mph (50 kph)

Visibility Vests Along with warning triangles, these are usually in the boot of hire cars, but check before driving off. If you break down on the motorway or dual carriageway, you cannot get out of your car unless you have a visibility vest. You will be fined if you fail to wear one.

Warning Triangle These are also compulsory and must be erected just up the road from where you have stopped. Remember, if you're travelling through France you are required to display a GB sticker and have headlamp deflectors fitted. Carrying spare headlamp bulbs is strongly advised.

Road signs:

Speed Limit a black number inside a red circle on a white background.

End of a Speed Zone black and white, with a black slash through the number.

Yield to Oncoming Traffic a red circle with a white background, a black arrow pointing down, and a red arrow pointing up.

Yield Ahead a point-down red-and-white triangle.

Pedestrian Zone in town, a simple white circle with a red border or the words *zona pedonale* or *zona traffico limitato*. You can drop someone off, however.

One-way Streets a white arrow on a blue background. Also the sign *senso unico*.

No Entry a red circle with a horizontal white slash.

Not Allowed like the UK, any image in black on a white background surrounded by a red circle indicates you can't do it.

No Parking a circular sign in blue with a red circle and slash.

Parking: To park your car either find a *parcheggio* (car park) or park on the street. White lines indicate free public spaces and blue lines paying public spaces, usually marked by a *pagamento a sosta* (pay to park) sign. Find a meter, punch in how long you want to park, then stick the ticket somewhere visible. If you park in an area marked *parcheggio disco orario*, look for the cardboard parking disc in your hire car's glove compartment (or buy one at a petrol station). Here you just dial up the hour of your arrival and display it on the dashboard. You're allowed *un ora* (1 hr) or *due ore* (2 hr) of free parking depending on the sign. **Car parks** have ticket dispensers and/or manned booths. You pick up your ticket as you drive in, and pay at the booth or automated machine as you leave.

By Train Italy's nationally owned train network is comfortable, regular and reliable. It's also incredibly good value, astoundingly so when you compare it to Britain's ramshackle network. For example you'll pay about 20€ for a journey between Milan–Venice, 12€ Verona–Milan and 8€ Trieste–Venice. Even one-horse towns get a service of sorts.

If you are intending to use the train, before you leave for Italy visit the Trenitalia website (***www.trenitalia.com***) or the new version for English speakers (***www.italiarail.co.uk***), to check routes, timetables and fares.

There is little difference between first and second class, the only real benefit being more space if you're travelling overnight. If you avoid rush hours you are sure to get a seat. However, on the faster routes between cities, you will need to book a seat to ensure you are all together. *La Ferrovia Italiana* has quite a few different types of train:

ES (Eurostar) are fast trains connecting major Italian cities.

EN (Euronotte) are the overnight version of these, with sleeping cars or couchettes.

EC (Eurocity) are high-speed international trains connecting main European and Italian cities.

IC (Intercity) trains are similar to *Eurocity* trains, in that they offer both first- and second-class travel and require a supplement, but they never cross an international border.

P (Pendolino) is the 'pendulum' train that zips back and forward between Rome and Milan, only stopping at Florence and Bologna. It's the fastest, but most expensive, option (first class only, meal included); it has its own ticket window at stations and requires a seat reservation.

E (Espressi) stop at all major and most secondary stations.

IR (Interregionale) make more stops than the *Espressi*.

R (Regionale) stay within a region (e.g. the Veneto) and stop at every station.

A D (Diretto) not what it sounds like – these stop at virtually every station.

L (Locale) stop at every small station, and sometimes just stop!

When buying a regular ticket, ask for either **andata** (one-way) or **andata e ritorno** (round-trip). If the train you plan to take is an ES/EC or IC, ask for the ticket *con supplemento rapido* (with speed supplement) to avoid onboard penalty charges.

Most importantly, **stamp your ticket in the little yellow box** on the platform before you board. It is not unheard of for tourists to get a hard time from guards for unstamped tickets.

Children under 12 always travel half-price, and those under 4 travel free. If you are under 26, you can buy a 26€ (£17.50) **Carta Verde** (Green Card) at any Italian train station. This gets you a 15% discount on all FS tickets for 1 year. Over-60s can get discounts by buying a **Carta d'Argento** (Silver Card).

The **Trenitalia Pass** is another discount card. It works similarly to the Eurail pass, in that you have 2 months in which to use the train on a set number of days. The base number of days is four, and you can add up to six more. For adults, the first-class pass costs £142; the second-class version is £114 for adults; for youths under 26, the price is £95. You can get different deals or buy extra days and get savings if two adults travel together. You must buy this before you go to Italy: contact **Rail Europe** (☎ *08708-371-371 www.raileurope.co.uk*).

Timetables for all routes are displayed on posters in stations. Useful schedules for all train lines are printed biannually in booklets available at any newsstand. You can also get official schedules (and more train information, some even in English) on the web (see *www.trenitalia.com*).

Stations tend to be well-run and clean, with luggage storage facilities at all but the smallest, and usually a good bar with surprisingly palatable food. *Binario* means platform. If you pull into a small town with a shed-sized or non-existent station, find the nearest bar or *tabacchi* to buy your tickets and ask for information.

By Bus Regional buses are called *pullman,* though *autobus,* the term for a city bus, is also sometimes used. It's not easy getting hold of a timetable for local buses, but ask in the tourist office or the *tabacchi* nearest your stop. A town's bus stop is usually either in the main piazza or on the outskirts. The nearest newsstand or *tabacchi*, or sometimes a bar, will sell you tickets. Remember to stamp these using the yellow machine when you get on.

By Taxi Like the UK, licensed taxis have regulations. Unlike the UK, many drivers pay little regard to them. If you find a great taxi driver, tip him well. It helps if you have an idea about what sort of fare to expect before you climb in. At an airport, ask at the information desk how much your journey is likely to cost. A rough figure can be helpful when faced with a brazen chancer who insists on three times the price. To help you out, here are three golden rules:

- **Always** ask how much the fare is likely to be or fix a price before setting off.
- **Always** check that the meter is on.

Travel Times

Cities	*Distance*	*Car Travel*	*Train Travel*
Genoa to Turin	110 miles (160 km)	2 hr	1 hr 50 min
Turin to Milan	90 miles (145 km)	1 hr 50 min	1 hr 45 min
Milan to Verona	100 miles (160 km)	1 hr 45	1 hr 50 min
Verona to Venice	75 miles (123 km)	1 hr 40 min	2 hr
Venice to Trieste	102 miles (164 km)	2 hr	2 hr 5 min
Trieste to Bolzano	114 miles (184 km)	4 hr	6 hr 30 min
Bolzano to Milan	230 miles (370 km)	4 hr 30 min	3 hr 30 min

Handy Phrases for the Bus

I'd like to find out about the bus timetable please?

Vorrei sapere gli orari del Pullman per favore? *Voh-ray sa-peh-reh yee o-rah-ree dehl pool-man pehr-fah-vor-eh?*

I'm getting off at Verona Porta Nuova.

Scendo a Verona Porta Nuova. *Shehn-doh a Veh-roh-na Por-tah nwo-vah*

Can you let me know when we approach Verona Porta Nuova please?

Mi fa sapere quando si avvicina a Verona Porta Nuova per favore? *Mee fay sa-peh-reh kwan-doh see a-vee-che-na a Veh-roh-na Por-tah nwo-vah pehr fah-vor-eh?*

It's the next stop/ Is it the next stop?

E` la prossima fermata (?) *Eh la pross-ee-mah fehr-mah-ta?*

May I please get off?

Posso scendere? *Poh-ss-oh sh-ehn-deh-reh?*

Are these places free?

Sono liberi questi posti? *So-no lee-beh-ree kweh-stee?*

● **Always** ask to see the laminated price list for supplements (extra persons, baggage, after midnight, weekend/holiday rates, etc.).

There is still a chance you might get ripped off, but letting them see you're on the ball can help.

Only in the bigger cities can you hail a cab – elsewhere find a taxi rank or call one. Information is provided in the relevant chapters.

TIPS ON EATING OUT

Dining

You'll start the day with **colazione**, or breakfast. This is usually orange juice and croissants (*cornetti*) filled with marmalade, chocolate or custard (*crema*), all washed down with milky caffé latte or cappuccino. Supposedly it's not form to drink either of these after midday, but you're in Italy, so make like the Italians and ignore the rules if you feel like it. You often get cold meats and cheeses, which can be tucked into brioche, wrapped in a napkin and smuggled out of the breakfast room for later. Everybody else is doing it.

If you are feeling peckish before lunchtime, know the name of the game before you order. If you stand at a bar – *al banco* – you'll be charged the minimum for your drinks, ice cream or *panini*. If you sit down, you incur a cover charge and heftier prices for exactly the same food. Sit outside the bar and you pay even more. A simple *panino* (flattened, toasted bread with a cheese, ham or vegetable filling) or *tramezzini* (triangles of soft white-bread sandwiches with the crusts cut off) can cost anything from 1.50€ to 5€ (£1–3.35).

Pizza will be the thing your children most remember about their trip, and along many thoroughfares you can buy it by the slice from a **pizza à taglio** or **pizza rustica**. If you want to sit down and pay a bit extra, a **pizzeria** will prepare your favourite toppings. Check to see it has a wood-burning oven if you want something close to the original Neapolitan DOC. A **rosticceria** is the same type of place with chickens roasting on a spit in the window. In Venice, you can buy *cichetti* (fishy bites and vegetable fritters) at bars throughout the day, even in the morning (sardines and pickled squid for breakfast anyone?). This is not a cheap option, especially if your eyes are bigger than your belly.

Pranzo (lunch) or **cena** (dinner) consists of **antipasti** (appetizers), **primo** (first course) of pasta, soup or risotto, and **secondo** (second course) of meat or fish, possibly

Ristoranti, Trattorie, Osterie...What's that all about?

There used to be more marked differences between the types of eateries in Italy: the boundaries may have blurred in recent times, but in general *un ristorante* is the most sophisticated and formal, having a printed menu and wine list. A trattoria is a more homely establishment serving fewer dishes, often without a written menu, and the service is less polished. An osteria (or Hostaria) is a tavern that serves a limited choice of hearty dishes often in rustic, relaxed surroundings; the meals of the day are displayed on a blackboard. In recent years a new breed of urban wine bar, the enoteca, has sprung up, offering wine by the glass accompanied by cheese and cold-cut platters, as well as small tapas-like dishes. Pizzerie of course serve pizzas, but increasingly they have a selection of other meals. A tavola calda (meaning hot table) is usually a place where you eat standing up and a rosticceria has roasted meats and veggies for people in a hurry. A paninoteca sells panini and other snacks and a pasticceria is a pastry shop that often has a selection of hot and cold drinks. Italians pop into un bar for a quick espresso or cappuccino and sweet pastry in the mornings and later on for more espressi or a snifter perhaps. Un caffè is usually a little more sophisticated, having waiter service as well as tables inside and out.

Piatti Tipici: Northern Italian Dishes for You and Your Children to Try

Fiori di zucchini – courgette flowers stuffed with fish mousse or ricotta, and fried in a light batter.

Insalata di frutte di mare – a mixed seafood platter with *vongole* (clams), *cozze* (mussels), *polpi* (octopus), *calamari* (squid) and *gamberi* (prawns).

Pesto – basil, garlic, olive oil, pine nuts and parmesan pummelled by a pestle and served with pasta.

Polenta – maize porridge served gloopy with stew, or firm and grilled with a sauce.

Risotto alle seppie – risotto made with cuttlefish ink. Turns tongues black!

Tiramisu – coffee-soaked sponge with custard and mascarpone cream. The original pick-me-up.

Tortelli con zucca – pasta stuffed with sweet pumpkin.

accompanied by a **contorno** (side dish) of veggies, finished off with **dolce** (dessert) and a **caffè** (espresso coffee). Don't feel compelled to order every course: *primo* and *dolce* will suffice for most children. Menus often have English subtitles, but if not, don't be afraid to ask.

A word of warning: the **pane e coperto** is a bread and cover charge of anywhere from 50¢ to 8€ (£0.33–5.35) that you pay for the privilege of sitting at the table, even at a bar. To request the bill, say '*Il conto, per favore*' (eel con-to payr fa-vor-ay). A service charge of 15% is usually included these days, but if unsure ask '*è incluso il servizio?*' (ay een-cloo-soh eel sair-vee-tsee-oh?).

SUGGESTED ITINERARIES: NORTHERN ITALY IN 1 & 2 WEEKS

These whistlestop one- and two-week tours of northern Italy's must-see sights start in Milan. The one-week tour could be done by train or car. The second week involves lots of driving. These journeys are designed to give you an idea of how much ground you *could* cover. Understandably, most families will opt for a more leisurely itinerary. So get yourself a large map and plan a route to suit your family's needs.

NORTHERN ITALY ITINERARIES

Northern Italy in 1 Week

Day 1: Arrive in Milan

Check out Milano's main sights, mostly near the Duomo, peruse the chic shops and explore the **Leonardo da Vinci Science Museum**, before dining at one of the city's excellent eateries.

Day 2: Lake Como

Get a boat pass and spend the day criss-crossing the lake, starting at **Como**, dipping into beguiling **Bellagio** for lunch and an ice cream, before sampling the delights of **Menaggio** and **Varenna**. You can catch a train to Bergamo via **Lecco** from this side of the lake.

Day 3: Bergamo and Verona

Take the funicular and amble around Bergamo's *citta alta*, enjoying refreshments in **Piazza Vecchia**, before exploring the evocative streets and city walls. Travel to Verona in the afternoon where the children can let their imaginations wander at the **House of Juliet** and the Castelvecchio. Families with older children here in July or August should go to the opera at the magical Roman **Arena**.

Day 4: Vicenza & Padua

Visit the fabulous Renaissance city of Vicenza with its Palladian splendours, where teens will especially enjoy the shopping, before heading to Padua for a gander at the **Scrovegni Chapel**.

Days 5 & 6: Venice

Save at least a couple of nights to stay in Venice. It may be pricey, but children will never forget their first dream-like wander amid the *canali*, *campi* and *calli*. Check out what festivals and events are taking place. If you're lucky or have planned it, there'll be a colourful procession along the Grand Canal to delight little ones, or the Biennale will be in full swing for trendy teens.

Day 7: Last Day in Milan

It's not too far to reach one of the many airports by rail or road. It's a 3-hour ride back to Milan, so you might have time to do some last-minute shopping (big chunks of *parmiggiano* are always worth picking up).

Northern Italy in 2 Weeks

Begin with the first six days of the previous tour, then rent a car in Venice. You'll need it to explore the remote corners of the Dolomites, Liguria and Piedmont. Drop the car off at your departure airport.

Day 7: Treviso, Asolo, Bassano del Grappa & Trento

After spending the morning enjoying Treviso's canalside attractions and bustling **fish market**, head towards Asolo (whizz through its hilltop centre if you have time) and then on to Bassano del Grappa. Children can unwind in the laid-back piazzas or by the river. The scenery will become more epic as you near Trento, where you can stop to enjoy the city's cosy cafés and handsome *Centro Storico* including the **Castello di Buonconsiglio**. Stay the night here, or if you enjoy driving and the children aren't whining, take the **Great Dolomite Road** to Bolzano.

Day 8: Bolzano & Trento

Children can meet Ötzi, the 5000-year-old '**Ice Man**', at Bolzano's archaeological museum. Mountain-loving families should spend a night in this spellbinding landscape; alternatively, head south to Lake Garda.

Day 9: Lake Garda

Active families with an interest in history can check out the western shore: windsurfing at **Riva del Garda,** d'Annunzio's eccentric **Il Vittoriale** at **Gardone** and Mussolini's old haunts at **Salò.** Fun-seekers should head east to one of the theme parks, like **Gardaland**. On the way, visit picturesque Malcesine and grab an ice cream by the port at Torri di Benaco. If you have time and it's outside high season, visit the castle and Roman villa ruins at Sirmione.

Days 10 & 11: Mantua, the Cinque Terre & Portofino

In the morning head to Mantua and discover the moody delights of Mantegna's city. Families with older children who like walking on the wild side should head to the Cinque Terre. If that's not your lot, head further up the Riviera di Levante to Portofino. The day trippers should have left by the time you arrive.

Day 12: Genoa & Piedmont's Wine Country

Children will adore Europe's largest **aquarium** in **Genoa** and the Old Port attractions, including the **Bigo tower**. Sample the city's seafood and pesto, before setting out towards Turin, passing through the vine-covered hills of the Wine Country. Spend the night in one of the area's enchanting towns, like Alba or Brà.

Day 13: Piedmont's Wine Country & Turin

Drive to Turin and spend the rest of the day savouring its family-friendly sights, including the Egyptian Museum and the iconic **Mole Antonelliana** tower, which houses a fantastic Cinema Museum. Savour the dramatic ride in a sleek glass lift that accesses a gallery with breathtaking views of the city and Alps beyond.

Day 14: Lake Maggiore & Milan

Depending on when and where your return flight is departing, you could take in some more sights: Malpensa-bound passengers could visit Lake Maggiore.

Anyone Linate-bound should visit the impressive **Certosa di Pavia**. Either way, don't forget to stop off at a supermarket or Autogrill to stock up on fine food for the fridge.

GETTING CHILDREN INTERESTED IN NORTHERN ITALY

Get the children excited about the trip by watching a few films and suggesting some books to read. The classic films are a good place to start: *Cinema Paradiso* (the shorter version is the child-friendly one), *Life is Beautiful* and *Pinocchio*. Watch *The Italian Job* to lap up the Torino sights, classic lines and Quincy Jones soundtrack.

The *Adventures of Pinocchio* by Carlo Collodi is a great read for small children. For primary-school youngsters, try *Follow the Dream* by Peter Sis, which explores the life of Christopher Columbus. Books about da Vinci will get imaginations running wild before a visit to his museum: check out Heinz Kaehne's *Dreams, Schemes and Flying Machines* and *Leonardo da Vinci for Kids: His Life and Ideas – 21 Activities* by Janis Herbert. Check out the museum website (**www.museoscienza.org**) for other ideas. *Tony's Bread* by Tomie de Paola is a sweet tale for little ones. Venice-bound children could try *Venice* by Renzo Rossi and the teen-friendly *Stravaganza: City of Masks* by Mary Hoffman. *Thief Lord* (by Cornelia Funke), recently made into a film, captures the mystery of the most serene republic. Under-10s will enjoy *Ice Mummy: The Discovery of a 5000 Year Old Man* by Mark Dubowski. Italo Calvino's enchanting and bizarre Italian Folktales is a great book to dip in and out of for kids and adults alike.

Italian Pop is always a winner for a singalong in the car (although the kids might not agree). You can pick up great-value CDs of San Remo Festival hits at any Autogrill. Check out Laura Pausini for heartbreaking yet uplifting tunes. Morricone's soundtracks for the Sergio Leone Spaghetti Westerns are perfect for epic mountain drives: children whistling along to *The Good, the Bad and the Ugly* will thank you in years to come. Honest.

FAST FACTS: NORTHERN ITALY

Alcohol There is no minimum age for drinking in Italy (in a nation that prides itself on ignoring laws, maybe a good thing). There are no restrictions on when you can purchase alcohol in shops.

Business Hours Regular hours are 9am–1pm and 4–7.30pm, or thereabouts. Banking hours are generally from 8:30am-1:30pm and 3–4pm.

Car Rental See 'Getting Around', earlier in this chapter.

Chemists A chemist (or drugstore in American) is called a *farmacia*. Your hotel will be able to tell you where you can find one and give you the lowdown on out-of-hours opening.

Climate See 'When to Go', earlier in this chapter.

Currency The euro. See 'Money', earlier in this chapter.

Driving Rules See 'Getting Around' earlier in this chapter.

Electricity Like other European countries, Italy uses 220 V, 50 Hz. Some older hotels may still use 125 V. Power sockets have two or three holes and do not have their own switches. Buy an adaptor at home.

Embassies & Consulates All of these are in Milan:

British Consulate at Via San Paolo 7 (*02-230-01*)

Irish Consulate is at Piazza S. Pietro in Gessate 2 (*02-5518-8848*)

Australian Consulate at Via Borgogna 2 (*02-777-041*)

Canadian Consulate at Via Pisani 19 (*02-675-81*)

New Zealand Consulate at Via Arezzo 6 (*02-4801-2544*)

US Consulate at Via Principe Amadeo 2/10 (*02-290-351*)

Emergency Numbers

113 Police

112 Carabinieri (also deal with crimes)

115 Fire department

118 Medical emergency

There is also a number for child protection, *114*, for children at risk.

Internet Access It's easy enough to find an Internet café in cities and major towns. Remember to take your passport to ensure you comply with Italian regulations. Wi-Fi isn't quite as widespread as at home, but you'll find a hotspot in most large towns.

Language English is widely spoken, but where's the fun in that? Marlon Lodge's *Rapid Italian: 200+ Essential Words and Phrases Anchored into Your Long Term Memory with Great Music* (available in audiobook or audio CD) is a fun way to learn and, more importantly, have the confidence to speak. If you're really keen, get a copy of *Basic Italian Grammar* by C. A. McCormick. See Appendix A for a glossary of useful words and phrases.

Legal Assistance The Italian section on the British Embassy website (***www.britishembassy.gov.uk***) has a list of lawyers, under 'When things go wrong'. Your travel insurance company can also advise on how to get help.

Maps Most car hire companies will furnish you with a decent map of the region, but for more detail and smaller roads (the ones where you are more likely to get lost) get an AA or Michelin map. These cost around 8€ (£5.35) for a fold-up one or 18€ (£12) for the hardcover version, and are widely available.

Newspapers & Magazines If it's British newspapers you're after, they don't reach Italian newsstands until the next day. However, yesterday's *Guardian*, *Times*, *Financial Times*, *Mail* and *Mirror* are readily available.

Passports See 'Entry Requirements & Customs', earlier in this chapter.

Post It costs 65¢ (£0.44) to send a postcard (or anything up to 20 g) home by *posta prioritaria*. Stamps can be bought in *tabbachi*, some shops and post offices.

Radio Italian radio stations all seem to offer generic Europop with a smattering of palatable cheese.

Registering with the Police Legally, you are required to register with the police within three days of entering the country; however, the police don't pay too much attention to this if you're a EU citizen. If you are staying at a hotel, they will do this for you (that's why they take your passports).

Smoking Smoking in public places, including bars, restaurants, discotheques and offices, is banned.

Telephones Public telephones are plentiful and have instructions in English. Calling from your hotel room can be very expensive, so it will save you money to go out to make that call. If you can't find a phone box, some cafés and bars have a red phone symbol, which means they have a public telephone.

To call an Italian number from the UK: First dial ☎ *00*; then ☎ *39*; next you dial the area code (dropping the 0 it begins with); then the number. For example, if you wanted to call Marco Polo airport you dial ☎ *00-39-41-260-9240*.

To call home from Italy: To make international calls from Italy, first dial ☎ *00*; and then the country code (UK ☎ *44*, Ireland ☎ *353*); then the area code (dropping the 0 it begins with); then the number. For example, if you wanted to call British Airways customer services you would dial ☎ *00-44-191-490-7901*

For directory assistance: For operator-assisted international calls dial ☎ *170*. Dial ☎ *12* if you're looking for a number within Italy, dial ☎ *176* for numbers in Europe, and ☎ *1790* for numbers outside Europe.

For operator assistance: If you need operator assistance to make a call, dial ☎ *172-0044* to reach BT in the UK or ☎ *172-0353* for Ireland.

Telephone Cards If you are not taking a mobile phone, buy a *carta telefonica* from a tobacconist for use in public phones. They come in a number of denominations and are easy to use.

Time Zone Italy is one hour ahead of the UK and Ireland.

Tipping Check to see if service is included in the bill. Otherwise, 10–15% is the norm. Don't tip bad service. However, let them know why you aren't.

Weather Forecasts Check what the weather is like at **www.bbc.co.uk/weather/world** or **www.meteo.it**.

3 Lakes & Mountains

Northern Italy's mountainous arc stretches from the Alpi Marittime in Liguria to the Friulian Dolomites on the Slovenian border. For families who love the outdoors, the options are almost limitless. Moving from west to east: the Valle d'Aosta has spectacular alpine massifs for skiers and adventurers; the lakes of Maggiore, Como and Garda offer aquatic pleasures, child-friendly activities and plenty of cultural sights (as well as a theme park or five); and Trentino–Alto-Adige and the Dolomites surprise visitors with a hybrid Italo-Germanic culture, wild terrain and spectacular peaks.

For those wanting to dip in and out of the lakes and mountains, use this chapter alongside others in the book: remember that wherever you are in Piedmont (Chapter 7), Lombardy (Chapter 6), the Veneto (Chapter 5) and Friuli (Chapter 5) even if you are in the flatter Po basin you are never far away from more rugged terrain and one of the lakes. You can comfortably combine a city break with a ski trip, camping tour or lakeside holiday.

Just remember, a trip to the mountains often involves twisting mountain roads, so take frequent breaks – everyone will need a breather. Bring something (see p. 23) for children who suffer from car sickness, too. Boat trips, cobbled lanes and fields are tricky with pushchairs, so plan your route to avoid hassles and tears. The weather can be unpredictable in these wilder environments, so pack clothing layers including waterproofs (vital outside the summer months and on high-altitude cable cars), high factor sun cream, hats, snacks, water and a first aid kit. Touring Club Italiano produces good general maps of the regions, while Kompass and Casa Editrice Tabacco publish detailed maps for hiking and trekking. All are widely available when you get here. If you're going walking, skiing or cycling in the mountains, or taking a boat, common-sense precautions are vital: write down the time of departure and planned return, as well as details of where you are going, and leave it with someone (hotel reception, boat hire company). Bring a mobile phone, but remember you may not get reception everywhere. And don't forget your camera!

VALLE D'AOSTA (AOSTA VALLEY)

Aosta: 113 km (70 miles) NW of Turin, 184 km (114 miles) NW of Milan; Courmayeur-Entrèves: 35 km (22 miles) W of Aosta, 148 km (92 miles) NW of Turin

For fresh air, alpine pastures, outdoor activities and stunning scenery, the Valle d'Aosta is hard to beat – and it's only two hours from Turin. Italy's tallest mountains are here: Monte Bianco (Mont Blanc) bordering France and Monte Cervino (the Matterhorn) bordering Switzerland. Children will get a kick out of cable car rides up the craggy slopes. Families of skiers and adrenalin junkies flock to the resort of Courmayeur all year round to explore the pistes and bike trails. Aosta itself has Roman ruins and nearby fairy-tale castles, and the Gran Paradiso National Park has wildlife and wilderness aplenty.

Essentials

Getting There

By Train Two dozen trains a day link Aosta with **Turin** (2 hr) and **Milan** (3 hr, changing at Chivasso).

By Bus The bus station is located opposite the train station. Eight buses a day go to and from **Turin** (3 hr); most require a change at Ivrea. Four daily buses also connect Aosta and **Milan** (3 hr) as well as other popular destinations, including **Courmayeur** where you can pick up the shuttle bus to the La Palud cable car (see 'Monte Bianco Cable Cars', below) and **Cogne**, gateway to the **Gran Paradiso National Park** (see p. 57). For bus information, call ☎ *0165-262-027*.

By Car The A5 from Turin bisects the Valle d'Aosta, en route to France and Switzerland via the Mont Blanc and Grand-St-Bernard tunnels. Turin to Aosta takes around 1½ hr by car; expect heavy traffic on Friday afternoons, around Ferragosto (August holidays) and during the ski season (December to April). The stretch between Aosta and Courmayeur takes about 30 min., while the scenic route, on the S26, takes around 1 hr.

VISITOR INFORMATION

The Aosta **tourist office** (Piazza Chanoux 8. ☎ *0165-236-627*; ***www.regione.vda.it/turismo***) has tons of information on hotels, restaurants, attractions, wine trails, campsites, hiking footpaths, bike rentals, ski-lift tickets and adventure sports. On the road to Monte Bianco, the **tourist office** in Courmayeur (Piazzale Monte Bianco 8. ☎ *0165-842-060*. ***www.comune.courmayeur.ao.it/turismo***) is an excellent source of information. The **tourist office** in Cogne (Piazza Chanoux 34–36. ☎ *0165-74-040*; ***www.cogne.org***) is the place to go for hiking maps and information about the Gran Paradiso National Park.

Festivals & Markets

Aosta comes alive to celebrate its patron saint with dancing, mulled wine and a craft fair at the **Fiera Sant'Orso** (last two days of January). The **Batailles de Reines (Battles of the Cows)**, as the name suggests, is a series of bovine brawls; the competition starts in the spring with qualifying contests throughout the region and culminates in the grand final at Aosta's Arena Croix Noire on the third Sunday in October (see ***www.amisdesreines.it*** for a schedule). Equally bizarre are the various

Arco di Augusto

giochi di rimando (*tsan*, *fiolet*, *rebatta* and *palet*): traditional games played in large fields, involving the launching and hitting of balls using wooden implements and levers. Contact the Aosta tourist office or check their website (see above) for upcoming tournaments. In the **Gran Paradiso National Park**, on 10th August, the people of Cogne and Val Soana climb the 2000 metres to the Sanctuary of San Besso, in celebration of their patron saint. Aosta's **weekly market** (Tuesday at Piazza Cavalieri di Vittorio Veneto) has stalls selling food, clothes, crafts and household goods.

Around the City

Aosta is a small mountain city surrounded by snow-capped peaks, with a rich history, chic shopping and outdoor pursuits on the doorstep. Vestiges of its days as the Rome of the Alps can be seen in the two Roman gates: **Porta Praetoria,** at the western entrance to the Roman town, and the **Arco di Augusto** (or Arco Romano), at the eastern end, built in AD25 to commemorate a Roman victory over the Celts. A **Roman bridge** spans the River Buthier, east of the Arco and just north of the Porta Praetoria you can see the facade of the **Teatro Romano (Roman Theatre)** alongside the remains of an **amphitheatre** that once had a capacity of 20,000 (follow the yellow signposts). The theatre and nearby **Forum** are open daily in summer from 9:30am to noon and 2:30 to 6:30pm, in winter from 9:30am to noon and 2 to 4:30pm; admission is free. Aosta's **Archaeological Museum** AGES 5 AND UP (Piazza Roncas 12; ☎ *0165-238-680*. Free admission. Daily 9am–7pm) will fascinate children with its many ancient finds.

Pop into the 10th century **Duomo** AGES 3 AND UP (Piazza Giovanni XXIII. ☎ *0165-40-251*. Free admission. Treasury: 2.20€ (£1.50) adults, 1€ (£0.67) under 10s. Mon–Sat 8am–12:30pm and 2:30–5:30pm, Sun 12:30–5:30pm; Treasury open April to September) with its 19th century façade and numerous alterations, to discover a couple of captivating treasures: beautiful 12th century mosaics before the altar and an ivory diptych (AD 406) that depicts the Roman emperor Honorius in the Treasury.

On the eastern outskirts of the *Centro Storico* you'll find the **Collegiata dei Santi Pietro e Orso** AGES 5 AND UP (Via Sant'Anselmo 9. ☎ *0165-262-026*. Affreschi Ottoniani: April to September 9am–7pm, October to March 10am–5pm), which displays a mishmash of architectural styles from the 6th to the 18th centuries. Worth seeking out is the 11th century fresco cycle recounting the life of Christ and the Apostles, housed in a room marked Affreschi Ottoniani, above the nave on the left aisle. The 12th century cloister also has 40 masterfully carved columns.

SIDE TRIPS FROM AOSTA

Castello Di Fenis (Fenis Castle) ★★ AGES 5 AND UP The turrets, dungeons and atmospheric wooden *loggias* here are bound to be a hit with the children. The Challant counts who built it decorated the living quarters with elaborate Gothic frescoes: seek out the one in the courtyard depicting St George rescuing a damsel in distress from

On the Scent of the St Bernard

The Great-St-Bernard pass, north of Aosta, links Italy with Switzerland, and is named after Bernard of Methon, an 11th century vicar of the city who founded schools, churches and inns for mountain travellers. Traversing the Alps was a hazardous business, so trained dogs were used to track down wayfarers buried in the snowdrifts: these 'St Bernards' are the ancestors of Swiss herding dogs and can handle deep snow and sniff out lost people. They are known for their gentle nature, being especially good with children. According to legend they carried small casks of brandy around their necks to warm those they rescued.

the ferocious dragon. After the compulsory tour (takes 30 min.; in Italian only), unfurl your picnic rug and enjoy the alpine vistas. A word of warning: get here early in the summer – tours are very popular. The nearby village of Nus has a train station and is worth a visit for its rustic stone buildings and to stock up on snacks.

0165-764-263. 5.50€ (£3.35). March to June and September 9am–7pm; July and August 9am–8pm daily; October to February Wed–Mon 10am–5pm (until 6pm Sun). Admission: 5.50€ (£3.70) By car: take the S26 east of Aosta 12 km (7miles); By bus: 30 min. from Aosta.

Breuil-Cervinia & The Matterhorn ALL AGES The **Matterhorn's (Monte Cervino** in Italian) distinctive profile dominates the Valtournenche as you approach overdeveloped Breuil-Cervínia –not the prettiest Alpine town, but one stuffed with excellent intermediate slopes with skiable access to Zermatt in Switzerland, and even summer skiing on the glacier (daily lift passes 24€ (£16) in summer and 34€ (£22.80) during the winter). Alternatively you can just enjoy the wonderful cable car ride to the Plateau Rosa (3480 m) and Little Matterhorn at 3883 m (25€ (£16.75) round-trip; closed 10th September to mid-October). The **tourist office** (Via Carrel 29. *0166-949-136; www.montecervino.it* or *www.cervinia.it*) dispenses useful information about family-oriented activities, including hiking and climbing, as well as skiing. To get here by car from Aosta (1 hr) take the A5 and S406. The best route via public transport involves taking a Turin-bound train to Chatillon (20 min.), followed by a 1 hr bus journey to Breuil-Cervínia.

Monte Bianco Cable Cars ★★ AGES 3 AND UP A series of

The Matterhorn

Courmayeur Resort

cable cars departing from La Palud (a 10-minute shuttle bus ride from Courmayeur; departs hourly) let you dangle above glaciers and soar among grand Alpine peaks. Although a multi-legged excursion to Chamonix may be too gruelling for younger children (definitely not advisable for under 3s because of the altitude), and seriously taxing on your wallet, you could easily go to Punta Helbronner: at 3462m (11,000 ft) the views of the Mont Blanc glaciers and the Matterhorn are unforgettable. The trip lasts 20 min. each way and costs 32€ (£21.50) for a round-trip or 88€ (£59) for a family pass, valid for two adults and two children aged 4–15. In summer, it's worth hopping off on the way at Pavillon Frety (2173 m) for a look around the Giardino Botanico Alpino Saussurea **AGES 3 AND UP** (☎ *333-446-2959*; ***www.saussurea.net.***; 2.50€ (£1.68) adults, 1.50€ (£1) 10–15, under 10s free. Open late June to end of September). The next stop is Rifugio Torino (3375 m) before going on to the last station in Italy, Punta Helbronner (3462 m) where there are more stunning views over the Ghiacciaio del Gigante, and a small museum full of rock crystals. A family ticket for two adults and two children (4–15 years) as far as here costs 98€ (£65.70). You can then continue over to the spectacular French outpost **Aiguille du Midi** ★★★ (takes 30 mins and costs an extra 18€ (£12), the highest point on the entire journey at 3642 m. If anyone in your group suffers from vertigo, be warned: the tiny gondola hangs 2300 m (7544 ft) in mid-air over the glacier and Vallée Blanche. This leg takes half an hour and costs 20€ (£13.40). From Aiguille du Midi you descend to Plan de L'Aiguille (2137 m) and then to Chamonix, on the French flank of Mont Blanc: this trip is 50 min. each way and costs 50€ (£33.50). If you fancy doing all five legs from Courmayeur to Chamonix, in France (no passport required), followed by return coach to Courmayeur, there is the Trans Mont Blanc ticket: 82€ (£55) adults; 70€ (£47) 12–15 years; 57€ (£38.20) under 12s. Because of weather conditions the service can be sporadic, but generally it runs every 20 min. from 7:20am (8:20am in the autumn and spring) to 12:30pm, and 2 to 5:30pm (all day 22nd July–27th Aug; closed 2nd Nov–10th Dec). The Helbronner–Aiguille du Midi cable car is open May to September. Apart from on the special package deals, children aged 4 to 15 get 50% off the journey prices from the La Palud ticket office. Senior citizens (over 60) get a 10% discount. For more information, call ☎ *0165-89-925* (***www.montebianco.com***). For a detailed weather report, ☎ *0165-89-961*.

Plans are afoot to upgrade this route, so expect some closures in coming years. It is also very popular, often meaning a long wait on a clear day. An alternative, cheaper and alas less thrilling, Val Veny cable car departs from Entrèves. Its just outside the village ascending to Val Veny. The round-trip fare is 10€ (£6.70), and it's free for children shorter than 1.3 m (4 ft. 4 in.). Cars depart every 20 minutes (9am–12:50pm and 2:15–5:40pm. closed late August to late December).

On all these trips make sure you bring warm clothing (temperatures can dip well below zero even in the summer), sun cream, sunglasses, bottled water and snacks.

La Thuile and Dolonne ★

AGES 3 AND UP 8 km (5 miles) from Courmayeur is the quieter village of La Thuile, whose wide beginners' slopes make it ideal for budding skiers. A top tip is to hire lockers on top of the mountain to avoid lugging your ski gear up every morning. And wrap up warm for a day's skiing here: the resort is known by locals for its cold winds. The excellent lifts are also used by mountain bikers and trekkers in summer. There are miles of trails, many suitable for family jaunts. If the children fancy a piece of the action, the local **Società Guide Alpine** (Strada Villair 2, 11013 Courmayeur. ☎ *0165-842-064*; ***www.guidecourmayeur.com***) runs courses and excursions for all abilities and ages. For more information about outdoor activities in the area check out ***www.vallemontebianco.it***; ***www.lathuile.net***; and ***www.lathuile.it***.

A short trip south-west of Courmayeur at Dolonne is a great **fun park** for children **AGES 3 AND UP** ★★★ **FIND**, full of funky ways to enjoy the snow: inflatables, snow tube pistes, ski foxes, snow bikes, *il Moon*

Walker and safe games for toddlers. In summer they have mini quad bikes and a pool. It is open from 9am to 4:30pm in the winter and until 7pm in the warmer months (Strada Statale 26/34, 11013 Courmayeur. *0348-591-6217*; email funpark.courm@yeur.net). It costs 6€ (£4) for a day on the *gonfiabili* (inflatables), and 12€ (£8) to have a go on everything both in summer and winter.

Gran Paradiso National Park

This magnificent national park covering 3626 sq. km (1414 sq. miles) straddles the Piedmont–Valle d'Aosta border and is a great destination for families seeking fresh air and rugged wilderness. Whether it's a day trip visit or a week's camping, there's a good chance of spotting the park's wild animals, including the protected ibex (a goat with large curved horns), marmot, chamois, small antelope and golden eagle. These craggy outcrops, wild forests and alpine fields were the hunting grounds of King Vittorio Emmanuele before it was donated to the Italian government in 1922. The principal gateway to the park on the Valle d'Aosta side is the small town of **Cogne**, 29 km (18 miles) south of Aosta via the S35 and S507. The village has decent services and nearby campsites.

There are hundreds of miles of well-signposted hiking trails, suitable for different family groups, from gentle strolls to more technical treks. A good place to start, for those with small children especially, is the village of Valnontey near Cogne, home to the **Giardino Alpino Paradisia** ALL AGES (*0165-74-147*. 2.50€ (£1.68) adults, 1€ (£0.67) 12–18-year-olds. 10th June to 15 September; daily 10am–6:30pm (5:30pm June and September)). From Valnontey, fit families with older children could consider the trek to the Vittorio Sella mountain lodge, where you can view roaming ibex at the Lago del Lauson, explore the mountain hamlet of Herbetet and picnic below a glacier. Don't hike anywhere without a decent map: the Istituto Geografico Centrale 1:25,000 map 101: Gran Paradiso, La Grivola, Cogne covers this part of the park.

Family-Friendly Accommodation & Dining

Expect hearty mountain food: beef stew, polenta, buttery cheeses like fontina and rustic salamis. If the children aren't into the flavoursome fayre, pizzas and classic pasta dishes are available everywhere.

Aosta

Milleluci This chalet-style hotel perched above Aosta has a swimming pool and views to die for. The functional rooms are comfy (ask for one facing south for mountain views) and there are different sizes for families, including spacious suites tucked under the eaves. Service is fantastic and the excellent buffet breakfast is a feast to fuel the family. It's a 25-minute walk into town.

Roppoz, 11100 Aosta. (☎ 0165-23-5278. fax: 0165-235-284. www.hotelmilleluci.com). 31 units. 95€–160€ (£63.50–107) double; 200€ (£134) suite; 190€–240€ (£127–161) adjoining rooms for 4. Rates include breakfast. AE, DC, MC, V. Free parking. Amenities: concierge; courtesy car; outdoor pool (heated); sauna; jacuzzi; children's playground; tour desk; limited room service; babysitting. In room: TV, dataport, hairdryer, minibar, safe.

Caffè Nazionale is bound to impress with its pastry treats and 19th century interiors, including a frescoed chapel room once used by the Dukes of Aosta.

(Piazza Chanoux 9. ☎ 0165-362-130)

Grotta Azzurra If you're tired of munching mountain fare try this decent pizzeria which does a mouthwatering margherita with fresh pomodori and mozzarella di bufala, as well as seafood delights.

Via Croix de Ville 97. (☎ 0165-262-474). Primi 4€–9€ (£2.70–6); secondi 5€–13€ (£3.35–8.70); pizza 4.50€–8€ (£3–5.35).; Thu–Tue (daily in summer) noon–2:30pm and 7–10pm).

Courmayeur and La Thuile

Atahotel Planibel Residence This complex offers good value and loads of facilities for families. It's right next to the ski runs (including nursery slopes) and chairlifts, and is also handy for the hiking trails in summer. Apartments are generally spacious with a small kitchenette – there's a supermarket nearby, a ski hire shop and restaurants. Look out for the hidden costs (final cleaning fee, towel charge, sports): these can add up.

*La Thuile, 11016 Aosta. (☎ 0165-884-541; fax: 0165-884-535. **www.atahotels.it**). 230 apartments. 7-night package depending on season: 1-bedroom apartment 300€-850€ (£200–570); 2-bedroom apartment 630€–1100€ (£422–737); final cleaning 30€ (£20). AE, DC, MC, V. Free parking. Amenities: two pools; gym; jacuzzi; sauna; children's mini-club; sporting club with games room and disco; tour desk; massage. In room: sat TV, hairdryer, kitchenette, safe.*

Baita Ermitage A wonderful terrace with views of Monte Bianco and tasty dishes using local ingredients like wild mushrooms make a visit here a real treat. And everyone loves the hot Alpine raspberries with ice cream.

Loc. Ermitage. (☎ 0165-844-351). Primi 5€–11€ (£3.35–7.40); secondi 7€–15€ (£4.70–10). Thu–Tue noon–2:30pm and 7–10:30pm Take the road to Entrèves and then the steep road to Ermitage.

Cogne and Valnontey

Hotel Gran Paradiso ★★ FIND Set in a dramatic spot, deep in the mountains with access to walks and lots of family activities, including cross-country skiing and mountain bike trails, this place is a bit special. Rooms are spotless and there's a cosy lounge with a fireplace for evening reading, chatting and games playing. The restaurant serves quality Italian fayre, and there's a shop next door, handy for picnic supplies if you're hiking. Family options (triples, quads and quintuples) are available on request.

*Pont Valsavarenche. (✆ 0165-953-18; [fax] 0165-950-74. **www.hotelgparadiso.com**). 8 units. Double 50€–70€ (£33.50–47). Triple 65€–90€ (£43.50–60). Half-board for two people 70–100€ (£47–67). 20–50% discount on triples and quads according to season. Breakfast included. AE, DC, MC, V. Free parking. Amenities: bar; restaurant. In room: TV, hairdryer.*

Camping Lo Stambecco For families seeking fresh air, spectacular scenery and outdoor activities a go-go, this campsite surrounded by peaks and pine trees is a good bet. It's just down the road from Cogne (connected by a regular bus service), and there's plenty of room for children to play. Bring a tent or caravan and enjoy the fantastic mountain biking, horse riding and walking trails nearby.

*0165-741-52; fax: 0165-749-213. (**www.campinglostambecco.com**). Family of four 35€ (£23.50) approximately per night for a pitch. AE, DC, MC, V. Free parking. Amenities: bar restaurant; tourist info; barbeque; washing and showering facilities; electricity.*

Brasserie Du Bon Bec This is a fun and fascinating place for a family meal, as the waiting staff are dressed in traditional *contadino* (peasant) garb and the place is full of village antiques. As well as hearty classics like *polenta concia* with fontina cheese, they have a good children's menu for 15€ (£10.

Via Bourgeois 72, 11012 Cogne. (✆ 0165-749-288). Primi 5€–10€ (£3.35–6.70); secondi 6€–13€ (£4–8.70). Tue–Sun noon–2:30pm and 7–10pm.

Lake Maggiore, Stresa

LAKE MAGGIORE (LAGO MAGGIORE)

Stresa: 80 km (50 miles) NW of Milan; Verbania: 95 km (59 miles) NW of Milan, 16 km (10 miles) N of Stresa

Lago Maggiore, Italy's second-largest lake, became renowned throughout Europe during the 19th century. Its shimmering waters and mountainous backdrop made it a Grand Tour destination *de rigeur*. The shoreline is dotted with promenades and small private beaches, and there are alluring attractions to visit, including the Borromean Islands, botanical gardens and a dramatic gorge. You can even pop over the border to Switzerland.

The major resorts are on the western (Piedmont) shore: starting in the south with **Arona** (uninteresting besides the views from inside the copper statue of St Charles Borromeo); followed further north by busy **Stresa** with its promenades and ferry links; quieter **Baveno** with its campsites and beaches, famed for its pink granite and the 1879 springtime sojourn of Queen Victoria at Castello Branca; largish **Verbania** incorporating Pallanza and Intra, which has a curious mixture of tourist facilities, industry, ferries and the Villa Taranto gardens; **Ghiffa**, a scattered conurbation with hotels and beaches; **Cannero Riviera**, a charming resort backed by Monte Carza (1118 m); **Cannobio**, with medieval buildings and access to the Parco Nazionale Val Grande (*www.parcovalgrande.it*) via the Val Cannobina; and finally the Swiss frontier with the Brissago Isles and towns of Ascona and Locarno beyond.

The eastern (Lombardy) shore is less interesting, though there's excellent walking terrain in the hills and some pleasant towns: **Luino** hosts the biggest market on the lake each Wednesday; **Laveno** is linked by ferry to Intra, with a cable car to Sasso del Ferro, used by paragliders, and a ceramic museum in nearby Cerro; **Santa Caterina** has a dramatic monastery set into the cliffs; **Angera** is known for its attractive waterfront and nearby castle, Rocca Borromeo; and **Ranco** is famed for its fascinating **transport museum** ★ (☎ *0331-975-198*. *www.museo-ogliari.it.* Admission free. April to October: 10am–noon, 3–6pm; October to April: 10–noon, 2–5pm).

Essentials

Getting There & Around

By Train Stresa is connected to Milan by around 20 trains per day (regional: 1¼ hr; high-speed: 58 min.).

By Boat Boats link Stresa with the Isole Borromee (Borromean Islands) and other lakeside spots, arriving at and departing from Piazza Marconi; the main company running these is **Navigazione Sul Lago Maggiore** (☎ *02-467-6101/ 800-551-801*; *www.navlaghi.it*).

By Car The A8 runs between Milan and Sesto, at the southern

Maggiore Facts

It is also known as 'Verbano', from the Roman name Verbanus, in reference to the herbaceous vervain plant that grows abundantly here and has small blue, white, or purple flowers. The Lake has a surface area of 213 sq km, is around 60 km in length, and is 12 km at its widest point. It's 372 m at its deepest point, off Ghiffa.

end of the lake; from there take the S33 which follows the western shore to Stresa (1 hr)

VISITOR INFORMATION

The **tourist office** is in Piazza Marconi (✆/[fax] *0323-31-308*. March to October:10am–12:30pm, 3pm–6:30pm). Other useful resources are ***www.stresa.it***, ***www.lagomaggiore.it*** and ***www.borromeoturismo.it***)

Festivals & Markets

Settimane Musicali (✆ *0323-31-095*; ***www.settimanemusicali.net***) is a classical music festival that runs from July to September. It attracts an international crowd to venues in Stresa and elsewhere on the lakeside.

Friday is market day in Stresa; in Verbania, it's Saturday. It's usually interesting to visit some of the smaller local markets in the morning as part of an excursion.

Verbania (Saturday) and Cannobio (Sunday) both have a relaxed atmosphere. There's a list of all the markets at: ***www.lagomaggiore.net/community/mercati.asp.***

THE BORROMEAN ISLANDS (ISOLE BORROMEE)

A boat trip to these three gorgeous islands, named after the Borromeo family, makes a fun journey for children and a refreshing break from the traffic. Each island has its own character and charms; Isola Bella and Isola Superiore are free to wander around, while Isola Madre has gardens you have to pay to visit.

There are two departing public ferries an hour from Stresa's Piazza Marconi (see 'Getting There & Around', above); buy an 8€ (£5.35) day-pass to visit all three. You'll also save 1€ (£0.67) if you buy your admission tickets for the island attractions at the Stresa ferry office. There is always a crowd of touts dressed as sailors in front of ticket booths trying to entice you on to their private boats. Be careful, they charge exorbitant prices, so unless you're in a large group with negotiating power, take the ferry. (For large groups, the prices can be reasonable; do your negotiating on the dock before you get on the boat.).

Isola Bella I is a genteel experiment in garden perfection – its 17th century terraces resemble a wedding cake in a Lewis Carroll fantasy. You half expect the Mad Hatter or scurrying Mr Rabbit to appear from behind a classical statue, exotic plant or fountain. The palace is equally whimsical in a stunningly baroque fashion. Children will love the marionettes, armoury and preposterous escapism of *le Grotte*: a series of artificial grottoes adorned with stones, shell mosaics and nymphs. The room where Napoléon stayed seems mundane in comparison. The palace and gardens are open daily:

Isola dei Pescatori

March to September 9am–noon and 1:30–5:30pm (to 5pm 1st–24th October). Admission: 10€ (£6.70) for adults and 4.50€ (£3) for children aged 6–15. Audio tours are available for 3.50€ (£2.35) each or 5€ (£3.35) for two headphone sets. Picnics are not allowed. For more information, call *0323-30-556*.

Narrow **Isola Superiore** (or Isola dei Pescatori) has remnants of its fishing village past, though it's rather dressed up for the tourists these days. Nevertheless, outside June, July and August, when the place is mobbed, a walk around the intimate lanes strung with fishing nets and little shops is a relaxing enough jaunt, and one that young children will enjoy.

Walking around the fragrant gardens of **Isola Madre** ★★, after the half-hour trip from Stresa, you could be fooled into thinking you'd landed in the subtropics . Even the vibrantly kitsch chapel façade has a pungent whiff of the Hispanic Americas. It's the largest and most tranquil of the islands, and the most rewarding to visit with children. The enchanting 8-acre **Orto Botanico** ALL AGES (*0323-31-261*) is full of colourful flora and exotic birds, including outrageously endowed peacocks and game fowl, which strut their feathery stuff under flowery pergolas and around the 16th century villa. Inside there is an exquisitely designed antique puppet theatre by La Scala scenographer Alessandro Sanquirico. Horticultural highlights include a large Kashmiri cypress, banana, eucalyptus, palms and spectacular early spring blooms of camellias and azaleas that frame shimmering vistas of Laveno and Santa Caterina del Sasso. The botanical garden is open daily: late March to September 9am–noon and 1:30–5:30pm, and 1st October to late October

Animal Sounds – Talking Italian

Italian animals make different sounds and, believe it or not, speak a different language.

Dogs (*cane*) go bau bau *bow bow*

Roosters (*galli*) go chicchirichí *keekeereekee*

Birds (*uccelli*) go cip cip *cheep cheep*

Sheep (*pecore*) go *beeeeh* (using e sound in bell)

Mice (*topi*) go squitt squitt *skweet skweet*

Chicks (*pulcini*) go pio pio *peeo peeo*

Frogs (*rane*) go cra cra *kra kra*

Donkeys (*asini*) go I-oo I-oo *ee-oo ee-oo*

9:30am–12:30pm and 1:30–5pm. Admission: 9€ (£6) for adults and 4.50€ (£3) for children aged 6–15.

Other Sights Near Stresa

Parco della Villa Pallavicino
★★ ALL AGES This wonderful zoo where animals wander amongst the visitors is a great place to spend a couple of hours. Formal gardens and mature woodland can be explored on foot (parts are quite hilly, a little awkward for pushchairs): the cool shade here provides welcome relief from the midday sun. The real draw is the wildlife, a cornucopia of beasts including zebras, kangaroos, flamingos, llamas, deer, raccoons, skunks, macaques and eagle owls. Families should wander among the entertaining Tibetan goats, that the children can feed and pet. Be careful what they munch on, though. The facilities include a playground, shop with animal-related goodies, open-air café and the La Scuderia restaurant. A mini-train connects the park with Piazzale Imbarcadero di Stresa, passing through the centre of town (9:30am–4:30pm).

Via Sempione Sud 8, 28019 Stresa. ☎ 0323-31533. ***www.parcozoopallavicino.it***. 8.50€ (£5.70) adults, 5.50€ (£3.70) 4–14 years. March to October daily 9am–6pm.

Funivia Monte Mottarone
There are superb hiking and mountain biking trails above Stresa, accessed via the Stresa Mottarone cable car, which runs every 20 minutes from 9:30 am–12:30pm and 1:30–5:30pm. Half-way up you can stop off at the **Giardino Botanico Alpinia** ALL AGES (adults 2.50€ (£1.68), 2€ (£1.34) 4–12 years) for the rare plants and stunning lake views. There are even more jaw-dropping vistas from the grassy summit – a great place to have a picnic. To hire specialized bikes or find out about their

TIP Airborne Adventures

As you approach the eastern shore at Laven, you'll notice paragliders, hang-gliders and other aeronautical acrobats descending from the Sasso di Ferro peak. If you or any older children fancy a go, contact the friendly **Club Icaro 2000** (Via Molin, 21014 Laveno. ☎ *0332-626-212*) which organises weekend beginners' flights.

mountain bike school as well as trekking, climbing, canyoning and rafting excursions in the area, contact **Bicico** (Piazzale della Funivia. ☎ *0331-324-300*; ***www.bicico.it***).

*Piazzale Lido 8. (☎ 0323–30295. **www.stresa-mottarone.it**) 13.50 €, 8€4-12 years return; runs every 20 minutes from 9:30 am to 12:30pm and 1:30-5:30pm daily.*

Villa San Remigio and Villa Taranto AGES 5 AND UP The pristine formal gardens of **Villa San Remigio** above Pallanza are well worth a visit if you have older children – their hilly terraces are tricky for little ones. If you are unable to secure a place on the guided tours (you must book a place in advance; ☎ *0323-503-249*), don't despair as the nearby **Villa Taranto** botanical gardens are also open to the public. The lavishly landscaped grounds are the fruit of a visionary Scot, Captain Neil Boyd McEacharn, who saw the villa for sale in an advertisment in *The Times* in 1930. Take a leisurely stroll around the extensive grounds filled with water fountains and exotic plants, including rare Australasian tree-ferns and giant South American water lilies.

*Verbania Pallanza 28922 (☎ 0323-56667. **www.villataranto.it**). 9€ (£6) adults, 6€ (£4) 6–14 years. Open 8:30am–6:30pm*

Stresa-Mottarone Cable Car

Family-Friendly Dining

There are lots of family-friendly eateries to choose from (many in Stresa and Verbania), serving everything from lake-caught fish to pizza.

Stresa

Osteria degli Amici ★ ITALIAN/PIZZERIA The cosy interiors and vine-shaded terrace attract a steady stream of Italians to enjoy the delicious pizzas, lake perch (*persico*), steaks and pasta creations.

Via A. M. Bolongaro 33. (☎ 0323-30-453). Reservations recommended. Primi 5.50€–8€ (£3.70–5.35); secondi 9€–15€ (£6–10); pizza 4€–10€ (£2.70–6.70). MC, V. Thurs–Tues noon–2:30pm and 7pm–midnight. Closed January and November.

Isola Superiore

Verbano ★★ ITALIAN For a real family treat, this restaurant on the fairytale Fisherman's Isle is hard to beat. Expect lots of fresh fish and vegetables served on a flowery terrace looking out to Isola Bella and beyond.

Isola Superiore dei Pescatori. (☎ 0323-32-534). Reservations recommended. Primi 5.50€–11€ (£3.70–7.40); secondi 10€–21€ (£6.70–14). AE, DC, MC, V. Daily noon–2:30pm and 7–10pm (closed Wed in winter). Closed January.

Verbania

La Lampara ★ VALUE ITALIAN/SEAFOOD Local families crowd into this friendly local, where smiley *ragazzi* and *bambini* feast on lake fish and tasty pasta.

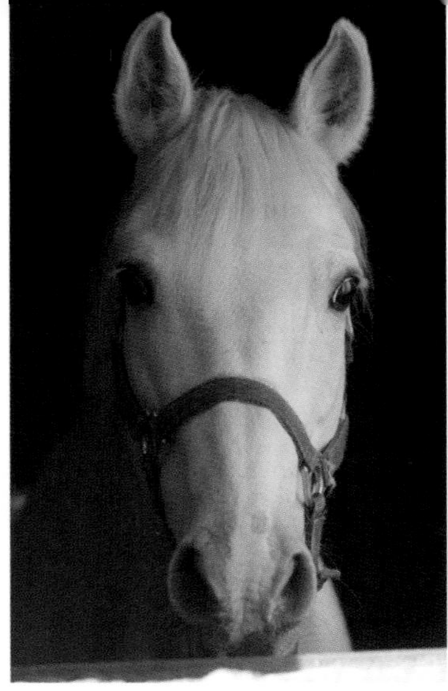

Agriturismo Monterosso

Vicolo Freschetto 1, on the corner of Via Canova. (☎ 0323-581-446). Primi 5€–8€ (£3.35–5.35); secondi 8€–14€ (£5.35–9.40). MC, V. Noon–2:30pm and 7pm–11:30pm

Family-Friendly Accommodation

The majority of the best resorts and hotels are on the western shoreline, close to the main family attractions. If your budget is tight, consider one of the agriturismi or campsites. Contact the Stresa tourist office (see Essentials above) for a comprehensive list.

Cannobio

Residenza Patrizia ★★ Families should have no trouble finding something suitable at this snazzy complex near the Cannobio shoreline. It incorporates a four-star hotel and spacious apartments. Interiors are contemporary and stylish, and many rooms have balconies. Children will love the two pools (indoor and outdoor), and there are watersports and other activities to keep you all busy.

Via Vittorio Veneto (☎ 0323-739-713) fax: 0323-739-778 ***www.residenzapatrizia.com****). 51 units. Double 120€–140€ (£80–94). Apartments 110€–265€ (£74–178). Breakfast included. AE, DC, MC, V. Free parking. Amenities: bar; restaurant; two pools; gym; sauna; Turkish bath. In room: A/C, sat TV, hairdryer.*

Verbania Pallanza

Agriturismo Monterosso ★★ FIND The adventure begins with an exhilarating drive round dozens of hairpin bends up to this historic farmstead turned agriturismo, which sits atop Monterosso. The French, Germans and Italians who regularly return for the great-value regional dishes and relaxed rural atmosphere are on to a winner. Children will love the farmyard animals and the outdoor activities, including horse riding and mountain biking. Contact the amiable owners, Iside and Giorgio, for more details on the variously sized functional apartments with kitchenettes and terraces. Get in quick: they are often snapped up months in advance.

Ristoro di Monterosso. (☎ 0323-556-510; fax: 0323-519-706. ***www.ilmonterosso.it*** *10 units. Double 75€ (£50). Apartments for 2–6: 300€–600€ (£200–400) per week plus 2.50€ (£1.68) per person per day for services. Breakfast included. AE, DC, MC, V. Free parking. Amenities: bar; restaurant; bike hire. In room: sat TV in apartments.*

Baveno

Hotel Rigoli The Rigoli sits in a superb position away from the main road with fantastic views of the Borromean Islands. There's lots of sporty things to do for children, rooms with balconies and a wonderful little beach. The hotel has an okay restaurant, but your best bet for a longer stay is to visit the nearby eateries that offer better value and quality. For those seeking independence, the hotel's nearby Residence Ortensia has apartments for 2–5 people that are great for families.

Via Piave 48. (☎ 0323-924-756; fax: 0323-925-156. ***www.hotelrigoli.com****). 31 units. Double 100€–120€ (£67–80). Triple 150€ (£100). Quadruple 170€ (£114). Apartments 2–5 people 75€–145€ (£50–97). Breakfast included. AE, DC, MC, V. Free parking. Amenities: bar; restaurant. In room: A/C, safe, sat TV, hairdryer.*

Camping

Conca d'Oro There are dozens of campsites along the shoreline, many with small private beaches and excellent facilities and sports. Some have noisy evening entertainment while others are quieter – ask lots of questions before you choose, so you get one that suits your family's needs.

The Conca d'Oro is a good bet near Verbania. It is set in a nature reserve at Feriolo. Children will love the private beach, and there are excellent facilities including a great-value restaurant. Renting a maxi caravan for four costs 50€–90€ (£33.50–60) per night depending on the season. A family of four can expect to pay around 45€ (£30) per night for a tent/caravan pitch.

*Via 42 Martiri 26, Feriolo di Baveno. (0323-28-116; fax: 0323-28-538. **www.concadoro.it**). Amenities: washing and cleaning facilities; bar-restaurant; children's playground; bike hire; sports activities including football, ping pong, horse-riding, watersports.*

LAKE COMO (LAGO DI COMO)

Como (town): 78 km (48 miles) N of Milan; Menaggio: 35 km (22 miles) NE of Como and 85 km (53 miles) N of Milan; Varenna: 50 km (31 miles) NE of Como and 80 km (50 miles) N of Milan

Surrounded by wooded slopes with the jagged outline of the Alps beyond, Lake Como's dreamy waters and bougainvillea-clad villas drew English Romantic poets like Byron, Shelley and Wordsworth during the 19th century. Its fishing villages soon became genteel resorts. Mass tourism and the car have slightly tarnished the otherworldly beauty and serenity that Pliny the Elder and Younger enjoyed when they sojourned here, but the whiff of aristocratic old-money is still in the air, embellished with jet-set glamour – not least in Bellagio where Americans peer through the tinted windows of passing Lamborghinis hoping to catch a glimpse of George Clooney, who has a house nearby. Fortunately you can mix boutique-browsing *passeggiate* and touristy visits to lavish villas with explorations of the wilder, mountainous corners of the lake and nearby valleys. The lavish hotels and restaurants may be

Lake Transport

more suited to honeymooning couples, but there are plenty of boat trips and lakeside activities to keep children amused, too. A word of warning about swimming and messing about on the water: be vigilant, as Lake Como gets deep very quickly and remember it's freshwater, so lacks the buoyancy of the sea.

Essentials

Getting There & Around

By Train There are 1–3 hourly trains between Milan and Como's **Stazione San Giovanni**: the regional train (1 hr) leaves Milan's Piazza Garibaldi station while the Intercity (40 min.) departs Stazione Centrale. To reach Bellagio and the other towns and resorts on the lake, you need to catch a bus or boat.

By Boat From Como, boats stop first at Bellagio: it takes 2 hr by ferry and 45 min. by hydrofoil. Next stop is Menaggio, a further 15 min. by ferry or 5 min. by hydrofoil. Many boats also stop at Varenna, and there are a number of short-haul ferries from Bellagio and Menaggio to Varenna. Ask about the day tickets if you want to hop around the lake from one resort to another.

You can take your car on to many of the ferries for an additional fee. Schedules vary with the season, but from Easter to September a car ferry or hydrofoil makes the trip from Como to Bellagio and other towns along the lake at least hourly. For more information, contact **Navigazione Lago di Como** (☎ *800-551-801* or *031-579-211*) ***www.navigazionelaghi.it***); the office is on the lakefront in Como, on Lungo Lario Trieste.

By Bus 1–3 **SPT** buses (☎ *031-304-744*) an hour travel from Como to Bellagio (about 1⅙ hr). Hourly buses to Menaggio take 65 min. Buses leave Como from in front of the main train station; buy tickets at the bar inside the station.

By Car Bellagio is connected to Como by a lakeshore road, the S583, which can be a tortuous yet exhilarating drive in summer: it's often crowded and locals driving towards you do not budge an inch, even on narrow corners. The A9 links Como with Milan (1 hr). From Como, Menaggio is reached via the S340 along the western shore of the lake. For Varenna, take the S342 to Nibionno, and pick up the S36, which runs north through Lecco and along the eastern shore.

Visitor Information

The **regional tourist office** is in Como (Piazza Cavour 17. ☎ *031-269-712* or *031-264-215*; ***www.lakecomo.org***. Open 9am–1pm, 2–5pm; closed Sun in winter).

Festivals & Markets

The **Sagra di San Giovanni** ★★ (last weekend in June) sees folkloric festivities and fireworks in Como.The **Festa del Lago** in Varenna re-enacts the

A Lakeside Walk in Como

Starting at Piazza Cavour, follow the avenue of lime trees to the **Giardino Pubblico**, a child-friendly expanse of greenery. The rotund **Tempio Voltiano** AGES 5 AND UP (Lungo Lario Marconi. *031-574-705*. 3€ (£2). Tuesday to Sunday 10am–noon, 2–4pm April to September. 10am–noon, 3–6pm in winter contains an exhibition in honour of physicist Alessandro Volta, who invented a rudimentary electric battery in 1799 – we name-check him when we talk about 'volts'. A design for a power station by Sant'Elia is the basis of the 1933 stark **modernist war memorial** nearby. Further along the prom, there's the chance to spy on the gardens and boathouses, and admire Belle Époque villas including **La Rotonda** and **Villa Pallavicino**. At the end of this stretch, formal Italian gardens provide a stately entrance to the creamy-hued, neoclassical **Villa Olmo** AGES 5 AND UP (Via Cantoni. *031-252443*. Monday to Saturday 8am–6pm. Art shows: 9€ (£6), 6€ (£4) 6–16-year-olds), which hosts fine temporary exhibitions (Magritte, Picasso and Mirò of late) in sumptuous *saloni*. The real treat here for families is around the back: a sprawling garden perfect for play and picnics.

1169 torching of the Isola di Comancina by Comaschi that was supported by Holy Roman Emperor Frederick I Barbarossa (Redbeard). Each September, the **Palio di Baradello** recreates the struggles against Barbarossa in the 12th century, with Middle Ages costume dramas. Also in September is the **Palio Remiero del Lario**, a traditional boat race on the lake.

Como's **food market** is on Tuesday and Thursday mornings and all day Saturday. Wednesday is market day in Varenna. For a full list of local markets see ***www.lagodicomo.com/english/mercati***.

In and Around Como

The town of Como on the Southern Tip of the lake has a fine *centro storico* worth exploring for a few hours: don't be put off by the congested outskirts and silk factories, as the heart of the city has characterful narrow streets, handsome buildings and an attractive lakeside promenade. Head straight for the 14th century **Duomo** AGES 3 AND UP (7:30–noon and 3–7pm daily), built entirely of marble and housing giant 16th century tapestries, vivid stained-glass windows and a dome built by Juvarra (of Turin fame) with gilded flourishes. You can't miss the elegant grey-and-pink-striped **Broletto** (13th century town hall) and the **Torre del Comune**. In stark architectural contrast is the nearby **Casa del Facsio** (built in 1936 over the railway track), one of Italy's most revered modernist buildings.

Narrow medieval streets with wooden-eaved buildings surround the pentagonal 12th century **San Fedele** (8am–noon and 3:30–7pm) church, which has a charming cobbled square in front of it. Further along Como's main street, Corso Vittorio Vittorio Emmanuele II, is the **Musei Civici** AGES 5 AND UP (Piazza Medaglie d'Oro 1. ☎ *031-271-343*. 3.50€ (£2.35) adults, 1.50€ (£1) children. Tuesday to Saturday 9.30am–12.30pm and 2–5pm; Sunday 10am–1pm) which has fascinating archaeological finds, natural history exhibits, a Risorgimento museum, an Egyptian collection and a section dedicated to World Wars I and II. Going west a few streets is the **Pinacoteca** AGES 7 AND UP (Via Diaz 84. ☎ *031-269-869*. Free admission. Tuesday toSaturday 9:30am–12.30pm and 2–5pm; Sunday 10am–1pm), housed in 17th century Palazzo Volpi, where you'll find Carolingian sculptural fragments and Futurist sketches by *Nuove Tendenze* member and influential Como architect Antonio Sant'Elia among the artistic treasures.

For stunning views and a grand picnic spot, take the **funicular** AGES 3 AND UP ★★ (☎ *0131-303-608*. ***www.funicolarecomo.it***. 1€ (£0.67) each way. 6am–3pm every 15 minutes, 3:30–10:30 every half-hour) from Lungo Lario Trieste, on the eastern waterfront, to the forested Brunate hill (713 m) above Como. There is a further 10-minute walk up a gentle incline to the viewing terrace. To go even higher, take the 10-minute bus ride from Brunate to San Maurizio (every half-hour where the **Faro Voltiano** lighthouse at 871 m offers yet more lake vistas. Keen walkers can follow several trails from Brunate – ask at the tourist office (see 'Essentials', above) for detailed maps.

The *Centro Lago* & Bellagio

Most visitors to Lake Como make their way to the central areas where the Como and Lecco arms meet. Positioned on a headland surrounded by cypress groves, lavish villas and exotic gardens, ever-popular **Bellagio** retains much of its traditional Lombardy character in its narrow cobbled lanes and buildings. A dash of glamour is provided by boutique shops, pastel-coloured hotel fronts and the odd yacht, flash car and poseur prancing along the promenade. You can easily spend a couple of hours ambling around, dipping in and out of shops selling craft objects, local silk creations, fashions and so on. For beautifully crafted olive-tree woodcrafts check out **Luigi Tacchi** on Via Garibaldi (☎ *031-950-836*). Sporty children will find Giro d'Italia cycling tops and footie shirts, as well as outdoor gear, at **Arco Sport** (Salita Monastero 6; ☎ *031-950-959*).

Slip into a seat at one of the waterfront cafés or restaurants,

Bellagio

put your shades on and enjoy an entertaining stint of people-watching and boat envy. No doubt the children will be itching for a dip – try the private beach at the **Lido**, at the end of the promenade, open daily from Easter to October, 8am–midnight.

There are a couple of famous villas with pleasant gardens to visit in Bellagio. **Villa Melzi** AGES 4 AND UP (*031-951-281*. Admission: 5.50€ (£3.70). Late March to early November: daily 9am–6pm) is a Belle Époque palace built by Francesco Melzi and frequented by Napoleon and Franz Liszt. You'll be dizzy at the sight of the steep formal garden terraces and sublime views as you stroll around admiring the plants and Egyptian sculpture. On the hill above town, **Villa Serbelloni** AGES 4 AND UP (*031-951-555*. Admission: 7€ (£4.70). April to October tours at 11am and 4pm, Tuesday to Sunday) is more Brahms than Liszt: its romantic gardens, grottoes and elegant fountains make for an even more intoxicating visit than its neighbour. Phone in advance to book a tour.

Varenna & The Eastern Shoreline

The charming little town of **Varenna** has narrow stepped streets and a small port that can only be accessed by foot. There's a promenade with great views of Bellagio and Villa Serbelloni, and a couple of attractive churches (San Giorgio and San Giovanni). Nearby, there is a couple of grand villas with extensive gardens. **Villa Cipressi** is now a hotel, but you can wander the terraced grounds filled with cypresses and wisteria.

Via IV Novembre 18. (01341-830-113). 2€ (£1.34) adults, 1.50€ (£1) under 10s. Open daily 9am–6pm April to October; the steep paths are tricky with small children.

Next door is **Villa Monastero**, a former monastery dissolved in

Como Facts

The lake covers an area of 146 sq km and has maximum depth of 410 metres.

It is the third-largest lake in Italy after Lake Garda and Lake Maggiore.

Two winds, known as the Breva and the Tivano, blowing from the south and north respectively, hit the lake, attracting windsurfers.

Villa d'Este, 3 miles north of Como at Cernobbios, was the centre of a 19th century scandal when lewdly dressed Caroline of Brunswick, the Princess of Wales, exiled herself here after leaving her rotund corset-wearing libertine husband the Prince Regent.

Isola Comacina, Lake Como's only island, was sold to Belgium by a local and is now run by a joint Italian/Belgian commission.

You may recognize the lake from the film *Star Wars Episode II: Attack of the Clones* as the planet Naboo.

In 1944, Mussolini and his mistress Claretta Petacci were shot dead at Mezzegra, just inland from Lenno.

the 17th century when the nuns started bearing proof of their intimacy with nearby priests. This has even more impressive gardens. Apart from opening an hour later at 10am, it keeps the same hours: combination tickets to see both are available, costing 4€ (£2.70) and 3€ (£2) for under 10s and over 60s. A renowned spring and the shortest river in Italy (at 250 m long), **Fiumelatte** emerges from rocks about 1 km out of town.This frothy milk-like (*latte* in Italian) torrent is active from May to October and was studied by Leonardo da Vinci: 'The Fiumelaccio falls from on high dropping more than 100 fathoms from the vein which gives it birth, falling sheer into the lake with the noisiest of rushes'. On the way, you can make a short detour to **Baluardo**, a scenic spot nearby. It's an easy enough walk with older children.

Apart from the lush central areas around Varenna and Bellagio, there are few child-friendly attractions on the eastern shoreline. **Lecco** is a busy commercial centre and most of the sprawl holds little interest, apart from **Bellano**, a town of small silk mills with the dramatic '**Orrido**' gorge. Specially constructed walkways allow spectacular views of the Pioverna torrents and canyon cliffs. But the ground is very uneven here, so it's not a trip recommended for families with small children. Anyone who enjoys walking should find out about the **Sentiero del Viandante**, an old 'Wayfarer's Track' that hugs the eastern shoreline, linking **Abbadia Lariana** near Lecco with Colico and Piantedo in the

Valtellina (Kompass does a series of maps and there's info at *www.valtellina.it*).

Menaggio & the Western Shoreline

Menaggio on the western shore is a bustling place with a waterfront piazza and narrow cobbled lanes leading to a castle. It's a good base if you love swimming, watersports and fancy hiking and cycling in the nearby mountains. Children can make a splash at the Lido (Via Roma 4. ☎ *0344-311-50*) which has a 25 m pool, a second pool for small children and a beach. The fantastic Ostello di Primula (see 'Family-Friendly Accommodation & Dining', below) is a hive of activity, renting out bikes and organizing courses and events. The beautiful countryside inland around Monte Bregagno, Monte Grona, Sasso Rancio and Rezzonico is worth exploring on foot foot (Kompass do the best maps of the area) with older children.

There are dozens of interesting villas along the western shoreline, including **Villa del Balbianello** ★★ AGES 3 AND UP near the ferry port at Lenno, run by the FAI (Italian Environmental Fund). Children will enjoy the exhibits documenting the expeditions of former owner Guido Monzino, the view from the fairytale *loggia* and the pristine gardens, where scenes from the latest Bond film *Casino Royale* were shot.

Via Comoedia, Lenno. (☎ 0344-56110. ***www.fondoambiente.it***). Villa and garden 11€ (£7.40), 4€ (£2.70) 4–12 years; garden only 5€ (£3.35), 2.50€ (£1.68) 4–12 years. Mid-March toNovember 10am–4pm. Closed Mon and Wed except public holidays.

Further up the coast is:

Villa Carlotta, which lies between the elegant resorts of Tremezzo and Cadenabbia. The 18th century interiors where Prussian royals inspired

A Side Trip for Active Families

Jungle Raider Park ★★ AGES 5 AND UP Adrenalin rushes are a given at this fabulous obstacle course in the conifers. Children and adults are safely harnessed and let loose to explore the network of gangways, Nepalese bridges, lianas and platforms. Choose from four routes of varying difficulty to suit all ages and abilities. There's a restaurant on site, a playground and mountain bikes (with trail guides).

Piano Rancio, Civenna, 22030 Como. (☎ *031-963-651*. ***www.jungleraiderpark.com***). 10–17€ (£6.70–11.40), 10€ (£6.70) under 14s. March, April and October Mon–Fri 10am–7pm; May to September 1am–7:30pm; other times by appointment only. By car: from Bellagio drive towards Magreglio and follow signs for Piano Rancio. By train: hourly to Canzo Rasso from Milan Ferrovie Nord.

Menaggio

the writer Stendahl are suitably lavish and pompous, but it's in the flower-filled botanical gardens that children will have most fun.

Via Regina 2, 22019 Tremezzo. (0344-40405. **www.villacarlotta.it**). 8€ (£5.35), free for under 6s. Second week in January to 30th March and October: 9–11:30am and 2–4:30pm; April to September 9am–6pm.

North of Menaggio there are several small resorts with pleasant beaches, quieter campsites and fantastic mountainous interiors leading to Switzerland. Places to consider are **Musso**, with its imposing fort, and **Dongo**, which isn't an Australian colony, but a great spot for watersports, swimming and excursions into the Alto Lario mountains. Indeed, if you love the outdoors, ask the tourist office about trips into the mountain valleys and passes along this stretch, including the **Val Darengo** and **Passo San Jorio**.

*Piano Rancio, Civenna, 22030 Como. (031-963-651. **www.jungleraiderpark.com**). 10–17€ (£6.70–11.40), 10€ (£6.70) under 14s. March, April and October Mon–Fri 10am–7pm; May toSeptember 1am–7:30pm; other times by appointment only. By car: from Bellagio drive towards Magreglio and follow signs for Piano Rancio. By train: hourly to Canzo Rasso from Milan Ferrovie Nord.*

Family-Friendly Accommodation & Dining

Como

Albergo del Duca/Le Colonne

★ For an overnight stay in Como you can't do much better than a stay at this *piccolo palazzo* set on a charming cobbled square: it's convenient for the railway station and the sights, has excellent options for families and even has a homely little restaurant, Le Colonne', specialising in fish and pizza. It lacks a lift though.

*Piazza Mazzini 12. ☏ 031 264-859. fax: 031-2439-69. **www.albergo delduca.it**. 8 units. 90€–120€ double; 20€extra bed. Rates include breakfast. AE, DC, MC, V. 10€ per day parking. Amenities: Internet, restaurant. In room: A/C, hairdryer, TV, minibar, safe. Le Colonne (Italian/ Pizzeria): Primi 6€–10€; secondi 8€–15 €.*

Bellagio

Hotel Bellagio This is a good value family choice in pricey Bellagio, although it's a bit of a hike up 38 steps for little legs and pushchairs. It lies in a quiet quarter and has a good choice of rooms for various sized groups – ask them about those with balcony views. Some rooms at the back are dark and gloomy. Guests have access to the Bellagio Sporting Club's pool and tennis courts and receive a 10% discount at the excellent Risorante Du Lac (see below). The only down side is the patchy service.

*Salita Grandi 6. (☏ 031-952-202; fax: 031-951-966. **www.hotelmilleluci.com**. 29 units. 80€–160€ (£54–107) double; 100€–190€ (£67–127) triple. Rates include breakfast. AE, DC, MC, V. Free parking. Amenities: gym; limited room service. In room: TV, minibar, safe.*

Bar Café Rossi ★ SNACKS Children will be raving about the pastries and breaded snacks at this lakefront local. Grab a table outside if you can, and don't forget to look inside at the handsome Liberty-style interiors.

Piazza Mazzini 22/24. (☏ 031-950-196). Sandwiches 3€–4.50€ (£2–3). AE, MC, V. April to September daily 7:30am–midnight; October to March Fri–Wed 7:30am–10:30pm.

Ristorante Du Lac ★★ For a real family-dining treat in Bellagio, this well-run lakefront establishment overlooking the main street is hard to beat. They do innovative Italian dishes like king prawn and courgette tempura (great to share), sublime pasta dishes like *fusilli* with smoked fish, and huge Florentine steaks. They'll even prepare some fab *contorni* (side dishes) to order for the children. Book a table outside and soak up the atmosphere.

Piazza Mazzini 32. (☏ 031-950-320). Primi 6€–10€ (£4–6.70); secondi 9€–16 € (£6–10.70). AE, DC, MC, V. Daily noon–2:30pm and 7pm–midnight.

Menaggio

Ostello La Primula VALUE This is not your run-of-the-mill hostel: it has superb value family suites with bunk beds. Most rooms have a view of the lake and the hostel is the focus of several sports activities, making it an ideal choice for active families. You can hire bikes and kayaks, play ping pong or just hang out making new friends on the large terrace. The set menu has lots of child-friendly pasta dishes, and costs just 12€ (£8).

*Via IV Novembre 86. (☎/fax: 0344-32-356. **www.menaggiohostel.com**). 35 beds. 15€ (£10) per person in dorm; 15€ (£10) per person in family suites (sleep 4–6 people) with private bathroom. Breakfast included. No credit cards. Open mid March to early November. Office open 8–10am and 5–11:30pm. Amenities: bar; restaurant; bike rental; washing machine.*

Varenna

Milano / La Vista ★★ It's a bit of a hike up to this fabulous spot (problematic if you have a pushchair, toddlers and heavy luggage) but it's well worth the effort for a couple of nights' stay. The doubles and triples are elegant, fresh and clean. Rooms 1 and 2 have large terraces with stunning views. The hotel's La Vista terrace restaurant also serves fresh Mediterranean-style fayre at 25€ (£16.75) per head for a three-course meal. Book early.

*Via XX Septembre 29. (☎/fax: 0341-830-298. **www.varenna.net**). 8 units. 120€–140€ (£80–94) double; 170€–190€ (£114–127) triple. Rates include buffet breakfast. AE, DC, MC, V. Closed late February to March. Amenities: bar; concierge; tour desk; limited room service; Internet; laundry service; massage; dry cleaning.*

Camping at Dongo

Magic Lake This fine little campsite on an idyllic stretch of the northern lake offers lots of sports activities including sailing, cycling and windsurfing. Parents and children can spend time on the beach splashing about in the Alpine waters. Expect to pay about 40€ (£27) for a family of four to pitch a tent or caravan. There is a small B&B on-site with doubles for 62€ (£41.50) and triples at 84€ (£56.30).

*Via Vigna del Lago 60. (☎/fax: 0344-80282. **www.magiclake.it**). Amenities: bar; laundry; bike and kayak rental. B&B has 5 units.*

Villa Rental

Vacanze Lago VALUE For affordable family accommodation, you could do worse than renting a villa from this agency based in Colico. They have a superb choice of properties (some with pools) – expect to pay anything from 300€ (£200) to 1600 per week € (£1072).

*Via Mazzini 13, 23823 Colico Lecco. (☎ 0341-940-327; fax: 0341-930-576. **www.vacanzelago.com**).*

Lake Garda

LAKE GARDA (LAGO DI GARDA)

Sirmione: 127 km (79 miles) E of Milan, 149 km (92 miles) W of Venice; Riva del Garda: 170 km (105 miles) E of Milan, 199 km (123 miles) NW of Venice, 43 km (27 miles) S of Trento

Lake Garda is the largest of the Italian lakes, renowned for its exotic plants, lemon groves, cypresses and deep waters backgrounded by Alpine peaks. The flatter southern stretches are a favourite with holidaying families from Lombardy, the Veneto and neighbouring German-speaking countries, who flock to handsome resorts like Sirmione, and to the theme parks including Italy's largest, Gardaland. Many roads, lakeside beaches and proms are jammed in the summer, but you can still find a dose of the serenity and magic that drew Byron and Churchill here.

Getting There

By Train Sirmione: The nearest station is **Desenzano del Garda** on the Milan–Venice line. From the Via Anelli bus stop in Desenzano it's a 20 minute bus ride.

By Bus Sirmione: An hourly bus service links the resort with **Verona** (1 hr) and **Brescia** (1 hr). For detailed information, contact **SAIA buses** in Brescia (*030-223-761*) or **APT** in Verona (*045-800-4129*).

Gardone di Garda: there is a bus service from Riva del Garda which takes about 1 hr. From Sirmione, you have to change at Desenzano del Garda. There are also buses from Milan (3 hr) and Brescia (1 hr).

Riva del Garda: There are six buses to and from Desenzano del Garda (2 hr). Most buses between Sirmione and Riva del Garda require a change at **Peschiera** (2 hr). There are a dozen trips to **Limone sul Garda** (20 min.) and 25 daily buses connect Riva with **Trento** (2 hr). There are over a dozen daily buses from Verona (2 hr), and five from Brescia (2 hr).

The Provincia di Verona publishes a very handy leaflet detailing all the seasonal public transport timetables available from the tourist offices.

By Boat Ferries and hydrofoils are operated by **Navigazione Lago di Garda** (*800-551-801*; ***www.navigazionelaghi.it***). One or two hourly ferries and four daily hydrofoils link Sirmione with Desenzano del Garda (20 min. by ferry; 10 min. by hydrofoil). Two daily ferries and three daily hydrofoils connect Sirmione with Gardone (1½ hr by ferry; 1 hr by hydrofoil), Limone sul Garda (2 daily; 3 hr by ferry; 1⅔ hr by hydrofoil), and Riva del Garda (4 hr by ferry; 2 hr by hydrofoil). There is a reduced service between October and April. A car ferry links the eastern and western shores, running between **Torri di Benaco** and **Maderno**.

By Car Sirmione: exit the A4 between Milan and Venice. The journey from Milan takes about 1 hr; from Venice allow at least 90 min.

Riva del Garda: The A22 runs along the east side of the lake passing Garda and Torri di Benaco before reaching the Mori turnoff, 8 miles east of Riva del Garda. The western shore has a scenic route between Riva del Garda and **Salò** that clings to cliffs and tunnels through miles of rock. Riva del Garda is about 1 hr from Verona and 45 min. from Sirmione.

Visitor Information

The **tourist office** at **Sirmione** (Viale Marconi 2. ☎ *030-916-245; www.bresciaholiday.com*) is outside the Old Town near the castle. Information is available in **Torri di Benaco** (Piazzale Lavanda. ☎ *045-722-5120*) near the small marina. The **Riva del Garda** office (Giardini di Porta Orientale 8. ☎ *0464-554-444*; *www.garda.com* or *www.gardatrentino.com*) is near the lake. Gardone's **tourist office** is at Corso Repubblica 8 (☎/fax: *0365-20-347*). They all dispense a wealth of information and will even book your hotel accommodation.

Festivals & Markets

There are a number of annual musical festivals, including the **Flicorno d'Oro** (*www.flicornodoro.it*), a marching band competition that takes place at Riva del Garda each April. **Il Festival del Garda** (*www.ilfestivaldelgarda.it*) incorporates a number of events including concerts, art exhibitions, a beauty pageant and a body-painting competition.

Desenzano holds its historic market each Tuesday; **Torri di Benaco** has one each Monday.

Sirmione & Desenzano

Sirmione sits at the tip of a narrow peninsula of olive and cypress groves, on the southern shore of the lake. It's renowned for hot springs, pleasant lakeside proms and idyllic spots for family bathing, including the **Lido Bionde**, which hires out sun loungers, parasols, kayaks and pedal boats. A stroll around the old town with its tacky gift shops and fortified buildings will excite younger children – although the crowds in summer are a real pain, especially on German bank holiday weekends and the last week in May. Imaginations will run wild at the sight of the turreted castle,

Sirmione

Lake Garda: Fruity Facts and Trivia Bites

Il Lago di Gardo was known as lacus benacus to the Romans and is Italy's largest lake: it's 52 km long, 5–17 km wide and covers an area of 370 square km. It's maximum depth is 346m and it is separated from the river Adige river valley by Monte Baldo (2,218 m). It receives the River Sarca and leaves as the River Mincio, a tributary of the Po. The northern reaches are narrow and fjord-like. Lake Garda is the northernmost citrus commercial growing spot (300 m) in the world. The lemon is a cultivated hybrid deriving from wild species including the citron and mandarin. The Riveira Bresciana is fertile strip of land between Gargnano and Salò on the west side of the lake. In this lush area lies the Heller Garden, whose owner Andrè Heller designed the iconic Fussball-Globe for the 2006 football World Cup in Germany, which was placed near the Brandenburg Gate.

Rocca Scaligera AGES 3 AND UP (☎ *030-916-468*). 4€ (£2.70). Tue–Sun April to October: 9am–8pm; November to March: 9am–1pm) built by the della Scallas and offering fine views from the 30m tower. Follow the Via Emmanuele to the **Grotte di Catullo** AGES 4 AND UP ★★ (☎ *030-916-157*). 4€ (£2.70) Tue–Sun 9–dusk), the evocative ruins of a Roman villa amid olive trees and wild flowers where the poet Catullus is said to have lived. On the road to Desenzano, turn off before Rivoltella for **San Martino della Battaglia**, where there is a tower commemorating the joint Piedmontese–French victory over the Austrians in 1859, a decisive battle in the unification of Italy. After thrilling the children with the climb and stunning views from the top, head to the **museum** (Via Ossario. ☎ *030-991-0370*. 5€ (£3.35). Open 9–12:30, 2–6:30pm and the nearby **Capella dei Conti Treccani** AGES 7 AND UP for a poignant and rather creepy experience. The ossuary houses 1274 skulls and the bones of 2619 souls killed in battle.

Desenzano is an attractive town with a picturesque quay, a cute lighthouse and arcaded piazza – a fine place to relax, eat ice cream and dine al fresco. A 4th century **Roman villa** AGES 3 AND UP (Via Crocefisso 22. ☎ *030-914-3547*. Free under 18s. 9:30am–6pm), the best in northern Italy, will fire children's imaginations with its grandiose octagonal hall and colourful mosaics. Bronze Age and neolithic finds and models of lakeside dwellings on stilts can be seen at the **Museo Civico Archeologico 'Giovanni Rambotti'** AGES 3 AND UP (Chiostro di Santa Maria de Senioribus, Via T. Dal Molin 7/c. ☎ *030-914-4529*. Admission free. Tue–Sun 3–7pm).

The Western Shoreline

North of Desenzano, the coastline around **Moniga** and **San Felice di Benaco** is known for its clean waters. **Salò,** where Mussolini ran his short-lived puppet republic in 1943, is perhaps the most attractive town here. It's a magical place, perfect for a wander around narrow streets with curious covered passageways and floral balconies. The magnificent late Gothic cathedral is worth a gander for its 15th century tabernacle and paintings.

Sheltered **Gardone Riviera** has lush parks and a fantastic attraction that visitors with children might easily overlook: **Il Vittoriale** ALL AGES ★★ (*0365-296-511. www.vittoriale.it.* Gardens and tour of house: 11€ (£7.40), 8€ (£5.35) 7–14 years; gardens only: 7€ (£4.70), 4€ (£2.70) 7–14 years. April to September 9:30am–7pm; Reduced hours October to April) was the sprawling, idiosyncratic residence of poet, Italian nationalist and fighter pilot, Gabriele d'Annunzio. It's crammed with eccentric objects that give an insight into this larger-than-life character, including the plane in which he famously flew over Vienna. Children will love the equally bonkers grounds, where they'll find fountains, monuments, an amphitheatre, the prow of a ship and a bubbling brook descending from the Acquapazza Valley. Book early, as tickets to see the house are limited. There is an extraordinary **botanical garden** ALL AGES ★★ nearby, originally created by amateur botanist Arturo Hruska and now the home of artist Andrè Heller (Via Roma 22. *336-410-877. www.hellergarden.com.* 8€ (£5.35), 4€ (£2.70) 5–11 years. Mid-March to mid-October 9am–6:30pm). Funky art installations by Roy Lichtenstein and Keith Haring as well as mystical sculptures have been placed amid giant tree-ferns, orchids, waterfalls, ponds and boulders.

Toscolano-Maderno is an interesting resort, worth stopping in if you fancy windsurfing, swimming (there's a beach and diving platform) or investigating the western shore's principal Roman settlement, **Benacum**: four Roman columns stand by the **Chiesa di Santi Pietro e Paolo**. Linger at a waterfront *caffè*, pop into the 12th century **church of Sant'Andrea** and hit the splendid beach.

The landscape becomes lusher on this stretch of coast, where the

TIP Lakeside Magic

The headland of Punta San Vigilio, south of Torri di Benaco, is one of the lake's magic places: park your car and follow the cypress avenue past Villa Guarienti and the church of San Vigillio, to a small, sheltered cove where children can swim in relative seclusion.

TIP Lakeside Sports

There's lots for sporty families in and around the lake. Children can learn windsurfing and sailing at Malcesine with WW Wind (☎ *045-740-0413*. ***www.wwwind.com***), near Riva at Vasco Renna (☎ *0464-505-993*. ***www.vascorenna.com***), or through Sailing Du Lac (***www.sailingdulac.com***), which also rents out mountain bikes for 20 € per day. Windsurfing courses cost about 150 € for ten hours. To hire a boat, ride a banana boat or find out about sports like wake-boarding, contact Nautica Gardamare at Manerba (☎ *030-961-846*. ***www.gardamare.it***). For family trips into the mountains, get in touch with expert local guides at Garda Trekking (☎ *0464-422-273*. ***www.gardatrekking.eu***). From 31€ for a trek up Monte Baldo.

Romans grew lemons – there is less development until you reach the little port of **Gargnano**. For the most spectacular views of the lake and a peek at **Villa Feltrinelli** (now a luxury hotel), where Mussolini lived out his last hurrah, take the inland road to **Madonna di Monte Castello**: don't forget the camera!

Limone sul Garda was surrounded by terraced gardens with special growing pavillions until the 1930s, when the town first became accessible by road. Once beloved of the poet Goethe, it soon lost its romantic allure when building speculators moved in during the 1950s – it's filled mainly with German tourists, trashy shops and cheap restaurants now.

Limone sul Garda

Riva del Garda

The northernmost town on the lake is a lively resort with an attractive cobbled *Centro Storico* filled with Renaissance churches, medieval *torri* and a 14th century castle, **La Rocca**. There's a lengthy promenade and pebbly beaches. Windsurfing is superb here, too (see 'Lakeside Sports', below). Inquisitive children will enjoy the armoury collection and archaeological finds from the Lago di Ladro Bronze Age lake dwellings at the **Museo Civico** AGES 4 AND UP (Piazza Battisti 3. ☎ *0464-573-869*. ***www.comune.rivadelgarda.tn.it/museo***. Free admission. March to November 10am–6pm; closed Mon). When the water level is low, some of the 20,000 wooden stakes from these lake huts can be seen near **Molina.** There is also a reconstruction of a Bronze Age straw-roofed dwelling and a small museum here: **Museo Tridentino di Scienze Naturali** AGES 4 AND UP, Molina (*0464-508-182*. 2.50€ (£1.68), 1.50€ (£1) 12–18 years, free under 12s. March to November, Tue–Sun 10am–1pm, 2–5pm).

The Eastern Shoreline

The 2000 m peaks of Monte Baldo flank the east side of the lake. It is an area renowned for its varied plant life, from olive and citrus groves lower down to Alpine species like mountain avens, gentians and succulent saxifrages on the ridges. For a close-up look at these natural wonders and jaw-dropping lake vistas, take the cable car at **Malcesine** and picnic on the summit of Monte Baldo (*045-740-0206*. ***www.funiviamalcesine.com***. 16€ (£10.70), free for children under 1 m. Reductions for families with four paying members. Early April to November: 8am–6pm; last descent 6:45pm) – you can even take your mountain bike up there. Malcesine itself is a charming resort, with a small port and narrow streets filled with cafés and shops. The well-preserved **Castello di Scaligeri** AGES 4 AND UP (Via Castello. *045-657-0963*. 4€ (£2.70), 1€ (£0.67) 6–14-year-olds, family tickets 8€–10€ (£5.35–6.70)) has great views from the *revelino* (artillery platform) and a few exhibition spaces: a natural history museum, Venetian galley finds, sketches by Goethe and changing art and photography shows. Concerts are held here in the summer: contact the venue and the tourist office about the latest programme.

Torri di Benaco has a great atmosphere and is, thankfully, not overrun with tourists: you can easily pass a couple of hours at the quayside cafés and strolling around up and down the long promenade eating ice-cream. Duck into the cool halls of the **Castello Scaligero** AGES 3 AND UP (Viale Fratelli Levanda 2. *045-629-6111*. 3€ (£2), 1€ (£0.67) 6–14 years. October- March: 9:30am–12:30pm, 2–6pm; April to September 9:30–1pm, 4:30–7:30pm) which has exhibits exploring the local fishing industry and olive production, as well as fine views from the tower.

Passing **Punta San Vigillio** (see 'Lakeside Magic', below) and the Bardolino vineyards there is a great spot for children: the **Lido di Cisano** ALL AGES, with a promenade, beach, ice cream vendor, playground and toilets. South of **Lazise**, a former Venetian stronghold, the flatter terrain and proximity to the motorway network mean lots of development. It may be the least attractive part of the lake but families flock here for the cheesy theme parks, Gardaland and Caneva World (see below), where you can enjoy a traditional medieval banquet of chicken and chips. Right in the south-eastern corner of the lake sits **Peschiera**

di Garda. Despite its impressive Venetian fortifications, and apart from using the train station to stock up on supplies, or to watch the boats gliding down the River Mincio into the lake, there is no reason to stop here.

Theme Parks

Gardaland ★★ ALL AGES Italy's biggest theme park has been packing them in for years. The various attractions take you on fantastical journeys from Africa to Atlantis. A Tarzan-aping, loincloth-wearing character shows you around his jungle home, Tunga. The fabled kingdom of *Atlantide* is brought to life with colossal statues and dizzying descents on round rafts. Rollercoaster rides include the Sequoia Adventure, Blue Tornado, Magic Mountain, Jungle Rapids and Fantasy Island. To cap it all, there are a dozen shows including an ice-skating gala, a Broadway extravaganza and a magic show. Top bill goes to the aquatic acrobatics of the dolphins. As always, there are various eateries with hilariously OTT décor to help you part with your money.

*Castelnuovo del Garda, 37014. (☎ 0456-449-777. **www.gardaland.it**). 1 day 26€ (£17.50), 22€ (£14.75) under 10s, free under 1 m; two consecutive days 42€ (£28.15), 35€ (£23.50) under 10s, free under 1 m; any 3 days 54€ (£36.20), 44€ (£29.50) under 10s, free under 1 m. By Car: from A4 exit at Peschiera or Sommacampagna; from A22 exit at Affi or Verona Nord.*

Caneva World Resort ALL AGES You'll be repeating 'I'm living in a movie' as you hurtle around the Movieland studios, getting up close to *Terminator II* in the cyber labs and Freddie Kruger at the Horror House. Adrenalin-junkies will enjoy the rollercoasters, water flumes and action-packed trucking adventures. The live shows include Blues Brothers, Stuntman Academy, Legend of Zorro, Rambo Action and Cartoon Network. Next to this in-your-face Hollywood-style excess, Acqua Paradise offers healthier action on a fantasy tropical island – it's more suited to younger children, who'll make almighty splashes on the water slides and in the pools. Also on-site is an American-style diner, Rock Café and the Medieval Times banquet hall, which delivers a heady mix of trumpeting, jousting, jesting, pizza and chips.

*Via Fossalta, 1, 37017 Lazise sul Garda. (☎ 0456-969-900. **www.canevaworld.it**). 1 day, 1 park: 20€ (£13.40) adults, 17€ (£11.40) under 1.4m height, free under 1m; 1 day, 2 parks: 26€ (£17.50) adults, 22€ (£14.75) under 1.4 m, free under 1 m; 2 day, 2 parks: 31€ (£20.80) adults, 26€ (£17.50) under 1.4 m, free under 1 m. Early April to July and September to mid October: 10am–6pm; 7th July to August: 10am–7pm with some late night openings to 11pm. By Car: from A4 exit at Peschiera.*

Parco Natura Viva ★★ ALL AGES Children will have a hoot at this animal kingdom near Peschiera di Garda: take your vehicle around the park where you'll meet giraffes, lions, tigers, chimps, zebras, rhinos, and hippos. The Parco Faunistico is explored on foot – you'll come across several protected species involved in an international breeding programme, including wolves, Madagascan lemurs, snow leopards and red pandas. Tropical birds flap around the greenhouse, exotic fish swim in the Aquaterrium's coral reef and scaly constrictors hiss at tarantulas in the Rettilario. Facilities include a playground, picnic area, café and souvenir shop.

*Località Figara 40, Bussolengo 37012. (☎ 045-717-0113. **www.parconaturaviva.it**). 15.50€ (£10.40), 12.50€ (£8.40) 3–12 years. 9am–6pm daily; November to March restricted hours according to weather conditions. By Car: from A4 exit at Peschiera del Garda or Sommacampagna; from A22 exit at Affi or Verona Nord.*

Family-Friendly Accommodation & Dining

Desenzano

Villa Maria ★★ FIND Fabulous gardens filled with olives and flowers, superb service and spacious accommodation, make this a real find for families. Sporty children will enjoy the huge pool, tennis courts, *bocce* (boule pit) and free use of mountain bikes. Alongside the hotel, there are 24 three-roomed villas in the grounds, all of which sleep up to six, as well as a fine restaurant with terrace.

*Via Michelangelo 150. (☎ 030-990-1725; fax: 0365-290-504. **www.gardalake.it/villa-maria**). 40 units. 24 villas. Rates per person. 51€–80€ (£34.20–54) double; 43€–62€ (£28.80–41.50) triple; 40€–55€ (£27–37) quad; 76€–180€ (£51–120) suite; free cots; 30€ (£20) extra bed, per day. Hotel rates include buffet breakfast (10€ (£6.70) for villa guests). AE, DC, MC, V. Free parking. Amenities: concierge; bar; restaurant; Internet; laundry service; pool; children's playground. In room: A/C, TV, hairdryer, safe, kitchenette in apartment.*

Sirmione

La Roccia ITALIAN/PIZZERIA There are two-dozen pizzas to choose from at this popular trattoria-pizzeria. With the children taken care of, adults can pick from the many menu highlights, which include roast trout, grilled meats and a plethora of pasta creations. In the summer you can eat in the garden.

Via Piana 2. (☎ 030-916-392). Primi 6€–11€ (£4–7.40) ; secondi 9€–16€ (£6–10.70); pizza 5.50€–9€ (£3.70–6). DC, MC, V. Fri–Wed 12:30–3pm and 7–10:30pm. Closed November to March.

Gardone Riviera – Toscolano

Residence Borgo Degli Ulivi ★ This spanking new complex offers a choice of comfortable flats with balconies, as well as fabulous grounds with two pools (including a small kiddies' one) and a playground. Ask for an apartment with views. There is air conditioning in the main living areas, but the bedrooms can get very stuffy in the summer, so you'd better bring a small fan.

*Via Panoramica 46. (☎ 0365-206-52; [fax] 0365-290-504. **www.residenceborgodegliulivi.it**). 43 units. 2–6 person apartments 90€–250€ (£60–168). 7€/15€ (£4.70/10) cot/extra bed, per day. Rates include breakfast. AE, DC, MC, V. Free parking. Amenities: concierge; two pools; jacuzzi; children's playground; babysitting; laundry service; games room. In room: A/C in living room, TV, hairdryer, kitchenette, safe.*

Agli Angeli ITALIAN Located near Il Vittoriale (see 'The Western Shoreline', above), this charming little trattoria spills out on to a cobbled square and serves seasonal creations including lake fish, game and a smattering of tasty side dishes to please fussier children and veggies. The coconut ice cream with chocolate sauce will go down a treat. They also have 12 rooms and a couple of suites suitable for families (100€–160€ (£67–107)).

*Piazza Garibaldi 2. (☎ 0365-20-832. **www.agliangeli.com**). Reservations recommended. Primi 6€–11€ (£4–7.40); secondi 9€–14€ (£6–9.40). V. Daily 12:30–3pm and 7–10:30pm. Closed November to mid-March.*

Riva del Garda

Hotel Gabry Immersed in lush grounds, the Donatinis' Hotel Gabry has an array of room options, including family accommodation with bunks. There's a small but perfectly formed pool and the nearby stretch of lake offers plenty of aquatic activities and courses, including swimming, sailing, diving and windsurfing. If you fancy mountain biking, you can use the hotel's bikes for free to explore the rugged terrain nearby. Riva is a 20-minute stroll away along a lakeside prom.

*Via Longa 6. (☎ 0464-553-600; fax: 0464-553-624.**www.hotelgabry.com**). 39 units. 80€–100€ (£54–67) double, 120€–150€ (£80–100) triple, 140€–170€ (£94–114) family room. Children's discounts. AE, DC, MC, V. Free parking. Amenities: bar; free bike and surfboard hire. In room: A/C (6€ (£4) per day on request), TV, hairdryer, safe.*

Birreria Spaten ITALIAN/TYROLEAN There's something for everyone at this atmospheric beer hall cum restaurant – it's been packing them in since 1968 and is a perennial hit with families. Children will love the pizzas, dads will love the beer and brainy mums should try the fish – oh, and the chocolate ice cream. For a change, order a Tyrolean platter of spicy meats, dumplings and sauerkraut. Riva is in the Trentino, after all.

Via Maffei 7. (☎ 0464-553-670). Primi 5€–8€ (£3.35–5.36); secondi 6€–14€ (£4–9.40); pizza 4.50€–7.50€ (£3–5). MC, V. Thurs–Tues 11am–3pm and 5:30pm–midnight. Closed November to February.

Torri di Benaco

Hotel Romeo ★★ VALUE For families looking for Garda's quiet side, the charming town of Torri di Benaco and the nearby Hotel Romeo will do just fine. There's lots for children to do: the leafy grounds have a curvy pool and a tennis court, while Torri's stretch of lake has watersports a go-go. Golfers should try the course at nearby Marciaga. Ask for one of the rooms at the front, which are more spacious and have balconies. It's worth going half-board: their restaurant serves excellent 3-course meals. Bring a portable fan in the summer.

*Via dell'Oca Bianca 31. (☎ 0457-225-040; fax: 0456-296-588. **www.hotelromeo.com**). 44 units. 80€–130€ (£54–87) double half-board; free for children up to 4 years; 5–11 years 50% discount; cot 10€ (£6.70) per day. AE, DC, MC, V. Free parking. Amenities: bar; restaurant; pool. In room: A/C (6€ (£4) per day on request), sat TV, safe.*

TRENTINO–ALTO ADIGE & THE DOLOMITES

Trento: 230 km (143 miles) NE of Milan, 101 km (63 miles) N of Verona, 57 km (35 miles) S of Bolzano; Bolzano: 154 km (95 miles) N of Verona, 118 km (73 miles) S of Innsbruck, 57 km (35 miles) NE of Trento; Cortina d'Ampezzo: 133 km (82 miles) E of Bolzano, 166 km (103 miles) N of Venice

The provinces of Trento and Bolzano contain the unspoiled mountain territory of the South Tyrol and upper Adige river valley – a region famed for its curious Italo-Germanic culture, where German becomes the principal language the further north you go, and pasta gradually gives way to potatoes and dumplings. As a family destination, it's hard to beat: from leisurely soirees in alpine towns

Lake Dobbiaco, The Dolomites

and castles that jut out of the dramatic Val d'Adige; to forays into the Dolomites for mountain pursuits, including skiing and trekking, to wow children and old folk alike. Between the cities of Trento and Bolzano is the **Strada del Vino** (Wine Road) – you'll see many hillside vineyards that produce plenty of quaffable Pinot Grigios and Pinot Noirs, among them some outstanding wines. Outdoorsy families can head to one of the region's many national parks, where children can see wild animals like ibex and bears. Anyone looking for ski pistes and hiking or biking trails can choose between numerous small towns with charm and chairlifts, and swanky resorts like Cortina d'Ampezzo with its miles of cable cars, fancy shops and lavish hotels.

Essentials

Getting There

By Plane There is a number of airports handy for reaching the Dolomites, including Brescia, Verona, Treviso and Venezia (See Planning Chapter and Appendices.)

By Train Trento and Bolzano lie on the line between Italy and Austria and are served by over 20 daily trains from Verona (around 1 hr), from where there are connections to Milan, Venice, Trieste and destinations south. There are frequent trains connecting Trento with Bolzano (45 min.). Cortina's closest train station is **Calalzo di Cadore,** 30.5 kilometres (19 miles) south. From here, there are frequent buses outside the railway station to and from Cortina.

By Bus **Atesina buses** (☎ *0461-821-000*; *www.atesina.it*) serve the mountain towns surrounding Trento. Bolzano is the hub of a bus network run by **SAD** (☎ *0471-450-111; www.sad.it*). You can also get to and from Garda and Cortina from here. **SIT** runs the only public transport to and from Cortina (☎ *800-846-047* in Italy; *www.sii.bz.it*).

By Car The A22 connects Trento with Verona (1 hr) and the A4 (Torino–Milan–Venice). The A22 links Trento and Bolzano (30 min.) as does the slower S12. The **Grande Strada delle Dolomiti** links Cortina with Bolzano. Cortina–Venice is a 3-hour journey along the S51 and A27.

Visitor Information

The **Trento tourist office** (Via Manci 2. ☎ *0461-983-880;* fax: *0461-232-426*; *www.apt.trento.it*) is close to the Duomo. The **Bolzano tourist office** is at Piazza Walther 8 (☎ *0471-307-000*; fax: *0471-980-128; www.bolzano-bozen.it*). For local event listings visit *www.bobo.it*. For Internet access go to Multimedia Team (Largo Poste 59 Cortina d'Ampezzo. ☎ *0436-8680900*.

Festivals & Markets

Trento hosts a couple of very popular annual festivals. May and June see music in suitably evocative settings as part of the **Festivale di Musica Sacra (Festival of Sacred Music).** In late June, the **Festive Vigiliane** involves a medieval pageant, goose races and fireworks in the Piazza del Duomo. From late June to September, **Superfestival** is another winner with the children, with fun musical performances and re-enactments of medieval and Renaissance legends in spectacular castle settings. In Bolzano, the October **Festival del Teatro di Strada** attracts family-friendly street performers including puppeteers. The **Bartolomeo Horse Fair** (24 August) is a colourful equine event on the Renon plateau about 10 km north east of Bolzano.

Trento hosts a **food market** on Piazza Alessandro Vittorio each day from 8am to 1pm.

Pinocchi

Each Thursday there is also a **weekly market** with household goods and clothing.

Bolzano's **produce market** in Piazza delle Erbe (Mon–Sat 8am–7pm) is great for children, but not as magical as the pre-Yuletide **Mercatino di Natale (Christkindlmarkt)** ★★★ which is chocker with christmas shoppers bagging wooden toys and crafts, and has plenty of mulled wine. Cortina's **Piazza Italia** is the venue for a general market (Tue & Fri 8am–1pm): expect local produce, big cheeses, clothing, knick-knacks and household goods.

Trento

Trento occupies a stunning position encircled by mountains on the banks of the Adige river, where light-hued stone streets come with a fresh hit of Alpine air after the flat terrain, uniformity, and oppressive atmosphere of the Po valley delta. Its relaxed café-society pace makes it a great family base for exploring the region's castles, folkloric attractions and natural wonders. This former Roman colony lies at the crossroads of the Teutonic and Latin worlds, yet unlike the Alto-Adige is unmistakably Italian, despite being ruled by German-Austrian prince-bishops for centuries. It feels far more Italian than Bolzano further north, for example. Its main claim to historical fame is the Catholic Council of Trent, who met here in the 16th century to address the threat from the Protestant Reformation.

View from Stresa

A fine place to start with a photo and ice-cream is beside the Neptune fountain on **Piazza Duomo**, surrounded by arcaded cafés and the Dolomites beyond. Pay a visit to the 13th century **Duomo** AGES 4 AND UP (*0461-234-419*. Mon–Sat 9:30–12:30pm and 2:30–6pm) where the Council of Trent established Europe's Counter-Reformation. The history might not impress the children, but the fresco fragments, huge marble baldachin (a symbol of authority) and spooky medieval crypt might. The neighbouring **Museo Diocesano Tridentino** AGES 6 AND UP (*0461-234-419*; ***www.museodiocesanotridentino.it***) contains paintings documenting the Council of Trent, tapestries and treasury objects. Admission: 4€ (£2.70) for adults, 1€ (£0.67) 12–18-year-olds, and free for children up to the age of 12; there is a family ticket available for 8€ (£5.36). Entrance is free on the first Sunday in the month.

A 10-min stroll north of the Duomo past handsome palaces with frescoed facades on Via Belenzani and Via Roma, is the magically maze-like **Castello di Buonconsiglio** ★★ AGES 4 AND UP (Via Bernardo Clesio 3. *0461-233-770*. ***www.buonconsiglio.it***. Admission: 6€ (£4) adults, 3€ (£2) children, 12€ (£8)

Victorian Grafitti

Take a closer look at Romanino's Ciclo dei Mesi (Cycle of the Months) frescoes at the Castello di Buonconsiglio: can you spot the drawn-in beards and scribbles? Barracked solders added these in the 19th century.

TIP Trento Card Savings 

If you're planning to visit the sights in town and to take the cable car, ask about the **Trento Card at the main attractions and tourist office**. A 24-hour ticket costs 9€ (£6) and includes entrance to the Musei di Trento, the Botanical Gardens at Alpino sul Monte Bondon, guided visits to wine cellars, free public transport, a ride on the Funivia Trento–Sardagna (see 'Side Trips From Trento', below), bike hire and other discounts. The 48-hour (14€) version includes all the above plus free entrance to the MART di Rovereto (Musem of Modern and Contemporary Art), Castel Beseno and the ethnographic museum, and the Museo Usi e Costumi della Gente Trentina at San Michele all'Adige. For more details check ☎ *0461-216-000* or visit ***www.apt.trento.it***.

family ticket, 8€ (£5.36) cumulative castle ticket, including admission to **Castel Baseno** and **Castel Stenico**. (April to September: Tues–Sun 9am–noon and 2–5:30pm; October to March: Tues–Sun 9am–noon and 2–5pm. Bus: B, 5, 7 or 10). Several Council meetings were held at this bishop's fortress, which is really two castles: the 13th century **Castelvecchio,** and the **Magno Palazzo** built in 1530. It's a bit of a trek to get here, but children will be thrilled with the fairytale battlements, Eagle's Tower and Renaissance *loggia del Romanino*.

SIDE TRIPS FROM TRENTO

For a thrilling ride to Sardagna, a mountain village high above Trento, hop on the **Trento–Sardagna Cable Car** ALL AGES ★★ at Ponte San Lorenzo, near the train station. Bring a picnic hamper and unfurl your blanket on the lush mountain meadows near the summit – there's room for the children to tumble around here on a sunny day. The cable car (☎ *0461-822-075*) runs every half-hour from 7am to 10:30pm (Sat and Sun until 7:30pm) and costs 1€ (£0.67) each way.

Another invigorating jaunt is the **Giardino Botanico Alpino** on **Monte Bondone** (☎ *0461-948-050*. ***www.mtsn.tn.it***. 2€ (£1.34), free for under 12s, 4€ (£2.70) family ticket) set in floristically fabulous Alpine meadows. Children will be blown away watching the para- and hang-gliding daredevils. It really is activity-city here: ask the tourist office for maps and details about the trekking trails, horse riding and mountain biking. For detailed info on routes and the network of hotels that cater for mountain bikers go to ***www.trentino.to***. Alp Bike (Via Castel Flavon 101 Bolzano. ☎ *0349-883-6578*. ***www.alpbike.it***.) hire out bikes and run courses for kids.

Young children will especially enjoy the vivid recreations of Trentino village life in days of yore at the **Museo degli Usi e**

Costumi della Gente Trentina AGES 3 AND UP (Etnographic Museum) north of Trento at San Michele All'Adige. It's open Tue–Sun 9am–12:30pm and 2:30–6pm (0461-650-314; *www.museosanmichele.it*), and costs 4€ (£2.70) for adults, 2€ (£1.34) for children.

35 km east of Trento on the SS47 amidst the lunaresque landscapes of the Gruppo di Sella plateau is the **Arte Sella Park** ALL AGES ★★ (Val di Sella, Borgo Valsugana. 0339-209-9226. *www.artesella.it* 3€ (£2), free under 10 years. Open 10am–6pm June to September daily, Sat and Sun only in October). This unusual sculpture park is a fantastic place to explore with children. Among the exhibits, which are all fashioned out of natural materials, is the towering Cattedrale Vegetale, eighty columns made from tree trunks.

Trekking and Skiing Near Trento

North-east of Trento the valleys of **Valsugana** (SS47) and **Val di Fiemme** (SS48) lead to the iridescent pinnacles of San Martino, formed as a coral reef 60 million years ago. The cobbled streets of **Cavalese** are popular with ice-cream eating families; you can also take one of the town's cable cars up to the **Catena dei Lagorai**, to explore mountain lakes and crags. There's decent skiing here in winter. Take a walk on the wild side down the wooded **Parco Paneveggio** (*www.parcopan.org*) where you can see deer, wild cats and eagles. It has trails and campsites aplenty.

Experienced walkers with older children can find even more thrilling terrain high on the **Pale di San Martino** plateau and down the dramatic Val Canali, which borders the Veneto and the Dolomiti Bellunesi. For skiing families, the smart resort of **San Martino** has some thrilling runs. Cable cars and chair lifts take you up onto the spectacular Pale di San Martino plateau including the Alpe Tognola and Cima della Rosetta, both over 2200 m (7000 ft) above sea level. Another fine family skiing option is the **Val di Fassa**, a little further north (see 'Laurie's Five Top Tips', below).

Bear-Watching and Skiing in the Brenta Dolomites

North-west of Trento lies the **Adamello Brenta Natural Park** (*www.parcoadamellobrenta.tn.it*) which contains the saw-toothed

European Brown Bear

Bear Necessities

The Brown Bear is 1.3 m–2.5 m in length and can live for between 25 and 30 years in the wild.

It inhabits the Adamello Brenta Park's dense forests at an altitude of between 700 m and 1800 m, mainly in the Val d'Algone and Val dei Cavai.

Orso bruno's diet comprises 60% plants – the rest is made up of insects (ants and bees are a favourite).

It rarely hunts and lies dormant in a natural cave between November and March.

peaks of the Dolomiti di Brenta, glaciers and 80 lakes. If you go down into the Brenta woods one day, you may have a big surprise by coming across the *Orso bruno* (European brown bear). Don't worry, the bears here eat mainly plants and only attack to defend their cubs. If you don't fancy trekking deep into the forests, the best place to spot them is at the **Sportmaggiore visitor centre** ★★ **ALL AGES** (Via Alt Spaur 82 ☎ *046-1653-637.*) ***www.prolocospormaggiore.tn.it***. 2.50€ (£1.68), 1.50€ (£1) under 14s. Early June to mid September 9:30am–6:30pm). Bring your teddy bears along: there is a picnic area on site. Elsewhere in the park, there are heart-pounding ascents and descents (Ages 12 and up) on Vie delle Bochette and Vie Ferrate (paths with metallic climbing aids). Just up the road, **Madonna di Campiglio** is a swish resort with over 100 miles of ski runs served by 40 lifts. During the summer months, it's also a fine place for trekking and climbing. The local **Alpine Guide Group** organises year-round outdoor activities and excursions for all ages and abilities. They are based at Brenta Alta 16, 38084 Madonna di Campiglio (☎ *0465-442-634.* ***www.guidealpinecampiglio.it***

Bolzano

Bolzano really doesn't feel Italian at all – in fact, it's only been part of Italy since the end of World War I. The people here call it Bozen, and tend to speak in German; their Italian doesn't have those mellifluous melodies you associate with *la bella lingua*. Despite the initial shock, you'll find it has its own particular charms, and there are some fine family-friendly attractions in the medieval centre of this Tyrolean city. Inviting cafés fringe one side of Piazza Walther and the **Duomo** (☎ *0471-978-676*. Mon–Fri 9:45–noon and 2–5pm; Sun for services), complete with colourful tiles and a striking spire – take a look inside for its faded frescoes and intricately worked pulpit. Just west of the

Laurie's Five Top Tips for a Great Skiing Holiday in Val di Fassa

My name is Laurie Presswood. I'm 9 years old and learned to ski in Canazei and Campitello, at New Year 2006. Here's what you need to know:

1. The Dolomites are beautiful. When we were in the plane flying over them, I was just like 'Wowwwwwww!!!! They are AMAZING!!' Make sure you take the cable car to the top of Sass Pordoi – the view is even more amazing.
2. Even if you're an adult, you should book yourself in ski school, unless you're a great skier, and I mean *great*!! Not only can it be good for your skiing, it's also the best way to get to know the runs (if you're not in the *bambini* group), and meet new friends.
   The ski school I went to was called **Scuola Italiana Sci–Canazei Marmolada** (*0462-601-211* ***www.scuolascicanazei.com***). It was fab! The ski instructors were really nice and half-way through the lesson we would always stop and have a drink and a snack at a mountain café. Try to get in a group with friends or people your own age.
3. Get a hotel close to the ski-lifts (see 'Family-Friendly Accommodation and Dining', below) if possible – it will save you a lot of walking. Ski resorts can get very busy, so it is a good idea to get up early and have breakfast quick so you can get to the lifts and miss the rush hour. If you have to get a ski bus to the lifts, it is EXTREMELY important to get up early, because you might find the bus is full, and then you might have to miss ski school. Of course, this never happened to me...
4. A good time to go is New Year, as you get great skiing and the Italians really know how to party! We arrived on New Year's Eve just in time for the 15-course meal welcoming us, then a disco and fireworks in the village square.
5. Don't forget, in Italy it is against the law for under-16s to ski without a helmet. So get one!
6. When getting on and off ski-lifts, be really careful because you can easily fall off and cause your dad to fall on top of you. Not that that EVER happened to me...

Duomo is the 13th century **Chiesa dei Domenicani** (*041-973-133*. Mon–Sat 9:30–6pm; Sun for services), which has rich frescoes attributed to the Giotto School. Children will enjoy the daily produce market at bustling **Piazza dell'Erbe** ★. It's a great spot for picking up picnic treats like strudel, bread, cheese and fruit. Pedestrianized Via dei Portici has lots of intriguing shops, and over the River Talvera, the imposing Fascist edifices of Corso Lidet lead to the picturesque village of **Greis** and the **Passeggiata del Guncina** (a 20 min walk), a lush park perfect for pinics and play.

About a mile north of Bolzano (you can get here on bus no. 12),

TIP National Parks near Bolzano 

There are some outstanding national parks across the Dolomites for families seeking a walk on the wild side. North of Bolzano is the well-heeled town of **Merano**, the gateway to two: the **Parco Nazionale di Tessa** and the huge **Parco Nazionale dello Stelvio** ★★, which covers the entire Ortles mountain range and contains one of Europe's largest glaciers, the Ghiacciaio dei Forni. Animal-crazy children can seek out elk, deer, ibex and golden eagles here. For maps and details about local outdoor activities, including cycling trails in the Val Vanosta, contact the visitor centre at **Silandro** (*0473-730-155. www.valvenosta.is.it*).

perched on a dramatic cliff, is the **Castel Roncolo** AGES 4 AND UP (*0471-329-808*; ***www.comune.bolzano.it/roncolo/ie***), a sight to fire children' imaginations. The interiors of this 13th century castle are filled with frescoes depicting chivalrous deeds. It's a fascinating place and costs 13€ (£8.70) for a family ticket; it's open Tue–Sun, 10am–6pm.

Another must-see sight is the **Museo Archeologico dell'Alto Adige** ★★ AGES 4 AND UP (Via Museo 43. *0471-320-100*. ***www.archaeologiemuseum.it***. Adults 9€ (£6), 16€ (£10.70) family ticket for 2 adults and children under 14 years. Tue–Sun 10am–5:30pm; open daily July, August and September). Remember Ötzi, the 5000-year-old ice man found by two German trekkers in a melting glacier back in 1991? Well he's here, along with his shoes, bearskin hat, a flint dagger, an axe and some arrows. The ghoulish, fragile remains of old Ötzi are housed in a special chamber, and among the absorbing exhibits there's also a replica, which you can see at close hand. Forensic studies revealed that he was killed in a skirmish – shot in the back; the evidence and the rest of Ötzi's story are here.

For a flying visit to the mountains, take one of the **cable cars** (*0471-978-479*; ***www.rittnerhorn.com www.renon.com***. 7am–8pm hourly; 9€ (£6), 5€ (£3.35) 6–14 years, family discounts available) that soar above the city: from the terminal on Via Renon near the train station – it's a dramatic 15-minute trip up to the Altopiano del Renon. At the bar at SopraBozen, you can drink in the views and some refreshing beverages. Don't miss the truly magic landscape of rocky spires, known as the *le piramidi di terra (The Earth Pyramids)*, further up further up. If you have older children you can take the footpath; otherwise hop on the tram (included in the price of your cable car ticket. The cable car also gives access to lots of hiking trails suitable for children.

Cortina d'Ampezzo

Cortina has been a glamorous ski resort since the mid-19th

Cortina d'Ampezzo

century, and gained international fame when it hosted the 1956 Winter Olympics. It's a bit of a jet-set retreat, so expect high prices during the peak ski-season months (December to March), as well as in July and August, when wealthy Italians exchange *cin-cins* in this Dolomite amphitheatre. For skiers, this is Italy's premier resort: there are 50 cable cars and chairlifts, and nearly 100 miles of ski runs. There's a whole lot of posing going on during the winter months – to compete with the er... *fashionistas*, kit your squad out in lurid fluorescent outfits and wrap-around shades before doing the *passeggiata* down **Corso Italia**.

The town itself is worth a look around for its hotchpotch of boutique shops, cafés and sports outlets. Amidst the Tyrolean-style buildings is the 18th century church of **Santi Filippo e Giacomo**, which has an enchanting campanile. Cortina's main draw is up in the clouds, which you can reach via one of the fabulous *funiculari*. For jaw-dropping vistas get propelled by the **Freccia nel Cielo** (Arrow in the Sky), which leaves the Stadio Olimpico del Ghiaccio (Olympic Ice Rink) a short walk west of the centre. If you are a top skiing family, there are exhilarating routes at 3000 m (10,000 ft) near the highest station, Tofana di Mezzo. The second stop, Ra Valles at 2500 m (8400 ft), has equally spectacular views over glaciers and craggy peaks, and there is a handy café-bar here to boot. It's quite pricey for one person (25€ (£16.75) round-trip), but there are a number of family ticket offers available depending on how far you go; under 6s go free all year round (under 12s free in low season). The service is pretty frequent (every 20 minutes 9am–5pm) and runs from mid-July to late September and mid-December to 1st May.

Cortina is geared mainly to intermediate skiers, though there are some excellent beginners' runs and tricky descents for the advanced. There are two types of ski pass available: the **Valley Ski Pass** is adequate for a week's skiing, while the **Dolomiti Superski** pass offers options for families wanting to explore a little further afield. You get unlimited skiing and free use of the lifts/funiculars and shuttle bus. For the menu of options contact the **tourist office** (Piazzetta San Franesco 8. *0436-3231*. ***www.cortina.dolomiti.com***, ***www.dolomiti.org/dengl/Cortina/skipass***) or Dolomiti Superski (Via D.Castello 33, 3203 Cortina. *0436-862-171*. ***www.dolomitisuperski.com***). Ski lessons are run by the **Scuola di Sci Cortina** (Corso Italia. *0436-2911*. ***www.scuolascicortina.it***). Six consecutive days of group lessons costs 170€ (£114) in low season and 205€ (£137.35) during high season. Snowboarding lessons are very pricey, though: 205€ for six days of lessons. Active families can get stuck into any number of exciting activities. The **Gruppo Guide Alpine Cortina** (Corso Italia 69A. *0463-868-505*. ***www.guidecortina.com***) organises action-packed adventures; ask them about their trekking, canyoning, various types of skiing, *vie ferrate* and other climbing trips, including ice climbing. Ice-skaters can glide amid the grand Olympian surrounds of the **Stadio Olimpico del Ghiaccio** (Via del Stadio. *0436-4380*). Just north of the town in Guargne is an indoor swimming pool, the **Piscina Coperta Comunale** (*0436-860-581*. Open mid-afternoon onwards; seasonal variations).

Family-Friendly Accommodation & Dining

Many of the hotels here (especially in Cortina) are booked up well in advance during high season (August, Christmas, and the snowy months). Some hotels require you to stay for a number of days and take at least half-board. This is often a good value option for families, as restaurants can be pricey. When you're eating out, most children will love the fairytale alpine interiors but may be a bit picky about the hearty fayre; a safe bet is to choose a few *contorni* (side dishes) for them.

Trento

Accademia Hotel and Restaurant ITALIAN Located near the Duomo, this hotel offers functional accommodation for families staying for a couple of nights maximum. There's a good little restaurant here as well serving Italian and Greek food – book a table in the tranquil inner courtyard.

*Vicolo Colico 4–6 (off Via Cavour). 0461-233-600; fax: 0461-230-174. **www.accademiahotel.it**). 50 units. 145€–200€ (£97–134) doubles and triples; rates include buffet breakfast. AE, DC, MC, V. Amenities: restaurant; enoteca (wine bar); bike rental; concierge; tour desk; babysitting; laundry service; dry cleaning; limited room service. In room: A/C, TV, hairdryer, minibar.*

Birreria Pedavena

BEER HALL/PIZZERIA During the day this beer hall cum pizzeria is great for families, as it serves *Würstel* (hot dogs), pizzas and pasta dishes. For adults there are lots of beers and they even show live events (including Italian footie and Champions' League) on a big screen.

*Piazza Fiera 13 at Via Santa Croce. ☎ 0461-986-255. **www.birreria pedavena.com**). Primi 3.50€–6€ (£2.35–4); secondi 5€–10.50€ (£3.35–7); pizza 3.50€–6€ (£2.35–4). MC, V. Mon and Wed–Thurs 9am–12:30am; Fri–Sat 9am–1am; Sun 9am–midnight.*

Ristorante Al Vò

TYROLEAN/ITALIAN For an old *osteria* atmosphere and simple tasty dishes, which most children will devour, this is a good bet. Alongside traditional fish and meat *piatti* they do a fantastic *Gnocchi di pane alle verdure* (breaded gnocchi with vegetables) for those who like their greens.

*Vicolo del Vo' 11. ☎ 0461-985-374. **www.ristorantealvo.it**). Primi 7€–10€ (£4.70–6.70); secondi 8.50€–14€ (£5.70–9.40). AE, MC, V. Mon–Sat noon–3pm and 7–11pm (Thu and Fri only).*

Bolzano

Hotel Regina The centrally positioned Regina has bright spacious rooms for families – many have ample bathrooms. You won't get luxury – the rooms are quite spartan – but you get value and choice to suit your needs. They have a mansard quintuple (low ceilings but cheaper) below the roof.

*Via Renon 1. ☎ 0471-972-195 or 0471-974-099; fax: 0471-978-944. **www.hotelreginabz.it**). 40 units. 85€–105€ (£57–70.50) double; 110€–125€ (£74–84) triple; 120€–250€ (£80–168) quad; 130€ (£87) mansard quintuple. Rates include breakfast. MC, V. Free parking. Amenities: bar; tour desk; concierge. In room: TV.*

Vogele ★

TYROLEAN You'll find suitably hearty Tyrolean grub at this atmospheric and popular café-restaurant. Expect heaped platters of *speck* and smoked meats as well as potato and sauerkraut *frittelle* (fritters) and tempting strudel.

Via Goethe 3. ☎ 0471-973-938). Reservations Recommended. Primi 4€–8.50€ (£2.70–5.70); secondi 9€–17€ (£6–11.40) . MC, V. Mon–Fri 9am–midnight; Sat 9am–3pm.

Val di Fassa

Hotel Rododendro ★ VALUE

The Rododendro is one of the many small family-run hotels in Campitello, a traditional Dolomite village in the Val Di Fassa. The hotel and village offer a warmer alternative to the anonymous, concrete resorts elsewhere. The food, staff and location (on the ski-bus route and 5 min. walk from the cable car station) are ideal for a ski break. The hotel has a small gym, a sauna and there's swimming and ice-skating nearby.

Via Dolomiti 31, 38031 Campitello di Fassa. ☎ 0462-750-368; fax:

*0462-750-047. **www.infotrentino.net/rododendro**). 28 units. 50€–90€ (£33.50–60) double; 70€–140€ (£47–94) triple. Add 15€–20€ (£10–14) per person for half-board. Breakfast included. AE, DC, MC, V. Free parking. Amenities: restaurant; bar; gym; jacuzzi; sauna; games room. In room: sat TV, hairdryer, safe.*

Cortina

Hotel Menardi ★★ The Menardis' well-run hotel is housed in a handsome alpine farm building – it's been a family favourite for years. Expect wood-panelled interiors, impeccable service, spa facilities and a children's playground. The rooms near the autostrada can be a little noisy, so ask for one at the back, all of which overlook the wonderful garden. Many guests take half-board as the Tyrolean fayre is very good.

*Via Majon 110. (☎ 0436-2400; fax: 0436-862-183. **www.hotelmenardi.it**). 51 units. 180€–270€ (£120–180) double with half-board; children under 6 free; 6–12 years 50% reduction. DC, MC, V. Free parking. Closed mid-April to mid-June and late September to late December. Amenities: restaurant; bar; concierge; room service; laundry service; dry cleaning; courtesy car; 24-hr. bike rental; golf course; playground; special ski-hire rates. In room: TV, dataport, hairdryer, minibar, safe.*

La Tavernetta ITALIAN Children will love the former barn setting, near the Olympic ice-skating stadium, and the wholesome food should go down equally well. They do a number of *contorni* (side dishes), which should please even the fussiest eaters. Menu highlights include wild asparagus and venison served with berries and polenta.

Via d. Stadio 27 a/b. (☎ 0436-867-494). Reservations recommended. Primi 7€–13€ (£4.70–8.70); secondi 11€–20€ (£7.40–13.40). AE, MC, V. Thurs–Tues noon–2:30pm and 7:30–11pm.

4 Venice

Venice is a city of clichés and contradictions: it's the most romantic city in the world, it's sinking, it's stinking. You've heard them all. Whatever you think, though, first-timers *will* find it dreamlike and wide-eyed children *will* be mesmerised – for starters you get around on boats, not by car. Weird! For that alone, it's a fun place to explore as a family.

However, a visit to *La Serenissima* has never been painless or serene: its muddy, mosquito-infested islands were colonised by refugees fleeing barbarian invasions, and as Venice's power grew, so did its citizens' sin and corruption. When confronted with outrageous prices and tourist rip-offs some visitors may feel that certain Venetians still display the greed of their forebears – with an added ennui. Venice is the archetype of a city that lives in the past. As the Italians say, and Charles Aznavour sings, *Com'è triste Venezia*. How sad Venice is.

Yet, despite the excessive zeal of some inhabitants when it comes to relieving tourists of their money and San Marco's day-tripping hordes, there is still genuine magic in these crumbling campanili and algae-ridden lagoons. Otherworldly watery visions of art and architecture leave you gawping. These reflections from a different age take you on evocative journeys to the former maritime republic and exotic European gateway to the Orient. And should the crowds and rip-offs start to wind you up, your children's sense of wonder should be the spur to escape and explore: leave the Piazza San Marco's pigeons behind and follow the *calli* less trodden. There's myth, mystery and spooky places at every turn. And remember, your feet are never in contact with truly solid ground in the city of Venezia.

Child-Friendly Festivals & Events

Although Venice is a magical place at any time, you could make the trip doubly special for your family by picking a date when an event or festival is taking place.

The city's most fantastical annual event is the pre-Lenten **Carnevale** ★★(☎ *041-241-0570*; ***www.carnivalofvenice.com***). The wild Venetian version of the bacchanalian revelries reached its height in the 18th century and was revived in the early 1980s. Unless you get a personal invite to a masked ball, you'll have to handover a fistful of *pittura fresca* to attend one. However, there are free events and concerts held in the ampler *campi* (a *campo* is a Venetian *piazza*) and parades near San Marco. Buy masks for all the family and join in: these are surreal Fellini-esque moments to savour. Shrove Tuesday or *Martedi Grasso* (Fat Tuesday) sees the climax, with fireworks and events around San Marco.

The **Festa di San Marco** (25th April) is the festival of *La Serenissima*'s patron saint,

HISTORY The Venice Timeline

It was around AD 450 that refugees fleeing the barbarian invasions came to settle in the lagoon wetlands here. By the 11th century Venice had gained its own sovereignty and independence and thereafter grew in size as a maritime republic. Here's a rundown of the story so far.

452 Refugees fleeing Attila the Hun settled in the lagoon wetlands.

466 The first Venetian government was established: a council representing the twelve communities.

727 The first recorded Doge, Orso Ipato, was elected.

811–827 Frankish invasions led to the inhabitants moving en masse to the more protected islands, the Rivo Alto or 'Ri'Alto' (meaning high bank). It soon became the centre of activity and its area was expanded dramatically by landfill.

9th–12th centuries Venice's strategic position and influence in the Adriatic helped trade flourish, establishing Venice as a powerful city-state.

12th century Venice was flourishing and growing at an impressive rate. The Venetian Arsenale was built. Venice took control of the Brenner pass from Verona, opening the silver trade from Germany. The city's influence over the north-eastern Italian *terra firma* began.

1204 Constantinople captured by Venice and its Crusader allies. Venice took control of eastern trade routes and picked up some booty in the process.

1295 Marco Polo was the subject of much interest and scepticism on his return from the Silk Road.

14th–16th centuries Venice's control over Padua, Verona, Bergamo, Brescia, Vicenza and the Friuli waxed and waned. It added Cyprus to its empire.

16th century Palladio's villas and churches built.

16th–18th centuries Venice lost Cyprus, Crete and Morea to the Ottoman Turks.

17th century The *Settecento* was the high-water mark of Venetian arts, architecture and literature.

1755 Giacomo Casanova was imprisoned in the famous prison, *I piombi*, for his interest in witchcraft. In 1756 he made an extraordinary escape and fled to France.

1797 Napoleon marched into town, effectively ending Venetian sovereignty.

19th century The city was ruled by Austria until 1866 when Venezia joined the unified Italian state.

---

marked by solemn religious ceremonies and the tradition of giving a *bòcolo* (rosebud) to a loved one.

In May, on the Sunday following Ascension Day, **La Festa della Sensa** takes place, celebrating the city's marriage to the

Voga Longa

sea by re-enacting Doge Ziani's gesture of throwing a gold ring into the waters at San Nicolò. Children will love the colourful water-borne pageantry. Book a boat trip and join the throngs that shadow the re-enactment.

The **Voga Longa** ★★★ (meaning 'Long Row') is a colourful and fun-filled 30-kilometre (19-mile) rowing 'race' from San Marco to Burano and back again. It takes place on a Sunday in late May or early June. Grab a spot on the Canal Grande and watch the procession of vessels with their hilariously dressed oarsmen. There's even a boat giving out free wine to the competitors. If you want to enter see ***www.vogalonga.com***.

The **Festa del Redentore** ★★(third Saturday and Sunday of July) is an annual celebration marking the end of the plague of 1576. This floating festa involves a bridge of boats from the Zattere to Palladio's Redentore church. There's food and drink aplenty, as well as spectacular fireworks and festive crowds.

Movie-mad youngsters will love the **Venice International Film Festival** (late August to early September). If you can't get tickets for the red-carpeted premieres at the Lido's Palazzo del Cinema, there are lots of screenings around the city, including magical open-air flicks in the *campi*.

Art aficionados of all ages should visit the **Biennale d'Arte** ★★(early June to late November) in odd years: 2007, 2009 etc, the most prestigious art show of them all. It's always a good laugh and the only time that Venice, usually very inward-looking, opens up and feels international. Various countries have stunning pavillions in the Biennale Gardens; Tracy Emin is representing Britain in 2007. Up the Arsenale, the long *corderie* host miles of mind-blowing displays and there are shows all over the city. Less flamboyant but just as stimulating is the **Biennale di Architettura** (mid-September to late November), which takes place in even years. Children will be transfixed by the cities of the future and the often crazy new building projects coming to a town near you. Less accessible to younger children are the concurrent Biennali of contemporary music, dance and theatre (various venues; ***www.labiennale.org***. Admission: 13€ (£8.70) adults, 8€ (£5.35) under 26s, 32€ (£21.50) family ticket for 2 adults and 2 children under 14, free under 6s. 10am–6pm. Vap: Giardini).

The **Regata Storica**, an extravagant parade alongside three competitive races on the Canal Grande, takes place on the first Sunday in September. If you don't mind the crowds, grab a spot on the Rialto Bridge or at one of the closed *vaporetto* pontoons.

Canal Grande

The **Festa delle Salute** on 21st November celebrates the end of the 1630 plague. There's a religious procession across a makeshift pontoon bridge over the Grand Canal from Santa Maria del Giglio to La Salute.

Entertainments & Sports

As befits a city oozing with history and past glories, Venice's entertainments tend towards the classical and are held in suitably grand settings. Children and teenagers who enjoy ballet, orchestral music, theatre or opera will be suitably impressed by the lavish setting of **La Fenice** (San Marco 1965, on Campo San Fantin; ☎ *041-786-562)*, which recently rose from the ashes of a catastrophic fire in 1996. To buy tickets go to ***www.vivaticket.it*** or their own website ***www.teatrolafenice.it***. You can also buy tickets before you arrive via ***www.musicinitaly.com*** or ***www.selectitaly.com***.

Named after the celebrated Venetian playwright, the **Teatro Carlo Goldoni** (Calle del Teatro 4650/A, San Marco; ☎ *041-240-2011*) has a varied programme, including the odd pop concert and children's theatre production. It's usually in Italian, though theatrical teens might enjoy seeing a play by Wilde, Goethe or Pirandello.

There are a number of ensembles playing Vivaldi and other baroque favourites in various evocative Venetian settings: you'll see a gang of people in period dress loitering on *calle* corners handing out leaflets, in Campo Santo Stefano and elsewhere. To buy in advance see *www.classictic.com*.

Footie fans should make a surging run to the ramshackle Stadio Penzo, way out east at Sant' Elena, to watch **A.C. Venezia**, currently languishing in Serie C1. Expect firecrackers, flag waving and a lot of moaning in the curious nasal dialect. Tickets are available on the day from the stadium or via agencies (Agenzia Ve.La. S.p.a. on Piazzale Roma) around the city (*041-520-6899*; *www.veneziacalcio.it*. Under-10s get in for 10€ (£6.70)).

There are only a dozen or so dedicated spaces for **playing sports** in Venice, and they all belong to schools and private clubs. However, there are tennis courts on Lido at the **Tennis Club Cai del Moro** (Via Ferruccio Parri 6; *041-770-801*) and the Alberoni golf course (Via del Forte, Alberoni-Lido; *041-731-333*; *www.circologolfvenezia.it*). If you fancy taking to the water, try the rowing club Reale Societa Canottieri Bucintoro near la Salute, which runs classes for children: see 'For Active Families: Rowing', below.

Essentials

Getting There

By Plane For the easiest and most direct route to Venice by air use **Aeroporto Marco Polo**. Low-cost airlines like Ryanair fly to Treviso, Brescia and Bergamo, from where you'll have to negotiate the roads or rail system.

Top 10 Venice Experiences

1. Take a vaporetto ride down the Grand Canal.
2. Go up the campanile on San Giorgio Maggiore.
3. Hang out in a campo, sipping a spritz – Campo Santa Margherita has lots of space for hyper littlun's.
4. Get up at the crack of dawn and see San Marco and Rialto without the crowds.
5. Grab the freshest fish and cippolini (cute onions) at the old Pescheria and Mercato.
6. Take a breezy boat trip on the back of a vaporetto to the islands: hop off at Burano and Torcello.
7. Take a wobbly and exhilarating traghetto ride on a gondola across the Grand Canal.
8. Eat ice cream and relax on the sunny Zattere.
9. Stroke chins in an arty fashion in the Accademia, Guggenheim and at the Biennale.
10. Get lost like a nincompoop: preferably around the northern reaches of Cannaregio and Castello on a freezing foggy day.

Aeroporto Marco Polo is on the mainland, 7 km (4⅓ miles) north of the city (☎ *041-260-9260* or *041-260-9250*; ***www.veniceairport.it***). The cheapest way to get to and from this recently renovated airport is via the half-hourly ACTV bus no. 5 (☎ *041-541-5180*). It costs 1.50€ (£1) and takes about 40 minutes. You have to carry your luggage on to a normal bus, which can be tricky, and it's often mobbed with schoolchildren. A less stressful alternative is the **ATVO airport shuttle bus** (☎ *041-541-5180* or *041-520-5530*; ***www.atvo.it***), which takes about 20 minutes and costs 3€ (£2). Tickets for either service are available at the newsstand just inside the terminal building. Both connect with Piazzale Roma, near Venice's Santa Lucia train station; there is a short walk between Piazzale Roma and the nearby **vaporetto** stop (see 'By Train', below). A **land taxi** from the airport to Piazzale Roma costs about 30€ (£20). Remember that from Piazzale Roma you'll have to take a *vaporetto,* or water taxi, to your hotel. Pack light: a trip to Venice always involves lugging your bags around and negotiating crowded bridges.

Take to the lagoon for the most exciting way to arrive at Piazza San Marco. The nearby docks are connected to the airport terminal building by a 2-minute shuttle bus journey (1€ (£0.67) payable on-board). The **Cooperative San Marco/Alilaguna** (☎ *041-523-5775*; ***www.alilaguna.it***) runs a large *motoscafo* (shuttle boat) service from the docks: the Blue and Red lines take slightly different routes (check the website timetables), but both stop at Murano and Lido before arriving at Piazza San Marco. Check with your hotel as to the best route and nearest stop – this will avoid any hassle.

For sheer glamour, drama and convenience take a **private water taxi** (around 25 min.). It's pricey, though – you can easily spend 85€ (£57) to get to your hotel. Try negotiating a price at the **Consorzio Motoscafi Venezia** office in the airport (☎ *041-522-2303*) or chum up with another family and share the cost (which will invariably be quoted a bit higher).

By Train Trains arrive at the **Stazione Venezia–Santa Lucia** (☎ *848-888-088* or *147-888-088*; ***www.trenitalia.com***). A word of warning: all trains pass through and often stop at Venezia–Mestre but don't get off here. Mestre is the last stop on the mainland and has none of the magic of Venice. A few trains terminate at Mestre, meaning that you'll have to transfer to one of the 10-minute local trains to reach Venice proper. To avoid this, confirm that the final destination is Venezia–Stazione Santa Lucia.

The Fascist-era station sits above the Grand Canal: look down the broad set of steps and you'll see the *vaporetti* pontoons.

Go to the ticket booths on your left, nearest the bridge, for a *vaporetto* to Canal Grande. The no. 82 is more direct to San Marco (25 min.), stopping off at fewer places (S. Marcuola, Rialto Bridge, S. Tomà, S. Samuele, and Accademia) on the Canal Grande; the no. 1 takes 31 min. Both depart from here every 10 minutes. Remember that some no. 82s terminate at Rialto. If you are staying along the Zattere or Giudecca take the 82 that goes in the other direction to San Zaccaria via Tronchetto and the docks.

By Bus Venice is served by long-distance buses from all over Italy and Europe. They terminate at Piazzale Roma, where you'll need to find transport to your accommodation (see above).

By Car There are no cars in Venice. If you bring one, you'll drive across the Ponte della Libertà from Mestre before leaving it at a Tronchetto car park near Piazzale Roma: the cheapest is **ASM garage** (☎ *041-272-7301*; ***www.asmvenezia.it***), costing from 20€ (£13.40) per day for an average-size car. A word of warning: leaving your car here can be costly. Check with your hotel before arriving about parking, as some have special arrangements with garages that could save you money.

Visitor Information

Tourist Offices For a city flooded with visitors, the locals and officials make no great effort to welcome them, so expect indifferent service. At the Santa Lucia train station there's a small, under-staffed office. The main tourist information office **Venice Pavilion/Palazzina dei Santi** (☎ *041-529-8711*; ***www.turismovenezia.it***. Daily 10am–6pm) is near the San Marco *vaporetto* stop and Giardinetti Reali. Another office is at the west end of Piazza San Marco (☎ *041-529-8740*. Mon–Fri 9am–3:30pm). There's a counter in the arrivals hall at Marco Polo Airport, though its opening hours vary.

Every month the APT tourist information offices publish the useful **Un Ospite di Venezia** (***www.unospitedivenezia.it***), available in many hotels. Look out for the long and thin **VDV** guide (Venezia da Vedere) that has excellent events, eating and nightlife listings. The monthly **Venezia News** has in-depth listings and features on the arts. You can also pick up useful leaflets including the **Dentro Venezia** walking guides produced in association with the Touring Club Italiano.

Websites The official tourist-board site is ***www.turismovenezia.it*** and the city government site is ***www.comune.venezia.it***. Among the best independents are **Venice Word** (***www.veniceword.com***), **Meeting Venice** (***www.meetingvenice.it***) and **Doge of Venice** (***www.doge.it***).

City Layout

Venice is connected to the mainland town of Mestre and its industrial satellite Marghera by the 4km Fascist-built Ponte della Libertà. Once you are away from the messy modern set-up around the train station and Tronchetto, the otherworldly atmosphere of the aquatic city begins to reveal itself. Many of your journeys will be along the main artery of Venice, the **Grand Canal (Canal Grande)**, which snakes through the city like an inverted S.

The city is divided into six *sestieri* ('sixths' or districts).

Cannaregio covers the north and west of the city, from La Ferrovia di Santa Lucia (train station) to the Jewish Ghetto and the Ospedale Civile (Public Hospital) off the Fondamente Nuove, and on to the old German printers' area north of the Rialto Bridge.

Castello is the largest of the *sestieri*, spanning the area east of San Marco as far as Sant'Elena and the football stadium, which you can reach via a broad esplanade named the Riva degli Schiavoni, by Piazza San Marco.

San Marco occupies the central territory between the Canal Grande and Il Molo (the quayside). Piazza San Marco is the political, religious and symbolic heart of the city, while Rialto Bridge to the north is the focus of the city's commerce.

San Polo is north of the Rialto Bridge on the other side of the Grand Canal, spanning the area west of the Pescheria (fish market) as far as the Church of San Rocco and Rio Muneghette.

Castello Cats

Santa Croce follows the Canal Grande from Palazzo Corner to Piazzale Roma and a thin strip ending back on the Grand Canal at Palazzo Boldi.

Dorsoduro, the sixth and last *sestiere*, lies on the other side of the Accademia Bridge from San Marco and covers the arty area from the Punta dell Dogana (old customs house) to the residential Santa Marta. Sunny Dorsoduro has a south-facing esplanade, the Zattere, which runs along the Canal della Giudecca. It is home to many university buildings and studenty hangouts, including Campo Santa Margherita.

There are several other islands in the Venetian lagoon. Opposite the Zattere is **La Giudecca**, a residential working-class strip with the exclusive Il Cipriani hotel. The adjacent island of **San Giorgio Maggiore** across from Piazza San Marco

Venice in a Blur: A One-Day Itinerary

Kick off your dreamy day trip with a vaporetto down the Grand Canal to Rialto. Scale the bridge, take some pics, peruse the kitsch souvenirs and, if you have time, dip into the Peschiera and produce market nearby. Duck into Ruga Rialto for refreshments and cichetti snacks. If you enjoy shopping and don't mind crowds, thread your way through the Mercerie district following the yellow signs for San Marco. Spend a couple of hours in the famous piazza gawping at the Venetian glitz (the Basilica and Palazzo Ducale) taking photos and frightening the flapping piccioni. Head down the Riva degli Schiavoni to catch a glimpse of the Bridge of Sighs. If you crave respite from the tourist hordes head to the Arsenale, the Naval History Museum, Via Garibaldi and the Biennali Gardens. Arty types with well-developed thigh muscles should keep going and head to the Guggenheim and Galleria Accademia. To get to these Dorsoduro delights and experience a quick knee-trembler of a gondola ride, hop on a traghetto at Santa Maria del Giglio to the photogenic Salute church. Take a breather on the sunny Zattere and eat ice cream from Nico. If you have time wander around the Dorsdoduro: grab some food at Taverna San Trovaso, near the Squero (gondola boat yard) or a light snack at Caffe` Rosso on Campo Santa Margherita before heading back to Piazzale Roma or the railway station.

has a magnificent eponymous church. Further east beyond Castello is the thin strip of the **Lido di Venezia**, which has a sandy beach and is the centre of the Venice Film Festival.

Beyond the northernmost foundations of the city are a series of islands: from the Fondamente Nuove you can see the nearby **San Michele** cemetery island, and beyond are the islands of **Murano, Burano, Torcello and Sant'Erasmo**. Murano is the historical centre of the glass trade; Burano is famed for its colourful houses and lace making; sparsely populated Torcello has remarkable Byzantine mosaics; and Sant'Erasmo is Venice's market garden, producing much of the fruit and veg sold in the Rialto markets.

Getting Around a Piedi and by *Vaporetto*

On Foot Getting around Venice on foot can be bewildering and often hilarious. Expect to get lost frequently, and to experience the 'Venice walk of shame': when you find yourself in a dead-end *campo* or *calle* facing a *canale* and have to backtrack. The first thing to buy on arriving is a map, or *pianta della città*, which are widely available. Their quality varies so make sure you get a good one: the **Touring Club Italiano** produce very detailed

VENICE **VAPORETTO**

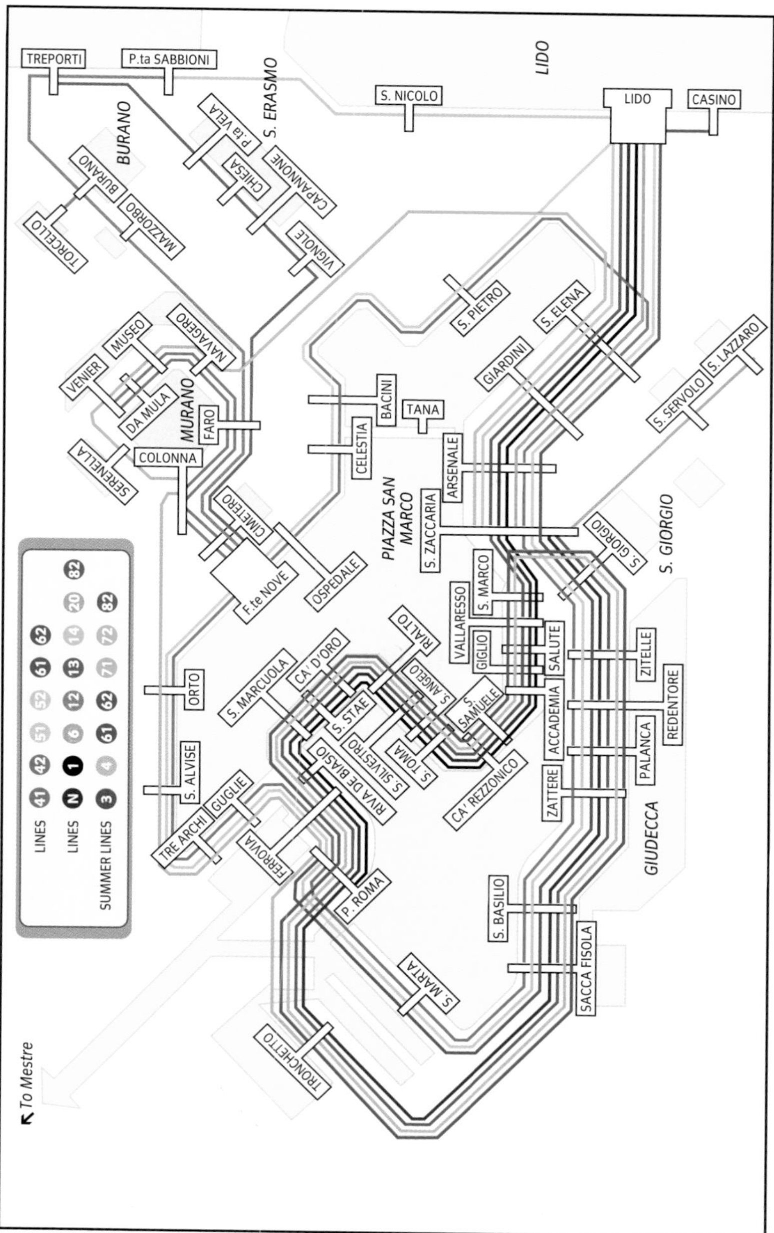

maps, though some are a little cumbersome. Storti Edizioni and Edizioni Zerella make compact folding maps. If you're in Venice for a while, invest in a copy of *Calli, Campielli e Canali* by Edizioni Helvetia, an A–Z format map book. Help is at hand with yellow signs posted around the city guiding the hordes to important locations: La Ferrovia (railway station), Piazzale Roma, Rialto, San Marco, Accademia and L'Arsenale. Venetian addresses are numbered consecutively by *sestiere*, without rhyme or reason to the order. However, most addresses are advertised with their relevant *calle* or *campo*, e.g. Campo Arsenale, Castello 2408.

By Boat The excellent *vaporetto* (water bus) system operated by the **Azienda del Consorzio Trasporti Veneziano (ACTV)** (Calle Fuseri 1810, San Marco; *041-528-7886*; ***www.actv.it***) is great for getting around, but can be extremely crowded and is now very pricey unless you are a resident. For families, the costs involved can be ludicrous. Unless you are travelling great distances with baggage or are heading to the islands, you're better off walking. The *vaporetti* mainly ply up and down Canal Grande and the larger waterways, so you have to walk most of the time anyway. You can pick up a map of the services from the tourist office or ACTV booth at many pontoons.

FUN FACT Andemo, tosi! Let's go, guys!

Listen out for locals speaking their harsh dialect, but you'll have to pinch your nose to get the authentic nasal sound of Veneziano

Ca' Abbreviation of 'Casa' (house) used here also for grand palazzi like Ca' d'Oro.

Calle Venetian word for street. Pronounced *cal-ay*, it is borrowed from Spanish. A *caletta* is a small alley.

Campo Venice's *campi* or smaller *campielli* are the dialect terms for a *piazza***.**

Canale The wide Canals are *Canali*, while each of the smaller ones are *rii* (singular: *rio*).

Fondamentae This is a walkway along a Canal.

Ramo A branch or side street.

Riva The promenades where goods are unloaded; and the name of the company that makes the gorgeous wood-veneered boats.

Ruga An old term for a *calle* flanked with stores, like Ruga Rialto.

Salizzada An alternative to *calle*: originally meaning 'paved'. These were the first streets in Venice covered with *masegni*, the Venetian paving stones.

Sottoportego This is a small passage under a building – children love them. There are lots around Venice, including a few Sottoportego dei Preti (priests' underpasses).

A one-way (*corso semplice*) ticket is a whopping 5€ (£3.35), valid for 60 minutes from the time it's validated. Some essential shuttle services (across the Grand Canal, and between Lido and Sant'Elena or San Giorgio and San Zaccaria) cost a more reasonable 2€ (£1.34). If you plan to be using the services a lot, it's worth considering the new **Venice Card** (see 'Planning Your Outings', below) or the **ACTV travel cards**: a 24-hour ticket costs 12€ (£8), a 72-hour ticket 25€ (£16.75) and the Young Person's 72-hour ticket 15€ (£10). Most lines run every 10–15 minutes from 7am to midnight, then hourly during the early hours. Most *vaporetto* stops have timetables posted and many have booths to buy tickets. As there are few bridges (Ponte degli Scalzi, Rialto, Accademia and a new one, Ponte Calatrava, soon to be completed) spanning the Canal Grande, seven *traghetti* (large gondolas manned by two *gondolieri*) ferry people across. See 'Gondola Rides' below.

INSIDER TIP

Most ticket booths close in the evenings, so if you board without a validated ticket, make sure you alert the conductor. It's your responsibility to do that: if caught without a ticket, expect a hefty fine, not sympathetic treatment because you're a visitor. At all times, make sure your ticket is stamped and validated using the machines at the vaporetto stop or else you will be fined.

Planning Your Outings

Negotiating the bridges and narrow bustling *calli* can be tricky with young children and a military exercise with a pushchair and luggage. Expect a lot of walking, so kit everyone out in comfortable shoes or trainers. You might need some plasters or 'second skin', so bring them along! You'll get into the rhythm after a while though, and distances can be covered in a short time here. Once you've seen the main sights around San Marco, be brave and head to the far-flung corners where real Venetians live. You'll be rewarded with fewer tourists and more space for children to play. In case you haven't all got mobile phones, agree on a meeting place should your group get split up: pick your own favourite spot or café depending on what part of the city you are in: the Torre del Orologio (astronomical clock) in Piazza San Marco is a favourite Venetian meeting place. As for the *Veneziani* themselves, they may not be the most welcoming, but at least the *vaporetti* staff let parents with babies get on first.

Just the Ticket: Venice Card, Museum Pass, Church Pass

Sightseeing and travelling on the *vaporetti* is an expensive business, so consider your options carefully. The **Museum Pass** costs 18€ (£12) for adults, 12€ (£8) for ages 6–14 years, and is free for under-5s. A family of at least two adults and two children aged 6–14 can get a family ticket for 54€ (£36.20) in total. It grants admission to all ten of the city-run museums and is valid for three months. It includes the following: Doge's Palace, Museo Correr, Museo Archaeologico Nazionale, La Biblioteca Nazionale Marciana, Ca' Rezzonico – Museo del Settecento, Museo di Palazzo Mocenigo e Centro Studi di Storia del Tessuto e del Costume, Casa di Carlo Goldoni, Ca' Pesaro (International Gallery of Modern Art and Oriental Museum), Museo Fortuny (temporary exhibitions), Glass Museum – Murano, Lace Museum – Burano.

If you are just planning to visit the San Marco museums (the first four in the list above) opt for the **Piazza San Marco Museum Card**, costing 12€ (£8), 6.50€ (£4.35) reduced, free for under-5s; or with a family of at least two adults and two children aged 6–14, one at full price and the rest reduced (so 31.50€ (£21.10) in total).

The **Venice Card** allows one, three, or seven days' unlimited transport, free access to the 10 civic museums, the 16 churches of the Associazione Chiese (see below), the casino and public toilets and changing facilities. It also includes a host of discounts, a document wallet, guide and map. You avoid the queues and messing about with cash – but it's pricey, especially for families. There are two versions, Orange and Blue. The Orange is the full shebang, while the Blue includes free transport but only discounted admission to the city's attractions. You can pay extra for the use of the Alilaguna service, handy for airport transfers. A one-day Orange card costs 29€ (£19.43) and 22€ (£14.75) for juniors (6–14), while the seven-day version is 76€ (£50.92) and 67€ (£44.90) (87€ (£58.30) and 96€ (£64) with Alilaguna services). For all the permutations and to purchase them slightly cheaper in advance, go to ***www.venicecard.it*** (*041-2424*).

The **Associazione Chiese di Venezia** (*041-275-0462*; ***www.chorusvenezia.org***) curates many of Venice's churches. A visit to one of the association's churches costs 2.50€ (£1.68); most are open Mon–Sat 10am–5pm and Sun 1–5pm. They are closed on Sundays in July and August.

If you plan to visit more than four of the churches below, buy the 8€ (£5.35) ticket or 16€ (£10.70) family ticket (two adults plus children up to the age of 18), but note, under-11s get in free. Cards are valid for a year. The card grants entry to the following churches: Santa Maria del Giglio, Santo Stefano, Santa Maria Formosa, Santa Maria dei Miracoli, Santa Maria Gloriosa dei Frari, San Polo, San Giacomo dell'Orio, San Stae, Alvise, Madonna dell'Orto, San Pietro di Castello, Il Redentore, San Sebastiano and the San Marco Basilica treasury.

INSIDER TIP

The Rolling Venice Card offers lots of discounts (in museums and restaurants, as well as bike hire on the Lido and on public transport) for 14–29 year olds – it costs 4€ (£2.70) and is valid for a year. Ask at the tourist offices or call 041-529-8711.

Picnicking & Food Shopping

Dining and snacks are expensive, particularly in San Marco, so plan a picnic and let the children run around. Bring a decent cool bag and backpack to a *supermercato* or market stall (the large one at the Rialto Pescheria is best). There are a couple of excellent Billa *supermercati*, at Cannareggio 3659 on Strada Nuova and Dorsoduro 1491 on Fondamenta Zattere; the Supermercato Giorgione on Via Cannaregio is worth seeking out on the way to the Fondamente Nuove. Once stocked up with goodies, head to one of the city's large *campi* where children can let off some steam. Ball games are officially banned, but the local children play footie regardless. The following large *campi* have market stalls, decent shops and pleasant cafés nearby: Campo Santa Margherita, Campo San Polo, Campo San Giacomo dell'Orio, Campo dei Gesuiti and Campo Santo Stefano. The sunny Zattere has the ever-popular Billa supermarket near the San Basilio *vaporetto* at the western end – on the eastern tip of the quayside is the Punta della Dogana, with fabulous Canal-side views. The Giardini is the only decent green space in the city, although there aren't any lush lawns – go for a food shop on nearby Via Garibaldi before picnicking here.

FAST FACTS: VENICE

Acqua Alta The tidal *acqua alta* (high water) floods the city during the winter months, leaving the lowest-lying areas ankle deep: Piazza San Marco being the lowest point is hit first. Expect occasional *acqua alta* between November and March, although it has been known to strike as early as September. As a warning, you will hear an eerie air-raid siren across the city. Unless it is raining heavily, the waters usually recede in a few hours. To combat the increased severity of high tides, a controversial system of hydraulic dams is being built.

Business Hours Standard shop opening hours are 9am–12:30pm and 3–7:30pm, Monday to Saturday. In winter, most shops stay shut on Monday morning and many food shops close on Wednesday afternoons. Most shops are closed on Sundays, apart from those in tourist hotspots. Restaurants close at least one day a week – that day varies from one eatery to another. On Sundays, many open just for lunch. Seafood trattorias usually close on Mondays, when the fish market is closed. Most restaurants close for a short holiday (*ferie*) over Christmas, in January before Carnevale, and for a spell during July and August.

Chemist Chemists (*farmacie*) take turns staying open all night. For the nearest one ask your hotel, check the rota posted outside all pharmacies or call ☎ *041-523-0573*. In San Marco try Italo Inglese (San Marco 3717 Calle della Mandola. ☎ *041-522-483*).

Climate May, September and early October are the most pleasant months weather-wise. July and August can be unbearably hot and humid. In April and October the weather can be temperamental.

Consulates The **UK Honorary Consul** in Venice is near the Accademia Bridge at Dorsoduro 1051 (☎ *041-522-7207*. Mon–Fri 9am–noon and 2–4pm. Vap: Accademia). The nearest **Irish Embassy** is in Milan (Via Largo Nazareno 3. ☎ *06-678-2541*).

Crime and Safety Venice is easily Italy's safest city, although incidents of street crime have increased in recent years. As always, be aware of opportunist strikes on bags and cameras, and pickpockets, especially on crowded *vaporetti*.

Discounts See 'Planning Your Outings', above.

Emergencies As elsewhere in Italy, phone ☎ *113* for the **police** or ☎ *112* for the military-style Carabinieri. For an **ambulance**, dial ☎ *523-0000*; and for the **fire brigade** call ☎ *115*, or the local number ☎ *041-520-0222*. For any tourism-related complaint (rip-offs, exceedingly shoddy service, and so on), dial the special English-speaking-agency **Venezia No Problem** freephone number ☎ *800-355-920*.

Internet Access **Teleradiofuga Internet Point** (2958 Campo Santo Stefano, San Marco; ☎ *041-894-6122*; Vap: S. Samuele, Giglio) is open 24 hours and charges 11€ (£7.40) per hour. For WiFi try Studioplan at Cannaregio 2116 (☎*041-099-4723*).

Laundry The best place near San Marco is **Gabriella** (San Marco 985; ☎ *041-522-1758*. Mon–Fri 10am–12:30pm, 2:30–7pm), off Calle dei Fabbri, on Rio Terrà Colonne, where they'll wash and dry your clothes for 15€ (£10) per load. The self-service laundry most convenient to the train station is the **Lavaget** (Cannaregio 1269; ☎ *041-715-976*), to the left as you cross Ponte alle Guglie from Lista di Spagna. Their rate is about 10€ (£6.70) for up to 4.5 kilos (10 lb).

Lost Property To report lost property go to the **Ufficio Oggetti Rinvenuti** (San Marco 4134; ☎ *041-788-225*. Mon, Wed and Fri 9:30am–12:30pm) at the Town Hall (Municipio), on Calle Piscopia o Loredan. It's near the Rialto Bridge by the *vaporetto* pontoon.

Other offices include: the airport lost property office **Ufficio Oggetti Smarriti**. (☎ *041-260-6436*) and the **Ufficio Oggetti Rinvenuti** at the train station (☎ *041-785-238*), at the end of *binario* (platform)14.

Luggage Storage The *deposito bagagli* in the train station is on platform 14 (☎ *041-785-531*. Daily 6am–midnight).

Post Office Venice's **Posta Centrale** is at San Marco 5554, on the San Marco side of the Rialto Bridge at Rialto Fontego dei Tedeschi (☎ *041-271-7111* or *041-528-5813*; Vap: Rialto). This office sells stamps at Window 12, Mon–Sat 8:30am–6:30pm (for parcels, 8:10am–1:30pm). If you're in Piazza San Marco and need postal services, walk through Sottoportego San Geminian, the cental portal at the opposite end of the piazza from the basilica on Calle Larga dell'Ascensione. Its usual hours are Mon–Fri 8:30am–2pm and Sat 8:30am–1pm. You can buy *francobolli* (stamps) at any tabaccaio (tobacconist's). The few mailboxes around town are red.

Toilets and Changing Facilities There are now ten public toilets around the city with changing facilities: Tronchetto, Piazzale Roma, San Bartolomeo, Diurno San Marco, Giardini San Marco, Bragora, San Leonardo, Rialto Novo, Accademia and San Domenico. For a map go to: ***www.venicecard.com***.

Tourism-Related Complaints If you're not happy with something (your hotel, a restaurant, service on the *traghetto*, and so on) call ☎ *041-529-8722/3* or send an email to complaint.apt@turismovenezia.it.

Family-Friendly Sights

If it's your first time in Venice you'll no doubt want to see the San Marco sights. Seasoned diggers of Venedig will be seeking new attractions away from the pesky pigeons and snap-happy snakes of tourists. Once you've got your bearings and have bagged the main sights you should head to Venice's far-flung, atmospheric corners and unearth the hidden gems in the less-trodden *calli* and *campi* of Castello, Cannaregio and the islands.

FUN FACT Spooky Venice: Crocodile in the Canali

It is said that across the Canal Grande towards the Punta della Dogana there is a hole where a sea monster lives. There have been various descriptions, but the most often recounted is that it has the jaws of a crocodile and a shiny black body. Sightings are rare, since it only comes out on the darkest nights in winter.

VENICE **ATTRACTIONS**

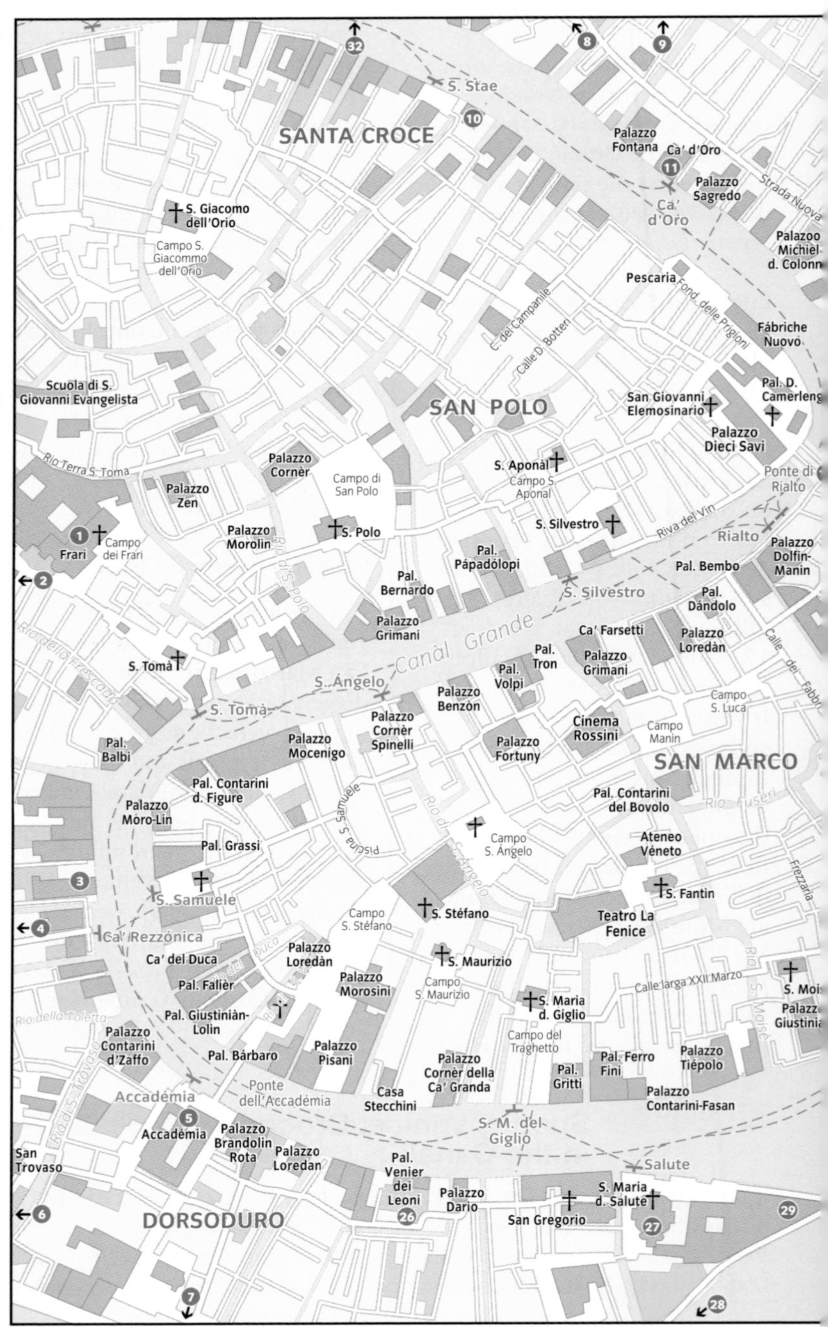

ademy Gallery
(Galleria dell'Accademia) **5**
idge of Sighs
(Ponte dei Sospiri) **18**
' d'Oro **11**
' Pesaro **10**
' Rezzonico **3**
mpanile di San Marco
(Bell Tower) **21**
iesa di San
Giorgio Maggiore **25**
iesa di San Salvador **15**
Chiesa di San Zaccaria **30**
Chiesa di Santa Maria
dei Miracoli **12**
Clock Tower
(Torre dell'Orologio) **22**
Correr Civic Museum
(Museo Civico Correr) **24**
Dogana da Mar **29**
Ducal Palace
(Palazzo Ducale) **19**
I Gesuati **7**
Il Redentore **28**
Madonna dell'Orto **9**
Museo Comunità Ebraica **8**
Natural History Museum **32**
Naval History Museum and
the Arsenal (Museo Storico
Navale & Arsenale) **31**
Peggy Guggenheim
Collection **26**
Piazza San Marco **23**
Piazzetta San Marco **20**
Rialto **14**
San Sebastiano **4**
Santa Maria della Salute **27**
Santa Maria Gloriosa
dei Frari **1**
Scuola di San Giorgio
degli Schiavoni **16**
Scuola Grande di
San Rocco **2**
Squero di San Trovaso **6**
SS. Giovanni e Paolo **13**
St. Mark's Basilica
(Basilica di San Marco) **17**

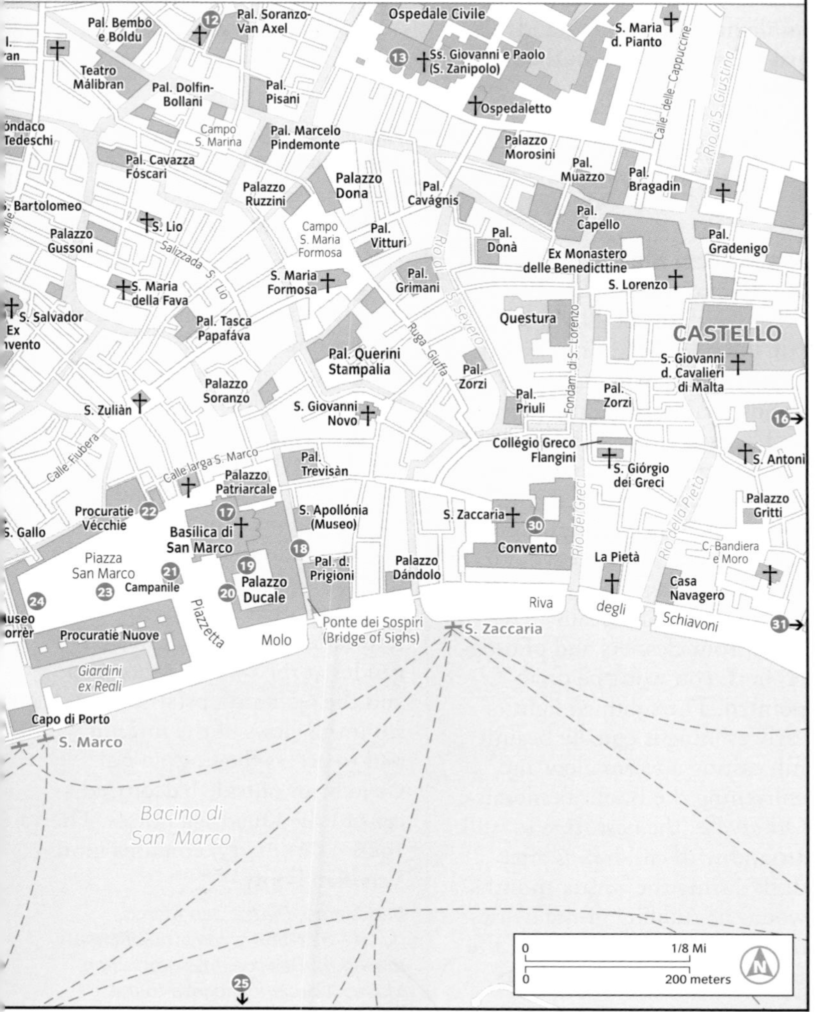

San Marco

Canal Grande (Grand Canal)

★★★ ALL AGES Cruising down the Grand Canal is a memorable experience – and a truly mesmerizing one for first-timers and children. It may be crowded, but you have to take the no. 1 vaporetto at least once in your life: try it during the photogenic golden hours of early morning and early evening when warm sunlight tones caress grand palazzi and sparkle on the water. If you can grab an outdoor seat at the prow, all the better.

From Piazzale Roma/Ferrovia (train station) and at Piazza San Marco. Tickets 5€ (£3.35). Vap: 1.

Piazza San Marco ALL AGES If you haven't been to Venice before with the children, then you'll no doubt want to spend some time soaking up the atmosphere, scaring the pigeons and exploring the sights around San Marco. Unfortunately, the place is usually mobbed with day-trippers and tour groups, so you'll quickly want to avoid it. If you can manage to see it at sunrise when it's practically deserted apart from cleaners and photographers, you won't be disappointed. The subdued light of early evening is equally beautiful, casting a warm glow and enlivening the Basilica's mosaics. Otherwise, the best time to walk around with children is after dusk during the winter months, when the tinkling of the ivories outside Caffé Quadri and Caffé Florian and the play of lights across the broad square are hypnotic. The **Basilica** and **Palazzo Ducale** are the must-see sights, while the **Museo Correr** (west side of the piazza. ✆ *041-271-5911*. Daily 9am–7pm) contains some intriguing artifacts and artworks, and is worth a look if you've bought a cumulative museum ticket or Venice Card.

INSIDER TIP

Be prepared to queue at the attractions – get here early if you can.

Basilica di San Marco ★★ AGES 4 AND UP The bulbous domes and intricately embellished Pala d'Oro (golden altarpiece) of the Byzantine basilica attest to Venice's historical position as the gateway to the Orient. The cavernous interior is ablaze with gilded flourishes and colourful mosaics, much of it plundered from further east. The unevenness of the 12th century floor shows how much the building has moved over the centuries – and is bound to impress even the moodiest teenager. If it's open (every so often it closes for restoration) you should have a gander at the **Museo Marciano** and the **Galleria** upstairs, for stunning views of the interior and to access the **Loggia dei Cavalli**, an outside balcony adjacent to the Quadriga horses. The **Tesoro (Treasury)** contains more Venetian booty.

*San Marco, Piazza San Marco. (✆ 041-522-5697; **www.basilicasanmarco.it**). Basilica, free admission; Museo Marciano (access to the*

View from San Giorgio Maggiore

Galleria and Loggia dei Cavalli), 3€ (£2), 1.50€ (£1) 6–14-year-olds; Tesoro, 2€ (£1.34), 1€ (£0.67) 6–14-year-olds. Basilica, Tesoro, and Pala d'Oro: April to October Mon–Sat 9:45am–5:30pm (November to March until 4:30pm). Museo Marciano: April to October daily 9:45am-5pm (November to March 9:45am–4pm). Vap: San Marco.

Campanile di San Marco
AGES 6 AND UP Children will love the view from the bell tower accessed via a lift – although the one at San Giorgio Maggiore is less crowded and has better views. Many Venetians avoid going up the campanile: it's meant to be unlucky – perhaps because it's collapsed four times since it was first built in the 9th century. The last time it collapsed was in 1902 (captured by a photographer – look out for the postcard); miraculously, the only victim was a cat.

San Marco, Piazza San Marco. (✆ 041-522-4064). Admission: 6€ (£4). April to June 9:30am–5pm; July to September 9am–9pm. Nov-Mar 9:30am-4:15pm Vap: San Marco.

Palazzo Ducale and Il Ponte dei Sospiri (The Bridge of Sighs) ★★ AGES 6 AND UP To the right of the Basilica is the pink and white marble Ducal Palace, whose sumptuous interiors and gruesome history will fascinate older children. For more than a millennium it was the seat of the Doges, the figureheads of a Venetian political system that was dominated by powerful aristocratic families. The present structure dates from the 14th and 15th centuries and is accessed via the Porta della Carta, which opens on to a handsomely arcaded courtyard. Beyond the aptly named Scala dei Giganti (Staircase of the Giants) by Sansovino are wood-panelled chambers decorated by Venetian masters Tiziano, Tintoretto and Veronese. Highlights include the Sala del Senato (Senate Chamber), Stanza del Consiglio dei Dieci (Room of the Council of Ten) where decapitations were ordered, and the huge Sala del

FUN FACT Know Your San Marco

- The Campanile is 98 m (321 ft) high.
- It has five bells: Nona rings the ninth hour, Marangona signals the start and end of the working day, Maleficio rang at public executions, while Trottiera and Pregadi called senators and magistrates to the Ducal Palace.
- The Torre dell'Orologio (Clock Tower) is a 15th century astronomical clock whose bronze moors strike the hours.
- Legend has it that Venetian merchants smuggled the remains of Saint Mark from Egypt packed in pickled pork to avoid the scrutiny of Turkish Muslim guards.
- The Quadriga of four gilded bronze horses date from the 2nd century and, along with the Lion of St. Mark, were brought back from the Crusades in the 10th century. The originals are housed in the Basilica's museum.
- Tintoretto's Paradiso in the Ducal Palace's Sala del Maggior Consiglio is said to be the largest oil painting in the world – it measures 7 m by 23 m (23 ft x 75 ft).
- The Bridge of Sighs got its present name in the 19th century, when poets described the condemned prisoners' final sighs of resignation.
- Near the Molo (quayside), two columns representing St. Theodore (first patron of the republic depicted standing on top of a crocodile) and Saint Mark (the lion), his replacement, mark the area where public executions took place.

Maggior Consiglio (Great Council Hall) containing the Doge's seat and Tintoretto's enormous *Paradiso*. Top billing goes to the much-photographed Ponte dei Sospiri, which links the Ducal Palace to the prisons. But for a real insight into shady Venetian politics and access to hidden passages and torture chambers, book a place on one of the **Itinerari Segreti** (Secret Itineraries) ★★ guided tours. Older children will particularly enjoy the story of Casanova's imprisonment and escape.

San Marco, Piazza San Marco. (☎ 041-271-5911). Admission on San Marco cumulative ticket or 11€ (£7.40) adults, 5.50€ (£3.70) students aged 15–29, 3€ (£2) ages 6–14 (includes cumulative ticket, free for children younger than 5). Daily 9am–5pm (until 7pm April to October; ticket office closes 1 hr earlier). Vap: San Marco.

Around San Marco

The Torre del Orologio marks the start of the Mercerie, the shopping district, which ends at Campo San Bartolomeo, the traditional meeting place of men of commerce. You'll find all the well-known shops and glitzy boutiques in this warren of calli. The gracefully arched 16th century bridge over the Canal Grande, Rialto, is overflowing with tourists and tat. Most children will probably find it exciting; parents might want to flee.

The food market is eye-catching, but you're better off going to the covered stalls over the bridge in San Polo near the Pescheria. Despite the hassle of dodging gormless snappers, you'll probably end up joining them – the passing water-borne traffic makes a great backdrop. Walking from the Rialto toward the Accademia, don't miss the fairytale spiral staircase, **Scala Contarini del Bovolo** (☎ *041-532-2920*. 3.50€ (£2.35). November to March Sat and Sun only 10am–4pm; April to October 10am–6pm daily. Take Calle della Vida off Campo Manin) named after the Venetian for snail, bovolo. If you don't fancy the extra expense to go inside, you can view the staircase from the calle, probably the best bet if you're in a large group. The

Torre dell'Orologio, Piazza San Marco

staircase was designed to allow the owner to ride his horse up to his living quarters.

Arising from the ashes of the catastrophic 1996 fire, the **Teatro di Fenice** (see 'Entertainments and Sports', above) on Calle del Teatro may interest older children who are into the performing arts. Just before reaching the Accademia Bridge, the wide expanse of Campo Santo Stefano is a welcome sight for energetic rascals.

Dorsoduro

On the southern side of the Accademia bridge, you'll find the city's arty and studenty haunts. As well as the classical masterpieces of the Galleria dell'Accademia and the modern works at the Collezione Peggy Guggenheim, the *sestiere* has lots of little galleries and interesting shops. The university buildings and schools near Ca' Foscari give the place a youthful feel. The focus of this is leafy Campo Santa Margherita, a large space with popular *caffes* and stalls, where local bambini play football and students pack the outdoor seating. At nearby Campo San Barnaba children can re-enact a scene from the latest Bond film, *Casino Royale.* There's also a wonderful greengrocers' boat around the corner near the Ponte dei Pugni – a fun place to visit. The long promenade facing the island of Giudecca, the Zattere, is a favourite spot for catching some rays and relaxing. It's also a perfect spot for a picnic. The Gesuati church is worth a butcher's for works by Tiepolo and Tintoretto. Look out for the Squero (boatyard) just off the Zattere on the Rio San Trovaso – in front of the Tyrolean-looking wooden structures you'll notice some gondolas being worked on.

At the eastern tip of Dorsoduro is the Punta della Dogana, the old customs house that has been undergoing restoration for nearly ten years now. When it's finished you'll once again be able to sit and enjoy the mesmerising views of San Marco and the Grand Canale. Around the corner is the Santa Maria della Salute church.

Galleria dell'Accademia (Academy Gallery)★★

AGES 5 AND UP The Accademia has Venice's most treasured paintings, which are exhibited chronologically from the 13th to the 18th centuries. You've probably heard of all the artists: Bellini, Tintoretto, Veronese, Mantegna, Canaletto, Tiziano and the beefy Dalmatian, Carpaccio. Here you can see them all in one place and finally work out who came first and who was pals with whom. Not only is it one of the greatest galleries in Europe, the paintings here provide a fascinating glimpse into Venice life over the years – it might not grab younger children at first sight, but some will be drawn in. Follow the development of Western art from the 14th century Byzantine world of Veneziano to the dramatic 18th century views of Guardi, who painted the Fire at San Marcuola, a spectral night scene filled with flames. Backed by wealthy patrons, Venetian artists created inventive and vivid works inspired by the city's light and water, which combined create dazzling and subtle effects. It also helped that the richest pigments from the city's Eastern trade links were widely available here. Venice further revolutionised Western art because the dampness here made fresco painting prone to disaster – the ideal solution was to stretch linen canvas brought from the Arsenale shipyards.

FUN FACT **Ponte dei Pugni (Bridge of Fists)** 

Place your feet on the footprints imprinted on the bridge and imagine this scene... It was here that men from the city's rival factions, the Castellani (with red caps) from Castello and the local Nicolotti (wearing black caps), would fight bare-fisted, roared on by baying crowds and spilling into the water. These city rivals also contested less violent games, called Forze d'Ercole (Forces of Hercules), at the end of Rio San Gregorio: the Castellani and Nicolotti would confront each other in human pyramids. A child capped each pyramid, which could reach as high as eight tiers of men.

FUN FACT Venetian Masters

Venetian *maestri* Tintoretto and Tiziano are the most ubiquitous artists in Venice some 450 years after their expert brush strokes transformed enormous blank canvases into sparkling Renaissance scenes. Jacopo Robusti (1518–1594) was called Tintoretto after his father's profession, *un tintor*, a dyer. He was a devout man who only once ventured beyond Venice.

Tiziano Vecelli (1488–1576) lends the English version of his name Titian to a brownish-orange colour, which he used frequently. He was approaching 90 when he was struck down during the plague of 1576.

Dorsoduro, at foot of Accademia Bridge. (📞 041-522-2247. ***www.gallerieaccademia.org****). Admission: 6.50€ (£4.35) adults, 3.25€ (£2.20) 18–25-year-olds, free for under 18s. Mon 8:15am–2pm; Tues–Sun 8:15am–7:15pm; last admission 30 min. before close (winter hours may be shorter). Vap: Accademia.*

Ca' Rezzonico (Museum of 18th Century Venice) ★

AGES 6 AND UP Nosey children and adults will enjoy this intriguing glimpse behind the heavy curtains of an 18th century Venetian home. This handsome *palazzo* on the Grand Canal was opened as a museum in 2001, and although a bit pricey, it has proved very popular. Ca' Rezzonico was built for a wealthy merchant family by Baldassare Longhena, the 17th century architect of La Salute church. He created a fabulous backdrop for paintings by Tiepolo, Guardi and Longhi, and the ornate furnishings. The English poet Robert Browning lived out his last days here in the 1880s.

Dorsoduro (on the Grand Canal on Fondamenta Rezzonico). (📞 041-241-0100 or 041-520-4036). Admission: 6.50€ (£4.35) adults, 4.50€ (£3) students. April to October Wed–Mon 10am–6pm; November to March 10am–5pm. Vap: Ca' Rezzonico (go to Campo San Barnabà, turn right at the piazza and over the small bridge; the museum entrance is on your right).

Collezione Peggy Guggenheim (Peggy Guggenheim Collection) ★★

AGES 5 AND UP Peggy Guggenheim (1898–1979) was a flamboyant, rich American art dealer whose friendship and patronage of a number of European artists helped them find a market for art that pushed the boundaries. This collection of surrealist, Cubist, abstract-expressionist and futurist art helps you work out when and why art stopped being about pretty pictures and started to be about something else altogether. Housed in Peggy's former home, Palazzo Venier dei Leoni on the Canal Grande, it opened in 1951 and is now looked after by the Solomon R. Guggenheim Foundation (her uncle) that runs the Berlin, New York, Bilbao and Las Vegas Guggenheims.

Modern Art: What's It All About?

Don't let knowing nothing about art stop you from enjoying it. Take this guide to the Peggy Guggenheim Collection and everything will fall into place...kind of.

Avant-garde people or works that are experimental or novel – they go beyond the norm. Sums up Peggy Guggenheim nicely.

Cubism was an early 20th century avant-garde art movement in which the object of the work was broken up, examined and then put back together in an abstracted way, letting you experience it from other perspectives. Look out for Picasso's *The Poet* and *The Studio*.

Dada or Dadaism is a cultural movement that started in Zürich during World War I and involved the visual and performing arts, literature and graphic design. Anti-war and anti-art, Dadaists rebelled against a social order that they believed inspired conflict, oppression and artistic supression. Look out for Jan (Hans) Arp's *Overturned Blue Shoe with Two Heels Under a Black Vault*.

Surrealism started around 1917 and stemmed from Dadaism. It was an artistic, cultural and intellectual movement which sought to free the unconscious mind, which was said to be truer and more real than the conscious. Look out for Dali's *Birth of Liquid Desires* and Magritte's *Voice of Space* (*La Voix des airs*).

Abstract expressionism picked up from surrealism and began after World War II. Its creations were spontaneous, fast and subconscious. Look out for Jackson Pollock's *Enchanted Forest* and *The Moon Woman*.

Futurism was about hating the old, accepted artistic and cultural ways, and loving the white heat of technology; about man's triumph over nature. Look out for Umberto Boccioni's *Dynamism of a Speeding Horse + Houses*.

*Dorsoduro 701 (on Calle San Cristoforo). (☎ 041-240-5411; **www.guggenheim-venice.it**). Admission: 10€ (£6.70) adults, 5€ (£3.35) children over 5 and students. Wed–Mon 10am–6pm (until 10pm on Sat April to October). Vap: Accademia (walk around left side of Accademia, take 1st left, and walk straight ahead following signs – you'll cross a Canale, then walk alongside another, until turning left when necessary).*

Santa Maria della Salute (Church of the Virgin Mary of Good Health) ★ AGES 4 AND UP

Popularly known as 'La Salute,' this 17th century baroque beauty is probably the second most recognisable Venetian place of worship, and one of the most photographed buildings in the world. It sits at the end of the Canal Grande near the Punta della Dogana (customs house), almost directly across from Piazza San Marco.

It was built to honour the Virgin Mary of Good Health for ending the plague of 1630. It took 50 years to build and is designed in the shape of a crown, probably in reference to the 'Queen of Heaven' mentioned in the Venetian prayer recited during the plague. Within the spacious and rather sombre octagonal interiors, under two impressive domes, are sumptuous artworks by Tiziano (Titian) and Tintoretto. Bring a picnic and sit outside on either the steps of the Campo della Salute or the Punta della Dogana nearby (when it's reopened) and watch the action on the Canal Grande.

Dorsoduro (on Campo della Salute). (☎ 041-522-5558). Church, free admission; sacristy, 1.50€ (£1). Daily 9am–noon and 3–5:30pm. Vap: Salute.

Around Santa Croce

The part of Santa Croce near the Piazzale Roma has many university buildings and quite a bit of incongruous modern development. It's pleasant enough, but has nothing to excite children. Going east, the maze of *calli* and small *campi* bordering San Polo offers photo opportunities, while the leafy and spacious Campo San Giacomo dell'Orio is great for play, picnic and pizzas. Amongst the historic *palazzi* on the Grand Canal are two gems with very different exhibitions: Ca' Pesaro houses modern art, while Palazzo Fontegio dei Turchi is a must for budding natural scientists.

Museo di Storia Naturale ★★

ALL AGES Over two million zoological wonders fill the large *saloni* of the Palazzo Fontego dei Turchi – the fossils, microbiological slides and aquarium creatures are a welcome escape from Venetian culture. The atmospheric Ligabue Collection will excite and spook children with ferocious beasts found on 1970s digs in the Sahara, including the *Ouranosaurus* and the massive crocodile, *Sarcosuchus imperator*.

FUN FACT **Spooky Venice: Revenge of the Skull** 

A young Venetian man walking with his fiancé near a cemetery kicked a skull into the canale as an act of bravado – and the young girl cackled with laughter. The couple forgot the incident and married a few months later, settling in the Dorsoduro area near La Salute. On their wedding night they heard a knock on the door. The groom opened it to find a beautiful girl. 'Who are you?' he asked. 'You don't remember me? I'm the one you kicked into a canale,' she answered. At that moment he remembered kicking the skull into the canale and in a panic slammed the door. He turned around to see the skin on his wife's face fade away, as she turned into a skeleton and her once pearly-white teeth fell to the floor.

Santa Croce

Santa Croce 1730 (Fontego Turchi). (☎ 041-275-0206). Free admission. Tue–Fri 9am–12.30pm; Sat and Sun 9am–3.30 pm. Closed Mon, 25th December, 1st January and 1st May. Vap: Riva di Biagio/ San Stae.

Ca' Pesaro AGES 6 AND UP This Renaissance palazzo's collections will stimulate anyone getting tired of high art and tourist tat. The fabulous Museo d'Arte Moderna (Museum of Modern Art) collection is a legacy of Venice's role as host to the world's greatest contemporary art show, the Biennale (see 'Child-Friendly Festivals & Events', above). The grandiose rooms house intriguing and often perplexing works by Matisse, Kandinsky, Klimt, Moore, Miró, Chagall, De Chirico, Manzù, Boccioni and Morandi.

Santa Croce 2076 (Fondamenta Ca' Pesaro). (☎ 041-524-1173). Admission: 5.50€ (£3.70), 3€ (£2) 6–14 years. Tues–Sun 10am–6pm. Vap: San Stae.

Around San Polo

Venice's smallest *sestiere* has some of its oldest buildings. Near the Rialto Bridge is the famous covered market, where you can feast your eyes on the freshest seafood and other colourful produce. The centre of San Polo life is the

TIP Gondola Rides

A cheaper alternative to an outrageously priced gondola ride is to take one of the *traghetti* across the Canal Grande. These gondolas, steered by two *gondolieri*, are not as plush as the tourist versions, but the short trip is thrilling for - children. The Venetians tend to stand up, which can be quite a wobbly experience – take younger children on last when the boat is steadier and sit down if you feel safer that way. **Tip:** the normally affable gondolieri are prone to swearing and threatening gestures if you take a photo near their boat. Ask their permission first. The fare is 0.50€ (£0.34). Catch one between the following jetties: **Fondamente S. Lucia (railway station)**; **Fondamenta San Simeón Piccolo**; **San Marcuola**; **Fóndaco dei Turchi** (by the Natural History Museum); **Santa Sofia** (near Ca' d'Oro); **Pescheria** (fish market); **Riva del Carbòn**; **Fondamente del Vin**; **Sant' Angelo**; **San Tomà**; **San Samuele**; **Ca' Rezzónico**; **Santa Maria del Giglio**; **Calle Lanza** (near the Salute church).

eponymously named *campo* – a large expanse where children can play while parents can sip a Spritz at one of the outdoor cafés. Heading west, yellow signs reading 'Alla Ferrovia' and 'Piazzale Roma' take you to the Frari church and Scuola di San Rocco.

Santa Maria Gloriosa dei Frari (Church of the Frari)

AGES 4 AND UP The colossal bulk of this 13th–14th century Gothic church will take your breath away, if the weaving in and out of passers-by getting here hasn't left you short of puff already. The locals call it 'i Frari,' the dialect version of *frati* (brothers); it was built by the Franciscans. The second-largest church in Venice is just a short hop, pizza slice and ice cream away from the Scuola Grande di San Rocco. Not surprisingly, given that it's dedicated to the humble bird-fancier and denouncer of worldly goods, St Francis of Assisi, the building is suitably austere, with plenty of niches for sparrows and pigeons on the largely brick exterior. There are a number of important artworks inside, including two Tiziano masterpieces, a Donatello wood-carving and a Bellini triptych. You can also see Tiziano's and Canova's tombs here. If you're particularly interested, ask about free English-speaking tours run by volunteers during the summer.

San Polo 3072 (on Campo dei Frari). (☎ 041-522-2637). Admission: 2€ (£1.34) or 8€ (£5.35) on a cumulative ticket. Mon–Sat 9am–6pm; Sun 1–6pm. Vap: San Tomà

Church of the Frari

Scuola Grande di San Rocco

AGES 6 AND UP The epic scale and intensity of Tintoretto's canvasses at this confraternity guild (*scuola*) is likely to impress old masters and, if you haven't already overloaded them with art, whippersnappers alike. The 50 dramatic works displayed took the artist around 20 years, so take your time over them before wolfing down a pizza slice on the way to the Frari. Highlights include the powerful *La Crocifissione (The Crucifixion)* in the gilt-ceilinged hall and the tumultuous energy of *La Strage degli Innocenti (The Slaughter of the Innocents)* downstairs. As light relief try and spot the Tiziano and Tiepolos.

San Polo 3058 (on Campo San Rocco adjacent to Campo dei Frari). (☎ 041-523-4864). Admission: 5.50€ (£3.70) adults, 4€ (£2.70) students, free for under-18s. Late March to November, daily 9am–5:30pm; November to late March 10am–5pm. Vap: San Tomà (look for red San Rocco sign).

Cannaregio

Spanning the large area east of Santa Lucia train station as far as the Rio dei Mendicanti, bordering Castello and the Ospedale (hospital), Cannaregio has plenty of space to escape the hordes and stumble across hidden gems. If your family doesn't mind walking, it's a fun place to get lost. Try and bypass the Lista di Spagna area near the station – there are better and cheaper places to eat and spend your money. Beyond the Ponte dei Tre Archi and north of the Napoleon-built Strada Nova (New Road) shops are Cannaregio's long *Fondamente* with interesting shops, characterful watering holes and eateries where locals and students hang out.

The Jewish Ghetto is a poignant place (see below) to visit and the mighty long, often sunny Fondamenta degli Ormesini ending at the sadly neglected Misericordia church makes an unforgettable stroll. On the northern extremities is the extravagantly baroque Gesuiti church, which looms out of the surrounding houses above a *campo* where local youngsters often play footie. Just around the corner on the Fondamente Nuove is the edge of Venice, where you can look out to the San Michele cemetery and, on a clear day, the distant Dolomites. There are a couple of inviting bars serving ice cream and snacks here near *vaporetti* pontoons; you can catch boats to Murano, Burano and Torcello here. Towards Rialto, don't miss Venice's sweetest church and favourite Venetian wedding venue:

Chiesa Santa Maria dei Miracoli ★ AGES 4 AND UP which sits beside a chilled-out *campo* that has a great little *café-gelateria* and arty bookshop (see 'Venice Shopping', below).

Rio d. Miracoli. 2.50€ (£1.68), 8€ (£5.35) on a cumulative ticket or 16€ (£10.70) family ticket. Mon–Sat 10am–5pm; Sun 3–5pm.

Ca' d'Oro (Galleria Giorgio Franchetti) AGES 5 AND UP The highlight of a child's visit to this once-golden Gothic palace is likely to be the view of the Grand Canale from the *loggia* – it's practically the same view that the Contarinis would have surveyed in the 15th century. The gilt-covered facade may have

Santa Maria dei Miracoli

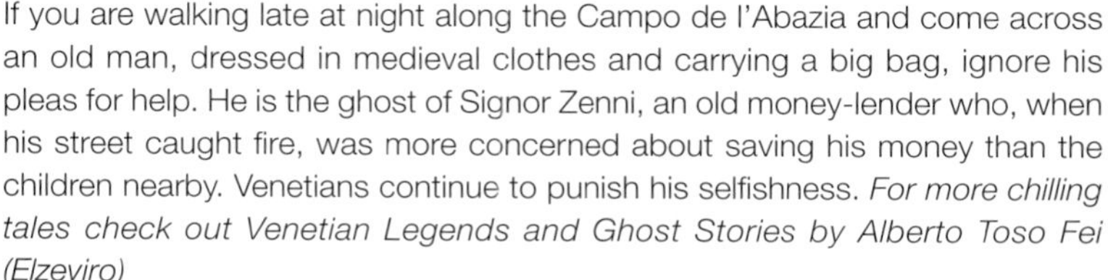

FUN FACT **Spooky Venice: Mind the Bagman**

If you are walking late at night along the Campo de l'Abazia and come across an old man, dressed in medieval clothes and carrying a big bag, ignore his pleas for help. He is the ghost of Signor Zenni, an old money-lender who, when his street caught fire, was more concerned about saving his money than the children nearby. Venetians continue to punish his selfishness. *For more chilling tales check out Venetian Legends and Ghost Stories by Alberto Toso Fei (Elzeviro)*

faded, but the beamed ceilings and grand interiors, filled with artworks bequeathed by former owner Baron Franchetti, are dressed to impress. Treasures not to be missed are Vivarini's *Passion Scenes* and Mantegna's *San Sebastiano.*

Cannaregio between 3931 and 3932 (on Calle Ca' d'Oro north of Rialto Bridge). (☎ 041-523-8790). Admission: 5€ (£3.35), free for children under 12. Mon 8:15am–2pm; Tues–Sat 8:15am–7:15pm (winter hours may be shorter). Vap: Ca' d'Oro.

Il Ghetto (The Jewish Ghetto)

ALL AGES Forget South Central, Brixton, Staines... the original ghetto is found in a quiet area of Cannaregio – home to Venice's Jewish population from 1516 to 1797. The area was originally a foundry – *getto* in Venetian. Jewish quarters around the world were subsequently given the name. Although they had to follow rules that limited their social and economic freedoms, worship was not restricted. In 1797 Napoleon destroyed the ghetto gates and disbanded the Christian guards who manned them, allowing Jews to move freely around the city. For a real insight into the history of the Venetian ghetto, take older children and teenagers on a guided tour of the area and its 16th century synagogues run by the **Museo Communità Ebraica**. Combine a visit with a meal at the excellent Gam Gam restaurant nearby (p. 146).

Cannaregio 2902B (Campo del Ghetto Nuovo). (☎ 041-715-359). Museum 3€ (£2) adults, 2€ (£1.34) children; museum and synagogue tour 8.50€ (£5.70) adults, 7€ (£4.70) children. Museum April to September Sun–Fri 10am–7pm, October to March Sun–Fri 10am–6pm; synagogue tours hourly 10:30am–4:30pm (until 5pm April to September). Closed on Jewish holidays. Vap: Guglie or San Marcuola.

Around Castello

The last and largest of the *sestieri* becomes less touristy the further east you go towards Via Garibaldi and St Elena. Away from the often cramped tourist routes, children will enjoy the extra space to run around, and can see how the last remaining real Venetians live. Before you strike out for freedom, don't forget the large *campi* with impressive churches on the western fringes – well worth hanging out

FUN FACT Spooky Venice: *Calle della Morte* 

'The Street of Death' is a narrow L-shaped *calle* on Campo Bandiera e Moro, where 'unofficial' executions took place. Among the many who met a gruesome end here were two innocent men mistaken for Genovese spies.

in. Up near the Ospedale, **Campo SS. Giovanni e Paolo** has a bulging Gothic church, a famous *caffé-pasticcerria*, **Rosa Salva** (p. 141), and a heroic-looking bronze equestrian statue of *condottiere* Bartolommeo Colleoni. **Campo Santa Maria Formosa**, the scene of outrageous carnival antics, is a fun place to linger, with space for children to play, a produce market and outdoor café seating looking on to the shapely church and baroque campanile. For respite from the crowds, head east of St Mark's to the Gothic-Renaissance **Chiesa di San Zaccaria** and its 13th century campanile on an attractive *campo* circled by handsome *palazzi*.

From the Molo di San Marco, you can escape the crowds by heading east along the wide **Riva degli Schiavoni** – on the way you'll reach the entrance to the Arsenale naval dockyards and the **Naval Museum** (see below), which is great for children. Further on is the spacious **Via Garibaldi**, lined with local shops, inviting *caffés* and *pasticcerie*. Keep your eyes peeled for the colossal cruise ships passing on the Canale San Marco – a surreal photo opportunity. Don't miss the statues of Garibaldi and a lion perched above a small pond on the leafy avenue.

If you all have the legs and are relishing the relaxed atmosphere way out east, head to **San Pietro di Castello**, once the city's principal cathedral and surrounded by greenery. Venice's largest green spaces are found at the Giardini Pubblici, which contain the Biennale pavilions (see 'Child-Friendly Events & Festivals', above) and the shady parks of St Elena, near the ramshackle football stadium.

Arsenale and Museo Storico Navale (Naval History Museum and the Arsenal)

★★★ **AGES 4 AND UP** The scale of the mighty Venetian Arsenale shipbuilding complex and the nautical exhibits in the naval museum are sure to blow the minds of children and adults. Take a walk down the Canale dell'Arsenale to admire the grand entrance with its flag-bearing towers, baroque statues and stone lions – a great photo backdrop. These days its impressive docks and long *corderie* warehouses are off-limits except for military personnel – you'll no doubt spot dapper naval officers grabbing an espresso nearby. During the various Biennale festivals, some of the cavernous spaces, where thousands once toiled outfitting gargantuan galleys, are used for performances and to exhibit contemporary art and architecture. For a glimpse of the shipyards, take *vaporetti* 41, 42, 51 or 52.

The **Naval History Museum** at Campo San Biagio is filled with fascinating naval artifacts including maps, weaponry, navigational devices and hundreds of model ships. Pride of place goes to a replica of the lavish ceremonial barge that belonged to the Doges, the *Bucintoro*. They also have a fine collection of shells and the *Padiglione delle navi* is a pavilion filled with historic vessels, including gondolas with *felze* (creepy cabins) and frigates.
*Castello 2148 (Campo San Biagio). (041-520-0276; **www.marina.difesa.it/venezia**). Admission: 2€ (£1.34), Tues–Sun 8:45am–1:30pm / until 1pm Sat; closed Sun and public holidays. Vap: Arsenale.*

Giudecca & San Giorgio

The Giudecca is a long, thin island, seldom visited, with a largely working class population. It has few obvious attractions apart from a lack of tourists and the celebrated **Chiesa del Redentore** Ages 6 and up by Palladio (2€ (£1.34) or 8€ (£5.35) cumulative ticket. Mon–Sat 10am–5pm; Sun 1–5pm. Vap: Redentore). It was built as votive thanks for the city being delivered from the great plague of 1575–77, which claimed 46,000 lives. If you're lucky enough to be here during the Festa del Redentore in July (see 'Child-Friendly Festivals & Events', above), children will enjoy the festivities and fireworks. Tucked away at the far eastern end is the exclusive Cipriani hotel and Cip's restaurant, a celebrity haunt. If the children fancy supplementing their pocket money with a paparazzo pic of Becks, Brosnan or Beyonce, book a table at the pricey Cip – no jacket required.

A short taxi ride away on a Riva, or a one-stop *vaporetto*

Arsenale

San Giorgio Maggiore

hop, is the small island of San Giorgio, where you can soak up the best aerial views in Venice from the campanile of the:

Chiesa di San Giorgio Maggiore ★★ AGES 4 AND UP Prolific Palladio designed the twin facades with mathematical precision and thousands of craftsmen built his harmoniously proportioned vision over the remains of previous structures – there was a church here as early as the 8th century. After the ostentation of St Mark's Basilica, the light, simplicity and spaciousness makes for a refreshing change. However, there are a few epic Tintoretto canvasses to view, including a famous version of the Last Supper with dramatic chiaroscuro qualities. What makes the trip truly unforgettable is the 360-degree views from the campanile gallery – don't forget your camera.

San Giorgio Maggiore; (☎ 041-522-7827). Free admission. Campanile lift 3€ (£2). Mon–Sat 9:30am–12:30pm; daily 2–6pm. Vap: San Giorgio Maggiore.

Sun, Sea and Sand: a Trip to Lido & its Beaches

Lido is worth a day trip if you're in Venice for a week or more, as younger children will love the sandy beaches. The thought of an idyllic beach a mere 15-minute *vaporetto* cruise from **San Zaccaria** sounds perfect, but the reality of polluted waters and overcrowded beaches can be hard to swallow. If you just envisage a quick run around and paddle, head to the **Spiaggia Comunale** (overcrowded in July and August). Remember the private beaches charge for the use of parasols, deck chairs and cabins. Your best bet for a few hours sand-castling is to take Bus B from Piazzale Elisabetta to Alberoni at the southern end of the island, where the dunes and fishermen's nets will occupy youngsters for hours.

If you're determined to have a few days or longer on the beach, the nearest okay resort is **Sottomarina**, near Chioggia. Cheap beach holidays are two-a-penny at **Lido di Jesolo**, a mosquito-infested marshland drained by Mussolini. Slightly less commercial is **Cavallino**, but for charm and character try **Caorle** further up the coast.

Lido itself is a little nondescript save for a few Belle Époque hotels, which regain some of their glamour during the Film Festival in August and September. The main street, the Gran Viale Santa Maria Elisabetta, has some odd-looking boutiques and a few decent *caffé-gelaterie* for the children. You can also rent bikes on the Gran Viale (see 'Cycling in Lido', below), which is a fun way of exploring the villa-lined leafy streets and far-flung sand dunes, toward the island of Pellestrina.

Campo dei Gesuiti

Palladio Was Here

Anyone who's been to Vicenza will know something about the architectural wonder boy, Palladio. He was commissioned to work on a number of Venetian buildings, and after his death in 1580 his loyal student Vincenzo Scamozzi completed his works.

Il Redentore (1576–1591) on Giudecca. The diameter of the dome is 15.25 m (50 ft). The length of the church (from the entrance to the rear wall) is 69.19 m (227 ft). Palladio used a proportional system to create a harmony in his architecture: the overall width of the facade is about the same as the height of the church to the base of the dome (83 vs. 87 Vicentine feet), and the height from the ground to the peak of the main pediment (68⅓') is half the overall height (137⅚').

San Giorgio Maggiore (1560–1580). The church is on an island just a short *vaporetto* ride from San Marco. It's a huge building: the diameter of its dome is 12.19 m (40 ft) and the Campanile is 18.29 m (60 ft) high. The façade was completed in 1610 by Vincenzo Scamozzi, 30 years after the death of the maestro. Although two-dimensional, it looks 3-D and resembles a classical temple portico.

TIP Cycling in Lido

If you fancy a ride along the proms of the Lido, or even on the neighbouring island strip of Pellestrina, via the ferry, contact **Lido on Bike** or **Gardin Anna Vallì**. An hour's bike rental is 3€ (£2); all day costs 9€ (£6). For a bit of family fun, they even have tandems and four-seaters. Gardin Anna Vallì offers a 20% discount with a **Rolling Venice Card** (see 'Planning Your Outings', above). **Lido on Bike**: Gran Viale 21, Lido di Venezia. 041-526-8018; ***www.lidoonbike.it***. April to October daily 8:30am–7:30pm / **Gardin Anna Vallì**: Piazzale S. M. Elisabetta 2/a, Lido di Venezia. 041-276-0005; ***www.biciclettegardin.com***. May to October 8am–8pm.

A DAY TRIP TO THE ISLANDS: SAN MICHELE, MURANO, BURANO & TORCELLO

Children will love taking the *vaporetto* to the islands in the northern lagoon. Each island has its own charm, and all except the cemetery of San Michele have ice cream. You'll need a few hours for the entire trip – if you're short on time skip San Michele and Murano; Torcello and Burano are the most attractive for a family day out. A word of warning though: older kids and some adults might find the islands a little dull. Catch a *vaporetto* at Fondamente Nuove – you could get here early and have breakfast or a snack in one of the bars near the pontoon, like **Algiubagio** (see 'Cafés, Snacks & Family-Friendly Dining', below).

First stop **San Michele** is a large cemetery studded with cypress trees, grand monuments and high-rise tombs. Enjoy the comparative silence while the children marvel at the lavish graves and monuments of the old Venetian families who desperately tried to outdo each other. Ask children to spot their three most over-the-top mausoleums, or hunt for the graves of Igor Stravinsky and Ezra Pound (clue: they died in 1971 and 1972, respectively).

Next stop **Murano** has a number of foundries which are great for children to watch the skilful art of glassblowing. There's also the **Museo del'Vetro** that has a sparkling collection of antique glass.

Fondamenta Giustinian 8, 30121 Murano. (041-739-586). 5.50€ (£3.70), 3€ (£2) 6–14 years. Free under-5s. November to March 10am–4pm, April to October 10am–6pm.

Burano is a beguiling fishing village with brightly painted houses and a multitude of lace shops – quieter than Venice, it's a charming place to stroll around, snapping the multi-coloured *calli* and eating ice cream. There are open spaces for lively youngsters to run around in, too.

Torcello has a different, vaguely spooky, feel, especially in winter. Less than 100 people live amid

VENICE & **LAGOON**

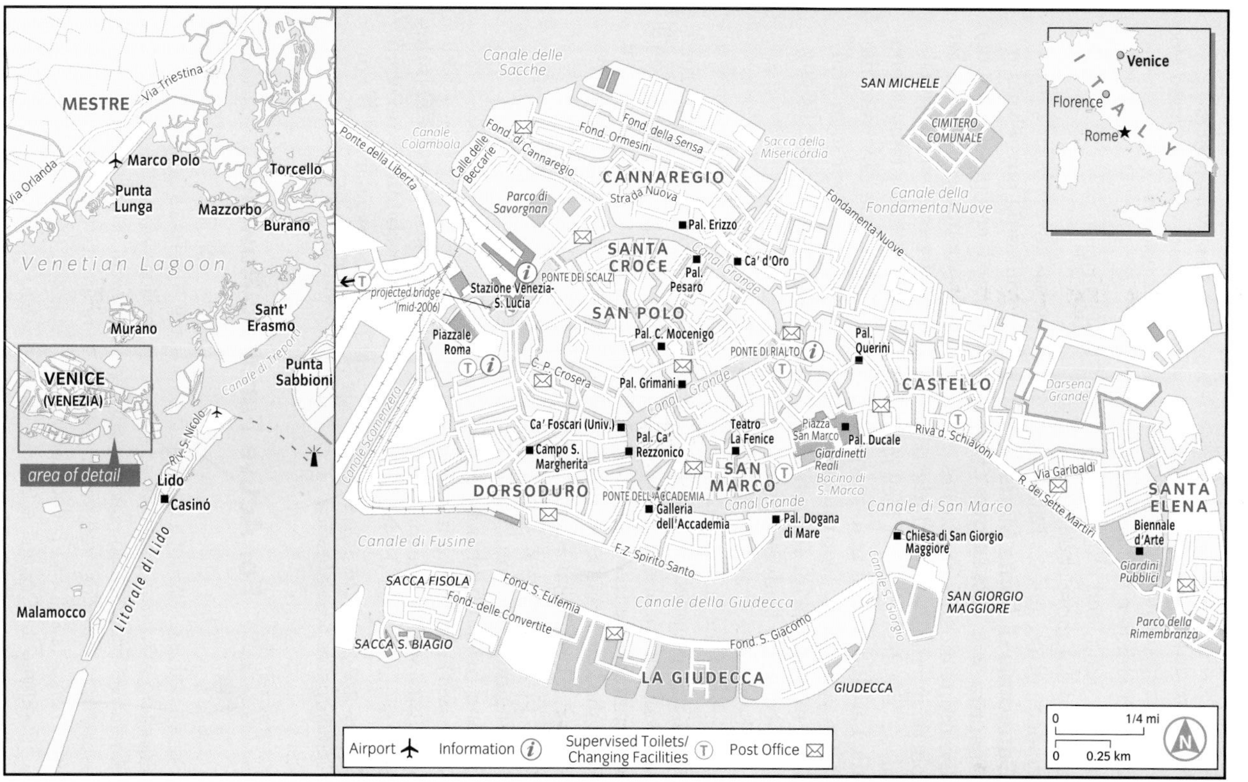

the grass-banked Canals and crumbling buildings, a far cry from the 20,000 refugees who fled here during the Dark Ages. After being cooped up in the city, younger children will appreciate a run around, and older ones can find out more about this desolate place, and it's haunting **Cattedrale di Santa Maria Assunta** ★★ AGES 3 AND UP The Byzantine mosaics and atmospheric interiors are worth the trip alone: the depictions of Hell in the Last Judgement send shivers down your spine. Don't miss two little museums with artifacts and archaeological finds next door. The better one is up the stairs to the right of the architectural fragments propped up against the wall – if it's not open, ask someone by the lace stalls. They keep the key. Bring a picnic, as there is a large lawn around the back, perfect for play. Take turns looking imperious on 'Attila's Throne' (it's probably a bishop's stone seat) and look out for the stray cats, which heartbreakingly used to number in the hundreds.

(☎ 041-270-2464). 3€ (£2), 8€ (£5.35) special ticket: basilica, museum and to climb the campanile. Museum & Basilica 5.50€ (£3.70), 3€ (£2) under-12s. March to October 10:30am–5pm. November to February 10am–4:30pm. Closed Mon and public holidays.

Shopping

Venice has always been a place where you could buy whatever you wanted, at a price. Although the main shopping area is in San Marco's *Mercerie*, where you'll find some of Italy's famous boutique names, you can avoid the crowds and discover some real gems scattered around the city.

Food

Pescheria ★★★ Perhaps the most stunning fish market you'll ever see, starring freshly caught squid, baby octopus and soft-shelled crabs.

San Polo (north of the Fabbriche Nouve, near Rialto). Mon–Sat 8am–1pm. Vap: Rialto.

Rialto Market ★★ VALUE Is this the cure for children who won't eat fruit and vegetables? If not, it's colourful, lively and a great

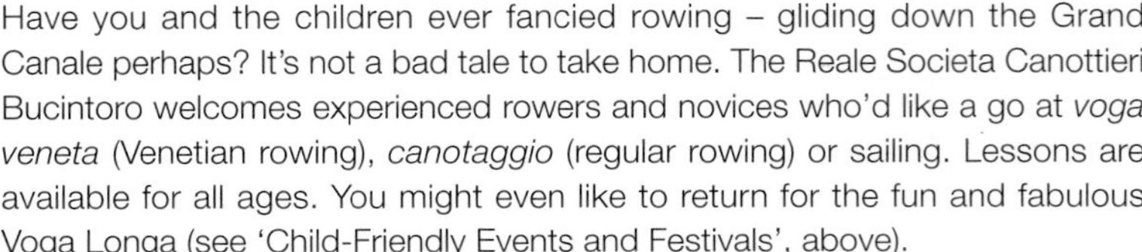

FUN FACT **For Active Families: Rowing**

Have you and the children ever fancied rowing – gliding down the Grand Canale perhaps? It's not a bad tale to take home. The Reale Societa Canottieri Bucintoro welcomes experienced rowers and novices who'd like a go at *voga veneta* (Venetian rowing), *canotaggio* (regular rowing) or sailing. Lessons are available for all ages. You might even like to return for the fun and fabulous Voga Longa (see 'Child-Friendly Events and Festivals', above).

Fondamenta Dogana e Salute 15, Dorsoduro 30123. ☎ *041-520-5630*; ***www.bucintoro.org***. Tue–Fri 10am–6pm, Sat 9am–6pm, Sun 8am–1pm. Vap: La Salute.

Rialto Market

reminder of what you don't find in supermarkets back home.

San Polo (by the Pescheria). Mon–Sat 8am–1pm. Vap: Rialto.

Casa del Parmigiano Next to the Pescheria, this house of cheese is a great place to stock up on cold cuts, olive oil and a slab of *caciocavallo*, *canestrato Pugliese* or good old Parmesan.

*Erberia Rialto. (☎ 0141-50-6525; **www.aliani-casadelparmigiano.it**) Vap: Rialto.*

Panificio Volpe Venice has perhaps the worst bread in Italy, so the Jewish bread and pastries from Volpe are often sold out by lunchtime. Come early.

Calle del Ghetto Vecchio, 1143 Cannaregio 30123 (next to the Tempio Israelitico). (☎ 041-715-178). Vap: Guglie.

Rosa Salva Wicked chocolates and sweets for immediate consumption or to take home.

Campo SS Giovanni e Paulo, 6779 Castello (on Salizzada SS Giovanni e Paulo). (☎ 0141-527-7949). Vap: Ospedale.

Masks

Il Canovaccio ★★ FIND This mask shop stands out because of its beautifully eccentric handmade animal masks that children love (from 20€ (£13.40) upwards).

Calle del Bande, 5369/70 Castello (between Salizzada San Lio and Rio San Zulian). (☎ 041-521-0393). Vap: Rialto or San Zaccaria.

Ca'Macana Famed for making the masks in Stanley Kubrick's *Eyes Wide Shut*, come here for the most elaborate handcrafted masks.

*Casin Lombardo, 3172 Dorsoduro (just south of Campo Santa Barbara). (☎ 041-277-6142; **www.camacana.com**). Vap: Accademia.*

Models, Toys & The Peculiar

Gilberto Penzo FIND Not really toys, but carefully constructed miniature gondolas and boats of all sizes and periods. Also sells kits to make your own.

Calle Seconda dei Saoneri, 2681 San Polo (between Rio Terra and Calle Saoneri). (☎ 041-719-372). Vap: San Toma.

Bambolandia Your daughter will either love or be freaked out by the scary porcelain dolls made by Italian artist Beatrice Perini. Also sells soft toys, puppets, mini-theatres and robust wooden toys.

Campo San Polo, 1462 San Polo (at the foot of the bridge that leads to Rialto). (☎ 0141-520-7502). Vap: San Silvestro.

Forma Nature-loving children will be fascinated by the fossils, minerals and mounted butterflies that this shop specialises in.

Campo San Rocco, 30125 San Polo (on Campo dei Frari). (☎ 0141-523-1794). Vap: San Toma.

Stationery & Books

Lyra If you like fancy stationery, Lyra has a splendid selection of coloured wax, quills, bronze stamps and embossers at fair prices.

*Merceria San Zulian, 714 San Marco (before the bridge over Rio Bareter). (☎ 041-241-0879; **www.lyravenice.com**). Vap: Rialto.*

Libreria Miracoli di Frizzo Luigi Don't miss this superb selection of books about Venice in Italian and English, as well as unusual art books. It's a stall next to the cutest church in Venice.

6062 Cannaregio (Campo Santa Maria Nova). (☎ 041-523-4060).

Glass & Jewellery

Vittorio Constantini makes creepy-crawlies wearable by encasing them in glass.

Ai Frari, 2603 San Polo (on Campo dei Frari). (☎ 041-717-719). Vap: San Toma.

Manna & Susanna Sent Funky, contemporary Murano vases, plates and jewellery that won't break the bank.

Campo San Vio, 669 Dorsoduro (between Palazzo Loredan and Palazzo Barbaringo). (☎ 041-520-8136). Vap: Accademia.

Venini The real deal in Murano glass, selling classic and contemporary pieces. Pricey, but they'll ship it home for you.

*Fondamenta Vetrai, 47–50 Murano (next to the Colonna vaporetto stop). (☎ 041-273-7211; **www.venini.com**). Vap: Colonna.*

Studio Genninger Who would believe that Leslie Ann Genninger, an American, is one of Venice's master bead-makers?

*Calle di Barcaroli, 1845 San Marco (between the Frezzeria and the Rio di Barcaroli). (☎ 041-522-5565; **www.genningerstudio.com**). Vap: Ca' Rezzonico.*

Paropàmiso Unusual beads made of glass and other

materials, and jewellery from all over the world.

Campo Santa Marina, 6051 San Marco (on the corner of Ramo Bragadin). (☎ 041-523-5888; www.paropamiso.com). Vap: San Marco.

Lace

Jesurum Sets the standard in Burano lace. Once you've seen the real thing, you'll easily spot a Chinese fake.

Procuratie Nuove, 60–61 San Marco (on the south side of Piazza San Marco). (☎ 041-522-9864). Vap: San Marco or San Zaccaria.

Annelie Beautiful lace-trimmed tablecloths, sheets and bed-clothes at buyable prices.

Calle Lunga Santa Barbara, 2748 Dorsoduro (on the calle that runs alongside Chiesa Santa Barbara). (☎ 041-520-3277). Vap: Ca' Rezzonico.

Clothes

Hibiscus Oriental boho for mature ladies. They have amazing accessories you'll not find anywhere else.

Calle del Olio, 1060/61 San Polo (between Calle Dolera and Calle Galizzi). (☎ 041-520-8989). Vap: Rialto or San Silvestro.

Laura Crovato Second-hand shops are few and far between in Italy, so you really pay for the privilege. Has some unique jewellery and handbag finds.

Calle di Botteghe, 2995 San Marco (to the north-west of Campo Santo Stefano). (☎ 0141-520-4170). Vap: San Angelo.

Pot Pourri Feels like you are stepping into someone's house during a dressing-up session. Beautiful imaginative clothes. Visit their website before your visit to arrange a 5% discount.

Palazzo Regina Vittorio, Calle di Barcaroli 1811M San Marco (between Calle di Fuseri and Rio di Barcaroli). (☎ 041-241-0990; www.potpourri.it). Vap: San Marco.

Camiceria San Marco Gentlemen's shirts for all occasions, as well as a bespoke service for fussier men – like Joe DiMaggio and Ernest Hemmingway.

Calle Vallaresso, 1340 San Marco (between Scallizza San Moise and the Grand Canale). (☎ 041-522-1432). Vap: San Marco.

Kirikù ★★★ FIND The coolest clothing for children and the most helpful shop assistants in Venice.

Calle de la Madonetta, 1465 San Polo (just off Campo San Polo). (☎ 041-296-0619). Vap: San Silvestro.

Zazu ★ The clothes and accessories are designed and made by the owner, so you can buy one-offs at amazing prices.

Calle dei Saonari, 2750 San Polo (between Rio Nomboli and Salizzada San Polo, just off Campo San Polo). Vap: San Toma.

Ottica Urbani Weird and wonderful frames, including their classic collaboration with Le Corbusier.

Frezzeria, 1280 San Marco (between Calle Zorzi and Bocca della Piazza).

(☏ 041-522-4140; **www.ottica urbani.com**). Vap: Rialto.*

Prevedello – Beggiora On the busting Rialto, this tiny shop has the most comprehensive selection of Italian and international football shirts and sportswear.

Ponte di Rialto, 547 San Polo (near the top of the Rialto Bridge). (☏ 041-522-5638). Vap: Rialto.

Shoes, Bags & Accessories

Fanny Gorgeous, soft leather gloves in every colour and style.

Calle dei Saoneri, 2723 San Polo (between Rio Nomboli and Salizzada San Polo, just off Campo San Polo). (☏ 041-522-8266). Vap: San Toma.

Calzoleria La Parigina Sells classic, stylish and affordable labels like Clarks, Camper and Timberland for men and women and children.

Merceria del Orologio, 727 San Marco (just before the junction with Calle Fiubera). (☏ 041-523-1555). Vap: San Marco.

Risuola Tutto di Giovanni Dittura Looks like a low-rent shoe shop, but closer inspection reveals divine slippers, made from velvet, silk and leather (for only 20€ (£13.40)). If you're here during *acqua alta* (see 'Fast Facts: *Acqua Alta*', above), they'll kit out the family in wellies.

Calle Nouva Sant'Agnese, 871 Dorsoduro (between the Accademia and Piscena Venier). (☏ 041-523-1163). Vap: Accademia.

Mori & Bozzi These quirky shoes, for adults and children, will get you noticed.

Rio Terà Maddalena, 2367 Cannaregio (to left of Calle Vendramin on the south side). (☏ 041-715-261). Vap: San Marcuola.

Calzature Casella Excellent service and a vast range of classic styles for anyone who's difficult to shoe.

Campo San Salvador, 5048 San Marco (on Campo San Salvador). (☏ 041-522-8848). Vap: Rialto.

Bottega Veneta Looking for an 'investment' handbag? This Venetian institution is sure to have a pricey (but superlative) something.

Calle Vallaresso, 1337 San Marco (bang in the middle of Calle Vallaresso). (☏ 041-522-8489). Vap: San Marco.

Furla If your housekeeping doesn't stretch to a Bottega Veneta handbag, Furla will have a wonder, at a price that won't make you faint.

Mercerie del Capitello, 4954 San Marco (just before Via 2 Aprile). (☏ 041-523-0611). Vap: Rialto.

Cafés, Snacks & Family-Friendly Dining

Eating in Venice is an expensive business for families, but with a bit of planning, food shopping and picnicking (see 'Planning Your Outings', above) you can eat fabulous food without breaking the bank. Venetians eat early, which suits families with young children – most kitchens close between 10pm and 10:30pm.

There are lots of small bars serving the Venetian staple snack, *tramezzini* – small, triangular white-bread sandwiches with plentiful fillings. Youngsters who like melted cheese and ham toasties should go for *un toast.* Neighbourhood bars (*bacari*) are great for adults to pop in out of the sun for a small glass of wine, known as an *ombra* (meaning shade). Many do *cicchetti*, tapas-style potato *crocchette*, calamari, octopus and olives. Remember it's much cheaper eating or drinking at the bar. **Antica Ostaria Ruga Rialto** (✆ *041-521-1243*) near the Pescheria serves fantastic *cicchetti* in a chatty atmosphere. Up on the Fondamenta dei Ormesini, **Al Mariner** (✆ *041-720-036*) serves great *cicchetti* to locals and passers-by and has outside seating in a tranquil Canal-side setting. In often charmless Venice, the *barista*, Caterina, is a breath of fresh air with her entertaining banter.

Unlike much of Italy, Venice doesn't excel when it comes to pastries: bread products are a big disappointment; especially the cloying and cardboardy white rolls sold everywhere. Notable exceptions are **Rosa Salva** (✆ *0141-527-7949*) on Campo San Giovanni e Paolo and **Rizzo Pane** on Campo Santa Margherita. Otherwise your best bet is a supermarket that sells Tuscan, Apulian or Neapolitan bread.

If you're hunting for cafés, **Florian** (✆ *041-520-5641*) and **Quadri** (✆ *041 -522-2105*) on Piazza San Marco are world-famous but extremely expensive and not especially child-friendly. Take a break from shopping in San Marco at **Black Jack** (✆ *041-522-2518*) on bustling Campo San Luca, a sweet little bar serving tasty snacks. There are some superb cafés with outdoor seating in the spacious child-friendly

Pescheria

CENTRAL VENICE

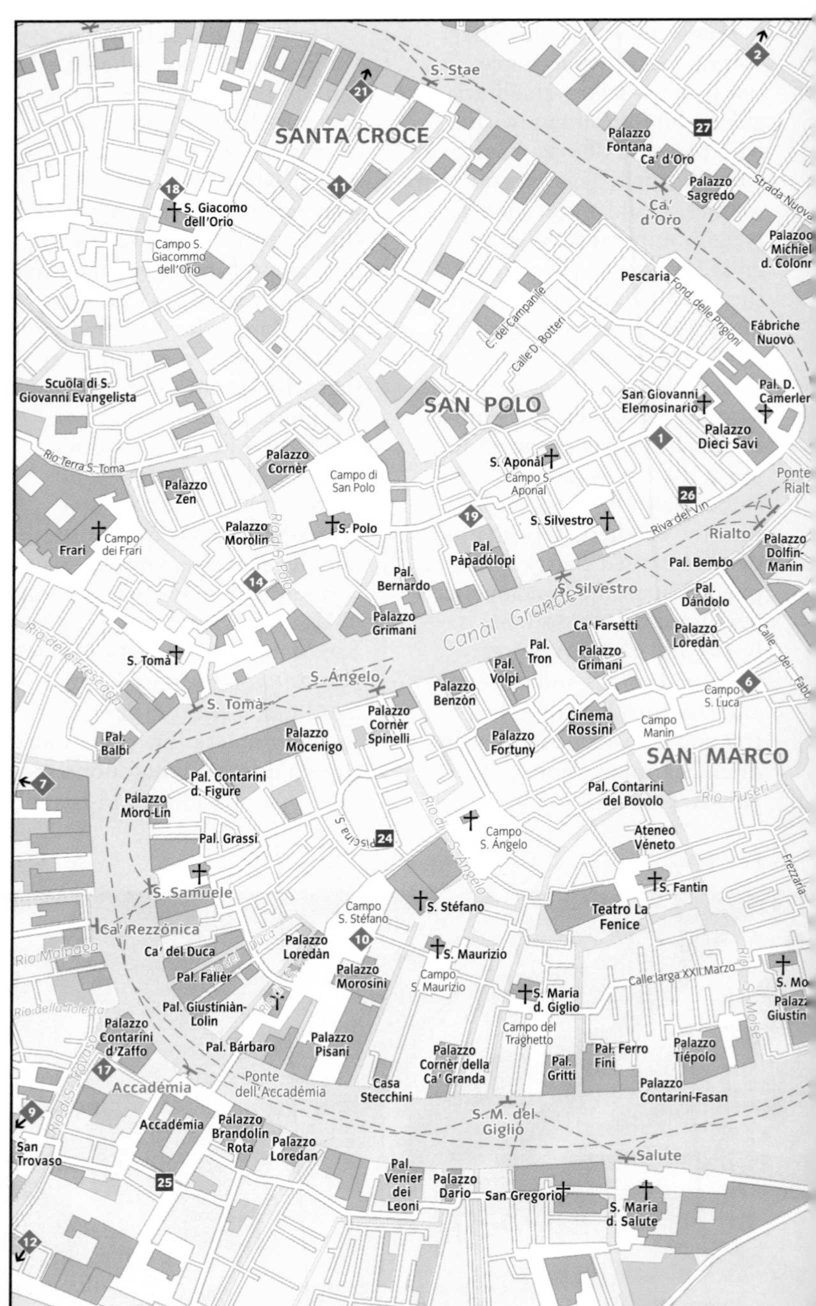

ning ◆
tica Osteria Ruga Rialto **1**
Mariner **2**
sa Salva **3**
rian **4**
adri **5**
ck Jack **6**
fè Rosso **7**
Algiubagio **8**
Suzie Cafè **9**
Gelateria Paolin **10**
Convertino **11**
Nico **12**
Gelateria Toscana **13**
Bar ai Nobili **14**
Le Bistrot de Venise **15**
Rosticceria San Bartolomeo **16**
Taverna San Trovaso **17**
Il Refolo **18**
Da Sandro **19**
Fiaschetteria Toscana **20**
Gam Gam **21**
Ristorante Corte Sconta **22**
Pizzeria 84 **23**

Accommodation ■
Locanda Fiorita **24**
Ca Pisani **25**
Antica Locanda Sturion **26**
Hotel Bernardi Semenzato **27**
Hotel La Residenza **28**

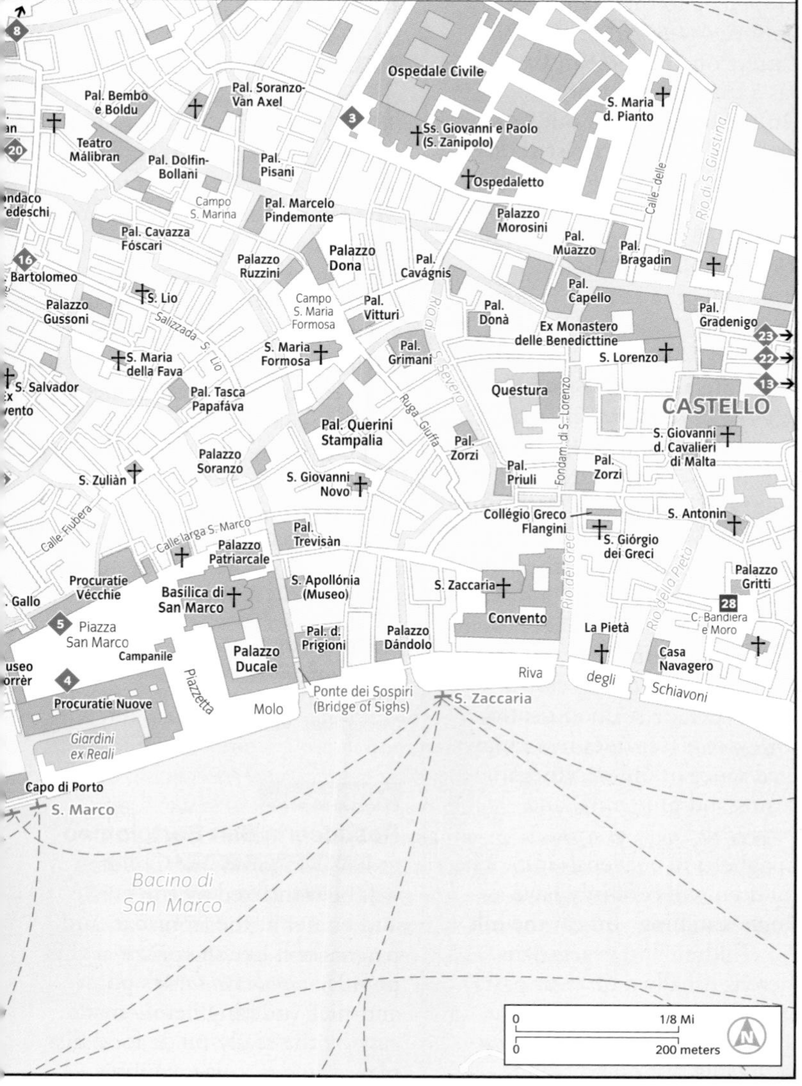

campi, like **Il Caffé** (*041-528-7998*) aka **Caffé Rosso** on Campo Santa Margherita which does mouth-watering *piadine* (thin, flat-bread sandwiches). Up on the Fondamente Nuove, pop into **Algiubagio** ★★(*041-523-6084*) for an ice cream, snack or refreshment while waiting for a *vaporetto* to the islands. **Suzie Café** (*041-522-7502*) off the Zattere on Campo San Basilio has a friendly, studenty vibe. Off the beaten track but worth checking out for its vast choice of panini displayed on funny wooden plaques is **Bar ai Nobili** FIND VALUE (*041-241-1841*), on Rio Terra dei Nomboli.

Among the best ice cream outlets are: **Gelateria Paolin** (*041-522-5576*) on Campo Santo Stefano, **Convertino** (*041-720-491*) on Salizzada San Stae, **Nico** on the Zattere near the Gesuati church and **Gelateria Toscana** (*041-523-0463*) on Via Garibaldi, which also has wonderful pastries and bite-sized *pizzette* for children,

Venetian cuisine relies heavily on fish and some may not be to your children's tastes: classic dishes include seafood risotto, *sarde a soar* (sardines in a tangy, aged sauce of onion, vinegar, raisins and pine nuts) and *spaghetti al nero di seppia* (spaghetti in cuttlefish ink). The children will certainly have a laugh watching you eat the ink. For children and vegetarians, there is usually a pizza or pasta option to satisfy – or you can always build a meal out of *contorni* (side dishes).

INSIDER TIP

The price of fish on a menu usually refers to weight (per *etto*/100g). The fish market is closed on Mondays: fish served then won't be fresh.

San Marco

EXPENSIVE

Le Bistrot de Venise ★★★

VENETIAN/FRENCH This laid-back eatery welcomes children and does a roaring trade, so book in advance. Poets and artists sit beside a steady stream of tourists who lap up the eclectic fare. You can have fun sampling old Venetian recipes like gnocchi without potatoes – there weren't any in 16th century Europe. The tasting menu is a good bet if you want to dig into an assortment. The wine list boasts the richest pickings of the Veneto, and children will love the *dolci*.

*San Marco 4687 (on Calle dei Fabbri). (041-523-6651. **www.bistrotdevenise.com**). Primi 8€–16€ (£5.35–10.70); secondi 14€–22€ (£9.40–14.75); Venetian tasting menu 35€ (£23.50); historical Venetian menu 45€ (£30). AE, MC, V. Daily noon–1am. Closed 10th to 25th December. Vap: Rialto.*

MODERATE

Rosticceria San Bartolomeo

★ ITALIAN/TAVOLA CALDA Children will be transfixed by the bustle and banter at the front bar, and parents will like the prices at this popular *tavola calda*. It's point-and-pick ordering here – made easy by the ready-made food displayed under a glass counter.

Feast your eyes on a wide choice of pasta, fish, seafood and meat dishes. The fussiest palates should be satisfied as they also do vegetarian *cicchetti*, pizza, panini and *tramezzini*. Pop in for some food on the ground floor and there's no *coperto* (cover charge). Eating in the upstairs dining room is a little pricey.

San Marco 5424 (on Calle della Bissa). (📞 041-522-3569). Snacks and primi 4€–8.50€ (£2.70–5.70); secondi 7€–13€ (£4.70–8.70); AE, MC, V. Daily 9:30am–10pm (until 3:30pm Mon). Vap: Rialto.

Dorsoduro

MODERATE

Taverna San Trovaso ★

VENETIAN The vaulted ceilings and relaxed youthful vibe of this value eatery near the Accademia and Squero (gondola yard), should mean the children are all right. The portions are plentiful: you could share a few *cicchetti*-style dishes or opt for a fixed menu. Highlights include the *insalata di mare* (seafood salad), grilled fish or the lightly-fried mixed seafood, *frittura mista*. There are plenty of pizza and pasta options to tempt the less adventurous.

Dorsoduro 1016 (Fondamenta Priuli). (📞 041-520-3703). Reservations recommended. Pizza and primi 7€–11€ (£4.70–7.40); secondi 8€–16€ (£5.35–10.70); menù turistico 18€ (£12). AE, DC, MC, V. Tues–Sun noon–2:30pm and 7–9:30pm. Vap: Accademia/Zattere.

Santa Croce

MODERATE

Il Refolo ITALIAN Children will love the outdoor setting on leafy Campo San Giacomo del'Orio. There are seasonal choices for veggies and budding epicureans should try the pizza topped with fig and prosciutto. Alternatively try the other menu page, which includes *rigatoni* with vegetables for *primo* and some mightily succulent lamb or chicken curry on the *secondi* list. For pud there's *panna cotta* with a variety of sauces, including chocolate, strawberries, fruits of the forest and *zabaglione*.

Campiello del Piovan Santa Croce 1459. (📞 041-524-0016). Primi and pizza 6€–14€ (£4–9.40); secondi 7€–18€ (£4.70–12). AE, MC, V. Closed Mon and Tue Lunch. Vap: San Silvestro.

San Polo

MODERATE

Da Sandro ITALIAN/PIZZERIA

Children will be chomping at the bit to try one of the forty fab pizzas here – there's spinach and ricotta for the veggies and *pizza alla Diavola* with spicy ham and mozzarella for carnivores. There's communal seating outside on both sides of the main street between Rialto and San Polo, which is great for making friends and people watching. Inside there is a cosy wooden-panelled room with some intriguing artwork to chat about. For parents they do a handy 10€ (£6.70) pizza with beer deal.

San Polo 1473 (Campiello dei Meloni). (☎ 041-523-4894). Primi and pizza 6€–16€ (£4–10.70); secondi 6€–18€ (£4–12); fixed-price menus 14€–18€ (£9.40–12) . AE, MC, V. Sat–Thurs 11:30am–11:30pm. Vap: San Silvestro.

Cannaregio

VERY EXPENSIVE

Fiaschetteria Toscana ★★

VENETIAN For a real culinary family treat this long-standing favourite of food critics and the public is perhaps the most reliable in town. The only problem is that it's so popular the waiters sometimes hurry you. Expect classic seafood, meat and game dishes, as well as a good selection of sides and alternatives to placate children and vegetarians. For a flash of flaming spectacle that children will love, order a *flambé*.

Cannaregio 5719 (Salizzada San Giovanni). (☎ 041-528-5281. www.fiaschetteriatoscana.it). Reservations recommended. Primi 11€–20€ (£7.40–13.40); secondi 13€–34€ (£8.70–22.80). AE, DC, MC, V. Wed–Sun 12:30–2:30pm; Wed–Mon 7:30–10:30pm. Vap: Rialto.

INEXPENSIVE

Gam Gam ★★ VALUE JEWISH

Gam Gam (meaning 'more! more!') is a famous kosher restaurant near the Ghetto with bright cheery interiors and outdoor seating on the Canale di Cannaregio. The staff are charming and great with children, helping you navigate through the unusual menu, which includes falafel, bourekas, salads and cous cous. Children might enjoy the latkes (potato pancakes) served with apple sauce. Come here for a light lunch and share one of the large platters. It's the one restaurant in Venice that you will leave genuinely feeling that you haven't been ripped off.

Sottoportico del Ghetto Vecchio, Cannaregio 1122. (☎ 041-715-284). Primi 4€–9€ (£2.70–6); secondi 7€–13€ (£4.70–8.70). AE, MC, V. Sun–Thurs noon–10pm, Fri noon–two hours before Shabbat. Vap: San Silvestro.

Castello

EXPENSIVE

Ristorante Corte Sconta ★

VENETIAN SEAFOOD The plain décor, marble floors and wooden tables hint at something a bit different from the Venetian norm. The informal atmosphere makes everyone feel comfortable: book a table in the small courtyard and savour the inventive fish dishes. Perennial favourites include marinated salmon, sea snails and scallops. For younger children, they'll knock up something special.

Calle del Pestrin 3886. (☎ 041-522-7024). Reservations recommended. Primi 12€–17€ (£8–11.40); secondi 12€–21€ (£8–14). MC, V. Tues–Sat 12:30–2pm and 7:15–10pm. Closed 7th January–7th February and 15th July–15th August. Vap: Arsenale.

INEXPENSIVE

Pizzeria 84 PIZZERIA This no-nonsense pizzeria is one of the best in Venice, run by an amiable, moustachioed Sardinian. Unfortunately, you can't get authentic Neapolitan DOC pizza here – fire restrictions prevent the use of wood-burning ovens. It's mighty popular with Venetians and students though, so you may have to hang about at the bar, or outside, until a table is free. Children will enjoy seeing their pizza made by the dexterous *pizzaiolo* behind the counter. They also do takeaways.

Salizzada S. Giustina, 2907A Castello. (☎ 041-520-4198). Open 5–9.30pm; closed Wed and Thurs. Vap: Santa Giustina.

Family-Friendly Accommodation

Like everything in Venice, accommodation is pricey (ludicrously so in the increasingly long high season). Many hotels don't have decent-sized rooms for families. Often the best option if you are staying for more than a couple of nights is to rent an apartment – it offers more space, independence and value-for-money. Various agencies have sprouted up to fill this demand in the last ten years, including **Venice Central Apartments** ★★ (dial 020-8133-4030 and they'll phone you back on Skype (**www.veniceapartments.org**) run by Michele Barison, who speaks English. They have about 60 properties, a luxury yacht and an old *vaporetto* with stylish lodgings which should be ready in 2007. Explore the options (the Gritti, Vendramin and Vivaldi are good value for larger families, costing 600€–1400€ (£400–938) for a week depending on the season) on their website and fire some questions at Mick and his staff.

San Marco

MODERATE

Locanda Fiorita ★★ The twin family attractions of Campo Santo Stefano with its *caffé-gelaterie* and Ponte dell'Accademia are just around the corner from the Fiorita. Wisteria vines cover the red-hued entrance that looks onto a little *campiello*, a wonderful place to relax and for children to play. Some rooms have exposed beams and most have eye-catching 18th century furnishings and decorative flourishes. The annex, **Ca' Morosini** (☎ *041-241-3800; [fax] 041-522-8043;* **www.camorosini.com**), offers additional lodging nearby.

San Marco 3457a (on Campiello Novo). (☎ 041-523-4754; [fax] 041-522-8043. **www.locandafiorita.com**)*. 16 units. 145€ (£97.15) double; 120€ (£80) double with shared bathroom. Extra person in room add 30%. Rates include continental breakfast. AE, DC, MC, V. Amenities: concierge; tour desk; limited room service; babysitting; non-smoking rooms. In room: A/C, TV, dataport (annex only), minibar (annex only), hairdryer, safe (annex only). Vap: S. Angelo.*

Dorsoduro

EXPENSIVE

Ca' Pisani ★ This is one for families who want to splash out on some stylish luxury, and who have children who'll dig a seriously cool hotel. Ca Pisani came like a breath of fresh air when it opened in 2000, swapping the ubiquitous Venetian glitz and chintz for stylish interiors inspired by the 1930s and 1940s. Smooth lines, exposed beams, Art Deco marquetry and Futurist artworks mix with sleek contemporary fittings. Individually designed rooms have a relaxing, sophisticated charm. Some bathrooms wouldn't be out of place in a Bond movie. Downstairs, La Rivista restaurant continues this theme and serves simple, contemporary and classic Italian cuisine. There's a sauna and access to a nearby gym.

*Rio Tera dei Foscarini, 979/a Dorsoduro. (☎ 041-240-1411; [fax] 041-522-2424. **www.capisanihotel.it**). 29 units. 210€–435€ (£140–291.50) double; 290€–550€ (£195–370) junior suite. Under-12s free in room. Rates include continental breakfast. AE, DC, MC, V. Amenities: babysitting; concierge; tour desk; room service; steam bath; Internet. In room: A/C, TV, dataport, hairdryer, minibar, safe. Vap: Ca' d'Oro.*

San Polo

MODERATE

Antica Locanda Sturion The Italo-Scottish owners are great with children and always happy to dispense top tips for sightseeing and dining. Ask them about the fascinating history of the building and you'll be regaled with exotic tales of shady Rialto merchants – it even features in Carpaccio's *Miracle of the Cross* (1494), housed in the Accademia. Marble floors, period furniture and rich Venetian décor, bordering on the kitsch, abound. Most guest rooms face a quiet *calle* but a few have grandstand views of the Canal Grande and the Rialto hubbub. There's no lift, making the staircase walk a bit of a struggle with baggage, but the in-room kettles mean you can at least have a cuppa when you get there.

*San Polo 679 (on Calle dello Sturion). (☎ 041-523-6243; [fax] 041-522-8378. **www.locandasturion.com**). 11 units. 130€–215€ (£87–144) double; 210€–260€ (£140–175) double with Grand Canal view; 170€–310€ (£114–208) triple; 235€–350€ (£157.50–234.50) triple with Grand Canal view; 210€–330€ (£140–220) quad; 280€–370€ (£188–248) quad with Grand Canal view. Check the website for latest family offers. Rates include buffet breakfast. AE, MC, V. Amenities: babysitting; bar; concierge; limited room service; Internet; tour desk. In room: A/C, TV, dataport, minibar, hairdryer, hot beverage-making facilities, safe. Vap: Rialto.*

Cannaregio

INEXPENSIVE

Hotel Bernardi Semenzato ★★ VALUE Not only does the Bernardi offer bargain prices, the location just off Napoleon's

Strada Nova is also perfect for families: it's near local supermarkets and the Fondamente Nuove boats to the islands. Renovation in the mid-1990s exposed the ceiling beams and the décor is understated. Rooms could do with some soundproofing work, however. Places in the nearby annex afford more space and comfort – parquet floors and Venetian furnishings give it the feel of a private residence. Families should request annex room no. 6, a suite with superb Canale views.

*Cannaregio 4366 (on Calle de l'Oca). (☎ 041-522-7257; [fax] 041-522-2424. **www.hotelbernardi.com**). Hotel:18 units. Annexes: 11 units. 90€ (£60) double with private bathroom; 105€ (£70.35) triple with private bathroom; 120€ (£80) quad with private bathroom. Rates include continental breakfast. AE, DC, MC, V. Amenities: concierge; tour desk; limited room service. In room: A/C, TV, dataport, hairdryer, safe. Vap: Ca' d'Oro.*

Castello

INEXPENSIVE

Hotel La Residenza ★ FIND Children will get wrapped up in the grand atmosphere of this hotel, once owned by the Gritti family. A bonus for parents is that it's also reasonably priced for Venice and looks on to tranquil Campo Bandiera e Moro. Behind the Gothic façade with its 10th century architectural details is a breakfast/lobby room with stuccoed walls – a great place to relax and have a tinkle on the baby grand piano. Seek out the refurbished rooms, which have a fresh, bright feel. The down-side is that there's no lift – but it's only 25 steps to the reception.

*Castello 3608 (Campo Bandiera e Moro). (☎ 041-528-5315; [fax] 041-523-8859. **www.venicelaresidenza.com**). 15 units. 80€–160€ (£54–107) double; 35€ (£23.50) extra bed. Breakfast included. AE, MC, V. Amenities: concierge. In room: A/C, TV, minibar, hairdryer (on request), safe. Vap: S. Zaccaria.*

Lido

MODERATE

Villa Beatrice Immersed in the green tranquillity of Lido's Alberoni district, Villa Beatrice is in a great spot. It's perfect for a couple of nights with children: nearby is the beach and a nature reserve, which you can explore on the hotel's free bikes. A recent refurbishment added modern facilities, interesting artwork and elegant 1930s-style touches. Guest rooms are clean and bright, and there are decently sized triples for families. Some have terraces and small outdoor spaces. Children can play in the garden while you relax on the patio quaffing Bellinis. The hotel has information on lots of sports activities and there's a golf course nearby.

*Via dei Villini 4, Alberoni, 30126 Lido di Venezia. (☎ 041-731-072; [fax] 041-5266101. **www.hotelbeatrice.com**). 10 units. 60€–150€ (£40–100) double; 60€–160€ (£40–107) triple. Breakfast included. AE, MC, V. Free parking. Amenities: babysitter; bar; Internet; free use of bikes. In room:*

TIP Saint Erasmus – A Tranquil Family Retreat for Active Families

Il Lato Azzurro FIND VALUE This friendly B&B/activity centre is popular with families and groups looking for something a bit different near Venice. The accommodation is basic and clean, and prices are a steal for the rip-off city, with variously sized rooms. The restaurant serves decent Mediterranean cuisine with veggie options: 20€ (£13.40) per head plus large discounts for children. They organise cultural events and can arrange courses and excursions including Italian language lessons and kayaking. You can also make the most of this market garden island on one of the centre's 50 bikes. They also have a couple of apartments in Cannaregio (750€ (£500) per week) and a very reasonably priced B&B (80€ (£54) double, 100€ (£67) triple, 120€ (£80) quad).

Via Forti 13, Sant'Erasmo. ☎/fax: *041-523-0642*. 15 units. ***www.latoazzurro.it***. 78€ (£52.30) double; 100€ (£67) triple; 112€ (£75) quad. 10% discount for six nights or more. Breakfast included. AE, MC, V. Amenities: Internet; free use of bikes. Vap: S. Erasmo.

A/C, ceiling fans, TV, minibar, hairdryer (on request), safe. Vap: Santa Maria Elisabetta (Lido) and then another vaporetto or bus to Alberoni.

Camping by the Beach

Camping Village Cavallino If you're set on a bucket-and-spade break near Venice, consider the Cavallino. This sprawling, well-equipped complex is set in green woodland that opens on to a sandy Adriatic beach. They've got it all: a shop, newsagent, launderette, cashpoint, restaurant and bar. Children and teens will enjoy the pool and can also enjoy al fresco ping pong, tennis and crazy golf. Various events, fitness sessions and children's clubs are organised, too. Check out their website to see the choice of bungalows, caravans and mobile homes, all with mod-cons and some with air conditioning. A family of four happy campers can expect to pay 35€–60€ (£23.50–40) a night to pitch a tent and up to 80€ (£54) for a caravan in high season.

Via delle Batterie164, Cavallino Venezia 30013. (☎ 041-966-133; [fax] 041-530-0827. ***www.baiaholiday.com****). Baia Bungalow for a family of 2–4: 40€–120€ (£27–80), Venezia Bungalow for a family of 6: 60€–125€ (£40–83.75). AE, MC, V. Closed mid-September to early March. Amenities: Internet point; newsagent; launderette; cashpoint; restaurant-pizzeria and bar. Vap: Punta Sabbione then bus to Ca' Ballarin.*

5 The Veneto & Friuli

VENETO/THE FRIULI

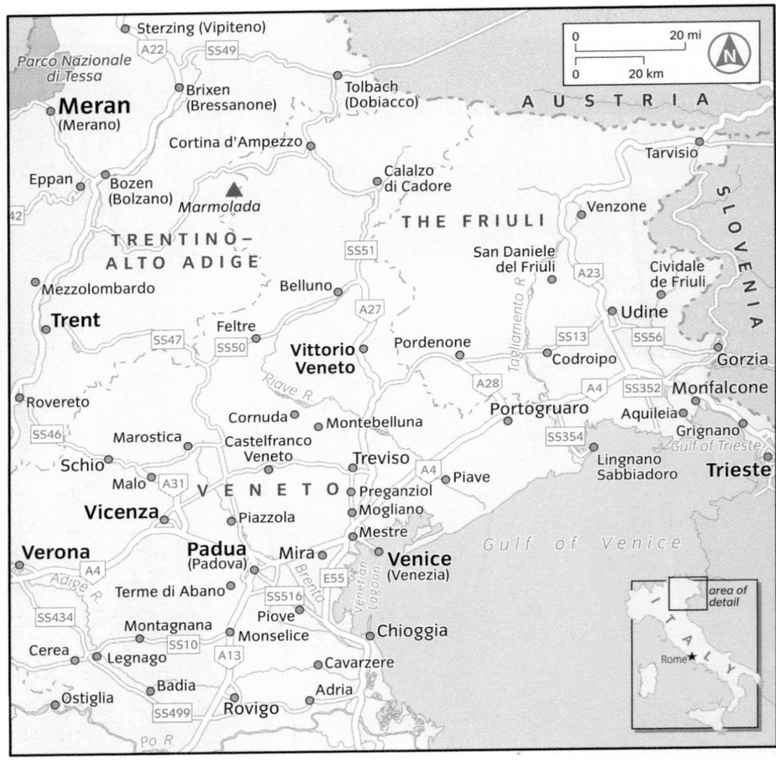

Venice ruled much of the north-eastern corner of Italy for centuries. Venetian influence, and its winged Lion of Saint Mark can be seen in the Veneto towns of Verona, Vicenza, Padua and Treviso, as well as in Friulian Udine. Visiting families can gorge themselves on the culture paid for by the wealthy patronage of *La Serenissima* – as well as the influential architecture by Palladio in the cities' *palazzi* and the grand villas along the Brenta Canal, there's Renaissance art by Giotto, Tiepolo, Tiziano, Tintoretto and Veronese that fill the region's churches and historic buildings. The allure and legendary deeds of Verona and its citizens prompted Shakespeare to write two plays set in a place he hadn't even visited: children will revel in a pilgrimage to the *Romeo and Juliet* sights, and the Roman Arena's dramatic presence will impress everyone.

There's always time to relax and space to play in these urban stage sets. Picnic opportunities and café breaks abound in and around Verona's grand gardens, Vicenza's Palladian piazzas, Padua's markets, Udine's castle hill, and beside Treviso's leafy canals. They're all great family stops. Up in the north-eastern corner of the Adriatic is mixed-up Trieste, once a major

Austro-Hungarian port and the least Italian city of them all. Little ones go mad for its open spaces, huge skyscapes and seaside treats, while grown-up children lap up the Istrian, outsider atmosphere and Mitteleuropean café culture. If the tourist hordes of the cities get too much, you can always visit one of the many smaller laid-back towns: Bassano di Grappa, Asolo, Aquileia, Cividale and Muggia are the highlights.

As well as its urbane attractions, the Veneto and Friuli have natural wonders: the Po Delta wetlands (p. 183), the eastern shoreline of Lake Garda (p. 76), the Dolomites of Belluno and Carnia, the Euganean hills and Adriatic lagoons. Families can easily find outdoor activities and swimming opportunities. The countryside also produces excellent wines, including sparkling Prosecco, Soave, Valpolicella and Collio, and the local cuisine has Germanic and Slavonic influences, so family dining is always full of surprises. Expect carbohydrate staples risotto and polenta accompanied by seafood or hearty mountain fare, although simple pasta dishes and pizzas are always easy to find. Listen, too, to the locals across the region who speak various dialects – the curious nasal accents will have cheeky children doing impressions.

A number of precautions apply when visiting the Veneto and Friuli. Near the Adriatic the wetlands and lagoons have always been infested by mosquitoes, so bring a decent spray low in Deet or (preferably) a natural concoction for children. Stock up at a chemist before you leave, or ask at any local pharmacy. A plug-in mozzie killer is a must for a comfortable night's sleep in rural and seaside areas. The area is hit by two unpleasant winds: the Scirocco from Africa brings humidity and rain in the autumn, while the Bora from Siberia brings strong icy winds, even occasionally in summer. Bring layers and waterproofs for you and the children just in case, especially if you are heading outside the cities.

Transport links are superb in the Veneto – you can get between the Renaissance towns easily by train or car, so there are lots of day trip options. For journeys, liquids are essential in the hot and humid summer months, so buy bottles of water cheaply from supermarkets and store them in a large cool bag.

As always, keep valuables safe and be especially vigilant in tourist towns; pickpockets prey on the unwary. To ward off an opportunist snatch of your snazzy camera, wrap the strap around your wrist a couple of times.

VERONA

114 km (71 miles) W of Venice, 80 km (50 miles) W of Padua, 61 km (38 miles) W of Vicenza, 157 km (97 miles) E of Milan

Whether it's the expanse of sky, the River Adige snaking through the city, the informal medieval charm (compared to the super-grand Venice and Vicenza) or the romance of Romeo and Juliet, children seem to love

Verona Street

Verona. Some of its more worthy sites are less interesting to children than to adults, but the Arena, the Teatro and of course Juliet's mythical balcony and tomb will certainly stoke their imaginations.

Shakespeare might have been inspired by the family feuds that dominated medieval Veronese life. The Della Scala (Scaligeri) dynasty jostled with its rivals for power from the late 1200s, bringing tension and extravagant displays of power. In 1405 the city surrendered to Venice, which ruled until Napoleon invaded in 1797. You only have to wander around the magnificent *palazzi* and the epic Piazza Brà to sense the city's tangled and proud history. Despite this, Verona has less pretence than most cities with a Roman, medieval and Renaissance cachet.

Essentials

Getting There & Around

By Train Verona sits on the east–west Venice–Milan line as well as the north–south Brennero–Rome line. At least 30 trains daily travel to Venice (1½–2 hr), and trains to Milan (1½–2 hr) are generally twice hourly. Vicenza is 30–50 min. away, whilst Padua is 35–50 min. and Bologna 1⅔–2 hr.

The **Stazione Porta Nuova** (✆ *045-590-688*) is some distance from Piazza Brà and the Arena but regular bus services (72 and 73) make it easy to get to. There are taxis available. For timetables and detailed info about Verona's public transport, check out ***www.amt.it***. The bus network within the historical centre is limited, so if you have luggage, you'll probably want to get a cab to your hotel. There are taxis available outside the train station and on Piazza Brà. Call RadioTaxi on ✆ *045-532-666*.

By Bus The bus station, **APT** (Azienda Provinciale Trasporti) is at Piazza XXV Aprile (✆ *045-887-1111*; ***www.amt.it***), beside the train station. Buses travel to all regional destinations but trains are more direct, just as cheap and a lot quicker.

By Car The *Serenissima autostrada* (A4) links Venice and Milan, passing Verona. To get into the city, the Verona Sud exit is the easiest to navigate. There's secure parking at piazza Cittadella, 4 (✆ *045-595-593*).

Visitor Information

A **central tourist office** is at Piazza Chiesa 34 (✆/fax: *045-705-0088*) – summer hours are Monday to Saturday 9am–8pm and Sunday 10am–1pm and 4–7pm (winter hours are shorter, and it's closed on Sundays). Another **tourist office** is at Via degli Alpini 9, adjacent to the Arena off Piazza Brà (✆ *045-806-8680*; fax: *045-801-0682*), open Monday to Saturday 9am–6pm. A **small office** at the train station (✆ *045-800-0861*) is open Tuesday to Saturday 8am–7:30pm and Sunday and Monday 10am–4pm. Their website (***www.tourism.verona.it***) has a children's version (***www.comune.verona.it/veronaforchildren***), with a list of parks and playgrounds.

City Layout

Verona has a compact city centre and everything is reachable on foot. The centre is tucked into the left bank of the curve of the Adige, between Ponte Scaligeri and Ponte Aleardi. The **Arena** and **Piazza Brà** lie between the bridges. Heading north from the piazza, **Via Mazzini**, pedestrianised and one of the main shopping streets, takes you to **Piazza delle Erbe** and **Piazza dei Signori.** The little streets and piazzas that branch off these are crammed with cafés and shops, and this is where you'll find the markets. You need to head over the river to reach the **Teatro Romano.**

Most sites are concentrated within these few history-steeped blocks. It's easy to venture off the shop-lined treadmill and seek out narrow, cobble-stoned side streets evocative of eras past. Little to no traffic is permitted in town, so stash your car in a parking area suggested by your hotel (where they'll probably have a special arrangement), and let your feet do the transporting.

Festivals & Markets

The Teatro Romano is known for its **Festival Shakespeariano** (you guessed it, the **Shakespeare Festival**) ★. Festival performances begin in late May and June with jazz concerts, moving on to contemporary dance and ballets (including Prokofiev's *Romeo and Juliet*) in July and August. Tickets cost from 13€ (£8.70) to 26€ (£17.50) plus booking charges and, if you leave it late, can often be picked up at 8pm, just before the performance, at the Teatro Romano box office (✆ *045-807-7500* or *045-806-6485*) or with the tourist office (see above or ***www.estateteatraleveronese.it***).

Young thespians will enjoy **Sognando Shakespeare (Dreaming Shakespeare),** a travelling band of young players in costume who can be found under balconies and wandering the lesser-known streets reciting *Romeo e Giulietta*. For information, contact the tourist office.

Piazza San Zeno hosts a **travelling antiques market** on the third Saturday of every month.

INSIDER TIP
Get here early, at about 8am for the best discoveries.

What To See & Do In Verona

Arena di Verona ★★★

AGES 4 AND UP This awe-inspiring Roman amphitheatre is in tremendously good nick, considering it was built in AD 100 and lost most of its outer arches in an earthquake. Built of pink marble, it dominates Piazza Brà. Now one of the world's most famous opera venues, from June to August it runs two or three shows per week, with the sets of the show in waiting stored out on the Piazza. Seeing a massive golden sphinx from *Aida* next to Renaissance buildings makes a great holiday snap. A night at the opera here is one the family will enthuse about for years. Unlike the snooty operatic audiences of other cities, you will find entire families with cushions (you can rent one) and picnics settling in for the spectacle. During the rest of the year, weather permitting, you can see classical concerts and ballets. Children under 4 are not permitted.

*Piazza Brà. (☎ 045-800-3204). Arena visit: admission: 3.10€ (£2.08). Mon 1:45–7:30pm; Tues–Sun 8:30am–7:30pm (last admission 45 min. before close); July to August summer opera season 9am–3:30pm. Opera performance: 23€ (£15.40) (stone steps) to 160€ (£107) (posh stalls) adults, various reductions for those under 26 and over 60. A booking fee is charged. Alternatively, if you are really keen, you can line up at 4 or 5pm for the 6pm opening of the gates; you might get a ticket for the 9pm performance. Via Dietro Anfiteatro 6b (☎ 045-800-5151;fax: 045-801-3287; **www.arena.it**) for opera tickets.*

Casa di Giulietta (Juliet's House) ★★ ALL AGES There is no actual proof that this was the house of love-struck Giulietta Capuleti but thanks to a little

TIP Verona On the Cheap

The VeronaCard, a *biglietto cumulativo* (cumulative ticket), lets you visit several of the city's sites for one fee. Two versions of the card are available. The 8€ (£5.35) card, valid for one day, allows you to ride the city's buses and enter its museums, monuments and churches, including the Castelvecchio Museum, the Arena, Juliet's House, the Teatro Romano, the Duomo and San Zeno, amongst others. The 12€ (£8) card offers the same places, but allows you three days rather than one. The VeronaCard can be bought at any of the major sites or by calling ☎ ***045-807-7774.***

Better still, visit the Castelvecchio Museum, the Roman Theatre and Juliet's Tomb on the first Sunday of any month and admission is free.

VERONA

Attractions ●
Arche Scaligere **1**
Arena di Verona **2**
Basilica di Sant'Anastasia **3**
Basilica San Zeno Maggiore **4**
Duomo **5**
Giardino Giusti **6**
Juliet's House **7**
Juliet's Tomb **8**
Loggia del Consiglio **9**
Museo Castelvecchio **10**
Piazza dei Signori (Piazza Dante) **11**
Piazza delle Erbe **12**
Archaeological Museum **13**
Romeo's House **14**
Parco Delle Colombare **15**

Accommodation ■
L'Ospite di Federica De Rossi **16**
Hotel Aurora **17**
Hotel Giulietta e Romeo **18**

Dining ◆
Caffè Filippini **19**
Balù **20**
Caffè Malta **21**
Pasticceria Bar Flego **22**
Carro Armato **23**
Hostaria Dall'Orso **24**
Antica Osteria-Trattoria Al Duomo **25**

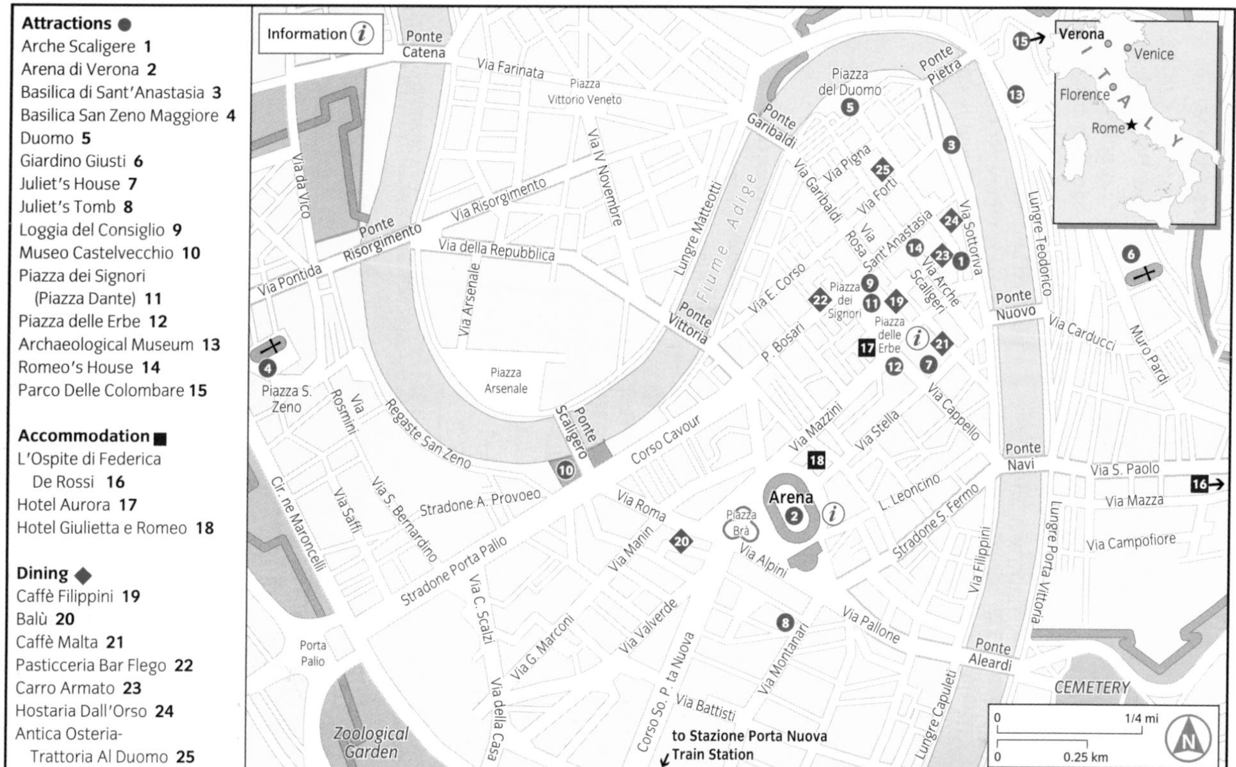

artistic licence by the ruling authorities, it has become the focal point for the hordes of tourists who dearly want it to be. Yet, for all the evidence that suggests *Romeo and Juliet* is without foundation, this doesn't feel like a contrived hotspot: thousands of teenagers have claimed it as their own and scrawled messages of love on the walls. The same authorities have passed a law to prevent people writing graffiti and impose a fine on those who get caught doing so. However, there are still some lovers who defy the rules and write of their love, whilst the meeker of heart use Post-It notes. You can enter the restored house for a fee and stand on the balcony.

Via Cappello 23 (south-east of Piazza delle Erbe). ☎ 045-803-4303). Courtyard free; admission to house: 3.10€ (£2.08) adults, 2.10€ (£1.40) children. Mon 1:30–7:30pm; Tues–Sun 8:30am–7:30pm; last admission 45 min. before close.

If you want to continue the homage to Juliet, **La Tomba di Giulietta (Juliet's Tomb)** **ALL AGES** (☎ *045-800-0361*) is about a 15-minute walk along the river just past Ponte Aleardi. Set inside the Capuchin monastery of San Francesco al Corso, Juliet's sarcophagus sits in dignified silence. The church next door is where Romeo and Juliet's secret marriage is said to have taken place.

Via delle Pontiere 5. Admission: 2.60€ (£1.75) adults, 1.50€ (£1) children, and free first Sunday of each month; Tues–Sun 9am–7pm.

Museo Castelvecchio ★

AGES 4 AND UP Commissioned by the Scaligeri warlord Cangrande II in 1354, this sturdy building survived centuries of tit-for-tat between warring families and the occupying Venetians, before being bombed by the Germans in World War II. The darling of Italian architecture, Carlos Scarpa, restored the vaulted walls

Juliet's Balcony

Romeo and Juliet? Fact or Total Fiction?

***Romeo and Juliet* is one of the Bard's most popular works:** it has been made into films by Franco Zeffirelli and Baz Lhurmand, and was Americanised to create *West Side Story.* But Shakespeare didn't make it all up. The Capuleti and Montecchi did exist: they were Veronese noble families. They no doubt did get involved in a bit of territory marking. But what of Romeo and Juliet themselves? Shakespeare relied on a well-worn formula of forbidden love that had been around so long it had made Greeks weep, and may even have been 'inspired' by the story-telling of Luigi da Porto. Da Porto was a gentleman of Verona who told of two misty-eyed but tragically doomed lovers, Romeo and Giulietta, whose *storia d'amore* was translated in the 16th century into English.

and network of mezzanines in 1964. Downstairs there are displays of statues and carvings of the Middle Ages, which are worthy but may just look like lumps of rock to children. Take them upstairs: the grand rooms where paintings by Tintoretto, Tiepolo, Veronese, Bellini and the Verona-born Pisanello hang are impressive enough, but it's the huge courtyard with the statue of Cangrande I ('Big Dog', d. 1329) astride his horse carrying a slayed dragon's head that tops the lot. In the days when artists lost their heads for unflattering likenesses, you can only wonder what happened to the poor sculptor who made this work. Finally, walk across the **Ponte Scaligeri** to appreciate the full size and might of the castle.

Corso Castelvecchio 2 (at Via Roma, on the Adige). ✆ 045-594-734 or 045-800-5817. ***www.comune.verona.it/Castelvecchio/cvsito****). Admission: 3.10€ (£2.08). Free 1st Sunday of each month. Mon 1:45–7:30pm; Tues–Sun 8:30am–7:30pm (last admission 45 min. before close).*

Arche Scaligere (Scaligeri Tombs) ★ **ALL AGES** Just off Piazza dei Signori in the grounds of the church of Santa Maria Antica are some elaborate funerary monuments by the Scaligeri family – you can admire them from behind the iron railings. Amid the intricately worked Gothic spires is the equestrian statue on Cangrande I's tomb. He was a renowned warrior and patron of Dante.

On Via delle Arche Scaligeri 2 nearby is the supposed 13th century home of **Romeo Montecchi** (Montague in Shakespearian). It isn't open to the public.

Teatro Romano (Roman Theatre) and the Museo Archeologico (Archaeological Museum) ★ **AGES 4 AND UP** Verona's oldest surviving Roman monument dates from the time of Augustus, when the Arena was built. As well as open-air performances of Shakespeare's *Two Gentlemen of Verona* and

Romeo and Juliet, it also hosts concerts. Included in the price is entrance to the small archaeological museum housed in the monastery building. It's a bit of an uphill walk (tricky with a pram or toddlers) but the views make the toil worthwhile.

Via Rigaste Redentore (over the Ponte Pietra bridge behind the Duomo, on the north bank of the Adige). (☎ 045-800-0360). Admission: 3€ (£2); free 1st Sunday of each month. Mon 1:30pm–6:45pm; Tues–Sun 8:30am–6:45pm; during theatre season 9am–3pm. Bus: 31, 32, 33 or 73.

Verona Duomo

For Parents Who Must Do the Churches

Not really for children, but if you can't visit an Italian city without taking in its most famous churches, look up the **Associazione Chiese Vive** (☎ *045-592-813*; ***www.veronatuttintorno.it/chiesevive/1000anni.htm***). Admission to any one church is 2.50€ (£1.68) or you can buy a cumulative ticket for 5€ (£3.35) for adults, granting admission to Sant'Anastasia, San Zeno, San Lorenzo, San Fermo and the Duomo complex (the last only between noon and 4pm on this cumulative ticket). The three beauties that churchaholics should certainly check out are:

Basilica San Zeno Maggiore Not quite in the main trawl, this church was built between the 9th and 12th centuries and is among the finest examples of Romanesque architecture in northern Italy.

Piazza San Zeno. (☎ 045-800-6120). Tues–Sat 8am–1pm, Tues–Sun 1:30–6pm (until 5pm November to February).

Basilica di Sant'Anastasia Not yet finished (it was only started in 1290) this splendid Gothic church has a 14th century campanile and atmospheric interiors filled with frescoes and sculptures.

Piazza Anastasia at Corso Anastasia. (☎ 045-592-813). March to October Mon–Sat 9am–6pm, Sun 1–6pm; November to February Tues–Sat 10am–4pm, Sun 1–4pm.

The Duomo Begun in the remains of a paleo-Christian church, it is worth visiting for the door alone. Round the back you can step right out of the church on to the oldest Roman monument in Verona, Ponte della Pietra bridge, which leads to the Teatro Romano.

Piazza Duomo (at Via del Duomo). (☎ 045-592-813). March to October Mon–Sat 9:30am–6pm, Sun 1–6pm; November to February Mon–Sat 10am–4pm, Sun 1:30–4pm.

Veronese Gardens

The **Giardino Giusti** gardens ★★ **ALL AGES** (Via Giardino Giusti 2. *045-803-4029*) are the stuff of dreams, with tiers of terraces hosting elegant watery delights, dreamy statues, fabulous staircases and a labyrinth. The gardens are open daily from 9am to dusk (closed Mon); admission is 5€ (£3.35). The **Parco delle Colombare** (Via Castel San Felice) is Verona's largest park with grottoes, fountains and playgrounds.

Shopping

The Veronese are shopaholics, and not just the men! With such demand, you can be sure that shopping in Verona offers variety and quality within a compact area, so you don't have to hoof long distances between shops. A good shopping area is complemented by a plentiful supply of cafés and *pasticcerie.*

Apart from the predictable souvenirs, the shopping is mostly for the *Veronesi*, and upscale clothing and accessories boutiques line the two most fashionable shopping streets: **Via Mazzini** (connecting the Arena and the Piazza delle Erbe) is chocker with upscale shops like Furla, Armani, Louis Vuitton and, for style-conscious teenagers, the best **Fiorucci** in this part of the country. **Via Cappello,** heading south-east from the piazza past Juliet's House has some interesting boutiques and bookstores, as well as **Coin**, the nation's favourite department store.

Corso Borsari and **Corso Sant'Anastasia** (heading west and east, respectively, off Piazza delle Erbe) have boutiques and antique stores. Back-streets like **Via Oberdan** have youth fashion outlets including **Green** at 1/B and **Bruschi** at 11/C. For travel books and maps try **Gulliver** (Via Stella 16/B. *045-800-7234*). Children will love the stationery inside and giant coloured pencils outside **Yola** (Via XX Settembre 1. *045-800-7866*) just across the Adige. You can check your email at the nearby Internet Train (Via San Paolo 8/a. *045-803-1690*).

Side Trips Outside The City

As well as being in easy reach of the Renaissance towns Vicenza (see below) and Mantova (p. 242), Verona is not too far from Venice (see Chapter 4). For dramatic scenery and outdoor pursuits head north along the Val Adige up to Trentino–Alto Adige or go west to Lake Garda for watery pleasures and theme parks (see Chapter 3). Towards Lombardy, there are a couple of family attractions amid the rolling hills of the Mincio river: **Picoverde** **ALL AGES** (Via Ossario 19, 37060 Custoza. *045-516-025*. ***www.picoverde.it***. Weekdays: 9€ (£6), 7€ (£4.70) 4–10 years, free for 3 years and under. Late May to early September 10am–7pm) is a water park with slides, pools and eateries; **Parco Sigurtà** ★★ ALL AGES (Via Cavour 1, 37067 Valeggio sul Mincio. ☎ *045-637-0959*. ***www.sigurta.it***. 9€ (£6), 6€ (£4) 5–14 years, free 0–4 years. Early March to early November 9am–7pm) has over 125 acres of luscious grounds with lawns, woodland and a dozen ponds filled with tropical fish. Hop on the mini railway and enter the fairytale vistas containing wandering animals, spectacular blooms and an enchanting castle. You can get to both via the A4 (exit at Sommacampagna) or by train to Valeggio sul Mincio from Verona's Stazione Porta Nuova. There are shuttle buses linking Peschiera del Garda station and Parco **Sigurtà** throughout the day (25 mins.).

Family-Friendly Accommodation

The traditional high season coinciding with Verona's opera season in July/August sees most hotels raising their tariffs. If you are having trouble booking a room contact **CAV** (Cooperativa Albergatori Veronesi), which represents dozens of hotels in various price categories (Via Patuzzi 5. ☎ *045-800-9844*; ***www.cav.vr.it***).

L'Ospite di Federica De Rossi ★★ VALUE FIND The ever-helpful Federica has six apartments, all perfect for families seeking independence and value. The building is just over the river in the Veronetta district, so is handy for the sights. Choose from studio flats and two-room apartments with kitchens. Ask for an apartment around the back for a quieter stay. There's a launderette, cafés and useful shops nearby.

Via XX Settembre 3. (☎/[fax] 045-803-6994. ***www.lospite.com****). 6 apartments. Studio apartment 60€–90€ (£40–60); two-room apartment 90€–150€ (£60–100). Under 3s free. Cots on request. Special family rates. AE, MC, V. Parking in car park 6 € per day – ask Federica for directions In room: A/C, TV, iron and board upon request.*

Hotel Aurora ★ The Aurora has some family-friendly rooms with views over Piazza delle Erbe and its bustling marketplace. The breakfast is bountiful with fruits, cheeses and meats to set you up for the day. Children will love the terrace overlooking the square. The top floor is ideal for larger families. There is no lift.

Piazza delle Erbe 2. (☎ 045-594-717; fax: 045-801-0860. ***www.hotel aurora.biz****). 19 units, 16 with private bathroom. 65€–140€ (£43.50–94) double; 125€–165€ (£83.75–110.50) suite. Rates include buffet breakfast. AE, DC, MC, V. Parking 10€ (£6.70). Amenities: bar; concierge. In room: A/C, TV, hairdryer.*

Hotel Giulietta e Romeo ★★ Near the Arena, this place offers great service and comfy accommodation for people travelling with children. Guest rooms are bright and complemented by wooden floors, while the bathrooms are a cut above the normal

Caffè Filippini

in this price range. Not surprisingly, they have Romeo and Juliet style balconies, but these rooms get snapped up quickly.

Vicolo Tre Marchetti 3 (south of Via Mazzini, 1 block east of the Arena). (✆ 045-800-3554; [fax] 045-801-0862. ***www.giuliettaeromeo.com****). 30 units. 115€–215€ (£77–144) double; 130€–240€ (£87–161) triple. Rates include buffet breakfast. AE, DC, MC, V. Parking nearby 15€ per day (£10). Amenities: bar; concierge; room service; laundry service; dry cleaning; babysitting. In room: A/C, TV, dataport, hairdryer, minibar, safe.*

Cafés, Snacks & Family-Friendly Dining

The most venerable of the cafés on Piazza delle Erbe is **Caffè Filippini** at no. 26 (✆ *045-800-4549*. Open 8am–1am; closed Wed in winter): the interiors have changed but its quality snacks and beverages still attract the punters to its grandstand seats, overlooking the market square. One of Verona's best ice cream makers is **Balù★** at Via Roma 1/C, just off Piazza Brà, and 57B Corso Porta Borsari (✆ *045-803-6341*). For refreshments and sugary treats, including their famous *Zaletti* biscuits, check out **Pasticceria Bar Flego** (Corso Porta Borsari 9; ✆ *045-803-2471*). Escape the Piazza delle Erbe crowds at **Caffè Malta ★**, which serves free nibbles with drinks on the quiet Piazzetta Navona (✆ *045-803-0530*). For quality deli foods go to **Gastronomia Stella** at Via Stella 11/A (✆ *045-806-8169*).

Carro Armato ★★ Carro Armato is named after Leonardo da Vinci's war machine, and occupies the ground floor of a 14th century *palazzo*. As you enter there is a bar piled with antipasti, assuring you that this place does much more than just sell scores of regional wines by the glass (1€–3€ (£0.67–2.00)). The relaxed atmosphere and mixed clientele makes family dining here informal; it's also great value for money. From cold platters to full-on plates of pasta with *salsa di pomodoro* and ricotta, the menu may not be extensive but it has something for all appetites.

Vicolo Gatto 2A. (☎ 045-803-0175). Primi 3€–6€ (£2–4); secondi 6€–11€ (£4–7.40). AE, MC, V. Mon–Fri 10am–2pm and 5pm–2am; Sat and Sun 10am–2am.

Hostaria Dall'Orso Amongst the trendy eateries on Via Sotto Riva is this great little place, with seating inside and out. The service can be a little slow but the atmosphere and superb cooking make it a great choice for families. They do scrumptious salads, superb pasta dishes with meaty sauces as well as *spaghetti al nero di seppia*: this tasty cuttlefish ink dish is potentially messy to eat and gives everyone a laugh.

Via Sotto Riva 3/C. (☎ 045-597-214) Primi 7€–9€ (£4.70–6); secondi 9€–14€ (£6–9.40). AE, MC, V. Noon–3pm and 7–11pm; closed Sun.

Antica Osteria–Trattoria Al Duomo ★★ VALUE This place comes highly recommended by the locals who frequent its characterful wooden rooms near the Duomo. There are simple pasta and gnocchi creations suitable for children and hearty plates for the adventurous, like grilled tuna with vegetables and Verona's equine dish, *Pastissada de Caval con polenta*. They even do *Roast Beef all'Inglese* sometimes. Ask the amiable staff about upcoming regular musical events.

Via Duomo 7/A. (☎ 045-800-4505). Primi 6.50€–8€ (£4.35–5.35); secondi 8€–13€ (£5.35–8.70). AE, MC, V. Noon–3pm and 7pm–midnight; closed Sun.

VICENZA

32 km (20 miles) W of Padua, 74 km (46 miles) W of Venice, 51 km (32 miles) E of Verona, 204 km (126 miles) E of Milan

Architecture enthusiasts swoon at the mention of Vicenza, and it is indeed one of the loveliest little cities in northern Italy. It's just the right size to saunter around and appreciate. As youngsters today might say, 'Palladio, I'm loving your work'. It won't take you long to clock that this is a wealthy city: Vicenza is the historic centre of Italy's gold industry (one-third of Italy's gold is manufactured here). It's also Italy's Silicon Valley: Federico Faggin, inventor of the silicon chip, was born here and it's now home to several component manufacturers. Made a UNESCO World Heritage Site in 1994, the magnificence of this university town will stimulate some sort of appreciation of classical buildings in children and adults alike. However, amongst the beauty lies decay. Come on a day where there has been rain and the seeping, weeping **Basilica Palladiana** will break your heart. How could they let it come to this? Apparently it's to undergo restoration soon – let's hope so.

Vicenza looks at its most elegant just after sunrise and a meander around its streets and *palazzi* as it comes to life is a memorable way to see it.

Palladio: Who's the Daddy (of Italian Architecture)?

1508 The year Michelangelo began painting the Sistine Chapel, Andrea di Pietro della Gondola was born in Padua to Mr and Mrs Pietro della Gondola.

1521 Andrea got an apprenticeship in stonecutting and sculpting in Padua at the age of 13, but chucked it in and went off to Vicenza, where he was lucky enough to get a second chance.

1537 Count Giangiogino Trissino became Andrea's mentor and got him all excited about classical Roman architecture. The Count gave him the nickname 'Palladio' after the Greek goddess of wisdom, Pallas Athene.

1540 Influenced by these 'new' ideas he began his first building, Villa Godi, in nearby Lonedo. Such was his flair, he soon wooed the Vicentine nobility, who were to commision him aplenty until his death.

1541 Now 32, he took himself off to Rome to study its ancient buildings and returned to Vicenza utterly inspired.

1545 He began the refurbishment of the majestic Basilica in Vicenza (completed in 1614 by his pupil Vincenzo Scamozzi, 34 years after Palladio's death).

1556 Palladio went to Udine and began work on Palazzo Antonini (completed in the year of his death). Back in Vicenza, he began Palazzo Thiene (finished in 1593 by Scamozzi).

1560s Vincenzo Scamozzi became his pupil.

1562 Palladio began work on an epic facade in San Giorgio Maggiore in Venice (finished in 1611 by Scamozzi). As jobs go, this was a biggy.

1567 He began designs for La Rotonda (finished in 1592 by Scamozzi; see 'A Side Trip to Palladio's Masterpiece', below).

1570 He was nominated as 'Illustrious citizen of Venice' and published his life's work, *The Four Books of Architecture*.

1574 Palladio published a book about Caesar.

1577 He began the construction of the Redentore (see p. 133) in Venice (finished in 1610 by Scamozzi).

1580 Palladio died in Vicenza at the age of 72.

Essentials

Getting There

By Train Step out of the **train station**, in Piazza Stazione, and you are met with the wide-open space of **Campo Marzio**, surely the most calming welcome any busy university town can offer. Every hour there are two or three services to Padua (20

Architectural terms made easy

The starting point is the three Grecian orders of columns

Doric – The first and most uncomplicated of the orders, it's straight up and down plainness is meant to symbolise man.

Ionic – Characterised by two large scrolls – or volutes. They are said to symbolise women.

Corinthian – The most decorative of the orders, this has a bell-shaped top adorned with acanthus leaves and volutes. Apparently, it symbolises virgins.

The Romans created two more styles: the **Tuscan order** which is without any decoration at all; and the **Composite order** – which is a mish-mash of the three Grecian orders.

Aedicule – A mini decorative structure, sometimes housing a statue.

Balustrade – An upright pillar or column that supports a handrail, perhaps of a stairway.

Caryatids – Sculptures of females used as columns.

Cornice – A horizontal moulding – or ledge. Inside, it's purely decorative; outside, it acts as a gutter, draining water away from the building.

Cupola – A dome on a roof.

Entablature – The bit that is held up by the column and includes the frieze and cornice.

Frieze – The centre of an entablature and often decorated.

Loggia – An open gallery or corridor on the facade of the building: like a portico but recessed.

Pediment – The gable end or front of a Grecian style structure. The bit supported by the columns and above the frieze and cornice.

Plinth – The lower part or base of a column.

Portico – The classical version of a porch!

Temples – The type of temple depends on the numbers of columns. A **Distyle**: two columns. A **tetrastyle**: four columns. An **Octastyle**: eight columns.

min.), Verona (30 min.) and Venice (52–67 min.).

By Bus The **FTV bus station** (☎ *0444-223-115*) is located on Viale Milano, just to the west (left) of the train station. Buses leave frequently for all the major cities in the Veneto, and to Milan.

By Car Vicenza is on the A4, linking Venice and Milan. It's 40 min. from Verona and 1 hr from Venice. If you're staying for more than one day the cheapest parking option is the park and ride on Via Bassano near the stadium. For short stays head to Piazzale Bologna.

Visitor Information

The **tourist information office** can be found at Piazza Matteotti 12 (*0444-994-770*; fax: *0444-994-779*; ***www.vicenzae.org***), next to the Teatro Olimpico. It's open April to September Mon–Sat 9am–1pm and 2:30–6pm, October to March Mon–Sat 9am–1pm and 2:30–5:30pm. During summer, an office at the train station is open Mon–Sat 9am–2pm and Sun 1–6pm.

City Layout

You can see almost everything in Vicenza on foot, needing a car or bus just for the two big Palladio villas on the outskirts. The train station lies to the south. From here, head straight ahead on Viale Roma; turn east (or right) at the gated gardens to head along **Corso Palladio** to the *Centro Storico.* Lined with shops, cafés and *palazzi*, the Corso splits the town. The streets heading south will take you to Piazza Duomo, and if you continue east you'll reach Piazza Matteotti and the Teatro Olimpico.

Getting Around

The *Centro Storico* is largely pedestrianised with access only for taxis, buses and residents. However, the city is small and compact enough to be able to pad about. Just pick up a map from your hotel or the tourist office and off you go.

Festivals

The **Concerti in Villa** ★ (*0444-399-104*) holds an outdoor series of opera and classical recitals in June and July, including venues like the Teatro Olimpico and Villa Rotonda. Contact the tourist office (see above) for ticket information. **Teatro Olimpico** (*0444-222-101* or *0444-222-154*; ***www.olimpico.vicenza.it***) hosts theatrical productions in September and October.

Piazza Dei Signori ★★★

This is the heart of the city, to the south of Corso Palladio. To the east lie **Piazza Blade** and the bell tower, **Torre Bissara**. Children will enjoy scampering around under the two Venetian columns, one with the winged lion of the Republic and the other sporting the Redeemer. To the north-west lies the **Loggia del Capitaniato**, the former seat of the Venetian Captain and now home to the local council. Built in 1571 by Palladio, it has

TIP Seeing Vicenza by Cumulative Ticket

The **Card Musei** is available from the top sights and tourist office and costs 8€ (£5.35) for adults, 5€ (£3.35) for children over 14 and students or there's a Family Ticket for two adults and a child at 12€ (£8); it includes admission to the **Teatro Olimpico, Museo Civico, Museo Naturalistico Archaeologico** and the **Museo del Risorgimento e della Resistenza.** Children under 14 go free.

splendour and ambition in bucketloads but does look out of proportion: you see only a building that is less than half of what Palladio intended.

Piazza dei Signori itself has a massive expanse for children to run around in and is sheathed by ostentatious buildings. Palladio may have only played the role of mere renovator of the **Basilica Palladiana** and died during its reconstruction, but it is true to his vision: awe-inspiring and with no expense spared. The commission involved revamping the Palazzo della Ragione (the lower part, which functioned as law courts and a meeting hall), built in the mid-15th century. The city was enjoying the patronage of Venice and was seeking a statement building in a High Renaissance style. Palladio was only 38 at the time and, eager to impress, decided on a lower loggia using Doric pillars, and an upper tier using Ionic columns. Both tiers are topped with entablatures and then crowned with a balustrade hosting 23 statues. The roof was destroyed by World War II bombing, but has been rebuilt in its original style. However, Vicenza has not looked after the Basilica. To see such a magnificent edifice cracked and crumbling and oozing water beggars belief. It is now closed and by 2007 plans are in place to swathe it in tarpaulin and renovate it, which could take five years. However, don't let that stop you having a look at those bits of exterior that will remain visible and enjoying its exalted presence on the piazza, despite the indignities it has had to bear. Behind the Basilica (to the south) is the **Piazza delle Erbe**, which you'll hear before you see: it's home to the daily **market**.

Corso Andrea Palladio

Vicenza's main street is lined with magnificent *palazzi* designed or influenced by Palladio. The tourist information office (see 'Visitor Information', above) has some great maps of the city and booklets about Palladio. If you want to amble along the Corso and take in the delights, your children may struggle to maintain the same level of enthusiasm. However, pointing out the never-ending display of weird doorknockers on the buildings may hold their interest just long enough for you

Knocker

to do the business. Corso Palladio is neatly packed with a stylish selection of shops and cafés, so stops for refreshment and retail are easy to accommodate. For anyone worried they aren't getting enough Palladio, **Palazzo Thiene** (Contrà Porti 12: now the headquarters of a bank) and **Palazzo Valmarana** (Corso Fogazzaro 16L) are notable examples of his work on streets just off Corso Palladio. At Corso Palladio 163 is the rather plain little *palazzo* that was Palladio's home.

When you reach Piazza Matteotti, you'll find the **Teatro Olimpico** AGES 4 AND UP Poor Palladio, building a whole city took its toll and much of his work was completed after his death. He began the Teatro Olimpico when he was 72 and, despite dying months later, it was finished by his protégé Vincenzo Scamozzi. It is considered to be his greatest work, taking classical theatres as his inspiration: his use of Greek and Roman design was a trademark. Seating 1000 in what was the first fully enclosed theatre in the world, the interior is designed to make you feel outside, with blue sky and fluffy clouds covering

Loggia del Capitaniato

the dome. Highbrow theatrical and musical performances dominate the hugely popular programme. Tickets start at 15€ and under 12s often get in free when accompanied by an adult.

*(☎ 0444-222-101 or 0444-222-154; **www.olimpico.vicenza.it**). Admission: 4€ (£2.70). April to September Tues–Sun 9am–7pm; October to March Tues–Sun 9am–5pm. Bus: 1, 2, 5 or 7.*

Palazzo Chiericati is across the piazza and houses the **Museo Civico (Municipal Museum)** AGES 4 AND UP. This is another of Palladio's celebrated buildings, again only completed after his death, and said to have been inspired by the Doge's Palace in Venice (p. 119). The way he situated rooms and created space and

TIP Touring the Villas

If your children are a bit older and have taken a shine to Palladio, or at least offer no resistance, try a guided tour of his buildings and villas in and around Vicenza. Palladio by the Hand run tours on Saturdays and Sundays, from 10€–12€ (£6.70–8) for adults, with children under 14 free. Contact the tourist information centre for details (☎ *0444-994-770*; ***www.vicenzae.org***).

A Side Trip to Palladio's Masterpiece

The **Villa Rotonda** (aka **Villa Almerico-Capra**) is a quick bus ride from the city centre. Its dream-like construction and gorgeous grounds make this a pleasant short trip for the whole family. Palladio's loyalty to classical standards and adherence to mathematical precision has resulted in what many claim is the perfect building. Listed by UNESCO as a World Heritage Site, it was begun by Palladio in 1567 and completed by Scamozzi 12 years after his death.

Via Rotunda 29. (☎ 0444-321-793; [fax] 0444-879-1380). Admission to grounds: 3€ (£2) adults; Mid-March to November, Tue–Sun 10am–noon and 3–6pm. Interior: 6€ (£4) adults. Mid-March to November, Wed and Sat only. 10am–noon and 3–6pm. Bus no. 8 from Viale Roma.

size was outlandish. The building's majesty is a perfect setting for the Tiepolos, Tintorettos and Veroneses displayed here.

(☎ 0444-222-800). Admission: 4€ (£2.70). Hours and details as Teatro Olimpico above.

Shopping

Corso Palladio is full of shops, from posh **Tods** at No. 59 (☎ **0444-547-810**) to high street **Zara** (☎ *0444-235-448*), but there are plenty of independent shops worth looking at, too. On the Corso at no. 67 is sleek **Vicenza Village** (☎ *0444- 540-430*), which has books, Internet access, Vicenza Calcio footie merchandise and a box office for local events. **Liberia Athena** ★ (Contra San Gaetano Thiene 2a; ☎ *0444-326-103*) just off Corso Palladio is a fascinating little bookshop in which to while away a half-hour or more. They have books in English and a great selection of children's stuff. Check out the architectural fragments in the adjoining courtyard of the Ca d'Oro. **Vestimi Tu** (Via Battisti 29) is a little shop selling children's clothing in vibrant colours as well as modish maternity wear. Another shop selling way-out children's clothing and shoes is **Surplus Kids** (Contra San Barbara 25, just off Piazza Blade) with labels like Diesel, Pinko, Levi's and Woz.

Antiques enthusiasts should check out the market on the second Sunday of every month in Piazza Signori.

Family-Friendly Accommodation

In January, May and September, the Vicenza international gold fairs make booking accommodation a bit tricky. However, outside these times you'll find it less busy than Padua or Verona. This wealthy city does not rely on tourism, so many of its hotels are aimed at businesspeople.

Campo Marzio ★ Just a few steps from the train station overlooking the vast expanse of green that is the Campo, this

Chocolates

hotel caters mainly for business folk but is so friendly and well run it's worth checking out. Some rooms are Palladian inspired with soft furnishings and architectural details. Bathrooms are small but well maintained. They also offer a fullsome breakfast buffet to set you up for the day.

*Viale Roma 21. (☎ 0444-545-700; [fax] 0444-320-495; **www.hotelcampomarzio.com**). 35 units. 140€ (£94) double; 166€ (£111.20) triple. Breakfast included. Free parking. AE, MC, V. Amenities: Bar, Restaurant. In room: Safe, Sat TV, hair dryer.*

Due Mori Just off Piazza dei Signori, Due Mori is one of Vicenza's best-known and oldest hotels. Inside an old *palazzo*, the rooms are modern and sparse – but attractively so. The location and prices make it ideal for families wanting to be close to the heart of the city. Book early.

Via Do Rode 24. (☎ 0444-321-886; [fax] 0444-326-127. hotelduemori@inwind.it). 30 units, 27 with private bathroom. 50€ (£33.50) double with shared bathroom; 75€ (£50) double with private bathroom; 84€ (£56.30) triple with private bathroom. Breakfast 5€ (£3.35). Free parking. AE, MC, V. Amenities: bar. In room: dataport, hairdryer (on request).

Ostello Olimpico di Vicenza Close to the Teatro Olimpico, this beautiful hostel is a real find for families looking for a low-cost way to see Vicenza. Family rooms have six or eight beds and are bright but basic, with a bathroom and sheets provided. There is no kitchen but there is a breakfast room. You must be back at the hostel by 11.30pm. Membership of Hostelling International is expected, although non-members can still stay but pay the higher price.

Viale Giuriolo 9. (☎ 0444-540-222; fax: 0444-547-762). 85 beds. 40€–60€ (£27–40) family rooms with bathroom. AE, MC, V. Amenities: TV room; Internet facilities.

Cafés, Snacks & Family-Friendly Dining

Vicenza has any number of great cafés to take in refreshment. Just off Corso Palladio is a tiny shopping centre where **Antico Café Nazionale** (Galleria Porti;

📞 *0044-323-477*) serves sweet espresso to a cross-section of Vicentine society. If you fancy putting together a picnic, **Il Ceppo Gastronomia** ★ at the far end of Corso Palladio (no. 196; 📞 *0044-544-414*; ***www.gastronomiailceppo.com***) has a jaw-dropping array of cold cuts, prepared seafood (try their *insalata di mare*), cooked pasta creations, local cheeses, roasted vegetables, marinated olives and bread (as well as bottles of chilled Prosecco and orange juice).

Caffé Natura ★★ FIND (Via Battisti 17; 📞 *0444-234-372*) just across from Vicenza's cute Duomo, is an excellent organic café and juice bar, with cakes and panini for staving off rumbles. Meanwhile, **Gran Caffè Garibaldi** (Piazza dei Signori 5. 📞 *0444-542-455*), overlooking Piazza dei Signori, has the best people-watching spot in Vicenza. Upstairs there is a posh restaurant with even better views, but the downstairs café is just perfect for a *panino* (3€ (£2)) or a salad (6€ (£4)).

Righetti VALUE VICENTINEITALIAN If you want to know why the *Vicentini* are so well off, come here and see for yourself how well they can eat for just a few euros. Busy with locals, this self-service restaurant on Piazza Duomo offers the very best Veneto cooking in a welcoming atmosphere. Choose your table, go to the counter and tell them what you'd like, and they'll bring it to your table, made fresh. From risotto on Tuesday and Friday to the evening selection of grilled meats, there is a good choice that'll please even the fussiest little eater.

Piazza Duomo 3–4. (📞 0444-543-135). Primi 2.50€–3€ (£1.68–2); secondi 4€–6€ (£2.70–4). No credit cards. Mon–Fri noon–2:30pm and 7–10pm.

ELSEWHERE IN THE VENETO: PADUA, TREVISO & AROUND

As well as the 'three Vs', there are a number of other towns and sights worth visiting in the Veneto, including Padua, the Brenta Canal, Bassano di Grappa, Asolo and Treviso.

Padua (Padova)

Padua has a rich history and lively *Centro Storico*, making it a stimulating place for a family day out. For tourist information and details about the money-saving **PadovaCard**, go to the office in the train station (📞 *049-875-2077*; ***www.turismopadova.it*** or ***www.padovanet.it***. PadovaCard 14€ (£9.40) for an adult and child under 12 allowing free admission to sights and free use of transport lasting 48 hours). As well as some quality fashion shopping for teens and parents, like Armani (Via San Fermo 41 & 61. 📞 *049-875-5965*), Gucci (Galleria Europa 2. 📞 *049-656-280*) and Ruco Line (Via Santa Lucia. 📞 *049-8766-390*), the city has one

FUN FACT Lost Your Larynx?

St Anthony is one of the Roman Catholic Church's most beloved saints. He is known for his powers to recover all lost things, be they door keys or love: check out the messages left on the tomb within his Basilica imploring the saint to wield his powers. Gruesomely enough, the eloquent preacher's **tongue and larynx** are kept in the Cappella del Tesoro and carried around Padua on 13 June, his feast day.

---

of the best food markets in the north of Italy in a grand setting alongside the imposing Palazzo del Ragione: from Monday to Saturday, Piazza delle Erbe, Piazza della Frutta and the surrounding arcades are filled with seasonal produce (look out for the spectacularly gnarly pumpkins in the autumn), deli foods, books, clothing and knick-knacks.

Millions of pilgrims a year visit the **Basilica di Sant'Antonio** ★ AGES 4 AND UP to pay homage to Saint Anthony. The enormous eight-domed edifice contains Donatello's seven **bronze statues**, including the *Crucifixion* towering over the main altar. Outside, don't miss the photo opportunity beside Donatello's colossal 15th century Venetian mercenary soldier ***Gattamelata*** – the first large-scale equestrian statue since Roman times.

*Piazza del Santo. (☎ 049-878-9722. **www.santantonio.org**). Free admission. Summer daily 6:20am–7:45pm; winter daily 6:20am–7pm.*

South of the basilica is the **Orto Botanico** ★ ALL AGES the oldest botanical gardens in Europe, dripping with exotic foliage.

Via Orto Botanico 15. (☎ 049-827-2119). 4€ (£2.70) adults, 3€ (£2) reduced. April to October: 9am–1pm, 3–6pm; November to March 9am–1pm.

Italy's largest piazza, the nearby **Prato della Valle**, with its bridges, moats, fountains, lawns and statues, is a grand place for children to run around. They'll be mesmerized by a peek into the world of magic lanterns, stereographs, early photography and myriad optical escapades at the **Museum of Precinema** AGES 4 AND UP in the Palazzo Angeli.

*Prato Della Valle 1/A. (☎ 049-876-3838. **www.minicizotti.it**). 3€ (£2), 2€ (£1.34) reductions. Mid-June to mid-September 4–10pm, mid-September to mid-June 10am–4pm. Closed Tue.*

North of the city centre is the must-see **Cappella degli Scrovegni (Scrovegni Chapel)** ★★★ AGES 4 AND UP, which contains the enthralling 14th century frescoes by Giotto that changed art forever. The vibrant colours, including the ubiquitous vivid blue and gold, will impress children and adults, Christians and heathens alike. This early Renaissance biblical cycle has a refreshing simplicity

Prato della Valle

and light that contrasts with the gloomy paintings that fill corners in churches all over the world. Not for nothing is Giotto known as the 'father of Western art'. Be warned though: during peak times there are long queues and you only get 15 minutes before you're shepherded out. It is essential to book in advance these days.

Piazza Eremitani 8, (off Corso Garibaldi). (☎ 049-201-0020 for reservations. ***www.cappelladegli scrovegni.it****). Admission (for Museo Eremitani, add 1€ (£0.67) per ticket): 12€ (£8) adults, 5€ (£3.35) ages 6–17, free for under 6s; free with purchase of PadovaCard. Summer: daily 9am–7pm; Mar-Oct last admission 9:40pm. Bus: 3, 5, 6, 8, 9, 10, 11, 12, 13, 15, 16, 18, 22, or 42.*

If you have the time and energy, check out the 13th century Romanesque **Chiesa degli Eremitani (Church of the Hermits),** which was almost completely destroyed by Nazi bombings in 1944. For really keen culture-vultures, the **Museo Civico Eremitani** next door houses the city's collection of ancient relics and Venetian art, including works by Tiziano, Tiepolo, and Tintoretto.

The Brenta Canal

The Brenta Canal runs between Padua and Venice, and is lined with elegant villas including the lavish **Villa Pisani** at Strà (☎ *049-502-074*. Admission: 5€ (£3.35), 2.50€ (£1.68) park only; April to September 9am–7pm, October to March 9am–4pm), which has Tiepolo frescoes and a hedge maze children will enjoy. Closer to Venice is Palladio's **Villa Foscari** AGES 7 AND UP (aka Villa Malcontenta, 'The Unhappy Woman'; ☎ *041-547-0012*. ***www.lamalcontenta.com***. May to October 9am–noon; otherwise by appointment.). If you're feeling flush and have older children you can take a serene cruise down the canal: the swanky boat **Il Burchiello** (☎ *049-820-6910*. ***www.ilburchiello.it***. 62€ (£41.50) adults, 44€ (£29.50) 12–18 years, 31€ (£20.80) 6–12 years) plies the canal between Padua and Venice, (stops at the della Pietà pier on the Riva degli Schiavoni in Venice), taking in the major villas on the way – it's a 9-hour trip. For more information about the canal and boat trips, check out ***www.padovanavigazione.it*** and contact the **Brenta Canal tourist office** (Via Nazionale 420, Rezzonico Foscari. ☎ *041-424-973* (***www.riviera-brenta.it***).

Bassano di Grappa and Asolo

A visit to Bassano di Grappa makes a refreshing change from the Veneto's congested cities. It's a peaceful little town where families can amble amid medieval and Venetian structures on largely traffic-free streets and piazzas (del Monte Vecchio, della Libertà and Garibaldi), dipping in and out of intriguing independent shops and cafés. There are lots of picturesque spots for a picnic down by the Brenta, where you can admire the cannily designed and often rebuilt covered bridge by Palladio, the timber of which flexes with the spring meltwaters. The top sight is the **Museo Civico** AGES 5 AND UP which has atmospheric cloisters, architectural fragments, Renaissance artwork and archaeological treasures. Included in the price is admission to **Palazzo Sturm** (1765–66), overlooking the Brenta on Via Schiavonetti: it contains interesting interiors and a ceramics museum.

*Piazza Garibaldi. (☎ 0424-522-235; **www.museobassano.it**). Admission: 4.50€ (£3), 3€ (£2) 10–26 years. Tue–Sat 9:30am–6:30pm, Sun 3:30–6:30pm.*

The town is of course famed for its *grappa*, a lethal grape spirit produced by distillers like **Nardini** (Ponte Vecchio 2. ☎ *0424-227-741*. ***www.nardini.it***), which has an atmospheric taverna, and the nearby **Poli** (☎ *0424-524-426*; ***www.poligrappa.it***) where you can learn about the

La Festa di Laurea & Palazzo Bo

If you hear cries of *'Dottore, Dottore'* and come across stumbling students covered in flour accompanied by a dressed-up entourage, it's a graduation party from the Università di Padova (Padua's university). Quite a few shamble through town during the year – it's hilarious to watch this odd ritual, which involves messy stunts and giddy dances. Follow in the footsteps of Galileo and Dante who studied at the old **Il Bo** (The Ox) university building, where you can wander atmospheric courtyards and sample the creepy **Teatro Anatomico** ★ AGES 6 AND UP, the oldest surviving medical lecture theatre in Europe.

Via VIII Febbraio (south of Piazza Cavour). ☎ *049-827-5111*. Admission: 3€ (£2) by guided tour only. Ask at tourist office for tours. Bus: 3, 8, 12, 16, 18 or 22.

production process in the small museum. The **tourist office** is at Lgo. Corona d'Italia 35 (☎ *0424-524-351*; ***www.comune.bassano.vi.it***; open 9am–1pm daily and 2–6pm Mon–Sat).

Around 20km east of Bassano di Grappa via the SS248 is the hilltop town of **Asolo**. There are a dozen buses (☎ 0423-493-464) from Bassano del Grappa (25 min.), which drop you off on the main road below **Asolo**– frequent shuttle buses ply the steep road up to the town itself. You could quite happily amble around its picturesque streets for a few hours, enjoying leafy gardens, fountains, artisan shops and cafés: indeed its atmosphere is so conducive to just, well... chilling, that poet Pietro Bembo coined the verb *asolare* to describe spending your time in agreeable aimlessness.

Treviso

Treviso is an intriguing fortified town known for its canals and medieval air. This 'Little Venice' is refreshingly unspoiled, although it took a pummelling from World War II air raids. For families seeking respite from the hordes of Venice and Verona, there are lots of leafy waterside spots for relaxing in and space for children to play. Don't miss the daily **fish market** ★ on a Canale Cagnan *isoletta* – children will enjoy the spectacle and you can pick up picnic supplies from the nearby **produce market**. Both take place from Monday to Saturday in the morning. The town's focal point, **Piazza dei Signori**, is an evocative space for relaxation, with inviting cafés and arcaded *palazzi*, including the rebuilt **Palazzo del Podestà** and 13th century **Palazzo dei Trecento. Bar Biffi** here does excellent *aperitivi*, cool drinks and snacks. The nearby **tourist office** on Piazza Monte di Pietà 8 (☎ *0422-547-632*; fax: *0422-419-092*) is worth a visit to check the town's latest cultural events for families. On Piazza San Vito, there are two medieval churches worth a gander: **Santa Lucia** has frescoes by Tomaso da Modena and **San Vito** has Byzantine-Romanesque treasures. They are both open daily from 9am–noon and 4–6pm. Photo opportunities of elegant frescoed buildings abound on **Via Calmaggiore** (it runs from Piazza dei Signori to the **Duomo**). The cathedral has impressive art including Tiziano's *Annunciation*, and *Adoration of the Magi* by Il Pordenone.

The **Museo Civico collection** AGES 5 AND UP includes Renaissance and Novecento artworks, as well

Local Heroes

Treviso is renowned for its radicchio rosso (red leaf chicory) and is the home of the fashion label **Benetton**. Check out its Treviso store filled with children's and adult clothing at Piazza Indipendenza 5 (☎ *0422-559-911*).

Palazzo dei Trecento

as archaeological finds, including some fancy swords. Its exhibits are displayed amid the cloisters next to the **Church of Santa Caterina**, also famed for its frescoes by Tomaso da Modena.

Where to Stay

Padua makes a good base for exploring the Veneto and dipping in and out of Venice – this way you avoid the exorbitant prices of the floating city.

Hotel al Fagiano It may not have the most auspicious of lobbies and many of the rooms are nothing to write home about but this place offers good family-value in a superb location – it's a short scoot west of Piazza del Santo and near the Basilica di Sant'Antonio.

*Via Locatelli 45. 35123 Padova. ☎ 049-875-0073. Fax 049-875-3396. **www.alfagiano.it**. 29 units. 85€ double; 95€ triple. Continental breakfast 6.50€. AE, DC, MC, V. Private parking 10€. Amenities: Bar; 24-hr room service; bike rental. In room: A/C, hair dryer, TV.*

Hotel Majestic Toscanelli ★ This place has classically themed rooms that may be a little lurid in colour but are comfy nonetheless. Public rooms, including the American Bar, have a colonial feel and the breakfast room has oodles of pastel-coloured panache. The largely traffic-free neighbourhood is full of interesting antique shops and is great for families as it's a leisurely stroll away from Piazza delle Erbe.

*Via dell'Arco 2, 35122 Padova. ☎ 049-663-244. Fax 049-876-0025. **www.toscanelli.com**. 34 units. 172€ double. 200€ suite. Rates include buffet breakfast. AE, DC, MC, V. Valet garage parking 19€ . Amenities: Bar; concierge; tour desk; courtesy car; limited room service; babysitting; dry cleaning; laundry service; WiFi. In room: A/C, TV, minibar, dataport, hair dryer, safe.*

Treviso has a dearth of decent accommodation, although **Hotel Scala** (Viale Fessissent,

31100 Treviso ☎ *0422-307-600*; fax: 0422-305-048; ***www.hotelscala.com***) has handsome rooms (doubles 110€, triples 135€) with A/C, TV, minibar and decent bathrooms) housed within an elegant villa. For unparalleled value and a more rustic experience try an agriturismo. **Al Moler** in Asolo (Via Risorgimento 1231011 Asolo ☎ *0423/55060*. Fax: *0423-950-511*. ***www.almorer.it***) has a comfy apartment sleeping 2-6 costing a bargain 60€ for a family of three or 100 € for six people. They even have a cot, a kitchen and a fab eatery nearby with wonderful terrace views.

UDINE, THE PREALPI GIULIE & THE ADRIATIC

Udine: 71 km (44 miles) NW of Trieste, 127 km (79 miles) NE of Venice

Compact, charming and vibrant, Udine is surrounded by lush hills with the stunning Carnic Alps to the north and the Friuli plains leading to Adriatic lagoons in the south. It's a refreshing place to walk around with children, noticeably different to the rest of Italy, even to nearby Veneto. Its piazzas somehow combine intimacy and grandeur, while outlying bits have a quirky, rural feel with streams bisecting Germanic-looking streets. During its history it's been governed by Venice and Austria, which is reflected in its eclectic art, architecture and culture: from the Lion of Saint Mark and Tiepolo paintings, to Teutonic buildings and Central European cuisine.

Essentials

Getting There

By Train There are frequent trains between Udine and Venice (2 hr) and Trieste (1½ hr). The train station is south of the city centre on Viale Europa Unità.

By Bus The bus station in Udine is a short walk from the train station on Viale Europa Unità. **SAF** (☎ *800-915-303*; ***www.saf.ud.it***) runs an extensive service throughout Friuli–Venezia Giulia, including frequent buses to Trieste (1½ hr).

By Car Udine is a 2-hr drive north and east of Venice: take the A4 east and then the A23 north. From Cortina d'Ampezzo and the Dolomites take the S51 into Belluno and then head east (toward Pordenone) on the S13 at Vittorio Veneto. The journey takes about 3 hr.

Visitor Information

For **tourist information** go to Piazza 1 Maggio 7 (☎ *0432-295-972*; ***www.turismo.fvg.it***; Mon–Sat 9am–1pm and 3–6pm). If you are planning to visit most of the main sights pick up the **Card Udine Museale,** a museum pass with no time limits that costs 6€ (£4) for adults and 3€ (£2) for 6–18-year-olds. It's available from the **Castello, the Museo Diocesano and the Galleria d'Arte Moderna**.

Festivals, Sport & Markets

Udine d'Estate is the city's major festival, running from July to mid-September with concerts and theatrical performances in churches and on Udine's beautiful *piazze*. An **outdoor food market** fills the atmospheric Piazza Matteotti daily from 8am to 1pm. Black-and-white-striped **AC Udinese** play in Italy's top division, Serie A. Tickets for their Stadio Friuli (Piazzale Argentina 3, località Rizzi. ☎ *0432-544-911*) fixtures are available at outlets around the city including **Riv. Tabacchi N. 3 Di Moretti Nadia** (Via Mercatovecchio 33. ☎ *0432-505-734*).

Out & About in Udine

Piazza della Libertà ★★

ALL AGES, the focal point, demonstrates Venice's pervasive influence: on the south-west side is the pink-and-white-striped façade of the **Loggia del Lionello,** the old Venetian town hall, built in the mid-15th century. It's a great place to shelter from the rain or sun, but watch you don't slip on the marble tiles. Looking across the piazza is the **Porticato di San Giovanni** ★★, a handsome Renaissance portico with a clock tower emblazoned with the Venetian lion. Two 19th century moors strike the hours. Fun opportunities for children to pose in photos abound. There's a 16th century fountain, two columns with the Saint Mark Lion and Justice, as well as impressive statues of Cacus and Hercules and the Statue of Peace.

Piazza della Libertà

Head under the Palladio-designed **Arco Bollani** up a steepish, curving road lined with Gothic porticoes. Children will love darting in and out of the columns and you'll be greeted at the top with a large open area with stunning views of the city and Alps beyond. The 13th century church of **Santa Maria di Castello**, restored after an earthquake in 1976, is unlocked by the museum on request. Dominating the space is the 16th century **Castello** ★★, which houses the **Museo Civico** **AGES 6 AND UP** (☎ *0432-502-872*. 3€ (£2) adults, free under 10s or with Card Udine Museale; open Tue–Sat 9:30am–12:30pm, 3–6pm; Sun 9:30am–12:30pm). There are a number of galleries inside housing an eclectic mix of ancient artefacts and historical photographs. Celebrated works by the town's favourite 18th century Rococo artist, Giambattista Tiepolo, are found in the **Galleria d'Arte Antica** AGES 5 AND UP. If you fancy a bit more Tiepolo, head to Piazza Duomo. The imposing **Cathedral** ★ AGES 4 AND UP (daily 7am–noon and 4–8pm) with its 14th century Gothic facade, has baroque interiors including paintings and frescoes by the great man. Across the piazza, the **Oratorio della Purità** ★ (*0432-506-830*; open on request) contains Tiepolo's *Fall of the Angel,* replete with cascading cherubs. Ask a sacristan in the Duomo if it would be possible to visit it. **Palazzo Patriarcale** or **Palazzo Arcivescovile** ★★ AGES 5 AND UP (*0432-25-003*. 5€ (£3.35), 3€ (£2) under 10s; Wed–Sun 10am–noon and 3:30–6:30pm), the former bishops' palace on Piazza Patriarcato, just north of the Duomo, has more Tiepolo treasures: mainly airy, pastel coloured Old Testament fresco scenes. Children may enjoy the dreamily atmospheric spaces of the Sala Rossa and Sala del Trono.

Charming **Piazza San Giacomo Matteotti** ★★ has lots of space for children, a 16th century fountain and cafés with outdoor seating. It's also known as Mercato Nuovo, so expect daily markets and Friulian costermonger banter.

Across town on Piazza Diacono, the **Museo d'Arte Moderna** ★ AGES 5 AND UP (*0432-295-891*. 3€ (£2), 1.50€ (£1) reductions. Free Sun mornings; Tue–Sat 9:30am–12:30pm, 3–6pm; Sun 9:30am–12:30pm) houses 20th century works by Picasso, Lichtenstein, de Kooning, Martini and Fontana.

Children with an interest in animals, plants and natural history will get something out of a visit to the **Museo Friuliano di Storia Naturale** ★ AGES 3 AND UP (Via Marangoni 39. *0432-584-711*. Mon–Fri 9am–12.15pm, Mon, Tue and Thu 3:15–4:45pm). Among the botanical, zoological, anthropological and paleontological exhibits is one of the oldest known flying reptiles, *Preondactylus buffarinii.*

Cividale dei Friuli

This beguiling town north-east of Udine on the banks of the River Natisone was founded by Julius Caesar and gave its name to the entire region. You can easily spend a few hours exploring the streets and enjoying a picnic overlooking the limestone gorge. The tourist office is at Corso Paolino d'Aquileia 10 (*0432-731-398*; ***www.comune.cividale-del-friuli.ud.it***; Mon–Fri 9am–1pm, 3–7pm). Pick up some supplies at the daily market on Piazza Diacono and enjoy refreshments by the 18th century fountain. The main street, Corso Mazzini, has plenty of shops and a 16th century palazzo with a frescoed facade. Piazza del Duomo lies on the site of the Roman forum and contains the 15th century

Furlan Marilenghe: find your Friulian tongue

As well as talking Italian with characteristic long vowels, many locals also speak Friulian, a language that grew out of the bastardised Latin spoken by Celts in the Roman colony of Aquileia. Not surprisingly, given its history and location, it has Slavonic, German and Venetian influences. It's still taught in some schools, and many road signs have the Friulian equivalent alongside.

Cathedral ★★ AGES 4 AND UP (9am–noon, 3–6pm; closed Sun morning). Within the stark interiors you'll find an 8th century Baptistery and the fabulous altar of the Duke of Ratchis (AD 744–49) ★★, a former Duke of the Friuli. Children will find it all very spooky and fascinating. The nearby Palladio-designed Palazzo dei Provveditori Veneti houses the **Museo Archeologico Nazionale** ★ AGES 5 AND UP (✆ *0432-700-700.* 2€ (£1.34); free under 18s. Tue–Sun 8:30am–7:30pm, Mon 9am–2pm), with ancient artefacts and walkways over excavations.

Follow the medieval lanes behind the palazzo through the Romanesque Porta Patriarchale gates, on to the Piazzetta San Biagio and the **Tempietto Longobardo** ★★★ AGES 4 AND UP (✆ *0432-700-867.* 2€ (£1.34), 1€ (£0.67) reductions. April to September 9am–1pm and 3–6:30pm; October to March 10am–1pm and 3–5pm). In the 8th century, the Lombards chiselled away at the limestone cliffs to produce this astonishing church and its stucco decoration, saintly monuments and exquisite friezes. It's been rebuilt several times after various earthquakes but this remarkable building still retains a spine-tingling aura.

Don't forget to visit the **Ponte del Diavolo** (Devil's Bridge): take the Corso Ponte d'Aquilea from the Piazza del Duomo for stunning river views.

Outdoor Activities in the Parco Naturale delle Prealpi Giulie

In the north-east of Friuli are the mountainous Prealps, home to rare flora and abundant fauna, including partridges, golden eagles, wild boar, lynx and the occasional brown bear. The former royal hunting grounds around Tarvisio provide a relatively unspoiled area for year-round outdoor adventures, mountaineering, mountain biking and dog sleighing: check out their website (***www.tarvisiano.org***). The **Scuola Italiano di Sci Tarvisio** (Via Preisnig 18, 33018 Tarvisio. ✆ *0428-2022.* ***www.scuolescifvg.com***) runs lessons for all ages and abilities. Active families with clambering children over the age of 3 should check out the **Parco Avventura Sella Nevea** ★★

AGES 4 AND UP (Scuola Sci–Piazzale Slovenija, 33010 Chiusaforte. ☎ *0433-54061*; ***www.sellanevea parco.it***), 3-6 years 7€, 7–10 11€, 11–16 14€, over 17 16€. May–Oct 10am–5:30pm) which has plenty of obstacles for little Tarzans.

A **visitor centre** at Prato di Resia (Piazza del Tiglio 3, 33010 Prato di Resia. ☎ *0433-53534/ 53483*. ***www.parcoprealpigiulie. org***. By car take the A23 from Udine or the more scenic S13 to Tarvisio) has child-friendly exhibitions about the park's wildlife and modest accommodation for families costing just 12 € and 5 € (under 10s) per night. They also organise excursions and sporting activities (including mountain biking and canyoning) throughout the year starting at 7€ per participant. Their website has more information, though most of it is in Italian.

Tarvisio

SEASIDE TRIPS & FAMILY FUN PARKS

During the warmer months, you could easily combine a trip to the north-east with a splash in the Adriatic. The resorts may not be to everyone's taste: they are largely commercialised and nondescript. So, it may not be the Riviera, but there are long sandy beaches, historic towns with fascinating sights, child-friendly attractions and campsites aplenty.

Aquileia was an important Roman town founded in 181 BC that retains remnants of its glorious past, including a forum, basilicas and the fascinating **Cripta degli Scavi** with its beautiful mosaics. The **Museo Archeologico Nazionale and Museo Paleocristiano** ★★ **AGES 5 AND UP** (Via Roma 1. ☎ *0431-91016*. ***www.museo archeo-aquileia.it***. Archeological Museum: Mon 8:30am–2pm; Tue–Sun 8:30am–7:30pm. 4€ (£2.70), 2€ (£1.34) 18–25-year-olds, free under 18s. Paleo-Christian Museum: Tue–Sun 8:30am–1:30pm. Free admission) contain some of Italy's most treasured antiquities: highlights include 1st century AD fish mosaics, remains of Roman houses, spooky sarcophagi, amusing graffiti, a ship and exquisite glass and stone objects.

If you're travelling by car and have time, continue to Belvedere and across a causeway over a lagoon to the island town of **Grado**. The concrete outskirts are ugly, but the *Centro Storico* retains charming alleyways, piazzas and some fine buildings, including the 6th century **Cathedral of Saint Eufemia**. Grado also has a thermal water park, minigolf, cycling routes and other amusements for families. The adjacent **Laguna di Grado** is a reedy, watery labyrinth of dunes, channels and small islands with primitive fishermen's *casun* huts dotted around. It's home to a large bird population: look out for swans, cormorants, hawks, teal and herons on your travels. For a closer look at the wetland wonders, contact the Grado tourist office (Viale Dante Alighieri 72 *0431-877-111*; ***www.gradoit.it***) for information about upcoming boat trips including exciting fishing forays. Heading west is the sprawling resort of **Lignano**, where you'll find long sandy beaches and a couple of fun attractions for families. **Aquasplash** (Viale Europa, 33054 Lignano Sabbiadoro. *0431-428-826*. ***www.aquasplash.it***. 18€ (£12); 14€ (£9.40) 3–8 years all day; 14€ (£9.40) and 12€ (£8) 3–6pm. Late May to mid-September daily 10–6pm) is a standard water park with slides and pools for children. Less pricey and hectic is the **Parco Zoo Punta Verde** (Via Scerbanenco 19/1, 33054 Lignano Sabbiadoro. *0431-428-775*. ***www.parcozoopuntaverde.it***. 10€ (£6.70), 8€ (£5.35) 3–11 years. April to September 9am–6pm; closed November to January. February, March and October reduced hours and mainly weekend opening), a lush park with native and exotic animals from alpacas to zebras.

Cafés, Snacks & Dining in Udine

After picking up picnic ingredients at the morning market on Piazza San Giacomo Matteotti, try one of the inviting cafés popular with local characters and student types that surround this large space. **Angelo Nero** is a good shout for drinks, which are served with free nibbles, while **Caffè Bistrot** does tempting pastries, ice cream, tasty snacks and light meals. Teenagers may like the cool **Caffè Contarena** on the corner of Piazza Libertà, which has drop-dead gorgeous interiors and bar staff, as well as tasty snacks including *piadine*. Parents can pick up Friulian wines like Tocai and Verduzzo from the adjoining *enoteca*.

Al Vecchio Stallo OSTERIA/UDINESE

If you're after a family meal in a place with bags of character, try this former post station. It serves hearty local specialities like *orzo e fagioli* (barley and bean soup) alongside Italian pasta dishes.

Via Viola 7 (off Viale Marco Volpe). (0432-21-296). Reservations recommended Primi 4€–7€ (£2.70–4.70); secondi 5€–9€ (£3.35–6). No credit cards. Thu–Tue noon–3pm and 6pm–midnight.

Concordia ★★ ITALIAN/PIZZERIA

Children will love the friendly parrot that sits in the large contemporary-style conservatory here, as well as the fab pizzas, including a mouthwatering *pizza alle melanzane e porcini* (topped with aubergine and wild mushrooms). Service is jovial and the atmosphere is relaxed. They also do omnivore and veggie-friendly salads and pasta creations.

Piazza Primo Maggio 21. (☎ 0432-505-813). Reservations recommended. Pizza 5€–10€ (£3.35–6.70); primi 4€–11€ (£2.70–7.40); secondi 8€–16€ (£5.35–10.70). MC, V. Tue–Sun noon–3pm and 6:30pm–midnight.

Family-Friendly Accommodation

Hotel Clocchiatti ★★★ This Liberty-style villa run by the amiable Clocchiatti family is just out of town and offers decent rooms for families. A fabulous annex has added stylish junior suites: think minimalist style with warm brownish hues, Philippe Starck bathrooms and gadgetry children will love. Many have patio doors looking on to a pool and understated Japanese gardens. Rooms in the old building have smallish bathrooms and there is no lift.

*Via Cividale 29, 33100 Udine. (☎/fax: 0432-505-047. **www.hotelclocchiatti.it**). 130€ (£87) double; 150€–180€ (£100–120) junior suite. Rates include breakfast. AE, DC, MC, V. Free Parking. Amenities: bike hire; concierge; limited room service; dry cleaning; laundry service; tour desk. In room: A/C, TV, dataport, minibar, hairdryer, safe.*

Hotel Europa For convenience and reasonable family deals near the train station, the Europa is a perennial favourite. Recent refurbishment has spruced up the interiors, modernised the bathrooms and installed air-conditioning. Ask for a room at the back, which looks on to a quiet courtyard. The ample triples allow families to squeeze into one room without spending a fortune.

Viale Europa Unità 47, 33100 Udine. (☎ 0432-508-731 or 0432-294-446; [fax] 0432-512-654). 44 units. 76€–90€ (£51–60) double; 100€–135€ (£67–90.45) triple. Breakfast included. AE, DC, MC, V. Parking 6.50€ per day (£4.35). Amenities: bar; concierge; tour desk; limited room service. In room: A/C, TV, dataport, hairdryer, minibar.

Camping Pino Mare There are a number of okay campsites along the coastal stretch around Lignano Sabbiadoro, many of which are huge sprawling beasts full of German families and loud Euro-House music. Pino Mare is one of the less noisy ones, but still has lots of life for children and is right on the beach. For most of their deals they throw in deckchairs and a parasol. The pools and sports facilities are first-rate and include tennis courts and a *calcetta* football pitch. As well as spots for your tent and/or caravan, there are variously sized rentable vans for 2–5 people costing anything between 80€ (£54) and 200€ (£134) a night, depending on the season. Avoid late July and August as it's packed.

*33054 Lignano Sabbiadoro. Riviera (just off the S354 from Latisana) (☎ 0431-424-424; [fax] 0431-424-427. **www.campingpinomare.it**). Caravan/tent pitch: 25€–65€ (£16.75–43.50). AE, DC, MC, V. Amenities: bar; shop; self-service restaurant; playground; washing and drying facilities; sports facilities including tennis, football, volleyball and sailing.*

TRIESTE

158 km (98 miles) E of Venice, 71 km (44 miles) SE of Udine, 408 km (253 miles) E of Milan

Trieste is a strange city – a border town and port caught between different worlds – and this identity crisis makes it a fascinating place for a short break, with excellent family-friendly sights and a bracing seafront. Its dockside boats have been whipped by the icy bora wind since time immemorial, and the town itself has been similarly battered and tossed around by different hegemonies: the Romans left their mark of course, and up until the early 20th century, Trieste was a prosperous Austro-Hungarian port. It was given to Italy after World War I, then became independent, was seized by the Nazis in 1943 and rejoined the Italian state in 1954. It is quite apt that the Italian word for sad, *triste*, is one letter short of Trieste: this oft-overlooked place with its melancholy air has attracted James Joyce, Franz Kafka and Graham Greene. So, while the children are enjoying the big open spaces and seaside treats, you can soak up Trieste's mixed up personality and atmosphere, reminiscent of an espionage novel. After visiting other Italian towns, you'll notice a faintly Viennese character: from the hybrid cuisine with Mitteleuropean influences to its pompous *palazzi* and Art Nouveau cafés. Since nearby Slovenia joined the EU, Trieste has started to reinvent itself again, so expect Slavonic accents and regeneration work.

Essentials

Getting There

By Train The rather nondescript **Stazione Centrale** is north-west of the city centre on Piazza della Libertà (*040-452-8111*). There are frequent trains to Venice (2½–3 hr); from there you can catch connecting trains to Milan and other destinations. A couple of trains an hour connect Trieste with Udine (1–1½hr).

By Bus Near the train station on Corso Cavour is the **bus terminal** (*800-915-303*; ***www.saf.ud.it***). There are lots of buses linking Trieste and Udine (1½ hr). Friuli's small provincial towns and villages are also well served.

By Car Trieste is 2 hr from Venice on the A4 and Ljubljana in Slovenia is 95km to the north-east.

Visitor Information

The main **tourist office** is at Piazza dell'Unità d'Italia 4B (*040-347-8312*; [fax] 040-437-8380; ***www.triestetourism.it***; open daily 9am–7pm). It can take quite a while to get information, though, as it's understaffed.

Getting Around

The city centre is okay for families getting around on foot, although getting up the

Capitoline Hill may prove too tricky with pushchairs and toddlers; in this case take the no. 24 line from the train station to the Castello di San Giusto or call a taxi (☎ *040-54-533* or *040-307-730*). There is an extensive network of buses and trams run by **ACT** (☎ *040-425-001* or *800-016-675* in Italy; ***www.triestetrasporti.it***). Tickets are available from tobacconists and cost 1€ (£0.67) for 60 minutes and 1.15€ (£0.77) for 75 minutes.

Festivals & Markets

July and August see lots of cultural events, including concerts and screenings at the Castello di San Giusto outdoor theatre. The **Barcolana Autumn Cup,** a spectacular sailing regatta, is held in the Golfo di Trieste in late September/early October. For the latest updates call ☎ *040-411-664* or visit ***www.barcolana.it***.

Footie fans should try and catch a **US Triestina** *partita* at the compact Stadio Nereo Rocco: tickets are on sale at the ground or from a number of outlets around the city including **Triestina Store** (Via Tarabocchia 4/B. ***www.triestinacalcio.it***), where you can also buy club merchandise.

Pick up food bargains and picnic fayre at the covered markets on Via Carducci and Via della Majolica (Mon 8am–2pm, Tue–Sat 8am–7pm). Also worth a gander is the Ponte Ponterosso open-air food and knick-knack market alongside the Canal Grande (Tue–Sat 8am–5:30pm).

The **antiques market** takes place each month on the third Sunday, in the **Cittavecchia** (Old City), while in late October and early November the important **Trieste Antiqua** (Stazione Maritima; ☎ *040-304-888*. ***www.triesteantiqua.it***) is a must for Lovejoy wannabes.

Around Town

Trieste's city centre is backed by hills and faces the sea – the main attractions are pretty close to each other, so getting about on

Canal Grande

Piazza dell'Unità d'Italia

foot as a family should be a cinch. The train and bus stations on **Piazza della Libertà** are at the northern end of the centre. Staying on Corso Cavour it's a 10 minute walk (a cab is easier as the traffic can be choking) to the grandiose **Piazza dell'Unità d'Italia.** The first sight of this huge space drops your jowls: children will be drawn to the fountain, and you can't help but be taken aback by the neoclassical Habsburg *palazzi*.

Before reaching this flamboyant focal point from the station you'll pass the 18th century **Canale Grande** and look down the waterway at handsome former warehouses, to the porticoed façade of the **Chiesa di Sant'Antonio Nuovo**. You will now be on Riva III Novembre where the scruffy dockyards stop and views of the sea open up. At the time of writing, this broad stretch of road is in a right mess; hopefully the revamp will mean less traffic intrusion on your waterfront stroll. Further along the waterfront is the **Molo Audace**, a long, wide stone pier frequented by canoodling couples and fishermen. It's a fab place for children, but keep an eye on them as there are no barriers and the water is deep. Following the quayside walk you can spot flash marina yachts and visit the aquarium next to the Molo Pescheria (see 'Family Attractions', below).

FUN FACT Caffè City

Trieste is a major importer of Arabica coffee beans and is home to Italy's leading brand, Illy. In 1935 Francesco Illy developed the modern espresso maker when he used steam instead of compressed air in a prototype machine. The city hosts a biennial trade fair dedicated to *caffé espresso*.

It's a bit of a climb but well worth the walk to the **Colle Capitolino (Capitoline Hill) ★★**, for a bit of history and some wonderful views from the castle. (If you have a pushchair and/or toddlers take the no. 24 bus from the station or a cab; see 'Getting Around', above). Start at Piazza Cavana, at the south-eastern tip of Piazza dell'Unità d'Italia, head to Piazza Barbacan and go through the ancient **Arco di Riccardo**, then follow Via Cattedrale up the hill to the **Cattedrale di San Giusto ★** AGES 4 AND UP (☎ *040-302-874*. Free admission. Daily 8:30am–noon and 4–7pm). The 14th century campanile lies on the remnants of a Roman temple. It incorporates two Romanesque places of worship, San Giusto (the town's patron saint) and Santa Maria Assunta. Nearby there are remains of a Roman forum and a poignant memorial to those lost in the Great War. Within the bastion walls that tower above lies the **Cortile delle Milizie**, where festival events are held and you'll also find the **Museo di Castello ★★** AGES 5 AND UP (☎ *040-309-362*. Castle: Daily 9am–7pm/5pm October to March; Museum: Tues–Sun 9am–1pm), which houses Venetian chambers, Flemish tapestries, Roman remains and weapons. A walk along the ramparts costs 1€ (£0.67) while a museum visit is 2€ (£1.34) (free for under 5s). If you and the children like archaeology, don't miss the **Museo di Storia ed Arte – Orto Lapidario** AGES 6 AND UP (☎ *040-310-500*. 2€ (£1.34), 1€ (£0.67) under 25s. Tues–Sun 9am–1pm; Wed until 7pm), which has Roman, Greek and Egyptian artefacts. If you are descending into town, take the leafy path that zig-zags through the **Giardini di Rimembranza** past touching personal war memorials inscribed on rocks – eventually you'll reach the ruins of the 1st century AD Roman amphitheatre, a great photo opportunity.

Family Attractions

Children love the **Acquario Marino ★** AGES 3 AND UP (Molo Pescheria 2. ☎ *040-306-201*. 3€

FUN FACT Literary Trieste

Bookish bairns may be interested in Trieste's former residents from the world of literature, although most children will be more entertained by the statues dedicated to them. James Joyce wrote part of *Ulysses* here and his friend, the native Italo-Jewish writer Italo Svevo, wrote several witty and angst-ridden novels that capture the atmosphere of the *fin de siècle* city. Look out for their statues: Joyce on the Canal Grande and Svevo in leafy Piazza Hortis. Sir Richard Burton was consul here and translated the more child-friendly *Thousand and One Nights* (otherwise known as the *Arabian Nights*) while staying in Villa Opicina. An unparalleled travelogue is Jan Morris's *Trieste and the Meaning of Nowhere*.

(£2), 2€ (£1.34) under 20-year-olds. Free under 5s. April to October 9am–7pm; November to March 9am–1:30pm; closed Mon and on religious festivals), which contains lots of marine species including the penguins Zigo and Zago, Adriatic invertebrates, tropical fish, amphibians and reptiles, all housed in a grand 1930s building. Animal lovers and scientists should check out the **Civico Museo di Storia Naturale** AGES 4 AND UP (Piazza A. Hortis 4. ✆ *040-675-8658*. 3€ (£2), 2€ (£1.34) under 20 years. Free under 5s. Tue–Sun 8:30am–1:30pm), a natural history museum with dinosaurs and the largest bear to walk the earth.

Arty types should check out the **Museo Revoltella** (Via Diaz 27. ✆ *040-675-4350*; ***www.museorevoltella.it***. 5€ (£3.35), 3€ (£2) reductions. Tue–Sat. September to mid-July: 9am–1:30pm, 4–7pm, Sun 10am–1pm and 3–7pm; mid-July to August 9am–1pm, 4–11pm, Sun 9am–2pm) two Renaissance *palazzi* with a large modern art collection, including an elegant Pietro Magni fountain. In the summer, don't miss a trip to the rooftop café, which has fab views and decent food.

Jaunts Around Trieste

Beaches and Parks ALL AGES

Along the coast are plenty of places to sunbathe and have a dip in the sea, though it's often chocker in the summer and the water isn't the cleanest. Outside high season, the **Riviera di Barcola** near the **Faro della Vittoria lighthouse** is an alluring pebbly stretch. There is also a small beach near the turrets of the **Castello di Miramare** ALL AGES ★★, four miles from central Trieste. The Austrian Archduke Maximilian built the castle in the 1850s with a suitably lavish interior. The real highlight of a visit is a walk around the stunning gardens, which is free. Within the grounds is also the **Parco Tropicale** (✆ *040-224-406*. ***www.parcotropicale.it***. 7€, 4€ under 14s, Free under 4s) where children can get close to exotic birds, insects and butterflies.

*Via Miramare, Grignano. ✆ 040-224-143. **www.castello-miramare.it**). Castle 4€ (£2.70) adults, 2€ (£1.34) ages 18–25, free for under 18s; grounds free. Castle: Daily 9am–7pm (last admission 30 min. before close). Grounds: April to September daily 8am–7pm; March and October daily 8am–6pm; November to February daily 8am–5pm. Bus: 36 (catch at Trieste train station). Parking available.*

The Opicina Tram and La Grotta Gigante ★★

AGES 7 AND UP A visit to this awe-inspiring cave with its other-worldly stalactites involves over 500 steps, but the exertion is well worth it. The 'Gigantic Cave' is the world's largest underground cavern open to the public. It measures 114 m high by 924 m long by 65 m wide (374 ft by 3031 ft by 213 ft). If you or the children have asthma, it might be an uncomfortable journey, though. Bring warm tops, as the caves are chilly all year round. If you can, take the famous tram from Piazza Oberdan in Trieste to **Villa Opicina**, which has stunning views of the city and beyond: if you have older kids and the weather is fine get off at the Obelisk, and walk for about 40 minutes to Prosecco. There are three trams (☎ *800-016-675. www.tramdeopcina.it*) an hour running from 7am to 7pm daily, and the fare is 1€ (£0.67). Tram no.411 is the oldest tram still operating in Europe.To reach the cave, take the no.42 bus from Villa Opicina.

Opicina. (☎ 040-327-312). Admission: 8€ (£5.35) adults, 6€ (£4) ages 6–12. Open Tues–Sun; tours every hour November to February 10am–noon and 2–4pm, March and October 10am–4pm; tours every half-hour April to September 10am–6pm. Bus: 42.

Muggia ALL AGES 11 km south of Trieste is this charming Istrian fishing port with colourful houses and Venetian history. You can easily spend a day here, exploring the *calli*, the 14th century castle and the ancient settlement of Muggia Vecchia, before enjoying a meal at one of the superb fish restaurants, like **Risorta.** ★ (Riva De Amicis 1/A.☎ *040-271-219*. Primi 7€-12€, Secondi 10€-17€. AE, DC, MC, V. Tue-Sat Noon-4pm, 7-11pm, Sun noon-4pm). You can get here by train or on the A4, but the best way to arrive, especially with children, is on a *traghetto* (ferry) from the Molo Pescheria in Trieste. There are 10 round-trips a day and it costs 6€ return *www.triestetrasporti.it*).

Café's, Snacks & Family-Friendly Dining

Trieste is renowned for its elegant cafés, including **Caffè degli Specchi** (Piazza dell'Unità d'Italia 7. ☎ *040-365-777*) which has tempting pastry treats, as does another Art Nouveau gem, **Caffè San Marco** ★★ (Via Battisti 18. ☎ *040-371-373*). Ice cream addicts should try the **Gelateria Zampolli** (Via Ghega 10. ☎ *040-364-868*; Piazza Cavana 6.

Speeding Sunflowers

040-306-003) which has dozens of delectable flavours to choose from. **Chocolat** at 15/b (040-300-524) has sublime chocolate, and ice cream too. Via Cavana is a great place to pick up treats, picnic snacks and food supplies: for starters it has a fabulous deli, **Buon Appetito** (Via Cavana 6. 040-312-838) filled with olives, meats, cheeses – everything you'd expect.The **Frutta e Verdura** at no.2 has fruit and veg, obviously. For fantastic bread, snacks (including delicious pizza slices) and drinks, try the café-bakery, **L'Angolo del Pane ★** (Via Cavana 5. 040-300-271). It has outdoor tables. If you are down by the Aquarium and fancy a snack or ice cream overlooking the marina, try **Il Pinguino** (Molo Pescheria 1. 040-306-969). You can sample Austro-Hungarian cakes like Rigojanci and other sweet treats at the historic **La Bomboniera** (Via XXX Ottobre 3. 040-632-752).

Fratelli La Bufala ★★

NEAPOLITAN This excellent Neapolitan pizzeria is great for families. It's got an intimate and relaxed atmosphere; so expect to be close to chattering locals and pizza conoscitori. The superb pizzas, calzoni packed with mozzarella and southern Italian dishes like Spaghettoni are bound to satisfy the children.

Via Roma 10. . 040-348-1316. Reservations recommended Primi 8€–11€ (£5.35–7.40); secondi 11€–17€ (£7.40–11.40). AE, DC, MC, V. Daily noon–3pm and 7:30pm–midnight.

Antica Trattoria Suban

TRIESTINE While in Trieste, why not try its traditional Mitteleuropean cuisine in this historic establishment, open since 1865? If the children don't like the sound of the hearty bean and sauerkraut soup Jota or the herb infused risotto alle erbe del carso, you'll find plenty of tasty side dish alternatives, and there's always chocolate soufflé and a pergola-shaded terrace to cheer them up!

Via Comici 2. (040-54368 MC, V. Reservations recommended. Primi 6€–10€ (£4–6.70); secondi 10€–15€ (£6.70–10). Wed–Sun, noon–3pm, 7pm–10.30pm; Mon 7pm–10.30pm.

Rex Café Gourmet

ITALIAN The Rex's quirky interiors have avanguardia appeal. They do healthy juices for children and tempting aperitivi for the longer in tooth. Choose from comfy seating inside or out on the street. It's a good option for light meals during the day, like a simple spaghetti con pomodorini e ricotta and healthy salads like Insalata Nicoise.

Galleria Protti 1. (040-367-878). Light meals 5€–10€ (£3.35–6.70). AE, DC, MC, V. Daily 7:30am–8pm.

Ristorante Le Maldobrie

ITALIAN Avoid the rip-off eateries near Piazza dell'Unità d'Italia and head to this great little *osteria* nearby, on a pedestrianised stretch of Via Malcanton. The amiable Arabic cook Zoubeir Saadi proudly displays his Italian cookery certificates alongside changing artwork in cosy wooden interiors. There are seats outside which are fine when the bora winds aren't blowing you and the table away. Fresh pasta dishes like *tagliatelle di gamberetti e rucola* (with prawns and rocket) go down a treat.

Via Malcanton, 040-349-86 41. Primi 7€–11€ (£4.70–7.40); secondi 10€–15€ (£6.70–10). AE, MC, V. Daily 12:30–3pm and 7:30pm–midnight.

Family-Friendly Accommodation

If the hotels below are full, you can book a room through **CAT** (☎ *040-452-8696*; ***www.cat-trieste.com***), who have an office in the train station.

Hotel Alabarda VALUE For families on a budget, the Alabarda is a good bet and handy for the sights. Rooms are simply furnished and compact but generally well looked after. Rates are so reasonable that you could splash out and give older children their own room. The staff are helpful and full of top local tips. Children will enjoy using the old iron cage lifts and there is Internet access in the hall. The only downside is that the breakfasts are very basic, involving a drinks machine and supermarket toast.

*Via Valdirivo 22. (☎ 040-630-269; [fax] 040-639-284. **www.hotelalabarda.it**). 10 units. Single 35€–55€ (£23.50–36.85); double with shared bathroom 50€ (£33.50); double with ensuite bathroom 75€ (£50). Rates include breakfast. AE, MC, V. Parking in garage. Amenities: Internet. In room: TV.*

L'Albero Nascosto ★★★ FIND VALUE The former antiques dealer who owns this place takes real pride in his small hotel and provides the warmest hospitality in town. Expect immaculate and homely accommodation in a number of options suitable for families. The understated mini-apartments are filled with interesting artwork and furnishings and most have handy kitchenettes. Breakfasts are top quality (rare teas, coffees, preserves and the freshest bread and pastries), served in a cosy café lined with fascinating books. Another bonus is that it's near the food shops of Via Cavana.

*Via Felice Venezian 18. (☎ 040-300-188; fax: 040-318-6666. **www.alberonascosto.it**). 10 units. Double 90€–135€ (£60–90.45); triple 100€–140€ (£67–94). Weekly rates: 570€–880€ (£382–590). Rates include breakfast. AE, DC, MC, V. Parking in garage. Amenities: bar; Wi-Fi. In room: A/C, sat TV, kitchenette.*

Hotel Colombia If you're after a hotel near Trieste's transport hubs, the train station and the Piazza Oberdan bus terminal, the Colombia in the Borgo Teresiano is not to be sniffed at. The staff is generally very friendly and there's a choice of accommodation for family groups. Superior rooms have free toiletries and tea/coffee-making facilities.

*Via Geppa 18. (☎ 040-369-333; fax: 040-369-644. **www.hotelcolombia.it**). 40 units. 130€–260€ (£87–174) double; free for children under 12 in parents' room. Rates include breakfast. AE, DC, MC, V. Parking in garage 18€ (£12) per day. Amenities: laundry service. In room: A/C, sat TV, hairdryer, minibar, safe, telephone.*

6 Milan & Lombardy

LOMBARDY

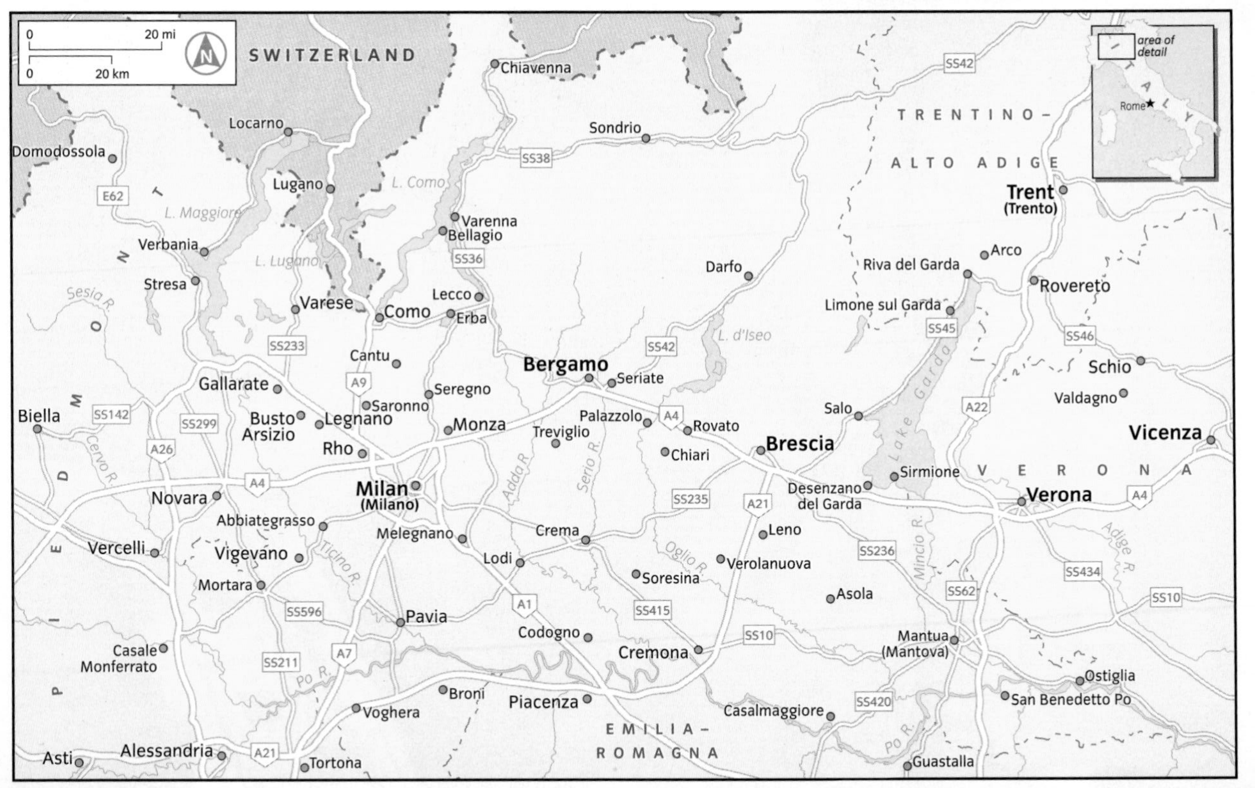

SWITZERLAND
TRENTINO – ALTO ADIGE
VERONA
EMILIA – ROMAGNA
PIEMONTE
ITALY
Rome
area of detail
0 20 mi
0 20 km
Domodossola
Locarno
Lugano
Verbania
Stresa
L. Maggiore
L. Lugano
L. Como
Varese
Como
Cantu
Lecco
Erba
Varenna
Bellagio
Chiavenna
Sondrio
Bergamo
Seriate
Darfo
L. d'Iseo
Brescia
Rovato
Chiari
Palazzolo
Treviglio
Monza
Seregno
Saronno
Legnano
Busto Arsizio
Gallarate
Rho
Milan (Milano)
Melegnano
Lodi
Crema
Codogno
Piacenza
Cremona
Soresina
Verolanuova
Leno
Casalmaggiore
Asola
Desenzano del Garda
Sirmione
Salo
Limone sul Garda
Riva del Garda
Arco
Lake Garda
Trent (Trento)
Rovereto
Schio
Valdagno
Vicenza
Verona
Mantua (Mantova)
Guastalla
San Benedetto Po
Ostiglia
Pavia
Broni
Voghera
Tortona
Alessandria
Asti
Casale Monferrato
Vercelli
Novara
Mortara
Vigevano
Abbiategrasso
Biella
Adige R.
Mincio R.
Oglio R.
Serio R.
Adda R.
Ticino R.
Po R.
Sesia R.
Cervo R.
A1
A4
A7
A9
A21
A22
A26
E62
SS10
SS36
SS38
SS42
SS45
SS46
SS62
SS142
SS211
SS233
SS235
SS236
SS299
SS415
SS420
SS434
SS596

Lombardy (Lombardia) has many urban attractions for visitors travelling with children. The sophisticated metropolis of Milan has the largest share, with its museums, art treasures, parks, fashion shopping and famous football clubs. The pace of life slows in Bergamo, Mantova, Cremona and Brescia, which have their own proud traditions and fabulous *piazze* to explore. For those seeking outdoor pleasures and fun, there are wonderful natural environments and theme parks to visit. The region's culinary specialities should be sampled, although the emphasis on butter over olive oil makes them a little less healthy than the Mediterranean diet eaten further south. Polenta and risotto often replace pasta here for primi, while main courses (secondi) are dominated by hearty meat creations like *osso buco* (braised veal shank) and *cotoletta alla Milanese*, a breaded veal cutlet.

Italy's financial capital, Milan, dominates the region economically, but Lombardy is much more than the modern preoccupations with industry, finance, fashion, football and shady politics. From the flat plains, rice fields and atmospheric wetlands in the south by the river Po to hilltop towns, Alpine peaks and shimmering lakes, the region has many cultural and geographical guises and a few surprises. History is everywhere, from architecture to the different dialects spoken. Indeed, Lombardy has fought and assimilated many invaders – Etruscans, Romans, Gauls and Huns to name a few. Some Lombards organised themselves in the 12th century forming the Lombard League of city-states which defeated their Germanic rulers. These fortified towns and hinterlands eventually fell into the hands of local rulers whose buildings and cultural legacies can be seen today: the Visconti and Sforza dynasties in Milan, Cremona and Brescia, the Republic of Venice in Bergamo and Brescia, and the Gonzaga in Mantua. The Spanish, the Austrians and Napoleon's Republican France all had a go at ruling the region – the Lombard people, freed from the shackles of tyranny, got a taste for new freedoms and, like many across the peninsula, eventually threw out their foreign dynasties. They joined a united Italy in 1870, but the Lombards' independent spirit has remained – it was in Milan that the corpse of Mussolini was hung upside down from a lamppost, the symbol of Italian Fascism crushed. It is here also, across Lombardy, where a significant minority want autonomy from the Italian state and the poorer south.

MILAN (MILANO)

552 km (342 miles) NW of Rome, 288 km (179 miles) NW of Florence, 257 km (159 miles) W of Venice, 140 km (87miles) NE of Turin, 142 km (88 miles) N of Genoa

When you first encounter Italy's financial powerhouse, it doesn't go out of its way to charm you – this is a modern city that may appear more impersonal than other Italian cities. You have to look beyond the sharp suits, unrelenting traffic and snooty boutiques to find the warmer Milanese soul. It can be stiflingly hot in summer and infamously foggy during the winter months. Once accustomed to the blur of grid-patterned streets and ever-busy Milanesi, you can seek out its family-friendly attractions, cultural gems, alluring districts, welcome open spaces and urbane haunts.

Essentials

Getting There

By Plane Both of Milan's airports are operated by SEA (✆ *02-7485-2200*; ***www.aeroportimilano.it***), while the increasingly popular Bergamo Orio del Serio airport (1 hr) is run by Sacbo (✆ *035-320-402*; ***www.sacbo.it***). **Milan Malpensa**, 48 km (30 miles) west of the city centre, is the newish international airport – it may have been beset by delays, cancellations and scandals during its first decade, but it seems to be a more reliable choice now and has an express train service that runs every half-hour to and from Cadorna, just north of the city centre. The **Malpensa Express** (✆ *02-9619-2301*; ***www.ferrovienord.it***) costs 11€ (£7.40) or 5.50€ (£3.70) if tickets are purchased in advance from the ticket office or automated machine. If you take the **Malpensa Shuttle bus** (✆ *02-5858-3185*; ***www.airpullman.com***), you will save some money but may be held up in traffic. The journey takes 50 min. at best. One-way fares are 5€ (£3.35) adults, 2.50€ (£1.68) for children aged 2–12 years. Tickets are available from Airport 2000 (Terminal 1), Air Pullman (Terminal 2) and SAP Passaggi/Colombo newsstand at Stazione Centrale. A taxi ride will cost around 70€ (£47) but is well worth it if you are in a larger group and running late outside the rush hour.
Milan Linate is a mere 7 km (4 miles) east of the city centre and handles European flights by the likes of easyJet and BA. Call ✆ *02-7485-2200* for information. The **Starfly Shuttle** (3€ (£2) one-way bought from the STAM office or on-board) runs every 30 minutes. The local ATM bus no.73 costs 1€ (£0.67) and links Linate with Piazza San Babila (✆ *02-7252-4360*; ***www.atm-mi***). Air Pullman also runs a shuttle bus between Malpensa and Linate, which takes 75 minutes (9€ (£6) adults, 4.50€ (£3) children).

Orio del Serio is located just outside Bergamo about an hour from Milan. There are a few bus companies that run to and from the side of Stazione Centrale including **Terravision** (✆ *06-4544-1345*; ***www.terravision.it***) which has buses every half-hour. Singles cost around 7€ (£4.70) and 3.50€ (£2.35) for children aged 5–12.

By Train Milan is a very busy rail hub, with regular connections to Europe's major cities. There are trains to and from Venice (3 hr) every half-hour, to and from Rome (5 hr), and hourly to and from Florence (3 hr). The imposing Fascist-built edifice of **Stazione Centrale** is about a half-hour walk northeast of the centre – there are connections to Piazza del Duomo by bus, tram and metro. The Metro stop Centrale F.S. is just 10 minutes away from the Duomo stop (four stops on the yellow line; direzione San Donato). For a look at the city en route, pass the usual street sellers, assorted characters and agile skateboarders outside the station and head to the bus and tram stops, which are on an island amid the honking traffic. The bus no.60 will take you to the Duomo. The traffic here can be very heavy, so it's advisable to avoid this method if you have young children. For a half-hour walk to the centre, follow Via Pisani to Piazza della Repubblica and then continue south on Via Turati and Via Manzoni to Piazza del Duomo.

You are likely to arrive at Stazione Centrale, although some trains serve Milan's other stations: **Stazione Nord** (services to and from Como), **Porta Genova** (services to and from Alessandria and Asti), and **Porta Garibaldi** (services to and from Lecco).

By Bus Italian trains are so affordable and regular, and the service so extensive, that the need for buses between major cities is almost obsolete. But if you do find yourself heading to Milan by Intercity bus, you'll arrive and depart from the front of the Castello Sforzesco on Piazza Castello (Metro: Cairoli). For more information consult ***www.autostradale.com***. (*☎ 02-339-107-94*).

By Car Milan has excellent motorway (autostrade) connections. The A1 (Autostrada del Sole) connects Milan with Rome (6 hr) and Florence (3 hr) and the A4 links Milan with Turin (1 hr) to the west and Verona and Venice (3 hr) to the east. In

Il Duomo

comparison with the often-chocker A4, the A7 which runs southwest toward Genoa is rather serene, by Italian standards. Avoid driving in the centre of Milan if you can: the traffic is heavy and the one-way system can be bewildering. Most hotels have special parking arrangements and some will even park your car while you check in – ask for the details when you make a reservation.

Visitor Information

The main APT **tourist office** is in the Palazzo del Turismo on Piazza del Duomo at Via Marconi 1 (☎ *02-7252-4301*; ***www.milanoinfotourist.com***). Office hours are Monday to Friday from 8:30am to 8pm, Saturday from 9am to 1pm and 2pm to 7pm, Sunday from 9am to 1pm and 2 to 5pm. There is an office in Stazione Centrale (☎ *02-7252-4360*) which is open Monday to Friday 8am to 7pm, Saturday 9am to 6pm and Sunday 9am to 12:30pm and 1:30 to 6pm.

There are lots of free leaflets, maps and listings to pick up, as well as the useful *Milano Mese*, *Hello Milano* (***www.hello milano.it***) and *EasyMilano* (***www.easymilano.it***), which have English versions and a wealth of up-to-date listings.

City Layout

The focal point of Milan is Piazza del Duomo – you can pick up a detailed map from the tourist office here and plan where you want to visit given your timeframe. A lot of the major attractions are within walking distance, but those with small children may want to plan using a metro or bus map (available at tourist information centres) to limit the amount of walking.

North of the Duomo is **Galleria Vittorio Emanuele II**, the *salotto dei Milanesi* (Milanese living room): an impressive Victorian-era iron and glass shopping centre. Just to one side of the central point of the Galleria you can follow Milanese tradition and make a wish whilst spinning on the shiny balls of the Toro (bull). To the north, you'll exit the Galleria and enter Piazza della Scala with its famous opera house. A short stroll along Via Manzoni, beyond the Via Montenapoleone intersection, and you are within the famed **Quadrilatero Della Moda** (The Quadrilateral of Fashion).

Further north-east along Via Manzoni, in and around the welcome shade of the **Giardini Pubblici** (public gardens), you'll find the **Gallery of Modern Art**, **Natural History Museum**, **Planetarium** and **Museo del Cinema**. Nearby, between San Babila and Porta Venezia metros, along Corso Venezia, are some of the finest examples of Milanese architecture down the ages, from the Renaissance-era Casa Fontana-Silvestri to the Liberty style Palazzo Castiglioni. Further north, toward the looming presence of the Stazione Centrale, the grid-patterned streets are flanked with some impressive Fascist-era buildings and less alluring modern structures – this part of the city was ravaged by World War II bombs.

The Brera district is a little further north of the Duomo, west of Piazza Cavour and the splendid public gardens. The Brera's boho atmosphere stems from its plethora of cafés, galleries, antique shops and markets. It also has the city's most impressive collection of art at the **Pinacoteca de Brera**, and beguiling botanical gardens over the wall.

West of the Duomo is the well-heeled Magenta district and the church of **Santa Maria delle Grazie**, which contains Leonardo's *L'Ultima Cena* (*Last Supper*). The **Archaeological Museum** on Via Magenta should spark the imagination of the family with its Roman remains. Further west is the Romanesque **Chiesa di Sant'Ambrogio**, devoted to Milan's patron saint, and the fantastic **Leonardo da Vinci Museum of Science and Technology**: children will love the interactive displays, gardens and hangers full of trains, planes, ships and submarines.

The imposing bulk and chunky towers of the **Castello Sforzesco** can be glimpsed if you look north-west along Via Dante. There are outdoor pleasures to be enjoyed in the lush **Parco Sempione** just beyond its courtyards and civic museums.

South of the Duomo (Metro: Porta Genova) is the Navigli district which has remnants of Milan's canal system. Head for the main canal, Naviglio Grande, for some quirky shopping, funky bars and eclectic market stalls. In summer (especially in June during the **Festa di Naviglio**) the place is buzzing with street fairs, concerts and al fresco dining on boats.

Getting Around

By Metro The Milan Metro system (Metropolitana Milanese), buses and trams make getting around a doddle, once you get the knack of buying and stamping your tickets. They are available from metro stations and *edicole* (newsstands) and it's advisable to buy plenty in advance. To avoid a fine, make sure you validate your ticket by using one of the usually yellow or orange machines as soon as you board a bus or tram. A *Biglietto ordinario urbano singolo* (single ticket valid for 75 minutes of transport above ground) costs 1€ (£0.67). A one-day travel card for unlimited travel costs 3€ (£2); a two-day version 5.50 €.The buses and trams run all day and night (barring strikes, which are quite frequent), while the Metro closes at midnight. Visit the ATM office at the Duomo metro stop for more information: it is open Monday to Friday 8:30am to 8pm and weekends 9am to 1pm, then 2pm to 7pm (until 5pm on Sundays; ✆ *02-7252-4301* or *800-80-81-81*; ***www.atmi-mi.it***).

By Car If you have a car, make sure your hotel arranges suitable parking in advance. For city sightseeing, leave the car and use public transport or taxis. The horrendous traffic, claustrophobic climate and infamous one-way system might induce a family riot. If you are feeling lucky and want to dip quickly into the city, you can park within the *sosta a pagamento* blue lines: the maximum stay is 2 hr. Pay and display *Sosta Milano* scratch cards are available from ATM offices, tobacconists and metro stations. Alternatively, there is a private car park at *Autosilo Borgospesso* (Via Borgospesso 18, close to the Cathedral, open 24 hours). For a less stressful experience, try one of the park and ride car parks run by ATM, next to metro stations (Bisceglie, Cascina Gobba, Famagosta, Lampugnano and Molino Dorino), which connect with Milan's Metro system: main roads indicate the nearest car park and number of spaces remaining.

For car hire try: *Avis*, at Via Corelli 150 (☎ 02-5530-5276; **www.avis.com**); Stazione Centrale, Galleria delle Carrozze (☎ 02-6698-0280) and at Piazza Diaz, near the Duomo (☎ 02-8901-0645). Or try *Hertz*, at Piazza Duca d'Aosta (☎ 02-6698-5151; **www.hertz.com**).

By Taxi Taxis are generally white and can be hailed on the streets – if you're very lucky they'll even stop! The best bet is to hire them at taxi ranks outside train stations (☎ 02-4040-8585 for location of nearest taxi rank). Alternatively, call one of these and you'll pay a small surcharge for a taxi to pick you up: (☎ 02-6767, 02-5353, 02-8585, 02-6969 or 02-4040). As always, make sure the meter is switched on.

Planning Your Outings

Milan is a huge city and, unfortunately, many of its sites are spread apart. This means a bit of realism is required when planning what to do. Look for sites that are close to each other or joined by a quick metro trip. For example, the **Aquarium**, **Castello Sforzesco** and **Triennale** (art gallery) are all in or near **Parco Sempione**, meaning you can see a site or two in the morning then take to the park in the afternoon. In the height of summer, when Milan can become stiflingly hot, it's a good idea to visit the indoor galleries and museums and enjoy their air conditioning during the midday period.

Start off with making sure you have a good supply of bus or tram tickets to get you there and back.

Toilets in railway stations and the bigger tourist attractions are, in general, plentiful and well looked after. When you're out and about it may be an idea to combine toilet trips with a water-buying/ice cream/quick espresso stop. Toilets in cafés and restaurants vary in cleanliness, so be sure to pack toilet paper and wipes in your bag.

Baby-changing facilities are available in most of the major sites, but be prepared to squeeze into toilet cubicles in some smaller visitor attractions (particularly churches), cafés and restaurants. Breastfeeding is perfectly acceptable in Milan, but a little discretion may be advisable in some restaurants and cafés. Some Italians can be quite disapproving of breastfeeding toddlers.

FAST FACTS: MILAN

Bookstores Milan's English-language bookshops are: **The English Bookshop,** Via Ariosto at Via Mascheroni 12 (☎ *02-469-4468*), open Monday to Saturday 9am to 8pm; and **The American Bookstore,** between the Duomo and Castello Sforzesco, Via Camperio 16 at the corner with Via Dante (☎ *02-878-920*), open Monday 1 to 7pm, Tuesday to Saturday 10am to 7pm (Metro: Cardusio).

Car Hire See 'Getting Around', above.

Embassies The **British Consulate,** Via San Paolo 7 (☎ *02-230-01*), is open Monday to Friday from 9:15am to 12:15pm and 2:30 to 4:30pm (Metro: Duomo); the **Irish Consulate** is at Piazza S. Pietro in Gessate 2 (☎ *02-5518-8848* Metro: San Babila); the **Australian Consulate** at Via Borgogna 2 (☎ *02-777-041*), is open Monday to Thursday 9am to noon and 2 to 4pm (Metro: San Babila); and the **New Zealand Consulate** at Via Arezzo 6 (☎ *02-4801-2544*), is open Monday to Friday from 9am to 11am (Metro: Pagano); the **US Consulate** is at Via Principe Amadeo 2/10 (☎ *02-290-351*) – it's open Monday to Friday from 9 to 11am and 2 to 4pm (Metro: Turati). The **Canadian Consulate** at Via Pisani 19 (☎ *02-675-81*) is open Monday to Thursday 8:30am to 12:30pm and 1:15 to 5:30pm (Metro: F.S. Centrale or Repubblica).

Crime and Safety For police emergencies dial ☎ *113* (a free call); for English-speaking tourist police staff call ☎ *02-863-701*. There is a police station at Stazione Centrale. The main police HQ, the **Questura,** is just west of the Giardini Pubblici at Via Fatebenefratelli 11, ☎ *02-622-61* (Metro: Turati). Places to be on guard, especially at night, are the Parco Sempione, the public gardens and around the Stazione Centrale: pickpockets operate here as on public transportation and street markets.

Chemists Opening hours rotate on 24-hr shifts; dial ☎ *192* to find which pharmacies are open or check schedules posted in most pharmacies announcing which shop is keeping a 24-hr schedule. The **Farmacia Stazione Centrale** (☎ *02-669-0935*), in the train station, is open 24 hours daily – some of the staff speak English.

Emergencies The general number for emergencies is ☎ *113.* For the police, call ☎ *112;* for first aid or an ambulance, dial ☎ *118.* All are free calls.

Hospitals The **Ospedale Maggiore Policlinico,** ☎ *02-556-812,* is centrally located, a 5-minute walk south-east of the Duomo at Via Francesco Sforza 35 (Metro: Duomo or Missori). Some of the medical personnel here speak English.

Internet **Grazie Internet Café** operates near Stazione Centrale at Piazza Duca d'Aosta 14 (☎ *02-6700-5430*). **AWBA Internet Café** is between the Duomo and Missori metro stops at Via Valpetrosa 59 (☎ *02-454-78874*). Linate and Malpensa airports have WiFi hotspots, as do many hotels and bars, including **Colonial Cafè** (Corso Magenta 85 ☎ *02 435-11-054*). For the full list go to ***www.jiwire.com.***

Launderette South of the Duomo at Via San Vito 5 is **Minola** (☎ *02-5811-1271*; Metro: Missori). Open weekdays from 8am to 6pm and Saturday from 8am to noon.

Lost Property The lost baggage number for **Aeroporto della Malpensa** is ☎ *02-7485-4215.* For **Aeroporto Linate** the number is ☎ *02-7010-2094.* The English-speaking staff at these offices cover luggage lost on most airlines at these airports. The **lost property office at Stazione Centrale** is open daily from 7am to 1pm and 2 to 8pm (☎ *6371-2667*). The **main municipal lost property office** is just south of Piazza del Duomo at Via Friuli 30 (☎ *02-551 6141*), it's open Monday to Friday 8:30am to 12:45pm and 2:15 to 5pm (Metro: Duomo or Missori).

Luggage Storage The luggage storage office in Stazione Centrale is open daily from 5am to 4am; the fee is 3€ (£2) per piece of baggage for each 12-hour period.

Newspapers and Magazines For English-language newspapers and magazines, check out the *edicole* newsstands in Stazione Centrale and around Piazza del Duomo.

Post Office The main post office, **Poste e Telecommunicazioni**, is west of Piazza del Duomo at Via Cordusio 4, ☎ *02-805-6812* (Metro: Cardusio). Service windows are open Monday to Friday 8:30am to 5:30pm and Saturday 8:30am to 1:50pm. Most branch offices are open Monday to Saturday 8:30am to 1:30pm. There is a post office inside Stazione Centrale, open Monday to Friday 8:15am to 5:30pm and Saturday 8:15am to 3:30pm.

Taxis To find a taxi in Milan, walk to the nearest taxi stand, usually located near major piazzas and major metro stops. In the centre, there are taxi stands at Piazza Duomo and Piazza della Scala. Or call a **radio taxi**

Tram

at 02-4040, 02-5353, 02-6767 or 02-8383.

Telephones There are public telephones throughout Milan. Phones accept coins or phone cards *(carta telefonica),* which are available at tobacco shops in denominations of 5€ (£3.35). Some telephones in the SIP/Telecom offices in Galleria Vittorio Emanuele and Stazione Centrale accept major credit cards. Telephone cards are also available here – both offices are open daily from 8am to 9:30pm. The area code for Milan is 02.

Toilets See 'Planning Your Outings', above.

What To See & Do In Milan

The cluster of sights around the Duomo are rich with artistic merit but may exhaust the most cultural of vultures, let alone their offspring. There are some great parks and excellent shopping to add some variety. If you only have an afternoon, the Duomo and Galleria are the focal point of the city, La Scala is a stone's throw away and the fashionista district just a hop and a jump beyond that.

In the Magenta neighbourhood, you can combine a visit to the Archaeolgical Museum with a visit to Santa Maria delle Grazie and the *Last Supper* (if you've booked). The fabulous Leonardo da Vinci Museum of Science and Technology offers lots of interactive models by the master as well as big spaces filled with planes, trains and submarines. Ask for an interactive tour with one of their well-informed staff. In this district you can also pay your respects to

CENTRAL **MILAN**

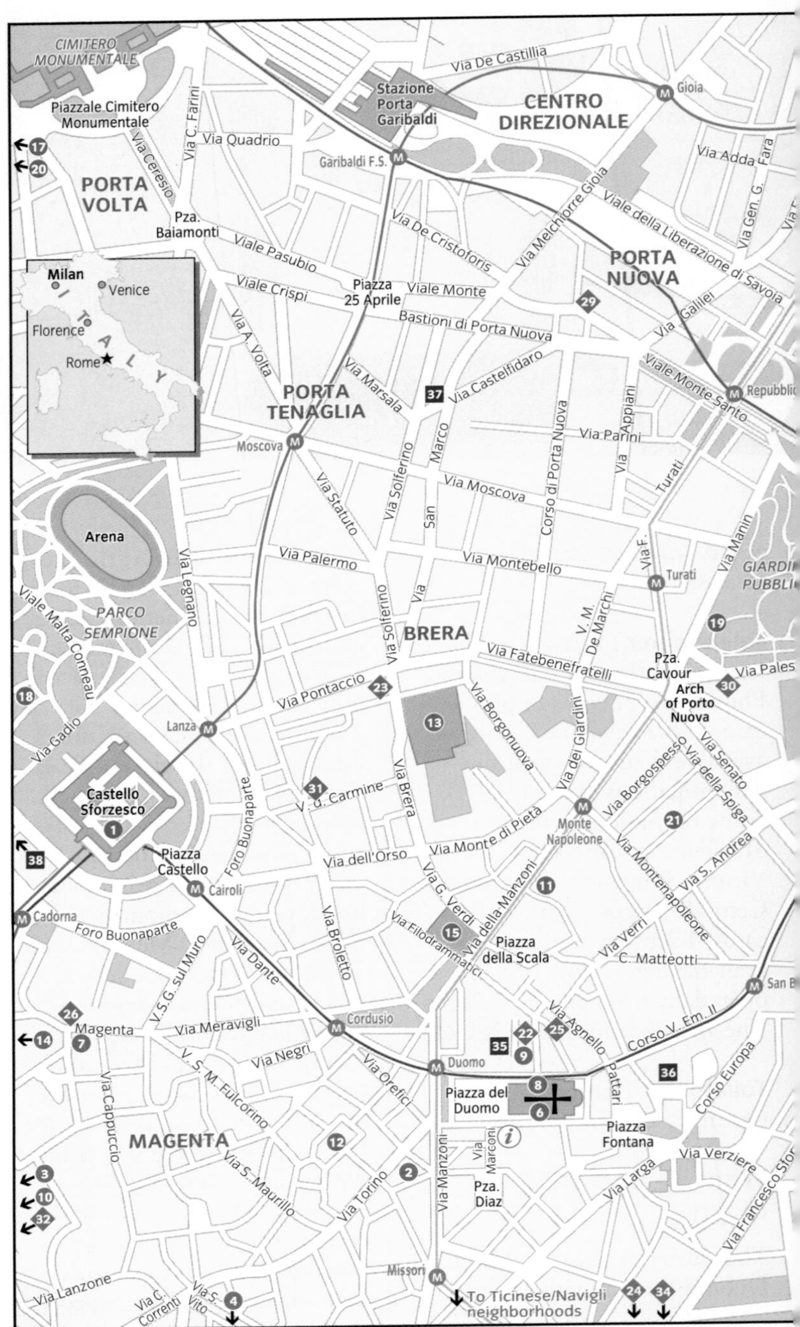

Attractions ●

Castello Sforzesco **1**
Chiesa Santa Maria **2**
Chiesa Di Sant'Ambrogio **3**
Chiesa di San Lorenzo **4**
Civic Gallery of Modern Art **5**
Museo Civico D'Arte Comtemporanea **6**
Civico Museo Archeologico **7**
Duomo **8**
Duomo Museum **9**
Leonardo da Vinci Nat. M **10**
Museo Poldi-Pezzoli **11**
Pinacoteca Ambrosiana **12**
Pinacoteca de Brera **13**
Santa Maria delle Grazie **14**
Teatro della Scala **15**
Museo di Storia Naturale **16**
Stadio Meazza (San Siro) **17**
La Triennale **18**
Palazzo Dugnani **19**
Ippodromo **20**
Quadrilatero d'oro **21**

Dining ◆

Caffè Miani **22**
Jamaica **23**
Sottosopra **24**
Luini Panzerotti **25**
Marchesi **26**
L'Osteria del Treno **27**
Pizzeria Spontini **28**
Taverna del Gran Sasso **29**
La Terrazza **30**
Trattoria del Carmine **31**
Anema e Cozze **32**
Angelo Azzurro **33**
Don Juan **34**

Accommodation ■

Park Hyatt **35**
Hotel Ambasciatori **36**
Antica Locanda Leonardo **37**
Hotel Lancaster **38**
Staranderson **39**
Hotel Terminal **40**
Hotel Del Corso **41**

0 1/4 mi
0 0.25 km
N

Milan's patron Saint at the **Sant'Ambrogio** and soak up the ancient atmosphere at the **San Lorenzo church**, which dates from Roman times.

Thankfully, there are some great parks to escape the Milanese hurly burly. You can mix old ramparts, museum masterpieces, an aquarium, the Triennale for design exhibits and a cool hangout, and fresh-air pursuits in and around Castello Sforzesco and Parco Sempione. The Giardini Pubblici is a shady place to relax amid ponds, fronds and follies, and for children to play – nearby attractions include the Planetarium, Museum of Natural History and Gallery of Modern Art. The **Navigli** warrants a few hours for a wander around its canal-side funky shops and eateries. If you are after an unusual souvenir try the Navigli flea market or the collectors' and antiques markets at Brera.

Football fans will get a kick out of making the pilgrimage to San Siro on the north-western outskirts – the nearby **Ippodromo** and park offers galloping horseracing fun, children's entertainment and cool places to eat. For something completely different, be flabbergasted at the elaborate tombs and get spooked with a visit to the magnificent **Cimiterio Monumentale**.

Top Sights

Duomo ★★ AGES 5 AND UP The building of this gothic goliath was started by the ruling Visconti family and the archbishop Antonio da Salubbio in 1386 – it was not finished until five centuries later when Napoleon completed the façade, in time to crown himself king of Italy. The façade may incorporate a myriad of styles, but its original design is attributed to Lombard masters Grassi and da Orsenigo, who were helped by German, French and Flemish craftsmen. There is ongoing restoration work in progress, hence the scaffolding and sheeting covering some of the ornate exterior and its 3400 statues and gargoyles. Take a close look at the huge bronze doors with bas reliefs recounting episodes from the lives of Sant' Ambrogio, the virgin and Milan itself. Amidst the darkened bronze, one of the character's legs is very shiny: you can see tourists going up to it and rubbing it superstitiously.

Il Duomo

Gasps and hushed 'wows' are in order as you enter the cavernous space dominated by 52 giant pillars that divide the aisles. The sombre mood of the interior is lifted by light shining through the impressive stained glass windows: behind the altar are the highest set examples in the world, *Le Vetrate del'Abside*, the latest section of which was added in 1988. The gruesome statue of St Bartholomew (Marco d'Agrate) depicts the martyr carrying his flesh over his shoulder having being flayed alive by the Astyages. Keep your eyes peeled for the Visconti insignia – a serpent swallowing a man – in the tracery of the apse windows.

Amid the monuments to Viscontis and cardinals is the tomb of Gian Giacomo Medici by Leone Leoni (1509–1590), which is reckoned to owe some of its design to Michelangelo. Below the main altar, the treasury contains medieval gold and silver. The **Battistero Paleocristiano** offers an atmospheric glimpse of the octagonal baptistery where Saint Ambrose is believed to have baptised Saint Augustine in 387. There are also remains here of 1st century Roman baths and the 4th century basilica of Santa Tecla.

If you fancy rising to the level of spires, flying buttresses and the gilded copper *Madonnina* (Milan's protectress), take to *Le Terrazze* (roof terrace: take the lift or scale the stairs behind the left, or north, transept). On a clear day you can see the Matterhorn, Monte Rosa and the Appenines. An audio guide is available for 2.60€ (£1.75) per person. If you are wearing shorts, or have bare shoulders, you will not be allowed in the Duomo. Be extra quiet and respectful if there is a mass going on so as not to disturb the congregation – and please remember to switch off your mobile phones when inside!

If you fancy seeing more of the Duomo's relics, including an early work by Tintoretto, and delving deeper into its history, head for the **Museo del Duomo**, across the piazza in Palazzo Reale. Little engineers in the making will enjoy the displays detailing its construction. For those interested in modern art, Italian Futurism and the post-Impressionists, check out the **Museo Civico d'Arte Contemporanea** on the second floor: amongst the collection of 3000 pieces are works by Boccioni, de Chirico, Cezanne, Gauguin, Kandinsky, Mondrian and Van Gogh. Whilst restoration work takes place on Palazzo Reale through 2007, some of the collection can be viewed at the **Museo del Permanente**.

Piazza del Duomo. (✆ 02-860-358 or 02-8646-3456). Duomo: Free admission; daily 6:50am–7pm. Roof: admission 3.50€ (£2.35), 5€ (£3.35); with lift; daily 7am–7pm. Crypt: admission 1.55€ (£1.04); daily 9am–noon and 2:30–6pm. Baptistery: admission 1.55€ (£1.04); Tues–Sun 10am–noon and 3–5pm. Museum: admission 6€ (£4) adults, 3€ (£2) children younger than 18 and senior citizens older than 65, ticket for museum and lift 7€ (£4.70); Tues–Sun 9:30am–12:30pm and 3–6pm. Metro: Duomo.

FUN FACT Know your Duomo

The Duomo:

- Is 157 m (514 ft) by 92 m (301 ft) at its widest point.
- Is the fourth largest church in the world after St Peter's in Rome, Seville's cathedral and Yamoussoukro, in the Ivory Coast.
- Contains a 4 m-high *Madonnina* (little Madonna) positioned 108 ft above ground level.
- Holds 40,000 people for services.
- Has 135 spires and 3440 statues.
- Is built of grey-pink Candoglia marble from quarries near Lake Maggiore.

Galleria Vittorio Emanuele II

ALL AGES Milan's precursor to today's shopping centre had a tragic start: architect Giusseppe Mengoni fell to his death from a girder a year before its inauguration in 1877. The colossal structure is famed for its magnificent glass and iron roof. Amongst the elegant shops and cafés is **Il Salotto**, a must for followers of iconic Italian cafés. Take refreshments at the bar or pay a pretty euro outside for a ringside view of the Milanese passeggiata. As you walk around you're bound to look up at the cupola, but don't forget to admire the mosaic tiles depicting zodiac signs and the four continents within the large Latin cross design. Check out the octagonal centrepiece and see if you can sniff out Taurus the Bull (known around these parts as *il toro di Milano*). Take turns in spinning on its golden balls and you'll be repaid with luck, so the locals say!

Between Piazza del Duomo and Piazza della Scala. Metro: Duomo.

Galleria Vittorio Emanuele II

Teatro della Scala/Museo

AGES 7 AND UP The world's most famous opera house has had a recent 50 million € (£33.5 million) overhaul, which includes the addition of a controversial elliptical edifice and new stage Flytower. The season opens on 7th December, on the feast day of Milan's patron saint, Sant'Ambrogio. You'll have to be well connected to attend the gala opening, which is often a mini-riot of mink-clad signore and anti-fur protesters. Children over the age of six are welcome and men are expected to dress dapperly in suit and tie. To purchase tickets for the lavish 1800-capacity auditorium, where Pavarotti got his big break, visit the website or box office at the Duomo metro station. The museum has a wealth of costumes, artwork, musical instruments and Verdi-related exhibits.

*Piazza Scala. Box office (☎ 02-7200-3744; museum ☎ 02-8879-2473 **www.teatroallscala.org**). Opera, ballet and concert tickets from 20€–180€ (£13.40–120). Museum: admission 5€ (£3.35), daily 9am–12:30 pm and 1:30pm–5:30 pm. Metro: Duomo.*

Pinacoteca di Brera/Botanical Gardens

AGES 5 AND UP To view the finest collection of northern Italian painting, look no further than this 17th century palazzo. The bronze statue of Napoleon I by Antonio Canova (the marble version is in London at Apsley House) marks the extraordinary way this vast collection came about. It was the diminutive Frenchman's policy of hording confiscated works from various collections in the palazzo, which ultimately benefited the Italian state. The various schools of the Italian Renaissance and Baroque painting are represented with works by Raphael, Bellini, Caravaggio, Piero della Francesca and Mantegna. The vast collection is housed in 38 rooms, which are often rearranged, so pick up the latest plan in the foyer. A word of warning: there's a lot here, so you might want to dip in and take a rest in one of the area's excellent cafés. Highlights include Mantegna's *Cristo Morto* (*Dead Christ*) and Raphael's altarpiece, *The Marriage of the Virgin*. Twentieth century works that may raise a few questions and a chortle for their surreal and angular shapes include Carlo Carra`s *Mother and Son* and Modigliani's *Portrait of Moise Kisling*. If you are wondering why Kisling looks cross-eyed and gormless, it's apparently due to the artist's fascination with African sculpture – or maybe he just looked like that. Works by Rembrandt, El Greco and Van Dyck are among the non-Italians on show. There are countless Venetian masterpieces, including Caravaggio's *Supper at Emmanus* (compare it with the other version in London's National Gallery).

*Via Brera 28. (☎ 02-722-631 or 02-8942-1146 (for reservations). **www.brera.beniculturali.it**). Admission: 6.20€ (£4.15). Tues–Sun 8:30am–7:30pm. Metro: Lanza or Montenapoleone.*

L'Orto Botanico **ALL AGES** was founded in 1774 and covers 5000 square metres. Although sadly neglected (it's apparently undergoing restoration), it's still an oasis of peace, with some fine old gingkos and a 30-metre-high lime tree.

Via Brera, 28. (☎ 02-8901-0419 or 02-5031-4774). Admission free. Daily 9am–12pm and 1pm–4pm. Metro: Lanza.

Santa Maria delle Grazie/ *The Last Supper* AGES 7 AND UP

The continuing clamour to see Leonardo da Vinci's *L'Ultima Cena* (*Last Supper*) in the Cenacolo Vinciano (refectory) has been amplified by recent popular works of fiction (or 'bottom juice' as Stephen Fry termed it), making it necessary to book well (months) in advance. The painting depicts the moment when Christ announces to his disciples that one of them will betray him. The history of the painting is as fascinating as the figures' expressions within it are captivating: it has certainly been through the wars since it was painted (1495–1497) for Duke Ludovico Sforza, and has been the subject of restoration on many occasions. The inherent problem stems from the artist's choice of technique: instead of painting a true 'fresco' onto the 'fresh' wet lime plaster, he applied tempera to the dry wall with later oil varnishes. This, combined with the humidity of the walls (in a place where the monks cooked), meant that by the 16th century the surface was flaking considerably. Worse was to come in the last century when Allied bombing during World War II destroyed the roof, exposing the work to the elements for three years. These calamities and many well-intentioned attempts to restore it (including oil applications in the 18th century) exacerbated the damage. The last restoration was more successful – it took 20 years, finishing in 1999. As a result, much of da Vinci's original colouring can be seen. On the opposite wall is a true fresco by Giovanni Donato Montorfano, entitled *Crucifixion* (1495). Only 25 people at a time are allowed to enter the refectory to view the works, ushered through pollutant filtering areas. Make the most of it as you are escorted out after 15 minutes. Tour companies swallow up many of the tickets, meaning that it is often booked up months in advance.

The church itself was designed by Guiniforte Solari and built between 1463 and 1490, largely in brick and terracotta. The choir, cloister and finely decorated dome, added not long after, have been attributed to Bramante, one of the initial architects to work on the basilica of St Peter's in Rome.

*Piazza Santa Maria delle Grazie. The Last Supper: (☎ 02-8942-1146. **www.cenacolovinciano.it**). Admission: 6.50€ (£4.35) plus a booking fee of 1€ (£0.67) Tues–Sun 8am–7:30pm (may close at 1:45pm in winter). Church: (☎ 02-467-6111). Free admission. Mon–Sat 7:30am–noon and 3–7pm, Sun 7:20am–12:15pm and 3:30–9pm (may close earlier in winter). Metro: Cardona or Conciliazione.*

Castello Sforzesco ALL AGES

The scale of this fortified castle complex replete with austere towers, magnificent courtyards and long salons will fire the imaginations of young and old visitors alike. The parkland surrounding it, including the Parco Sempione, has large green expanses for a relaxing picnic and a runaround. Its history is interlinked with Milan's two powerful dynasties: the Visconti built it in the 14th century and the usurping Sforza remodelled it into a Renaissance palazzo in 1451–1466. It has been used as a barracks and was heavily bombed in 1943, when many treasures were destroyed.

If you haven't a picnic, you can grab a snack, ice cream or refreshment outside on Piazza Castello, near the Fascist-era 'wedding cake' fountain, or in the huge Piazza d'Armi within the walls – careful though, as some kiosk vendors here are notorious for being *furbi* (sly), so check your change. For some shade and culture, head for the arcaded Rocchetta courtyard, designed by Bramante and Filarete, which formed the keep – the most defended area of the castle. The tower here contains the **Museum of Decorative Arts and Instruments**, which has a compass by Galileo, a spinet played by Mozart and a ballroom hung with tapestries. Budding Egyptologists should descend into the basement to examine the sarcophagi and other funerary relics. The prehistoric section contains objects from the Golasecca culture and Roman times. To the right is the charming Corte Ducale, which leads to the Pinacoteca and **Museo d'Arte Antica**. Check out the tombs and armour collection in the Sala Verde, da Vinci-designed frescoes in Sale delle Asse and Michelangelo's unfinished *Rondanini Pieta* in the Sala degli Scarlioni.

Piazza Castello. (☎ 02-6208-3940). Free admission. Tues–Sun 9:30am–5:30pm. Metro: Cairoli, Cadorna or Lanza.

The lush expanse of **Parco Sempione** is a great place to unwind and have a picnic – the 47 hectares were laid out in

Castello Sforzesco

1893 and contain ponds, a playful fountain by De Chirico awaiting restoration, an equestrian statue of Napoleon by Barzaghi and the triumphal **Arco della Pace**, marking the 182 km-long Simplon Road to Geneva, brainchild of Napoleon. The **Arena Civica**, former home of the Internazionale football team, hosts cultural, sporting (mainly junior athletics) and musical events. Some *Milanesi* claim the park has an amorous black-veiled female ghost, *La Dama Nera*, who walks the park at night. A fine Art Nouveau building houses the sublime:

Aquario Civico AGES 4 AND UP re-opened after its recent centenary, with recreated aquatic environments filled with creatures from the marine depths of the Mediterranean to freshwater Lake Como. Its scope is not that of Genoa's famous aquarium, but it's well worth a look.

Viale Grado 2. (☎ 02-804-487). Admission free; Tue–Sun 9am–5:30pm; Metro: Lanza.

For innovative decorative arts and design shows, check out the **Triennale**, incorporating the Palazzo d'Arte (see below).

For a pigeon's eye view of the park and the surrounding city from a height of 108 metres, visit the:

Torre Branca AGES 7 AND UP (opened in 1933 on the occasion of the fifth Triennale exhibition): the lift takes you to the viewing platform in just 90 seconds.

Torre Branca, Viale Camoens, Parco Sempione. (☎ 02-33-4120). Admission: 3€ (£2) mid-April to October, Wed 10:30am–12:30pm, 4–6:30pm; Fri 2:30–6pm; Sat and Sun 10:30am–7:30pm. Evening openings Tue–Sun 9:30pm–1am. Metro: Cadorna.

La Triennale and Milanese Design ★ AGES 5 AND UP Milan has long been a leading light in the contemporary design world, from its modernist architecture like the **Pirelli building** in piazza Duca d'Aosta, to stylish household objects like the Arco lamp. There are lots of design-related exhibitions around town, especially during **Milan Design Week** in mid-April – check the Triennale for the latest programme details. You'll find classic Italian design by Alessi and Castiglione exhibited here alongside architecture retrospectives and cool shows like 2006's *Fumetto International* about comics. It also has a fine bookshop and the stylish Fiat Café lounge that extends into the park during the summer. Among the many design events is the **Salone Internazionale del Mobile and Euroluce**, the most influential furniture and lighting fair on the planet. If you have children over 10 who like funky shapes and cool objects, it's well worth a day out at the Fiera.

*Viale Alemagna 6. (☎ 02-724-341. **www.triennale.it**). Admission free for most shows. Tues–Sun 10.30am–8.30pm. Metro: Cadorna. Fiera Milano exhibition complex at*

Milan with a Pram/Stroller

Start at Piazza del Duomo, where you can shoo the pigeons and have a quick gander at the cathedral. Enter the Galleria Vittorio Emanuele II, gazing up at the impressive canopy, down at the colourful mosaics and sideways at the chattering Milanesi in the swank caffès. Have a giggle spinning on the shiny toro. Walk down pedestrianized Via Dante where there are often interesting stalls and street entertainment toward the chunky towers of the Castello Sforzesco. Pick up an ice-cream and a granita (slushy ice drink) from the vendors outside, but check your change as some of them are chancers. Explore the bumpy courtyards of the castle and then enjoy the verdant delights of the park, where you can play games, lounge around and have a stylish refuel at the Triennale Caffè.

*Rho-Pero. (☎ 027-25941. **www.cosmit.it**). Metro: Rho-Fiera*

Museo Nazionale della Scienza e della Tecnologia Leonardo da Vinci (Leonardo da Vinci National Museum of Science and Technology) ★

AGES 5 AND UP With interactive exhibits based on the inventions of da Vinci and the fantastic collection of gadgets, machinery and transport, it's ideal for most children. Ask for a workshop visit at the entrance and you'll be treated to a hands-on explanation of the master's experimental machines. You can have a go at beating a wing (*ala battente*) and raising some heavy sacks by working the revolving crane (*gru girevole*). The impressive aerial screw *(vite aerea)* is a forerunner of a helicopter's blades. Before going, have a look at the museum website for films and explanations of the inventions, as well as a 3-D perspective on his ideal city. Elsewhere on the large site you'll find exhibits showing the development of various technologies and materials, including the radio, clocks, cameras and plastics. Set aside plenty of time to explore the hangars and grounds filled with steam trains, fighter planes, historic ships and streamlined submarines that make up the Rail Transport Building and the Air & Sea Transport Building. You can also go back in time and

Leonardo Da Vinci Statue

HISTORY The Life and Legacies of da Vinci 

His long white beard and smock belie the coolness of Leonardo da Vinci. In severely conservative and superstitious 15th century Florence, to be left-handed, vegetarian and probably gay did not bode well. But Leonardo's erudite charm, comprehensive genius and deep humanity allowed him to develop new disciplines and ideas, as well as to create works of mesmerising beauty.

1452 Born in Anchiano, near Vinci (*da Vinci* means from Vinci) on 15th April, he was brought up by his father, a notary (solicitor). His curiosity and deftness at drawing and ability to turn his hand to anything were recognised from an early age.

1466 to 1476 At the age of 14 he was apprenticed to the leading Florentine painter and sculptor, Andrea del Verrochio. As a studio boy he would assist in the preparation of canvases and paints, as well as learning to work with marble and bronze, and he taught himself to paint in oils. His time served in 1476, he went on to open his own workshop and take on his own apprentices.

1476 Following an anonymous accusation (put into a box or *tamburo* outside Florence's Palazzo Vecchio), Leonardo was arrested and held for two months for having an alleged homosexual affair with one of his models. He was acquitted.

1482 Painted the *Adoration of the Magi* at the monastery of San Donato a Scopeto, near Florence. Not really finished due to being...

1482 Appointed as painter to Ludovico Sforza, the Duke of Milan, a position he would hold for 17 years. This was his most productive period, both scientifically and artistically. The Duke called upon him to conceive elaborate pageants and festivals; design weapons of war (he rustled up a machine gun, the cluster bomb, an armoured tank and a submarine); amazing inventions (such as the deep-water diving suit, the aeroplane and the helicopter); beautiful buildings (with all the hoist, cranes and scaffolding needed to build them); and labour-saving machinery (the calculator and the cranked flywheel). Leonardo also produced his first anatomical studies.

1495 Leonardo began to keep notebooks of his ideas (and occasionally shopping lists) – all beautifully illustrated. To keep them private and stop some of the ideas from slipping into the wrong hands, he wrote them backwards using a mirror. Some of these can be found in the Louvre in Paris and, handily, Milan's Biblioteca Ambrosiana (Piazza Pio XI, 2 open Tues – Sun 10.00am–5.30pm) which exhibits the *Codice Atlantico*, a must for budding and fledged engineers, every year.

1498 After three years (quite quick for Leonardo), he completed the *Last Supper* in the refectory of Santa Maria delle Grazie. The prior of the convent was somewhat annoyed at how long Leonardo was taking, but his threat to use the nagging monk's likeness for the image of Judas secured him the time he needed to complete it.

1499 The Sforzas of Milan were routed by the French and Leonardo travelled around Italy looking for work. Commissions from the bloodthirsty Cesare Borgia – for weaponry of course – and a bridge to span the Bosphorus in Constantinople were the highlights. A version of the latter has been built in Norway almost 500 years after Leonardo designed it.

1504 His father Ser Piero died and his siblings deprived him of his inheritance.

1506 Leonardo completed the *Mona Lisa*. This is said to be one of the finest examples of the two new painting techniques he developed: *chiaroscuro* (using light and shade to define a form – look at her hands) and *sfumato* (subtle gradations in tone and colour, creating a hazy, smoky effect – look at her robes).

1511–1516 He spent three years in the Vatican. Banned from dissecting bodies, he turned his energies to developing solar power using concave mirrors to heat water.

1516–1519 When his patron, Giuliano de Medici, died, King Francis 1 of France took him on as 'Premier Painter, Engineer and Architect'. He and his *Mona Lisa* moved to Clos Luicé in Amboise and whilst his health was fading, he enjoyed a comfortable existence, which allowed him to continue teaching and drawing. Leonardo died on the 2nd May 1519 and was interred in the chapel that adjoins Château Amboise.

---

enter an old violin workshop, explore the world of navigation and life onboard a ship. If you don't have a picnic packed, there's a small café.

*Via San Vittore 21. (02-485-551 or 02-4801-0016. **www.museoscienza.org**). Admission: 6.20€ (£4.15) adults, 4.20€ (£2.80) younger than 18 and older than 60. Tues–Fri 9:30am–5pm; Sat–Sun 9:30am–6:30pm. Metro: Sant'Ambrogio.*

Cimiterio Monumentale FIND

ALL AGES It may not be an obvious choice, but Milan's grand cemetery (opened in 1866) is worth a visit for its stupendous monuments, mixing overblown

Leonardo da Vinci Museum of Science and Technology

displays of status with emotional poignancy conveyed through exquisite sculpture. Children who like to be spooked will love the atmosphere here, in the cold months especially.

Piazzale del Cimitero Monumentale. (☎ 02-8591-0419). Admission free. Tue–Sun 8:30am–5:30pm; Metro: Garibaldi.

More Churches, Parks, Museums & Ancient Wonders

Basilica di Sant'Ambrogio

AGES 5 AND UP It's well worth having a look at this beautiful Lombard church if you're near the da Vinci museum. It was founded in 379 by Saint Ambrose, Archbishop and patron saint of Milan, whose influence and eloquence were such that bees were said to fly into his mouth. The skeleton of Ambrose lies in the crypt. The 11th century structure set the standard for the Lombard Romanesque style, much copied in the region. Look out for the gold altar dating from the brief period when Charlemagne ruled the Western Roman Empire from the city. The small museum contains frescoes, tapestries and early Christian mosaics. On 7th December, the city celebrates with **La Festa di Sant'Ambrogio**: religious ceremonies take place here and more raucous *Oh Bei Oh Bei* street parties across the city.

Piazza Sant'Ambrogio 15. (☎ 02-8645-0895). Church: Free admission. Sacello di San Vittore: 2€ (£1.34). Mon–Sat 9:30am–noon and 2:30–6pm. Metro: Sant'Ambrogio.

Chiesa di San Lorenzo Maggiore

AGES 5 AND UP This 4th century octagonal basilica (rebuilt in the 12th and 16th centuries) is the oldest and most evocative in Milan. It's full of Roman relics including sixteen Corinthian columns lining the front, the remains of an amphitheatre and fine mosaics adorning the Chapel of St Aquilinus. Take a break in the attractive **Parco delle Basiliche** with its playgrounds, pastures and volleyball courts. If you still have an appetite for ecclesiastical ephemera, head towards the **Chiesa di Sant'Eustorgio** and the **Museo Diocesano**, at the southernmost tip of the park. Sant'Eustorgio (originally 11th century with many alterations, including a 19th century façade) has Milan's highest campanile and an early Christian cemetery beneath the nave. The museum brings together many collections and sacred objects from the Diocese of Milan.

*Corso di Porta Ticinese 39. No phone. **www.sanlorenzomaggiore.com**. Admission: 2€ (£1.34) adults, 1€ (£0.67) children. Mon–Sat 8am–12:30pm and 2–6:30pm; Sun 10:30–11:15am and 3–5:30pm. Metro: Missori.*

Chiesa Santa Maria Presso San Satiro

AGES 5 AND UP Renaissance architect Bramante created a magical illusion of space with his trompe l'oeil apse of arches, columns and dome in this beguiling church, dedicated to Saint Ambrose's brother. In the 13th and 14th centuries, word spread throughout Christendom that an image of the Madonna shed blood here, making it a magnet for pilgrims – a far cry from the shopping frenzy of present-day Via Torino outside. Look out for the terracotta Pietà by Agostino de Fondutis and a 13th century fresco on the high altar.

Via Torino. Free admission. Daily 9am–noon and 2:30–6pm. Metro: Missori or Duomo.

Civico Museo Archeologico AGES 5 AND UP All manner of objects from Roman-era Milan are crammed into this 16th century monastery building on Corso Magenta – there are even remnants of Mediolanum, the capital of the Western Roman Empire, around the back – not to be confused with the Berlusconi-owned bank that once sponsored his AC Milan team. Soak up the history of Greek, Etruscan and Ghandaran (North Indian) civilizations in the other fascinating sections – and it's free!

Corso Magenta 15. (☎ 02-8645-0011). Free admission. Tues–Sun 9:30am–5:30pm. Metro: Cadorna.

Giardini Pubblici, Palazzo Dugnani and Cinema Museum AGES 5 AND UP Need a breather from the crowds and fumes? The public gardens have lakes with ducks, lawns, flowerbeds, monuments, the occasional cultural event and some fine attractions to visit. The 18th century Palazzo Dugnani has frescoes by Tiepolo, and the Museo del Cinema has old projectors and apparatus designed by the Lumière brothers. If you are smitten by celluloid fever, they have an eclectic programme of film screenings, including cartoons for children at the weekend.

*Palazzo Dugnani/Museo del Cinema, Via Manin 2. (☎ 02-655-4977. **www.cinetecamilano.it/museo**). Admission: 3€ (£2) adults, 1.50€ (£1) children. Fri–Sun 3–6pm; Screenings 4pm and 5pm: phone to book seats. Metro: Turati or Palestro.*

Museo di Storia Naturale and Planetarium AGES 4 AND UP Perhaps more stimulating for children is the nearby Natural History Museum, the best of its kind in Italy. Walk amongst the dinosaurs (spot the tyrannosaurus), reptiles, plants, minerals and fossils. The largest sulphur crystal in the world and massive precious stones can be seen in the sparkling mineral collection. Reach for the stars through a telescope at the

Giardini Pubblici

Planetarium next door, which has interactive visits for children (*02-2953-1181* for latest programme).

Corso Venezia 55. (02-8846-3280). Admission free Tue–Sun 9:30am–6pm. Metro: Palestro.

Civica Galleria d'Arte Moderna AGES 5 AND UP The Civic Gallery of Modern Art housed in Villa Reale, where Napoleon once resided, shows the evolution of modern Italian art. Some of this is not quite 'Modern Art' as Brits know it, with works by Canova, Hayez, Carrà, Severini, de Chirico, Morandi and Fontana. For horsey types, there is an equestrian sculpture by Marini. Household names from the famous Grassi collection are on show, including Van Gogh, Gaughin, Lautrec and Cezanne. English Romantic-style gardens and lakes to the rear act as a venue for summer concerts and cultural events. Children must be accompanied by an adult.

Villa Reale, Via Palestro 16. (02-7600-2819). Free admission. Daily 9:30am–5:30pm. Metro: Porta Venezia.

High Art near the Duomo

Pinacoteca Ambrosiana AGES 5 AND UP It's a bit pricey but there are many artistic treasures to gaze over at this recently restored and highly celebrated gallery and library – the collection (24 rooms and over 1500 works) contains works by Botticelli, Titian, Raphael, Caravaggio and Appiani. A work (*Portrait of a Musician*) attributed to Leonardo is believed in many quarters to be really by Gaffurio – judge for yourself. Amongst the wonderful objets d'art is a reliquary containing a lock of Lucrezia Borgia's hair: Lord Byron is said to have acquired a few strands to send to his half-sister and lover Augusta Leigh. The library contains thousands of precious manuscripts, including Leonardo's *Codice Atlantico*, 1750 drawings and sketches made between 1478 and 1519.

*Piazza Pio XI 2. (02-809-921. **www.ambrosiana.it**). Admission: 7.50€ (£5) adults, 4.50€ (£3) children. Tues–Sun 10am–5pm. Metro: Cordusioor Duomo.*

Museo Poldi-Pezzoli AGES 5 AND UP Renowned 19th century art lover Giacomo Poldi-Pezzoli filled the variously styled salons here (from Baroque to Rococo) with art and objects from his collection. He bequeathed his residence to the city in 1881. Despite severe damage caused by World War II bombing, this house-museum contains many beautiful and enigmatic works, including Antonio Pollaiuolo's *Ritratto di Dama* (*Portrait of a Young Woman*).

*Via Manzoni 12. (02-794-889. **www.museopoldipezzoli.it**). Admission: 6.20€ (£4.15) adults, 4€ (£2.70) for 11–18-year-olds and those older than 60. Tues–Sun 10am–6pm. Metro: Duomo or Montenapoleone.*

Sport & Games

The city's two top football clubs, AC Milan and Internazionale (or Inter – never Inter Milan), play at the imposing 85,000-capacity:

Stadio Meazza ★ AGES 6 AND UP (aka San Siro). In 1908, Inter was established at a meeting of the more cosmopolitan members of the British-formed Milan Cricket and Football Club (now AC Milan) at the Orologio restaurant near the Duomo. The breakaway *nerazzuri* played at the Arena Civica until after World War II, when they began sharing a *campo sportivo* in the northern suburb of San Siro with their rivals (*i rossoneri*). The stadium was refurbished for World Cup Italia '90, when the distinctive cylindrical towers were added. Tickets for the cavernous stadium, renowned for its atmospheric steep curve, fireworks, smoke and colossal flags are available at club outlets and on the club websites. For less attractive fixtures you can pick them up at two ticket offices near the stadium, by gates 26 and 36.

AC's ultras (most notorious fans and hooligans) occupy the lower section of Curva Sud; the Interisti fill Curva Nord and the away fans at Inter games the Curva Sud (Gates 13 and 14). You're best to avoid these areas with children, as the smoke and boisterous behaviour might spoil the spectacle. The **San Siro Tour and Museum** (Gate 21, open daily 10am–5pm, matchday opening times vary) recounts the clubs' illustrious history and gives football fans the chance to see trophies, memorabilia and even life-size statues of Gianni Rivera, Karl Heinz Rummenigge, Marco Van Basten and Ruud Gullit. The shop is stacked with merchandise. On matchdays there is a free shuttle bus from metro stop Lotto or take tram 16 outside De Angelli metro. There are no shuttle buses after the match. There is however a large car park next to the Lampugnano metro station on Via Giulio Natta.

FUN FACT

Parliamo Calcio – footie talk

per che squadra tifi? what team do you support?

dai! forza ragazzi! come on! come on boys!

tira! shoot!

fuorigioco! offside!

l'arbitro è cieco! the referee is blind!

rigore! penalty!

un tunnel! nutmeg!

si è tuffato! he dived!

chi ha mangiato tutte le torte? who ate all the pies?

*Stadio Giuseppe Meazza, Via Piccolomini. Metro: Lotto. AC Milan tickets available at Cariplo bank branches: Via Verdi 8. Metro: Duomo; Inter tickets available at Banca Popolare di Milano. Piazza Meda 4. Metro: San Babila. Tickets can also be purchased at **www.acmilan.com** and **www.inter.it**.*

Ippodromo and Ippolandia ★

FIND AGES 6 AND UP Close to the Meazza stadium is the Ippodromo, home of horse and chariot racing, with its own sprawling bouncy castles, games area (Ippolandia), botanical gardens, fine Ristorante Lorenzo and al fresco Cheval Café centred around a handsome liberty-style palazzo. In the courtyard stands a massive equestrian sculpture, Il Cavallo, which was unveiled in 1999, exactly 500 years after French archers used and abused Leonardo da Vinci's original clay model. For a day out at the races, check the Ippodromo website and the magazine *Gallopo e Trotto* (**www.gaet.it**) for upcoming meetings. Expect fancy hats adorned with flowers for the big race meetings, the Gran Premio di Milano in June and the

L'Ippodromo

Jockey Club in October. Tickets from 20 €.

Piazzale dello Sport 6. Metro: Lotto and then 1 km walk.

Idro Park All ages. Centred around the idroscalo artificial lake, near Linate airport, the Idro Park is a great place to make a splash with its various water sports, beaches and sports activities. Activities include free climbing, mountain biking, nature walks, sailing, canoeing, swimming, tennis, fishing, inline skating and boating. Smaller children can bounce around in the Dolly Park, which brims with inflatables and games.

Via Circonvallazione, Peschiera Borromeo. (☎ 02-7020-0902/8388) 9am–9pm, Sat 2pm–9pm. To reach the lake, take Autolinea bus 73 from San Babila metro (Corso Europa).

Shopping

Quadrilatero d'oro (Golden Quadrilateral)

This is the priciest but certainly the most inspiring zone, with fabulous creations by Armani, Versace and Gianfranco Ferré that leave you awestruck.

Via Monte Napoleone, Via Sant'Andrea, Via Borgospesso and Via della Spiga. Metro: San Babila, Montenapoleone

Armani Megastore ★ This is a must; 8000 square feet with outlets for every line, including Armani Casa; flower, book and art shops; an electronics boutique; the Emporio Café; and a branch of New York's Nobu sushi bar.

Via Manzoni 31 (☎ 02-7231-8630).

Others worth a look, even in the window, are:

Dolce e Gabbana

*Womenswear at Via della Spiga no. 2 (☎ 02-7600-1155. **www.dolcegabbana.it**); menswear at Via della Spiga no. 26 (☎ 02-799-950); and its diffusion lines at Venezia 7 (☎ 02-7600-4091).*

Fendi

*Via Sant'Andrea 16 (☎ 02-7602-1617. **www.fendi.com**).*

Ferragamo

*Via Montenapoleone 20 (☎ 02-7600-3117. **www.ferragamo.it**); shoes at Via Montenapoleone 3 (☎ 02-7600-0054).*

Gianfranco Ferré

*Womenswear at Via Sant'Andrea 15 (☎ 02-794-864. **www.gianfrancoferre.com**), menswear at Corso Venezia 6.*

Fiorucci

Younger ladies will be mesmerised by the window here. Highly imaginative clothing at surprisingly decent prices.

Galleria Passarella 2 (☎ 02-7602-2452).

Gucci

*Via Montenapoleone 5–7, (☎ 02-771-271 **www.gucci.com**).*

Missoni

*Via Sant'Andrea at Via Bagutta, (☎ 02-7600-3555, **www.missoni.com**).*

Miu Miu

*Corso Venezia 3, (☎ 02-7601-4448, **www.miumiu.com**).*

Moschino

*Via Durini 14 (☎ 02-7600-4320) and Via Sant'Andrea 12 (☎ 02-7600-0832. **www.moschino.com**).*

Prada

*Womenswear at Via Sant'Andrea 21 (☎ 02-7600-1426 **www.prada.com**); Galleria Vittorio Emanuele 63 (☎ 02-876-979) underwear at Via della Spiga 5 (☎ 02-7601-4448); menswear at Via Montenapoleone 8 (☎ 02-7602-0273); bags, shoes and accessories at Via della Spiga 1 (☎ 02-7600-8636).*

Versace

*Via Montenapoleone 11, (☎ 02-7600-1982; **www.versace.com**).*

Sports and Toy Shops

Milan has some top-quality sports superstores and toy shops filled with weird and wonderful *giocattoli:*

Adidas

Corso Buenos Aires 88 ☎ 02-29523730

Cerchio Magico

(Toys and Games) Via Vincenzo Monti 41 (☎ 02-4692293

Decathlon

(Sportswear) Foro Buonaparte 7420121 ☎ 02- 8050-9755.

TofyToys

(Toys, Games and Models) Via Ruffini 9 ☎ 02-469-4776

Discount Shopping

You can still grab a bargain in the Quadrilatero d'Oro. Two of the best discount stores are:

Il Salvagente

Via Fratelli Bronzetti 16 (☎ 02-7611-0328).

DMagazine

Via Montenapoleone 26 (☎ 02-7600-6027).

TIP The right way to shop Milan

Shows Every January/February, June and October the city bursts with excitement when the world's highest ranking *fashionistas* descend on the city for the ready-to-wear designer shows.

Sales Bargain-hunting seasons are in mid-January and again in mid-July, when everything, steeply discounted, flies off the shelves.

Opening Some shops are moving to staying open all day, but generally the times are 9am–1pm and 4–7:30pm. Many are closed on Monday morning and in August.

Debit or credit card? Almost every shop of repute will take a credit or debit card (Switch/Maestro), but to avoid the chance of finding unwanted purchases on your next statement, stick to using these in the big names or respectable boutiques.

TIP Milan's Markets

Via Papiniano, Navigli (Metro: Porta Genova)
Tuesday mornings. Saturday flea market all day: antique–junk, alternative paraphernalia and clothing at rock bottom prices.

Mercatone dell'Antiquario, Naviglio Grande
Last Sunday of each month, all day: big antiques market.

Via Armorari, Off Piazza Cordusio (Metro: Cordusio)
Sunday morning: coin, stamp and ephemera collectors' paradise. (Metro: Cordusio)

Via Fiori Chiari, Brera (Metro: Moscova)
Third Sunday of each month, all day: antiques, collectables, jewellery and beads.

If you want style and utility, you'll have heard about:

Alessi who have worked with the likes of Philippe Starck and Frank Gehry to create kettles, pepper grinders and eggcups that are as wonderful to look at as to use.

*Main showroom on Corso Matteotti 9 (☎ 02-795-726. **www.alessi.com**); there's an outlet at Via Montenapoleone 19 (☎ 02-7602-1199).*

Corso Buenos Aires

North of the Giardini Pubblici is less upmarket but still heaving with choice and better prices than those in the city centre. (Metro: Lima and Loreto.)

Discount stores where you can pick up something wonderful with a label for a fraction of the price include:

Darsena

Corso Buenos Aires 16, (☎ 02-2952-1535).

Il Drug Store

Corso Buenos Aires 28, (☎ 02-2951-5592).

And for shoes:

Calzaturificio di Parabiago,

Corso Buenos Aires 52, (☎ 02-2940-6851).

Brera

The narrow streets of Via Brera, Via Solferino, Corso Garibaldi and Via Paolo Sarpi are packed with one-off boutiques, crafts and antique shops (Metro: Garibaldi and Lanza). Look out for:

Corso Como 10
This is a gallery, café and shop selling oh-so-stylish bags, home furnishings and trinkets.

Corso Como 10, (☎ 02-2900-2674).

Eclectica
You may find Georgio Armani himself here being inspired by

the myriad of **African and Asian Furnishings and Homewares**

Corso Garibaldi 3, (☎ 02-876-194).

Navigli

Both sides of the Naviglio Grande, on Via Ripa di Porta Ticinese, are packed with the weird and the wonderful. Children will love the games, comics and toy shops, whilst parents, and young girls, will love the vintage fashion, curiosities and bookshops, all of which are never more than a stride from a café.

SuperGulp
Boys of all ages will love this shop filled with masses of games, comics and role-play figurines.

Via Ripa di Porta Ticinese, 57, (☎ 02-837-2216).

Cafés, Snacks and Family-Friendly Dining

Milan is notoriously expensive compared to other parts of Italy, and dining near the Duomo can offer little value for money, especially for families. The best option is to escape the commercial hub and gullible tourists by hopping on the Metro, or better still, taking a cab to where *Milanesi* eat.

Light Bites

Caffè Miani in the Galleria is the place to sample a Campari and soda, and children will love the snacks here.

Metro: Duomo

Jamaica is the historic epicentre of the arty, Boho scene in Brera – it was also frequented by Mussolini in the 1920s.

Via Brera, 32. Metro: Lanza.

Navigli Flea Market

Sottosopra FIND

Funky chairs overlooking the canal and tasty *piadine* (rolled flat bread with various fillings) make this a great place to chill and chat.

Alzaia Naviglio Grande 56. Metro: Porta Genova.

Luini Panzerotti For snacks near the Duomo, try this Milanese takeaway institution serving crunchy *panini* and tasty pizza pockets (*panzerotti*) with various gooey fillings.

Via Radegonda 16. Metro: Duomo.

Milan's best pastries are at:

Marchesi

Corso Magenta 13. Metro: Cadorna and

Cova

Via Montenapoleone 8. Metro: Montenapoleone.

For **ice-cream**, try:

Toldo in Brera

Via Ponte Venero 9. Metro: Lanza and

Ecologica, which has organic *gelati*.

Corso di Porta Ticenese 40. Metro: Sant'Ambrogio

Gourmet food and picnic snacks can be found at:

Peck

Via Spadari 9. Metro: Duomo and:

Il Salumaio

Via Montenapoleone 12. Metro: Montenapoleone.

Near Stazione Centrale

L'Osteria del Treno MILANESE The outside may not look encouraging, but the Belle Époque style furnishings and tranquil courtyard make it a real find. While railway workers play cards in a side room, the friendly staff will educate your taste buds with their cheese and cold-meat platters – the osteria is a Slow Food member, so expect the best Lombardy produce. A good selection of pasta dishes should satisfy the pickiest of children's palates, while the more mature, discerning and wallet-carrying can savour the steak, duck and fish creations. Lunchtimes can get very busy, but it is worth considering for set menu deals.

Via Gregorio 46. (☎ 02-670-0479). Primi 8€–13€ (£5.35–8.70), Secondi 10€–17€ (£6.70–11.40). AE, MC, V. 12:30–2:30pm and 7–11.30pm. Metro: Centrale F.S.

Pizzeria Spontini ★ PIZZA This no-nonsense pizzeria with authentic wood-fired oven has been open since 1953 and its great value *pizza al trancio* (by the slice) heaped with mozzarella is a sure-fire family hit. The menu is simple – *trancio normale* or *abbondante*: normal or larger with extra cheese. A filling slice costs 4.50€ (£3). Otherwise, they serve mozzarella and Lasagne dishes at lunchtimes only. The choice of wines, beers and soft drinks is equally concise, but ample.

*Corso Buenos Aires 60. (☎ 02-204-7444. **www.pizzeriaspontini.it**). Highchairs. No credit cards. 11:45am–2:15pm, 6pm –11pm (12.30am Sat). Metro: Lima.*

Brera & Environs

Taverna del Gran Sasso ★★

FIND ABRUZZESE This family favourite has bags of rustic charm from the agricultural paraphernalia that fills the walls to the hearty fayre. The friendly crowd has been tucking in here since 1962: expect classic antipasti like *bruschette* and meaty mountain dishes of lamb, pork or chicken served with roast potatoes. Among the fun and flavoursome *primi* are *Spaghetti alla chitarra* (guitar-string pasta with tomato sauce) and risotto with aubergine and provolone cheese. Steak eaters can watch their meat sizzle on the grill. Reservations are a must.

Piazzale Principessa Clotilde 10. (☎ 02-659-7578). Highchairs. 12:30–2:30pm and 7:30pm–1am. Primi 7€–14€ (£4.70–9.40). Secondi 9€–17€ (£6–11.40). AE, DC, MC, V. Metro: Repubblica.

La Terrazza PASTA/FISH For a relaxed dining experience and rare views of the Giardini Pubblici and beyond, take the lift to the sixth floor of the Hotel Galles. During the day it's a wonderful place for dining, especially with older children and teens. At night, cocktails and candlelight make it an atmospheric venue. Alongside traditional pasta dishes, the Terrazza specialises in innovative fish creations like Trota alle mandorle in salsa di crema (trout with almonds in a creamy sauce). Reservations are recommended.

*Via Palestro 2. (☎ 02-7600-2186. **www.hotelgalles.com**). Set menus 35€–107€ (£23.50–71.70). AE, DC, MC, V. 12:30–2:30pm and 7–10pm. Sat and Sun: brunch only. Metro: Palestro.*

Trattoria del Carmine

PASTA/PIZZA/VEGETARIAN Just outside the bland banking district, life resumes at this Brera trattoria, which has covered seating on the intimate piazza in front of the Santa Maria del Carmine church. The service can be a little slow but the fresh food and location make up for it: they serve wonderful fresh salads in huge bowls, pizzas, seafood and a good selection of pasta dishes. Children like the simplicity of the *penne* with aubergines and tomatoes, or the cheesy fillings of the *tortellini di ricotta*. For picnic ingredients, or merely an interesting eyeful, there's a fabulous *salumeria* nearby, as well as a fishmonger's (Da Claudio) and friendly greengrocer's (Orto) around the corner on Via Ponte Vetero.

Piazza del Carmine 1. (☎ 02-8646-1234). Highchairs. Primi 8€–14€ (£5.35–9.40). Secondi 10€–17€ (£6.70–11.40). AE, DC, MC, V. 12:30pm–2:30pm, 8pm–11.30pm. Metro: Lanza.

Further Out but Worth the Journey

Anema e Cozze ★★ NEAPOLITAN: SEAFOOD/PIZZA This restaurant chain's jovial atmosphere, authentic Southern dishes and nautical-themed rooms make a visit an enlivening epicurean experience. On the *lista di pizze* are the *'A Rezza* (with tomatoes, prawns, mussels, clams, squid, octopus and rocket), fit for a Pliny the Elder, and *'O Purpo* (small tomatoes, octopus, black olives, basil) more suited to a Pliny the Younger. They do a fabulous *babà* pastry and the lunchtime fixed menu at 11.50€ (£7.70) is a steal. There are also a branch on Via Palermo 15 (Metro: Moscova).

Via Casale 7. (☎ 02-837-5459). Highchairs. Primi 6€–12€ (£4–8). Secondi 7€–17€ (£4.70–11.40). AE, DC, MC, V. 12:30–3pm and 7:30–midnight. Metro: Porta Genova.

Angelo Azzurro PIZZA/FISH A little out of town, towards Aeroporto Linate, but a warm Sicilian welcome, fantastic food and value, makes Angelo worth the effort. Their fresh fish (often swordfish and sea bass) should more than satisfy the adults, and the *pizza al taglio* (long pizzas with lots of topping options) will keep children busy. Sublime sweets include *Torta alle pere e alla nutella* (pear and nutella cakes). A veranda is open in the summer.

Via Battistotti Sassi 14. (☎ 02-719-350). Highchairs. Primi 7€–11€ (£4.70–7.40). Secondi 7€–19€ (£4.70–12.75). AE, DC, MC, V. 12:30–3pm and 7:30–midnight. Closed Tue, Sat Lunch. Bus: 27, 45 or 73.

Don Juan ARGENTINIAN Italy's best Argentinian restaurant and much-lauded grill serves mighty hunks of meat alongside lush salads, deliciously filled *empanadas* (pastry pies) and simply prepared vegetable side dishes. Its warm-hued South American décor is a favourite with footballers' families – the staff are very helpful and there is an excellent menu for *bambini.* Remember that a medium here is pretty raw for many in the English-speaking world, so specify *ben cotto* if you don't like your meat bloody. Children will love the *alfajores* cakes – be warned though: they are very rich.

*Via Altaguardia. (☎ 02-5843-0805. **www.ristorantedonjuan.com**). Highchairs. Primi 9€–14€ (£6–9.40), Secondi 9€–25€ (£6–16.75). AE, DC, MC, V. 7:30pm–0:30am. Closed August. Metro: Porta Romana.*

Galleria Restaurants

Family-Friendly Accommodation

There may be fewer foreign tourists than many other Italian cities, but Milan is often swelled with visitors attending trade fairs or cultural and sporting events. It is essential to reserve well in advance between March and October, and recommended at other times. Although staying near the Duomo is preferable for those seeking to do their main sightseeing on foot, other areas provide better value.

Near the Duomo

VERY EXPENSIVE

Park Hyatt ★★★ The Hyatt offers a haven of calm in a palatial building next door to the Galleria – so you get luxury, concierge service and the main sights on your doorstep. The circular main public area is reminiscent of the fabulous Art Deco space at Eltham Palace in Surrey so beloved of film producers – this skylit lounge in the old courtyard is a special place to relax and plan trips. Guest rooms are sumptuous and huge, so adding a bed or cot is not a problem. Bathrooms are equally impressive. Children will love the state-of-the-art gadgets and parents may want to use the spa and fitness centre downstairs. Ask for a room overlooking the Galleria.

*Via Tomasso Grossi 1, 20121. (☎ 02-8821-1234; fax: 02-8821-1235; **www.milan.park.hyatt.com**). 117 units. 470€ (£315) Double; 570€ (£382) Triple. Rates include breakfast. AE, DC, MC, V. 25 parking spaces in nearby garage. Amenities: babysitting; bar; concierge; dry cleaning; laundry service; gym and spa; restaurant; In room: A/C, cable TV, dataport, minibar, morning newspaper, safe. Metro: Duomo.*

MODERATE

Hotel Ambasciatori This hotel's entrance may be oddly placed in a shopping centre, smack in the centre of town near the Duomo, but the Ambasciatori offers practical benefits for those travelling with children. Rooms have patterned furnishings and en suite bathrooms that are ample for Milan. Connecting rooms are available. For excellent offers on family-friendly Junior Suites, including huge weekend discounts, book online.

*Milano Galleria del Corso 3, 20122. (☎ 02-7602-0241; [fax] 02-782-700; **www.ambasciatorihotel.it**). 93 units. 170–220€ (£114–147.40) Double; 170–350€ (£114–234.50) Junior Suite sleeping 1–2 adults and 1—2 children. Rates include buffet breakfast. AE, DC, MC, V. Amenities: concierge. In room: A/C, hairdryer, minibar, Internet, TV. Metro: Duomo/San Babila.*

Brera & Environs

MODERATE

Antica Locanda Leonardo This charismatic hotel down a cobbled lane, beloved of Marcello Mastroianni and *fashionistas*, has comfortable family accommodation in its rooms and small apartments. The bathrooms are a little small and there isn't a minibar in sight, but the atmosphere is welcoming and the location is great for shopping and sightseeing. For a quiet stay ask for a room overlooking the courtyard. As there is no breakfast room, everyone gets continental *colazione* in bed, which is always a treat.

*Via Castelfilardo 2, 20121. (☎ 02-657-0129; fax: 02-657-1361; **www.anticalocandasolferino.it**). 11 units. 150–250€ (£100–167.50) Double; 200–270€ (£134–181) Triple; 250–290€ (£167.50–194.30) Quad. Rates include continental breakfast. AE, MC, V. Amenities: car hire; concierge; laundry and dry cleaning service; In room: A/C (2 rooms), hairdryer, Internet, TV. Metro: Moscova.*

MODERATE

Hotel Lancaster Located in an elegant Belle Époque palazzo near Parco Sempione, this is well-placed for active children and the many attractions nearby. Cadorna metro is a 15-minute walk away, so take a cab (about 10€ (£6.70)) if you have heavy luggage. Rooms have been recently refurbished and the bathrooms are a decent size and well maintained. The English-speaking staff are very helpful, and provide cots free of charge.

Via Abbondio Sangiorgio, 16 20145. (☎ 02-344-705; [fax] 02-344-649). 30 units. 150–205€ (£100–137.35) Double; 200–250€ (£134–167.50) Triple; 250–290€ (£167.50–194.30) Quad. Rates include continental breakfast. AE, DC, MC, V. Amenities: bar; concierge; garage; laundry service; In room: A/C, dataport, hairdryer, minibar, safe, TV. Metro: Cadorna.

Stazione Centrale & Corso Buenos Airies

EXPENSIVE

Staranderson ★ This recently renovated modern building just over the road from Stazione Centrale houses a stylish boutique hotel offering convenience and understated luxury. There are quality fixtures and fittings throughout, from the cotton sheets to mini-TVs in the sleek bathrooms. The lounge bar has an adjoining library, a great place to relax after a long day sightseeing or travelling. Ask for a room on the upper floors, as there are rumbling noises from the nearby station. The rooms are fantastic but a little small to add an extra bed, so it's suitable for those with travel cots, or when two doubles are required. Although not quite as snazzy, sister hotel Starhotels Rosa near the Duomo (Via Pattari 5) has more room options for adding extra beds and cots for babies.

*Piazza Luigi di Savoia 20, 20124. (☎ 02-669-0141; [fax] 02-669-0331; **www.starhotels.com**). 106 units. 160–350€ (£107–234.50) Double. Rates include breakfast. AE, DC, MC, V. Parking 25 places. Amenities: babysitting; bar; concierge; dry cleaning; laundry service; gym; restaurant; Wi-Fi. In room: A/C, cable TV, minibar, safe. Metro: Centrale F.S.*

MODERATE

Hotel Terminal Close to the Stazione Centrale, the newly fitted-out Terminal offers great value for Milan and excellent transport links to boot. The simply furnished rooms are clean with wooden flooring and modern bathrooms. The bar and other public areas are great for families to relax in, and there is decent access for the disabled. For a 30% surcharge you can add an extra bed.

Via Ponte Seveso 38, 20124 (☎ 02-6671-1381; [fax] 02-6707-8366; ***www.hotelterminalmilano.com****). 42 units. 110–240€ (£73.70–161) Double; 150–300€ (£100–200) Triple. Rates include continental breakfast. AE, DC, MC, V. Amenities: bar; garage. In room: A/C, dataport, minibar, safe, TV. Metro: Centrale F.S.*

INEXPENSIVE

Hotel Del Corso ★ FIND This brand new hotel has immaculate minimalist rooms and bathrooms. It's very near Stazione Centrale and is well positioned for visiting the public gardens and heading toward the major sights. Public areas, including the breakfast area, are clean, sleek and enjoyable to spend time in. Their clearly laid out and easy-to-use website has a special direct booking engine for making reservations with children, and excellent offers and last-minute deals.

Via Pecchio, 2 20131 (☎ 02-2953-3330; fax: 02-2953-3302; ***www.hoteldelcorsomilan.com****) 70–90€ (£47–60) Double; 90–110€ (£60–73.70) Triple. Rates include continental breakfast. AE, DC, MC, V. Amenities: bar; garage; Internet; laundry and ironing service; In room: A/C, hairdryer, minibar, safe, TV. Metro: Loreto.*

PAVIA

This former Lombard capital on the river Ticino is famed for its fine medieval churches, grand *palazzi*, 14th century university and the magnificent charterhouse (**Certosa di Pavia**) on its northern fringes. You can easily spend a half a day exploring the cobbled streets between the Visconti castle to the north and the Ponte Coperto, the covered bridge straddling the river to the south. The **Castello Visconti** is worth a quick look for its fine courtyard – the antiques and art inside do not warrant a long visit. The university (founded in 1387) district has three 11th century towers, some very beguiling courtyards and the **Museo per la Storia dell' Università di Pavia**, which concentrates on the establishment's illustrious departments of medicine and physics. Check out the anatomical theatre where gruesome practices took place under the knife of surgeon Antonio Scarpa – although a celebrated figure, one of his students held a grudge against him and decapitated his dead body. Carry on down the **Strada Nuova** to the elongated and elegant **Piazza Vittoria** where you can visit the 12th century **Broletto** (town hall) and get refreshments in one of the cafés. The usual *maestri* suspects Bramante and Leonardo contributed to the design of the nearby **Duomo** (with Italy's third-largest dome). The elaborately ornamented church of

San Michele (off Via Capsoni) has an octagonal cupola and fine sculptural details. For a walk along the attractive **Lungoticino** riverbank, head for the **Ponte Coperto**, which is a replacement of the original 14th century bridge that collapsed in 1947. If you fancy a wander in the woods, there are many nature reserves near Pavia: ask at the tourist office (see below) for maps of the **Parco del Ticino**, **Parco del Vernavolo** and **Bosco Grande**. For a quality meal (including mushroom risotto, rabbit and yummy desserts) down by the river try Osteria della Malora *(Via Milazzo 79. ✆ 0382-34302. AE, MC, V. primi 7€–10€, Secondi 9€–14€. Closed Mon).*

Certosa di Pavia ★★

AGES 4 AND UP A gloriously embellished Carthusian monastery, 8 kilometres (5 miles) north of the city. Galeazzo Visconti commissioned it as a family mausoleum in 1397 – it was completed by the Sforzas in the 16th century. The ornate façade of differently hued marbles is adorned with many statues of saints, apostles and Roman emperors. During the winter months the enveloping *nebbie padane* (Padana Fog) gives the charterhouse a particularly haunting atmosphere. The Gothic interior is full of Renaissance motifs, elaborate altars and intricate marquetry. Look out for the tomb statues of Ludovico il Moro and Beatrice d'Este (sold by Milan's Santa Maria delle Grazie to raise funds) beneath the vibrant frescoes (1494) by Bergognone. A small arcaded cloister with a formal garden, terracotta saints and fountain leads to the large cloister, which has small dwellings for the industrious community of monks who sell toiletries, rice, scented soaps and their home-brew, *Liquore dei Monaci*, from their shop.

Free admisson. Tues–Sun 9am–11:30pm and 2:30–5:30pm, until 4:30pm November to February and 5:30pm September to October and March to April.

Oasi Sant-Alessio **AGES 3 AND UP**

This nature reserve, 6 kilometres north-east of Pavia, is a favourite of school children and families on holiday. There are acres of woods and pastures to explore and thousands of species to spot on your way, including peregrine falcons, pelicans and beavers. You can even watch the underwater life in a viewing tunnel. Within the grounds there is a medieval fortress, newly established beehive, tropical house, interactive museum and a hospital for injured animals. Picnic areas, a barbecue (Sundays and holidays) and a small café are available.

*Castello di Sant'Alessio 27016, Sant'Alessio con Vialone. (✆ 0382-94139; **www.oasisantalessio.com**). 10€ (£6.70) adults, 8€ (£5.35) for ages 3–12. By car: from Pavia take via Farrini and follow directions to Sant'Alessio.*

Getting There & Tourist Info

There are trains every half hour from Milano Centrale. From Pavia you can take a bus to the Certosa from the **Autocorriere station** (next to the train station); buses are every half-hour and it takes about 15 minutes. If you are travelling by car, the Certosa is about half an hour south of Milan off Autostrada A7 (follow exit signs).

The tourist office is close to the train station.

Via Fabio Filzi 2 (☎ 0382-22-156). Mon–Sat 8:30am–12:30pm and 2–6pm.

CREMONA

The violin workshops of this small city on the river Po, 92 kilometres (57 miles) south-east of Milan, have been famed since the 17th century. The present-day **Scuola di Liuteria** (violin school) is open occasionally for tours (ask the tourist office in Piazza del Comune) and during the annual **Cremona Mondomusica** festival, dedicated to handmade musical instruments. There are fascinating exhibits relating to renowned craftsmen Nicolo Amati and Antonio Stradivari (Stradivarius) at the **Museo Stradivariano** in the **Museo Civico** and at the **Raccolta dei Violini**. The latter is housed within the Gothic splendours of the **Palazzo del Comune**, in the Piazza del Comune. The square's wide and wonderful expanse is well worth lingering in: take a pew and relax with a drink and gelato at the **Portici del Comune** admiring the warm red-brick hues and terracotta details while the children play on the square.Then visit the 12th century pink marble-clad **Duomo** and scale the towering **Torrazzo** (Italy's tallest campanile at 111 m – 364 ft – and formerly known as Torrione). Set aside a couple of hours to see the 12th century baptistery next door and the 13th century handsomely arcaded **Loggia dei Militi** (former military command) opposite.

Torrone Nougat

Many of Cremona's towers may be long gone, since it was known as the 'city of a hundred towers', but there is a fair quantity of *Torrone* nougat, the affectionate 15th century nickname given to its tallest edifice, the Duomo

Stradivarius Sculpture

tower. According to folkore, this confection combining almonds, honey and egg whites was shaped into the tower to celebrate the marriage of Biana Maria Visconti and Francesco Sforza in 1441. Torrone addicts often bite off more than they can chew each November when manufacturers like Sperlari offer limitless chunks at the **Festa del Torrone** sweets festival.

Parco Della Preistoria ★

AGES 3 AND UP This fun and educational park is 25 kilometres (15.5 miles) east of Milan in the verdant pastures near the **River Adda**. As well as a museum full of fossils, there are lakes, lilyponds and woodlands teeming with wild flora and resident fauna, including deer, goats, ponies and peacocks. After a ride on the mini train, active children can enjoy the playground and labyrinth. There are excellent changing facilities and places to eat.

*Via ponte Vecchio 21, Rivolta d'adda 26027 (☎ 0363 78184; **www.parcodellapreistoria.it**) 10€ (£6.70) adults, 7€ (£4.70) children aged 3–13 Daily 9am – 7pm, closed December to January.*

Fantasy World **AGES 3 AND UP** is a theme park immersed in parkland, with its very own Mini Italia, replete with models of *bel paese* landmarks. Water rides, a Leonardo Museum and themed stage shows (including Peter Pan, wild west saloon and Blues Brothers) make for an action-packed day out.

*Casello di Capriate (☎ 020-9090-169; **www.fantasyworld.it**). Admission: 17€ (£11.40) adults, 12.50€ (£8.38) children 1–1.4 m in height. 9:30am – 6pm Easter to mid-September; Closed weekdays Mid-September to Easter. A4 Exit Capriate.*

BRESCIA

Lombardy's underrated second city has artistic and architectural riches aplenty, including Roman temples, two *duomi* and beautiful Renaissance *palazzi*. Slice through the industrialised suburbs (the area is famed for its cutlery and weaponry) and head for **Piazza della Vittoria** where the chequered flag is waved for the **Mille Miglia** vintage car race each May. Alas, throughout the year less attractive cars encircle this Fascist-era square with its nattily striped modernist post office. Make a beeline for the **Piazza della Loggia**, with its elegantly detailed Palazzo Pubblico attributed to Renaissance architects Palladio and Sansovino. The Venetian **Monte Vecchio di Pietà** (once a public pawnshop) and clock tower attest to the influence of *La Serenissima* over the town up to the late 17th century. On the eastern side above the gold-plated astronomical clock with signs of the zodiac, there are two statues, nicknamed '*i macc de le ur*' in Bresciano dialect (madmen of the hours) who strike the bell on the hour. To the east is **Piazza Paolo VI** where you can visit the 17th century:

Duomo Nuovo (New cathedral) and the more alluringly rotund Romanesque **Duomo Vecchio** (Old cathedral), aka *La Rotonda*.

Old Duomo: Wed–Mon 9am–noon and 3–7pm April to September; Sat–Sun 9am–noon and 3–6pm October to March. New Duomo: Mon–Sat 7:30am–noon and 4–7:30pm; Sun 8am–1pm and 4–7:30pm.

Brescia's medieval town hall, **Il Broletto** has a baroque courtyard loggia, the austere **Torre del Popolo** and the adjoining church of **Sant'Agosto**, replete with lion gargoyles that are sure to capture little imaginations.

Go west to the **Pinacoteca Tosio-Matinengo** AGES 5 AND UP for the city's best art collection, which has lots of Lombard masters (seek out local hero Moretto) alongside angelic Raffaellos and 18th century Ceruti street life.

*Piazza Moretto 4 (☎ 030-377-4999; **www.museiarte.brescia.it**) Admission: 3€ (£2). Mon–Sat 9am–7pm.*

If you have time, explore the streets to the west and seek out the **Santa Maria dei Miracoli** church, the 31-metre (85 ft) high, 13th century **Torre di Pallata** and wonderful fountains beneath with allegories of the town's rivers, the Garza and Mella.

Savour the atmosphere of the **Roman Capitolino** nearby, a temple built by Vespasian in AD 73, excavated in the 1820s and reconstructed in brick in the 1940s. The nearby **Teatro Romano**, once held 15,000 people and looks a little neglected. While the **Museo Romano** is being spruced up you can enjoy the Roman wall paintings and mosaics on a guided tour (every half-hour) of the **Monastero di Santa Giulia**. There are several more places of worship within the complex as well as cloisters and excavations.

The **Museo della Città** AGES 5 AND UP charts the city's history in detail and has some fascinating artifacts that span the ages.

Via dei Musei 1B (☎ 800-762-811). 8€ (£5.35) adults, 6€ (£4) under-17s and over-65s. Tues–Sun 10am–6pm June to September, and 9:30am–5:30pm October to May.

Up on the Colle Cidneo hill, the **Castello** ★ ALL AGES offers fine views and museums dedicated to the town's arms industry and the Italian Risorgimento. Children will love the medieval atmosphere, the drawbridge, the chunky **Torre della Mirabella** and the museum's collection of armour and weaponry. The surrounding park is a great place to have a picnic – check out the deli G.A. Porteri (Via trento 52 ☎ *030-380-947*) and go to **Pasticceria San Carlo** (Corso Zanardelli1. ☎ *030-422-72*) for pastries and refreshements. To reach the castle you can take the winding road from **Piazza del Foro**, or a more direct and arduous route from Piazza Paolo VI.

Cobbled lane in Bergamo

Via Castello 9. (☎ 030-293-292). Admission: 3 € (£2). 10am–1pm, 2:30–5pm; closed Mon.

Museo delle Mille Miglia This museum offers a taste of the *Mille Miglia* (meaning thousand miles, aka *La Freccia Rossa*) race that starts and finishes in Piazza Vittoria each May. Classic cars, posters and memorabilia are housed in the 11th century **Sant'Eufemia monastery**, near Porta Venezia. The shop is full of car-related gadgets and you can stop and fill a hole in your stomach at the **Taverna Mille Miglia**.

*Viale della Rimemberenza 3. (☎ 030-336-5631; **www.museomille miglia.it**) 10€ (£6.70) adults, 6€ (£4) for ages 6–12. Tues–Sun 9am–6pm.*

BERGAMO

With its wonderful and varied architecture, artwork, independent shops, greenery and bountiful food, this city nestled in the foothills of the Alps has it all within easy reach. Bergamo's two parts lie at the foothills of the Alps: the **Città Bassa**, the lower modern town with its spacious squares and the **Città Alta** crowning the hill, with its charming medieval and Renaissance architecture, and narrow streets crammed with interesting shops. These two parts owe their characters to Roman times, when the *civitas* (city) stood strategically atop the hill protected by fortifications, with the farms and villas of the *surburbia* below. A wonderful funicular railway connects them.

Essentials

Getting There

By Train There are hourly trains to and from Milan (50 min.) whilst services to and from Brescia are even more frequent. If you are planning to head to the Lakes you can take the train

Bergamasco countryside

to Lecco on Lake Como: an hourly service takes just 40 mins.

By Bus The bus station is beside the train station on Piazza Marconi. The service to and from Milan runs every half-hour and takes 1 hr (by **Autostradale** (*02-3391-0843*). There are five to six buses a day to and from Como run by **SPT** (*031-247-247*).

By Car The A4 runs alongside Bergamo, heading west to Milan and Turin and east to Brescia, Verona, and Venice. The trip between Milan and Bergamo takes a little over half an hour. Parking in or near the Città Alta, most of which is closed to traffic, can be difficult. It's a good idea to drive into the Città Bassa and park at the car park in Via Guiseppe Verdi (about 2€ –£1.34 – per hour) then take the funicular or the nearby steps up to the Città Alta.

Visitor Information

The **Città Bassa tourist office** is on Viale Vittorio Emanuele 20 (*035-210-204***;** fax: *035-230-184*; ***www.apt.bergamo.it***); it's open Monday to Friday 9am–12:30pm and 2–5:30pm. The **Città Alta office,** at Vicola Aquila Nera 2 (*035-232-730***;** [fax] 035-242-994), is to the side of Piazza Vecchia, and keeps the same hours.

Città Bassa

Often overlooked, the lower city's broad avenues and airy squares laid out in the 19th and early 20th centuries harbour some fine attractions including: **Galleria dell'Accademia** AGES 6 AND UP which owes its fine art collection to Napoleon's habit of purloining the region's treasures. Count Giacomo Carrara purchased the fine neo-classical building and founded the academy in 1780. The impressive collection fills 15 elegant salons and includes paintings by Bellini, Caravaggio, Rubens and Velasquez.

*Piazza Carrara 82. (☎ 035-399-640; **www.accademiacarrara.bergamo.it**). Admission: 3€ (£2). 10am–1pm. 2:30–5:30pm; closed Mon.*

Galleria d'Arte Moderna e Contemporanea AGES 6 AND UP has a small permanent collection (including a Kandinsky and a De Chirico) and temporary exhibitions.

*Via Tommaso 53, (☎ 035-399-521; **www.gamec.it**). Fees and opening hours vary show to show.*

The **Sentierone** (opened in 1762 and revamped in the 1920s) is the long avenue and gardens where *Bergamaschi* take their coffee and *passeggiate:* it has been so well trampled over the years that glistening new granite blocks have been laid recently. Elegant **Piazza Dante** nearby has some grassy open space (perfect for play and picnics) and is a venue for monthly markets, including antiques and crafts markets (second and third Sundays). Going north, **Piazza Libertà** is a broad square surrounded by austere Fascist-era and nondescript modern façades – it may not sound enticing but it plays host to cultural, sporting and musical events: summer concerts, *calcetta* (five-a-side footy) tournaments and a public ice-rink in winter. Further north at **Viale Vittorio Emanuele II** the Città Bassa meets the precipitous, leafy cliffs that rise to the Città Alta: it is time to hop aboard the **Funicolare railway** ★(opened in 1887) and head to the more charming part of Bergamo. With older children it's possible to scale the shady *scorlazzini* steps near the funicular stop in about 25 minutes, with a much-deserved breather or three thrown in.

Città Alta

The enjoyable *funicolare* ride allows glimpses of backyards and spectacular panoramas below, while mixing with the local characters. After all that excitement, refreshments may be in order – the small café within the station retains much of the Belle Époque atmosphere, boasts 50 beers on its decent menu and has wonderful views to boot. Step out on to the intimate **Piazza delle Scarpe** where the sight of seven cobbled roads only hints at the medieval and Gothic sights beyond.

There are options here – the steep Via Donizetti passes the **Casa dell'Arciprete**, a museum filled with religious relics occupying a Renaissance palazzo (by appointment only: ask at tourist office) and proceeds on to the main attractions, Santa Maria Maggiore and Piazza Vecchia. For an easier incline take **Via Gombito**, the main artery of the city, dipping in and out of the wonderfully varied shops en route to the *Centro Storico*.

The influence of Venice over the town can be seen in the buildings and monuments in the town's main adjoining squares – indeed the *Bergamaschi* still show some historical allegiance to Venice when they say that they 'turn east for inspiration, whilst showing their backsides to Milan'. At the north-east end of the intimately proportioned **Piazza Vecchia** is a hint of *La Serenissima*'s symbiotic relationship with the town over the centuries. The arcaded 12th century **Palazzo della Ragione** (Courts of Justice) display *Il leone di San Marco*, symbol of the Venetian Republic, over a balcony, arched windows and flower-lined covered staircase designed by Pietro Isabello. Thankfully, there's no traffic to disturb you and lots of al fresco café seating, as if anyone needs an excuse to linger. Here you can grab a seat outside the famous **Bar Del Tasso** (named after the poet who has a statue here), while the children play within sight around the spouting mouths of the **Fontana del Contarini**. Towering 51 metres (140 ft) above hangs the *campanone* (big bell) of the 12th century:

Torre del Comune AGES 6 AND UP
whose chime regularly resounds around the piazza – listen out at 10pm when it rings 100 times – echoing the ancient curfew bells.

Stairs only; open May to September 10am–8pm; or by appointment (☎ 035-247-116).

Within the 360-degrees of architectural finesse around the square, your eyes fall on the old

Piazza Vecchia

Venetian administrative HQ, the **Palazzo del Podestà Veneto**, the **Biblioteca Civica** (civic library) and through the archways, the **Piazza del Duomo**. This small piazza is crammed with fine religious buildings: the **Duomo**, the **Battistero** – which once stood inside the nearby **Basilica di Santa Maria Maggiore**, with an understated marble façade adorned with red lions and an exuberantly baroque interior. The colourful and whimsical Renaissance masterpiece chapel, **La Cappella Colleoni** contains the tomb of legendary mercenary Bartolomeo Colleoni, who served both the Viscontis and the Venetian Republic. Inside, the *condottiere* lies entombed alongside his daughter Medea, under Tiepolo frescoes.

Via Gomito leads into Via Colleoni and then onto Piazza della Cittadella and verdant Largo Aperto – follow your nose as you pass an array of shops including many patisserie; try **Cavour** ★ (famed for sweet treats including *La Polentina*) and the oldest **La Mariana**, a fabulous place to pick up picnic provisions. There are two great little museums on the way:

Museo di Scienze Naturali Enrico Caffi AGES 5 AND UP This has all sorts of flora and fauna to wow you.

*Piazza Cittadella 10. (☎ 035-286-011; **www.museoscienzebergamo.it**). Admission free. Open Tue–Fri 9am–12.30pm and 2.30–5.30pm and Sat, Sun and public holidays 9am–7pm.*

Museo Archeologico AGES 5 AND UP This has lots of Egyptian relics and remains of a nearby Roman house that many children will love.

*Piazza Cittadella 9. (☎ 035- 286-011; **www.museoarcheologicobergamo.it**). Admission is free. Open Tue–Fri 9am–12.30pm and 2.30–5.30pm and Sat, Sun and public holidays 9am–7pm.*

If you fancy a walk amidst succulents, Mediterranean bush, rare alpine plant species and wetland pondlife, pay a visit to the:

Orto Botanico Lorenzo Rota ALL AGES It has a decent path for pushchairs. The most elevated views in Bergamo can be sought by taking the *Funicolare* (see below).

*Colle Aperto, (☎ 035-286-060; **www.ortobotanico.comune.bergamo.it**.) Admission free. Daily 9am–12pm and 2pm–5pm; Sat, Sun and public holidays 9am–7pm.*

Funicolare San Vigilio ★★★ ALL AGES Take the *Funicolare* up to more serene environs at 461 metres (1264 ft), where you'll find the fantastic **San Vigilio Bar/pizzeria** (Via San Vigilio 34.☎*035-253-188*. ***www.ristorantepizzeriasanvigilio.it***).

You can explore the largely ruined **Castello** AGES 3 AND UP nearby, replete with four crumbling towers and surrounding parkland. For the fit, adventurous and well-prepared, the hills of Monte Bastia and San Sebastiano are well worth the ramble.

(☎ 035-236-285). Admission free. April to October 9am–8pm, October to March 10am–6pm and November to February 10am–4pm).

For Active Families

Enter via **Porta San Alessandro** and walk for about half a mile following the fortified walls of the town, taking in the splendid views. Next to **Porta Sant'Agostino** at La Fara, the footie mad and active amongst you can have a kick about on the pitch or play other games.

The **Cannoniera di San Michele** AGES 7 AND UP is one of 27 wall defences: get a soldier's-eye view of warfare from a

Bergamo city walls

tunnel and see where the cannons were placed after being dragged here by horses.

(☎ 035-251-233). Open by appointment.

If you still have the puff, follow the cobblestones further until you reach **Porta San Giacomo**: the spur of the walls and a great place to stop and drink in the panorama, and a beverage.

La Rocca ★★ AGES 4 AND UP
This impressive 14th century castle on the **Sant'Eufemia** hill has a boy's dream of a museum, dedicated to the *Risorgimento* and *Resistenza* and containing weaponry, aeroplanes and artifacts. Celts and Romans placed fortifications here, which were built upon by the Viscontis and then bolstered by the Venetians. The real fun in coming here lies in the tree-filled memorial park, where tanks and other World War I relics are scattered between pines and cypresses. Theatre productions and events dedicated to children often take place here in summer – check listings in local paper *L'Eco di Bergano.*

Piazzale Brigata Legnano. (☎ 035-221-040). 3€ (£2). Castle complex open Tue–Sun 9:30am–1pm and 2–5:30pm October to May; 9:30am–1pm and 2–5:30pm June to September; Sat and public holidays 9am–7pm. Park: Free admission daily 9am–8pm April to September; 10am–6pm October and March; daily 10am–5pm November to February.

Cafés, Snacks & Family-Friendly Dining

Take a snack break and fill your picnic hamper on your travels around the Città Alta at the aforementioned **Cavour ★** and **Nessi ★** (Via Gombito 7 and 34), which are crammed full of tasty pastries, sweet polenta treats and bread products. Of all the cafés on Piazza Vecchia,

Caffè del Tasso ★ is the only one to claim that Garibaldi's redshirts used to grab a snifter at the establishment before heading out to battle. **Cooperativa Città Alta** (Vicolo S Agata 19) has bargain antipasti dishes amidst a jovial backdrop of old men playing cards.

Da Mimmo★★ is well known for its family-friendly atmosphere and well-crafted dishes using the area's finest produce. Expect Bergamsaco favourites like *polenta taragna*, great *pizze* and vegetarian options including tagliatelle with spinach and the most flavoursome tomatoes. In summer they hold jazz and bossa nova concerts in the garden.

*Via Colleloni 17. (☎ 035-238-836; **www.ristorantemimmo.com**). Highchairs. Primi 9–13€ (£6–8.70) Secondi 9–15€ (£6–10). Mon–Sun noon–2:30pm and 7:30–11:30pm. Closed Tue.*

Book a terrace at **La Colombina** ★★ FIND for stunning views and regional classics like *casoncelli* (meat-filled ravioli) alongside taleggio cheese salads.

Borgo Canale 12. (☎ 035-261-402). Highchairs. Primi 7–12€ (£4.70–8); Secondi 7–13€ (£4.70–8.70). Wed–Sat noon–2:30pm and 7:30–11pm.

Parietti Piero Families flock here for the tasty seasonal dishes including swordfish, rabbit and beef.

Via Beltrami 52. (☎ 035-221-072). Highchairs. Primi 6–11€ (£4–7.40); Secondi 7–12€ (£4.70–8) noon–2:30pm and 7:30–11:30pm.

Cutting the Cheese

Family-Friendly Accommodation

Hotels in the Città Alta are few and far between and fill quickly, so reserve well in advance. Many of the hotels here are living off old reputations, lacking modern facilities and good customer service.

San Lorenzo This hotel housed in a former convent is tucked away in a tranquil piazza off Via Colleoni in the heart of the Città Alta, perfect for the *Centro Storico* attractions. Bedrooms are smallish but generally clean with simple furnishings and small balconies. The Roman ruins outside have halted the construction of an underground car park. Parking is available nearby though – ask for a permit at reception.

*Piazza Mascheroni 9A, Bergamo Alta, 24129. (☎ 035-237-383; fax: 035-237-958; **www.hotelsanlorenzobg.it**) 25 units. 110€–175€ (£74–117.25) double; 140€–210€ (£94–140) triple.*

Rates include continental breakfast. AE, DC, MC, V. Parking free. Amenities: bar; room service; laundry service; dry cleaning. In room: A/C, dataport, hairdryer, minibar, safe, TV.

The ever-popular **Agnello d'Oro** housed in a 17th century *palazzo* has 20 smallish units, which, although in need of updating, are adequate for small families should other hotels be full.

Via Gombito 22, Bergamo Alta 24129. (☎ 035-249-883; fax: 035-235-612). 20 units. 110€ (£61.64) double. Continental breakfast 6€ (£4) AE, DC, MC, V. Amenities: concierge; tour desk. In room: TV, dataport, hairdryer.

Mercure Bergamo Palazzo Dolci This stylish modern hotel may be in a busy part of the Città Bassa, but the fantastic double glazing keeps outside noise to a minimum. Public areas have cool, contemporary colours and vibrant artwork. Bedrooms are well-appointed and relaxing – children will like the satellite TV and gadgets. There is a supermarket nearby for water and picnic provisions.

*Viale Papa Giovanni XXIII 100, Bergamo Bassa 24121. (☎ 035-227-411; fax: 035-218-008; **www.accorhotels.com**). 88 units. 140€–180€ (£94–120) double; 160€–220€ (£107–147.40) triple. Rates include continental breakfast. AE, DC, MC, V. Parking free. Amenities: bar; room service; laundry service; dry cleaning and ironing service. In room: A/C, dataport, hairdryer, minibar, radio, safe, TV.*

Relais La Valetta ★★ FIND is immersed in the verdant **Colli di Bergamo** hills and offers comfortable family accommodation in variously sized cosy rooms with excellent facilities. The surrounding area is extremely peaceful with plenty of opportunities for adventurous pursuits: the owners can arrange horse-riding, trekking and mountain bike hire. They'll even ferry you to and from the airport.

*Via Castagneta 19. (☎ 035-242-746; fax: 035-228-1217; **www.lavallettabergamo.it.**) 6 units. 100€ (£67) double; 150€ (£100) suite. Rates include continental breakfast. Amenities: Internet; airport transfer. In room: A/C, minibar, TV.*

MANTUA (MANTOVA)

The brooding beauty of Mantova owes much to the Gonzaga family, who built the massive fortress-like **Palazzo Ducale** and whimsically epicurean **Palazzo Te** here between the 14th and 17th centuries, and to the River Mincio's swollen banks, forming the surrounding lakes that lend it a magically melancholic atmosphere. Indeed, its very name conjures up dark portents: according to Roman and Etruscan mythology the gods of the underworld Mantus and his wife Mania were associated with the town. The Roman poet Virgil was born here. Fittingly, Mantova was the destination Shakespeare chose for Romeo's exile and is the setting for Verdi's opera *Rigoletto*. Its compact scale and largely pedestrianised *Centro Storico*, full

Mantova

of historic *palazzi*, inviting cafés and tempting patisserie, make it a good family base for a couple of days.

Although the area's **Pianura Padana** plains and industrial outskirts appear rather nondescript, shrouded in an eerie fog for much of the year, there are some beautiful natural parks and hilltop villages further north by the **River Mincio**, while south towards the **Po**, there are wetland reserves. Both areas are perfect for family walks, boat trips and cycling.

Essentials

Getting There

By Train There are about a dozen trains each day from Milano Centrale (2 hr). If you are travelling from Verona, there are trains every hour.

By Car If coming from Milan take the autostrada towards Verona and then head down the A22 (2 hr). Via Trieste on the eastern outskirts is a good bet for metered-parking: pay and display your ticket and it's a 10-minute walk to Piazza Dante.

Visitor Information

The **tourist office** at Piazza Mantegna 6 (☎ *0376-328-253*; fax: *0376-363-292*; ***www.aptmantova.it***) is open Mon–Sat from 8:30am–12:30pm and 3–6pm and Sun 9:30am–12:30pm (closed almost every Sun January to February).

Festivals & Markets

The long-standing **Mantova Jazz Festival** is held in some atmospheric venues each spring. Piazza delle Erbe is the scene of a bustling **food market** Monday to Saturday from 8am to 1pm. On Thursday mornings, a **larger market**, filled with housewares, clothing and food spills out into the surrounding streets. From late November, the same *piazze* become a magical yuletide setting for stalls filled with Christmas-related foods, gifts and decorations.

Exploring the City

Once inside the historic centre, away from the traffic, walking around the series of handsome cobblestoned squares and arcaded streets is a scenic pleasure.

Approaching from the south, modern shop-fronts mix with historic *palazzi* before the imposing **Basilica di San Andrea** appears – looming over the beautifully proportioned **Piazza Mantegna** and **Piazza delle Erbe**, home to colourful weekly and seasonal markets. Medieval and Renaissance buildings catch the eye in every direction: the 12th and 13th century **Palazzo del Podestà** (Mayoral Palace) and porticoed **Palazzo della Ragione** (Law Courts), the perfectly formed **Rotunda di San Lorenzo** church and the **Torre del'Orologio**, a 14th century tower with an enigmatic astrological clock face.

Torre del'Orologio

Intimate **Piazza Broletto** leads to the grandest space, **Piazza Sordello**, with its crenellated **Palazzo Bianchi** (the Bishop's Palace since 1823), **Palazzo Bonacolsi** and austere **Palazzo Ducale**, which contains courtyards, gardens and over 500 rooms filled with the Gonzagas' artistic treasures. To the south, Giulio Romano's Mannerist masterpiece **Palazzo Te** contains dream-like fresco visions in the **Sala dei Giganti**. The surrounding park offers space to play and picnic. Open vistas can be found on lakeside walks, by hiring bicycles or on boat trips around the Mincio lakes and the Po, from nearby Castello di San Giorgio.

Palazzo Ducale AGES 5 AND UP

This massive, rambling fortress-palace gives you some idea of the wealth and art amassed by the Gonzagas – Mantova's most powerful family. The cultural life here really flourished under the patrimony of Isabella d'Este and Francesco Gonzaga, and their son Federico II – their loyal following of artists included Titian, Pisanello, Romano and court painter Mantegna. The latter took nine years to complete the ravishing **Camera degli Sposi** frescoes, a fascinating insight into 15th century court life.

There are over 700 rooms and 15 courtyards within the labyrinthine palace, which incorporates the **Palazzo di Capitano** and **Magnus Domus** facing Piazza Sordello; **Palazzo di Corte Vecchia**; the **Basilica di Santa Barbara**; **Castello di San Giorgio** and **Corte Nuova.** Although many rooms are not open to the public, there's still too much to see in one visit. For a breather, step outside into one of the courtyards and gardens.

*Piazza Sordello. (☏ 0376-382-150; **www.mantovaducale.it**). Admission: 6.50€ (£4.35). Tues–Sun 8:45am–7:15pm.*

Palazzo Te and Gardens ★★

AGES 5 AND UP In the midst of public gardens with lots of space to play lies this handsome 16th century summer villa commissioned by Federico II Gonzaga and built by Giulio Romano (protégé of Raphael) in the Mannerist style. This was a place for epicurean pleasures – the spacious salon's whimsical interiors include equine portraits, erotic scenes in the **Sala di Psiche** and the famous **Sala dei Giganti**, with its melodramatic frescoed depiction of the *Fall of the Giants*. Upstairs, there are Egyptian and Modern Art exhibits from the Museo Civico's collections.

Viale Te. (☏ 0376-323-266). Admission: 8€ (£5.35) adults, 2.50€ (£1.68) ages 12–18 and senior citizens over 65, free for children under 12. Mon 1–6pm; Tues–Sun 9am–6pm. Box office closes half an hour earlier.

Piazza Sordello

Basilica di Sant'Andrea

AGES 5 AND UP This elegant church by Leon Battista Alberi was commissioned by Ludivico II Gonzaga in 1470 – it was enlarged by Giulio Romano and the dome was added by Juvarra in 1732. The huge interior contains a spacious barrel-vaulted nave and side chapels, among them **La Cappella di Mantegna**, which contains the painter's tomb. The influence of Mantegna is also seen in the frescoes and terracotta detailing on the dome. A reliquary in the crypt is said to carry the blood of Christ, reputedly carried here by a Roman soldier called Longinus who speared Jesus's side.

Piazza Mantegna. Free admission. Daily 7:30am–noon and 3–7pm.

Boat Trips & Cycling

There are a number of companies running boat trips on the

Mincio and the lakes around Mantova.

Montonavi Andres Negrini ★★ ALL AGES has a fleet of five well-equipped boats that explore the area's waters and beyond, even as far as Venice and the Riviera del Brenta. You can embark at the Pontile Gonzaga on **Lago Inferiore** or Ponte dei Mulini on **Lago Superiore**, on a number of journeys (check website for latest details) including a 90-minute trip as far as Grazie di Curtatone.

*Via San Giorgio, 2 (☎ 0376-322-875; **www.montonaviandres.it**). Admission: 10€ (£6.70) adults, 9€ (£6) children from 4–14 years.*

Cycling around the largely flat terrain around Mantova is popular – there are easy lakeside routes from Porto Catena to **Parco Belfiore** and a rewarding 6 km (3.7 mile) track to **Bosco della Fontana** within the protected **Mincio park** – detailed maps are available at the tourist office. For cycle hire try La Rigola.

Lungolago dei Gonzaga and at Via Trieste (☎ 0376-366-677).

Café's, Snacks & Family-Friendly Dining

La cucina Mantovana mixes sophisticated dishes fit for Gonzaga banquets with rustic recipes using the territory's bountiful produce: fish from the lakes, pork, rice from the region's fields, and fruit and vegetables including pears, melons and pumpkins.

Although some children might turn their noses up at the sound of donkey stew, specialities like *tortelli di zucca* (ravioli filled with sweet pumpkin), the crumbly cake *brisolana* and *tagliatelle* cake should all go down a treat. For snacks, pastries (try their legendary *Papa di Mantova* cakes) and a sneaky *aperitivo*, pop into historic **Café Caravatti** on Piazza Broletto, and for picnic supplies try **Casa del Pane** at Via Verdi 65.

Il Cigno – Trattoria dei Martini ★ For an education in *La cucina Mantovana* reserve a table at the town's much-lauded eatery. What's great if you're here with children is that the clientele that dine in this historic 16th century palazzo are not precious foodies – the atmosphere is special, not stuffy. Enjoy classic dishes like *risotto alla pilota* (*Vialone Nano* rice with *Salamelle* minced pork and Grana Padano cheese), sweet and sour capon and their innovative take on *tortelli di zucca*. If you drink wine then you should definitely come here to imbibe a glass or two.

Piazza d'Arco 1. (☎ 0376-327-101). Primi 8€–13€ (£5.35–8.70); secondi 9€–17€ (£6–11.40). AE, DC, MC, V. 12:45–2:30pm and 7:45–11pm. Closed Mon, Tue and all of August.

Ochina Bianca ★★ A warm osteria welcome and fabulous Mantovano fayre make Ochina a perennial favourite for local families. Fresh fish from the Mincio, rabbit and pork feature regularly on the menu. If the children are big on trying exotic meat creations, they may enjoy their noodle-like bigoli pasta, served with pancetta bacon and fagioli (beans). One taste of their delicious homemade gelato and you'll come up in pleasurable goosebumps.

Via Finzi 2. (☎ 0376-323-700). Highchairs. Reservations required. Primi 7€ (£4.70); secondi 10€–12€ (£6.70–8). MC, V. Tues–Sun 12:45–2pm and 7:45–10pm. Closed last three weeks in August.

Family-Friendly Accommodation

As befits a town of architectural wonders, there are some handsome hotels here as well as comfortable, practical options – but they get booked up fast. An alternative, especially if you have your own transport and wish to have a more active holiday, is to base yourself in **agriturismo** lodgings (for a complete list go to ***www.agriturismomantova.it***) like Ca' Guerriera and Le Sorgive e Le Volpi (see below). There are also some basic, low-priced farmhouses out of town costing around 30€ (£20) per person, available via the tourist office.

Casa dei Poli This contemporary boutique style hotel in the centre of town offers convenience for sightseeing families and immaculately clean, stylish interiors. Parquet flooring, ample bathrooms and elegant design pieces make it a relaxing place to stay. It may be a little pricier than its dog-eared rivals, but quality details and the friendly staff make it well worth considering.

Corso Garibaldi 32, Mantova 46100. (☎ 0376-288-170; [fax] 0376-362-766). 27 units. 170€–210€ (£114–140) double. Rates include continental breakfast. AE, DC, MC, V. Parking free. Amenities: bar; room service; laundry service; dry cleaning and ironing service; spa and fitness centre. In room: A/C, Wi-Fi, minibar, safe, TV.

Hotel Mantegna ★ Recently renovated Mantegna is on a tranquil back street south of the *centro storico* and has an excellent choice of rooms for families of all sizes. Its clean, functional doubles, triples, suites and quads offer good value. Facilities include a TV lounge and bar, a comfy social space to watch Italian football *partite*, play board games and plan trips.

*Via Fabio Filzi 10, 46100 Mantova. (☎ 0376-328-019; [fax] 0376-368-564; **www.hotelmantegna.it**). 42 units. 150€ (£100) double; 160€ (£107) triple; 180€ (£120) suite. Buffet breakfast 8€ (£5.35). AE, MC, V. Parking free in courtyard. Closed 24th December to 7th January and for two weeks in August. Amenities: bar; concierge. In room: A/C, TV, dataport, minibar, hairdryer.*

Accommodation/Dining in the Province of Mantova

Heading south near the Po and beyond towards Emilia Romagna, the flat landscape of rice fields and marshy nature reserves is hardly frequented by tourists at all. Near Ostiglia there are two protected bird sanctuaries, the **Paludi di Ostiglia** (***www.life-paludiostiglia.it***) wetlands and **Isola Boschina**, a tiny island on the river Po, teeming with wild flowers, bird life and amphibians. At nearby **Revere**, there is a charming Ludovico Gonzaga palazzo, the grand 18th century church of the **Beata Vergine Annunziata** and the small **Museo del Po,** which has a collection of fishing, fauna and folk exhibits. In the hillier north of the province, the **Parco del Mincio** (***www.parcodelmincio.it***) by the river is popular territory for outdoor activities like boating, fishing and cycling, and general frolicking about on the *fiume*.

Ca' Guerriera ★ This well-established *agriturismo* near Ostiglia makes a superb base to enjoy the area's wildlife and activities like horse-riding (ask about the local equestrian centre, **La Conchiglia Centro Equestre** *(338-8290-368*) and cycling, or just to relax by the pool. Next door to the Marquis Guerrieri-Gonzaga's palatial residence, visitors enjoy the excellent value restaurant and immaculate accommodation designed by the family's architect daughter. For 20€ (£13.40) per head you can eat a wonderful three-course meal made with locally produced ingredients (they are members of Slow Food). The service can be a little haphazard, but overall it's a charming place. There's plenty of space for children to run around, farmyard animals to see and the imaginatively renovated dairy is occasionally used for small cultural events. Full and half-board are available.

Via Don Martini 91, Sustinente 46030. (0386-710-296; [fax] 0386-437-342). 86€ (£57.60) double; 120€ (£80) triple; 20€ (£13.40) extra bed; Children 0–2 free. Rates include basic continental breakfast. AE, DC, MC, V. Parking free. Amenities: Internet; restaurant; swimming pool. In room: A/C, dataport, hairdryer, safe, TV.

Le Sorgive – Le Volpi ★★ FIND 30 kms north of Mantova and just 10 km from Lake Garda, this *agriturismo* offers lots of activities for children within lush grounds. Its facilities include a swimming pool, riding school, martial arts and fitness centre, archery range, mountain-biking trails and a working farm whose produce is used in the rustic eatery. The owners can even organise cookery courses, scuba diving and boat trips on the nearby lake. Accommodation is within two renovated 19th century farm buildings – including well-equipped apartments suitable for families.

Via Piridello 6, Solferino 46040. (0376-854-252; fax: 0376-855-256; ***www.lesorgive.it****). 10 units. 45€–65€ (£30–43.50) per adult; 30% child discount. Includes buffet breakfast. AE, MC, V. Parking free. Amenities: restaurant; sports facilities; swimming pool. In room: A/C, TV.*

7 Turin & Piedmont

PIEDMONT/VALLE D'AOSTA

Piedmont lies at the foot of the Alps – *al piè dei monti* – bordering France and Switzerland. The region and its people have a whiff of the Gallic about them, sniffed out in the dialect, architecture and cuisine. Indeed, the Francophile House of Savoy, who came to preside over nascent Italy in the 1860s thanks to astute native Camillo Cavour, ruled for centuries from Piedmont's handsome capital. Turin's gracious street-plan contrasts with the messy set-up in other large Italian cities, especially neighbour and rival Milan. In the 19th century, its progressive economy and political class made it the natural choice as Italy's first capital, and a century later in the 1960s, companies like Fiat drove the Italian economic miracle, propelling Italy into the modern age. You can see these industrial legacies in the Lingotto test track, which starred in *The Italian Job,* and in the dreary suburbs that housed the southern Italians who came to work in the car factories. Fiat's might may have waned, but the city has reinvented itself, adding visionary architecture and infrastructure to the baroque palaces and sophisticated hospitality. Since the 2006 Winter Olympics gave it an overdue kick up the *culo*, the city is at last more geared to tourists than suits. It's now a fabulous place to visit with children.

Turin's fertile hinterland has rice fields to the east, at Vercelli, and to the south, the fertile rolling hills of the Monferrato and Le Langhe, covered in vineyards and dotted with hilltop villages. The region's gastronomic wonders, including the wines of Barolo and Barbaresco and the white truffles of Alba, are best sampled after a pleasurable day touring medieval villages, a spell by the pool of your rustic *agriturismo* and a late afternoon cycle ride with the kids around the magical landscape.

To the west and north of Turin rise the Alps: in the west are the Valli Valdesi, inhabited for centuries by Protestant Waldenses, and the Valle Di Susa, where *Torinesi* and *Francesi* converge on mountain passes and overdeveloped ski resorts. On the northern and eastern fringes of Piedmont are: Ivrea with its medieval castles; the Canavese, where subalpine valleys lead to the wonderful Gran Paradiso National Park; the southern faces of Monte Rosa and Monte Cervino (the Italian name for the Matterhorn) in the Valle d'Aosta; and the serene lakes of Orta and Maggiore. The best of these outdoor playgrounds for adventurers, skiers and holidaying families are covered in Chapter 3, 'Lakes & Mountains'.

Royal Palace Gates

TURIN

170 km (106 miles) NW of Genoa, 140 km (87 miles) E of Milan.

The positive effects of staging the Winter Olympics in 2006 make a visit to Turin a more pleasurable experience than even a couple of years ago. It's always had fine attractions for visitors with kids, but now the city has really got its act together. Turin's grid-plan Roman layout was embellished with handsome architecture in the 17th and 18th centuries by its French-speaking elite, the House of

Savoy. The elegant mix of broad Gallic avenues, neoclassical buildings, sumptuous cafés and Italianate arcades are a pleasure to walk around with kids, who will no doubt also have their eyes on Turin's fabulous chocolate grottos. Children with costume drama aspirations will swoon at the lavish *saloni* of the **Palazzo Reale**; most will relish their imaginations being spiked at the **Armeria Reale** next door. Spooky sights wait at the **Museum of Egyptology** and at the **Cattedrale di San Battista**, where the haunting image of the **Turin Shroud** might raise a thorny issue or two, beside the usual family debates over ice cream and spill-stains. What makes *Torino* even more stimulating are its more cosmopolitan flavours and metropolitan sights: the awesome glass-lift ride from the floor of the **National Film Museum**'s central hall to the viewing platform of the **Mole Antonelliana** takes some beating.

Essentials

Getting There

By Plane Caselle International Airport (✆ *011-567-6361; www.aeroportoditorino.it*) is 14 km (8¾ miles) north of Turin. Sadem buses link the airport with the city's main train stations, **Porta Nuova** and **Porta Susa** – a 30-minute trip costing 6 €. The **taxi** journey takes about 30 minutes and costs around 28€ (£18.75).

By Train Stazione di Porta Nuova (✆ *011-665-30984; www.trenitalia.it*) is the main train station, just south of the city centre on Piazza Carlo Felice. There are two dozen trains a day to and from Milan (110 min.). Many of these trains also stop at **Stazione di Porta Susa**. There are 16 trains a day to and from Venice (around 5 hr), 20 trains to and from Genoa (2 hr) and 20 trains to and from Rome (6–7 hr). Stazione di Porta Susa lies west of the city centre on Piazza XVIII Dicembre: it connects Turin with the rest of Piedmont. You can also take one of three TGV trains a day to Paris (6 hr).

By Bus Autostazione Terminal Bus at Corso Vittorio Emanuele II 131 (close to Stazione di Porta Susa) is the main bus station (✆ *011-433-8100; www.autostazionetorino.it*) connecting Turin with many destinations in Piedmont and beyond, including Milan (3 hr) and Chamonix (4 hr). You can buy tickets at the office between 7am and midday, and 3 and 7pm.

By Car The A4, A5, A6, A21 and A32 pass through the outskirts of Turin: the A4 connects Turin with Milan (1 hr); the A5 goes to Aosta; the A6 links Turin with the Ligurian coast in an hour (you can get to Genoa in 90 min. on the A10); the A21 reaches Asti and Piacenza (where you can pick up the A1 for

Florence, Rome and the South) before heading north-west to Brescia. **Parking** in the city centre can be tricky, so be prepared for some tight manoeuvres. Look out for the GTT *Sosta a Pagamento* (Parking scheme: 0.50–2€ (£0.34–1.34) per hr depending on zone) pay-and-display blue lines throughout the city. You might have to walk a bit to find a ticket machine, so buy tickets in advance from selected tobacconists and newsagents. You can also stop for an hour at Piazza Paleocapa, Lagrange, Carlo Felice, San Carlo, in Via Roma and at the Stazione di Porta Nuova (Via Sacchi and Via Nizza). Covered parking is available in 18 car parks scattered around the city – check out ***www.comune.torino.it/gtt/en/parking/*** for more information.

Visitor Information

Tourist offices are at **Piazza Solferino** (☎ *011-535-181;* fax: *011-530-070*; ***www.turismotorino.org***) and inside Stazione di Porta Nuova. The visitor services in Turin are among the most efficient and friendliest you'll find in Northern Italy. Their opening hours are Monday to Saturday from 9:30am to 7pm and Sunday from 9:30am to 3pm. They will book rooms for you up to 48 hours in advance. The tourist information at **Caselle International Airport** is open from 8:30am to 10:30pm.

Getting Around

Compared to many Italian cities, Turin is easy to get around **on foot.** There's also an excellent network of GTT (Gruppo Torinese Trasporti) trams and buses (☎ *800-019-152* in Italy, or *011-57-641*; ***www.gtt.to.it***). *Edicole* (newsstands) sell tickets for the city's public transport: 60 minutes' travel costs 0.90€ (£0.60). Remember to validate your ticket using the machines or you'll be fined if caught by an inspector. A carnet pack of 15 tickets costs 12.50€ (£8.40). The two types of **Torino Card** (see 'Planning Your Outings', below) include free transportation. An excellent way to see the city is by hopping on the **TurismoBus Torino** (starts and ends at Piazza Solferino. 6€ (£4), 4€ (£2.70) up to 12 years; free with the Torino card. 10am–6pm hourly. July to September and public holidays), which allows you to get off and explore at any of the 15 stops, before catching another bus to continue along the route. Turismo Torino **Guided Tours** (☎ *011-883-426*. 6€ (£4) per tour) are superb for first-time visitors, on Saturday mornings at 10am, as are the themed walks on Saturday evenings at 6pm. Ask at the tourist office for information on tours with titles like 'Tasty Turin', 'Literary Turin', 'Military Turin' and 'Walks under Artists' Lights', the latter exploring the city's outdoor light installations.

Piazza Castello

City Layout

The spine of the city's orderly grid layout runs north-eastwards from the Stazione di Porta Nuova to Piazza Castello, the centre of the city and a 20-minute walk away through a series of piazzas and handsome porticoed streets.

Piazza Carlo Felice, with its cafés and central garden, sits directly in front of the station. At the far end you enter Turin's principal shopping street, Via Roma, which leads to **Piazza San Carlo,** flanked by the churches of **Santa Cristina** and **San Carlo**. Arcaded Via Roma continues its elegant course, ending in the expansive **Piazza Castello,** containing understated fountains, classical statues and the imposing **Palazzo Madama.** This traffic-free space is great for children. The grandly proportioned **Palazzo Reale,** residence of the Royal House of Savoy from 1646 to 1865, is here, as is the Church of San Lorenzo.

For a closer look at Turin's modern symbol, the **Mole Antonelliana**, head past the bookstands of arcaded Via Po: the tower appears on your left at the junction with Via Antonelliana. At the end of Via Po is the eponymous river, before which you pass through Piazza Vittorio Veneto. The riverside has some great places for children, including the **Parco e Castello del Valentino, Botanical Gardens** and cafés by the water.

Child-Friendly Festivals, Sports, Entertainments & Markets

Turin celebrates its patron saint on 24th June in the **Festa di San Giovanni Battista,** with colourful events including costumed parades and religious ceremonies during the day culminating in a huge fireworks display on the Po. Torino and its surrounding area (notably Rivoli and Chieri) get into the spirit of **Carnival** each February by staging masked balls and child-friendly street processions. Nearly a million people descend on Piazza San Carlo for the 10-day **CioccolaTÒ** festival (*www.cioccola-to.com*) in late March, where you can taste the dark stuff in all its forms. Classical music, dance and theatre performances fill the first week of July, during the **Sere d'Estate**, and classical music concerts cram theatre schedules at the **Settembre Musica** festival (*www.settembremusica.it*). This might not sound like a child-fest, but some of the world music concerts are hugely popular with families. The **Torino Film Festival** takes place in November (*www.torinofilmfest.org*). The Slow Food movement was born in nearby Bra, and each year for **Salone del Gusto** (Lingotto Fiere. ✆ *0172-419-711*, *www.salonedelgusto.com*. Admission: 20€ (£13.40) adults, 14€ (£9.40) Slow Food members, 12€ (£8) ages 11–18, under 10s free. Late October. Bus: 1 or 35. Tram: 18) foodies gather to feast on Piedmont's bountiful harvest.

The daily market at **Porto Palazza**, in Piazza della Repubblica (weekday mornings 6:30am–1:30pm and all day Saturday until 7:30pm), is said to be the biggest in Europe: fill your picnic basket and loft space with cheeses and bargains. *Antiquariati* (antiques) and *mercato delle pulci* (flea-market) knick-knacks, household items, jewellery, clothing, and books can be examined at the **Balôn** (from 8am Saturdays; the larger **Gran Balôn** takes place on the second Sunday of the month). Check *www.turismotorino.org* for the full list of upcoming specialist markets.

Recently shamed and demoted **Juventus** (nicknamed *i bianconeri* or *La Vecchia Signora*: 'the black-and-whites' or 'The Old Lady') will join their rivals **AC Torino** (nicknamed *La Granata* after their maroon shirts) at the Stadio Grande Torino (the brand spanking new 27,000-capacity stadium used in the 2006 Winter Olympics), until at least 2008, while they await a new, more compact stadium, to replace the soulless Stadio delle Alpi. Matchday tickets are available from tobacconists and *TotoCalcio* football pools offices throughout the city. For the latest ticket information check out *www.juventus.it* (✆ *011-65631*) and *www.torinofc.it* (✆ *011-1970-0348*). The **Turin Marathon** (✆ *011-455-9959*. *www.turinmarathon.it*) has been going strong for over 20 years: each September, the **Topolino Marathon** ('Mickey Mouse Marathon') for 6- to 13-year-olds accompanies the main event, starting on the Viale Virgilio in the Parco Valentino.

Planning Your Outings

If you plan to see lots of sights and travel around the city, the

Torino Card, available at Tourist Information centres, will save a ton of money and hassle. There are two types, lasting 48 (16€ – £10.70) and 72 hours (18€ – £12). Each card allows free entry for one adult and a child under 12 to over 140 tourist attractions, free access to the Turismo Bus Torino and Mole Antonelliana panoramic lift, free unlimited travel on public transport and discounts galore. Thankfully, many of the city's baroque attractions, the Egyptian Museum and Mole Antonelliana are clustered around Via Roma. Many have decent toilets and changing facilities. Down by the river, the **Borgo Medievale** and surrounding **Parco Valentino** require some walking around, but at least you're away from the traffic. In the Parco it may be convenient to use the facilities in a riverside café: this gives you the chance to stock up on refreshments and *gelati* and enjoy the riverside setting. At the time of publication, the Museo dell'Automobile (Automobile Museum) (Corso Unita d'Italia 40. *011-677-666; www.museoauto.it*. Admission: 6€ (£4) adults, 4€ (£2.70) under 15s. Tues–Sat 10am–6:30pm; Sun 10am–8:30pm. Bus: 1, 17, 18, 34 or 35) – every boy and dad's dream museum – was about to close until 2008 for a refit. If you love a stylish Bugatti or Ferrari, check with the tourist office for the latest news about reopening.

FAST FACTS: TURIN

Bookstores Libreria Internazionale Luxemburg, (Via C. Battisti 7, *011-561-3896*. Mon–Sat 8am–7:30pm, Sun 10am–1pm and 3–7pm), has a decent selection of English-language material. Another good bet for books in English is the chain store **Libreria Feltrinelli** (Piazza Castello 19, *011-541-627; www.feltrinelli.it*).

Chemists Farmacia Boniscontro (Corso Vittorio Emanuele 66, *011-541-271*) is open most of the time (day and night), closing only between 12:30 and 3pm.

Car Hire You can rent a vehicle in Turin, from **Avis** (Corso Turati 15. *011-500-852; www.avis.com*), or **Hertz** (Via Magellano 12. *011-502-080; www.hertz.it*).

Consulates British subjects will find their consulate at Via Saluzzo 60 (*011-650-9202*), open Monday to Friday from 9:15am to 12:15pm and 2:30 to 4:30pm. Irish citizens can contact the embassy in Rome (*06-697-9121*) or the Honorary Consul (*25518-8848*) in Milan.

Crime and Safety In an emergency, call *113*; this is a free call. The central police station is at Corso Vinzaglio 10 near Stazione di Porta Susa (*011-558-81*). Torino was once notorious for petty and violent crime but it's recently cleaned up its act. However, be especially careful in and around Porta Nuova station, Via Nizza and in any of the parks.

Emergencies The general emergency number is *113*; for an ambulance, dial *118*. Both are free calls.

Internet For Internet access, the Internet Train (*011-543-000*; ***www.internettrain.it***), just down the street from the central Piazza Castello at Via Carlo Alberto 18, is open Monday to Friday from 9:30am to 10pm, Saturday from 9:30am to 8pm, and Sunday from 3 to 7pm. There are a number of Wi-Fi hotspots around town, including inside the Caffè Torino (*011-547-356*) in Piazza San Carlo.

Laundry Lavasciuga, a Laundromat/Internet point with seven locations across the city (*335-750-7583*; ***www.lavasciuga.torino.it***), charges 7€ (£4.70) for a wash-and-dry of a small load. They're open daily from 8am to 10pm. Their nearest location to the train station is Via S. Anselmo 9.

Lost Property Ufficio Oggetti Smarriti at *011-665-3315 /011-443-0753* is the place to contact regarding lost items.

Luggage Storage Luggage storage at the Porta Nuova train station costs 3€ (£2) per bag for each 12-hour period; it's open daily from 4:30am to 2:30am.

Newspapers and Magazines For English-language newspapers check out the selection at the Porta Nuova station *edicole* (newsstands).

Post Office Turin's main post office is just west of Piazza San Carlo at Via Alfieri 10 (*011-546-800*. Mon–Fri 8:30am–7pm, Sat 8:30am–1pm).

River Po

Taxis There are taxi ranks around the city. For a steady stream go to the ones at the train stations, as well as around Piazza San Carlo and Piazza Castello. Dial *011-5737*, *011-5730*, or *011-3399* for a radio taxi.

Family-Friendly Sights

Cattedrale di San Giovanni Battista ★★ AGES 4 AND UP No visit to Torino is complete without an inquisitive examination of the **Turin Shroud (La Sacra Sindone)**, or at least the replica on display. The real thing is rarely on view (the next public outing is scheduled for 2025), so you can only see a box draped in fabric (inside is a silver casket within an iron box) kept at the **Cappella della Sacra Sindone**, an austere dark-marbled chapel designed by Guarino Guarini. The shroud was reputedly wrapped around the body of Christ after he was taken down from the cross – the haunting image of a 5ft 7inch man with blood stains and wounds consistent with the cause of death was

Turin Shroud

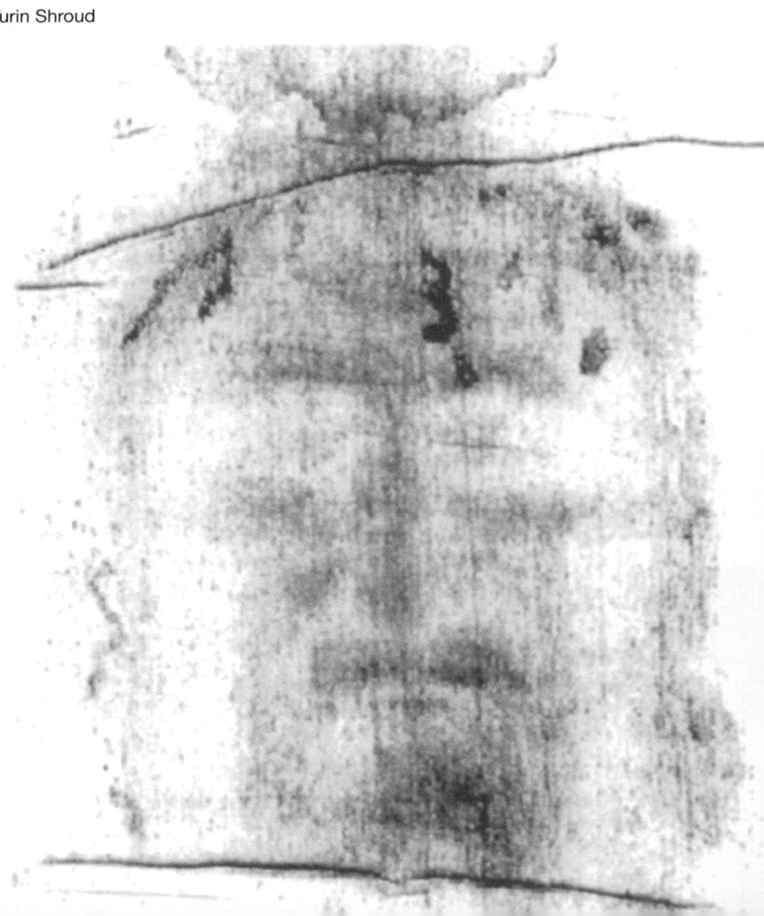

TURIN

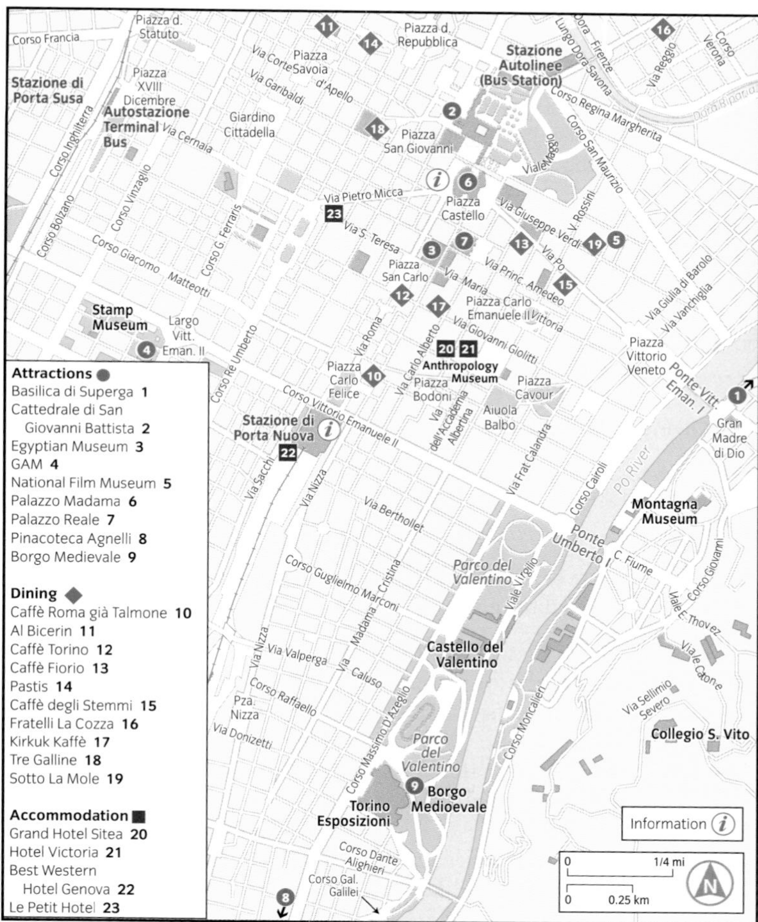

miraculously imprinted on the cloth. In 1988, carbon dating suggested that the shroud was made in the 13th or 14th centuries, but further forensic examinations and fabric historians have undermined the disbelievers' case. The shroud and the use of science and history to verify or dispute its status really catch the imagination of older children.

The **Museo della Sindone (Holy Shroud Museum)** at nearby Via San Domenico is full of evidence relating to the shroud.

*Via San Domenico 28 (☎ 011-436-5832; **www.sindone.org**) Admission: 6€ (£4) adults, 5€ (£3.35) under 14s, 9am–midday, 3–7pm daily*

Piazza San Giovanni. (☎ 011-436-1540). Free admission. Daily 7am–12:30pm and 3–7pm. Bus: 6, 11, 12, 27, 56 or 57.

FUN FACT The Italian Job

Before you go, don't forget to re-watch the 1969 classic film *The Italian Job***,** starring Michael Caine. The car chases involving nine Mini Coopers take place at some famous Turin landmarks. The traffic jam (instigated especially for the film by the city authorities) happens around Piazza Castello and Palazzo Madama; it's also here that the minis spin on the freshly mopped tiles. Down by the Po, the river was damned to allow the plucky little cars to cross at the weir – and nearby at the Ponte Vittorio Emmanuele bridge you'll recognise the Gran Madre di Dio church, where the stunt cars sped down 40 steps, criss-crossing a wedding party. A trip to the Pinacoteca Agnelli will bring back memories of the scene at the Lingotto test track. The final cliffhanger was filmed at Ceresole Reale, above a reservoir in the Gran Paradiso National Park about 45 miles north-west of Turin.

The Divine is in the Detail

- *La Sacra Sindone* measures 4.42 by 1.13 metres (14.3 – 3.7 ft).
- It is woven in herringbone twill consisting of flax and cotton.
- In 1898 Italian photographer Secondo Pia took the first photograph of the shroud, the negative of which illuminated a *chiaroscuro* (contrasting light and dark) image of a man. It whipped everyone into a frenzy: Was this what Jesus looked like?
- In 1988, microscopist Walter McCrone concluded that ordinary pigments were present, not blood. Subsequently, top chemist Alan Adler challenged McCrone by claiming that type AB blood was present.
- At the same time, a small part of the shroud was cut away and carbon-dated. These tests suggested the fabric was from 1260 and 1390, rendering the shroud nothing but a medieval fake.
- Other scientists have poo-pooed these results – saying that the piece used in the tests came from the part of the shroud that had been most handled over the years, giving a duff reading.
- The shroud has two dark parallel lines intersected by 29 roughly triangular holes surrounded by scorch marks. These happened during a fire at the Sainte-Chapelle, in Chambéry, in 1532: the silver storage cask melted, dropping red-hot silver on to the shroud.
- It was previously believed that the water stains had their origins in this fire incident, but fabric historians dispute this and suggest they come from damage incurred while it was rolled up in a clay jar, which was how precious fabrics were stored when Jesus was around.
- The cloth bears an unusual seam, only ever seen in fabric from around the 1st century

AD, found in the fortress of Masada near the Dead Sea.

GAM (Galleria Civica d'Arte Moderna e Contemporanea) ★ AGES 7 AND UP Turin's Modern Art museum was founded in 1863 and includes 18th- and 19th century works by late-neo-classical artists, so some of the collection predates what you'd usually call Modern Art. The exhibition is arranged chronologically, so is excellent for youngsters to get a grasp of the way art has developed. The rooms devoted to Italian art will definitely get some reactions from adults and children alike, especially the examples of post-war arte povera (translates as 'poor art' but is more about experimentation than art made by poverty-stricken artists, though many may well have been that too). There are over 600 works on display, including some by Canova, Hayez, De Chirico, Modigliani, Ernst, Warhol and Colombo. Temporary exhibitions feature contemporary artists and themed shows: recent exhibitors include photographer Paolo Mussat Sartor and American Jessica Stockholder. Tuesday is a great day to visit since admission is free all day.

*Via Magenta 31. (☎ 011-442-9518. **www.gamtorino.it**). Admission: 7.50€ (£5) adults, 4.50€ (£3) ages 10–25. Tues–Sun 9am–7pm. Bus: 5, 52, 58 or 62. Tram: 1 or 10.*

Mole Antonelliana & Museo Nazionale del Cinema (National Film Museum) ★★★ AGES 4 AND UP You'll have seen Il Mole from afar before you get the chance to gaze up at its steep ice-cream cone roof and elongated granite spire. This striking building looks like something from a retro-futuristic

FUN FACT Guess the film

Harry Potter e Il Calice di Fuoco

Guerre Stellari

I Puffi

Stanlio e Olio

Il Buono Il Brutto Il Cattivo

Tesoro, mi si sono ristretti i ragazzi

Tesoro, mi si è allargato il ragazzino

Lilly e Il Vagabondo

Il Padrino

Festa in Casa Muppet

Answers: *Harry Potter and the Goblet of Fire, Star Wars, The Smurfs, Laurel and Hardy, The Good, the Bad and the Ugly, Honey I Shrunk the Kids, Honey I Blew Up the Kids, Lady and the Tramp, The Godfather, Muppet Christmas Carol.*

FUN FACT Red Number Conundrum

What are the red neon lighted numbers on one side of the four-faced dome? A work of art called *Fibonacci Sequence* by Mario Merz: a progressive number sequence (1,1,2,3,5,8,13,21...) that represents a growth process model found in nature. Worked out the rules of the sequence?

Answer: Every number is the sum of the previous two.

film set with some Eiffel Tower thrown in: think Gotham City, Metropolis or Terry Gilliam's city in *Brazil*, which is apt as it now houses the National Film Museum. It's Turin's best attraction for children, who will love the dramatic trip to the viewing area via a glass lift that rises within the cavernous atrium and travels mysteriously through a hole in the colossal cupola. The 360-degree views of the city and Alpine peaks beyond from the platform are breathtaking. It was designed as a synagogue when work began in 1863, and subsequently became a monument to Italian unification on its completion in 1897. At 167 m (548 ft) it was once the tallest building in the world. It has been uncharitably called a glorified lightning conductor – ironic, as in 1953 the spire and angel at its zenith were severely damaged in an electric storm.

Film Museum

A small section of the museum tracks the early development of moving pictures, while the larger part is a fun-packed tribute to film, with reconstructed sets from period dramas and wild western saloon bars, as well as memorabilia and clips from celluloid classics like *Planet of the Apes*, *The Empire Strikes Back* and Fellini's *Satyricon*. In the immense Aula del Tempio hall, you can recline on a plush red chaise-longue, immersed in the soundtrack coming from the built-in speakers, gazing up at the main screen clips while the lift serenely rises and falls in your peripheral vision. It's the epitome of cinematic escape. The funky café is a cool spot for refreshments and food and the shop is worth a rummage as well.

*Via Montebello 20. (☎ 011-812-5658. **www.museonazionaledelcinema.it.**) Admission to museum: 5.20€ (£3.48) adults, 4.60€ (£3.08) ages 11–16;*

observation platform: 2.60€ (£1.75); museum and observation platform: 6.80€ (£4.55); under 10s free. Tues–Fri and Sun 9am–8pm; Sat 9am–11pm. Bus: 55, 56, 61 or 68. Tram: 13, 15 or 18.

Museo Egizio (Egyptian Museum) & Galleria Sabauda

★★★ **AGES 3 AND UP** This **Egyptian collection** is one of the world's largest and most important. The mummies, scarabs, papyrus scrolls and mighty statues on show will pique children's interest. A statue of Tutankhamun with the god Amon-Ra is said to be cursed, causing strange events to occur in its vicinity. This, the world's first Egyptian museum, owes much to the vision of Carlo Felice, who originally bought the Drovetti collection. Expeditions by Schiaparelli and Farina in the early 20th century followed. The museum played an influential role in the Nubia digs that rescued many treasures threatened by the waters of the Aswan dam: the recovered rock temple of Ellesiya can been seen here.

The House of Savoy amassed a sizeable collection of European paintings, which line the **Galleria Sabauda** *saloni* upstairs. Dutch and Flemish masters are well represented, including works by the Vans, Dyck, Eyck and der Weyden, as well as Rembrandt and Memling. Northern Italian artists from the Venetian, Lombard, Tuscan and Piedmontese schools also get a look in.

Statue of Amon-Ra and Tutankhamun

*Via Accademia delle Scienze 6. Museo Egizio. (☎ 011-561-7776. **www.museoegizio.org**). Admission: 6.50€ (£4.35) adults, 3€ (£2) ages 18–25, free for under 18s and over 60s. DC, MC, V. Tues, Fri, Sat–Sun 8:30am–2pm, Wed 2–7:30pm, Thurs 10am–7:30pm. Galleria Sabauda. (☎ 011-440-6903). Admission: 4€ (£2.70) adults, 2€ (£1.34) ages 18–25, free for under 18s and over 65s. Tues–Sun 8:30am–7:30pm (to 11pm Sat in summer). Bus: 4, 13, 18, 55 or 66.*

Palazzo Madama – Museo Civico di Arte Antica (Civic Museum of Ancient Art) ★

AGES 3 AND UP Beyond the baroque façade, added by celebrated architect Filippo Juvarra in the early 18th century, are a medieval castle (begun in 1276), the Roman Porta Praetoria, and several additions including a mighty marble staircase. Palazzo Madama gets its name from the *madame reali*, two regent widows who lived here in the 16th and 17th centuries and remodelled the building.

The **Museo Civico di Arte Antica** has been here since 1935 and contains 30,000 pieces, including Romanesque, Gothic and Renaissance sculpture and the celebrated *Hours of Milan* by Jan van Eyck. The first floor housed the seat of the Italian senate in the early 1860s and also contains the grand hall and royal apartments.

If all this royal refinement and fiddly detail fail to impress the children, the **Armeria Reale** at no.191 (a magnificent wing of the Palazzo Reale) will definitely fire their imaginations. This Royal Armoury is one of the best in Europe and includes some comical yet grotesque masks, and many fine examples of weaponry by Austrian and Bavarian craftsmen. Children will get a kick out of the 30 suits of armour, which include incongruously cute ones for regal youngsters and a dozen equestrian examples. The book-lined **Biblioteca Reale** next door conjures up fewer images of gore and knightly valour, with its displays of Renaissance drawings and miniatures collected by Carlo Alberto. Highlights include a sanguine self-portrait by da Vinci and prized pictures by Raphael, Dürer and Rembrandt.

*Palazzo Madama: Piazza Castello. (☎ 011-442-9911. **www.comune.torino.it/palazzomadama**). Free admission. Tues–Sat 10am–8pm; Sun 10am–11pm. Confirm hours with the tourist board as there is ongoing restoration work. Armeria and Biblioteca Reale: Piazza Castello 191. (☎ 011-543-889. **www.artito.arti.beniculturali.it**). 4€ (£2.70) adults, free for under 18s. Tue–Sun 10am–7pm. Bus: 6, 11, 12, 27, 56 or 57.*

Palazzo Reale e Giardini Reali (Royal Palace and Gardens) AGES 3 AND UP For a look around the opulent salons of this grandiose House of Savoy residence, begun in 1645, you'll have to join a 90-minute guided tour. Although the in-depth explanations of the lavish interiors by an expert guide in Italian (and in English via a headset recording) are fascinating, they may be a tad long for fidgety children. If you like tapestries, Chinese and Japanese vases and gilded flourishes, then you're in for a treat. The highlights are the evocative *Salone dei Svizzeri* and Juvarra's ingenious and elegant scissor-like staircase, the *Scala delle Forbici*. For a quick dip into the palace with smaller children, visit the cracking **Armeria Reale** (see above). For a well-earned breather from the regal frippery take a walk around the Royal Gardens, where there's plenty of open space for youngsters to let off steam.

Piazza Castello. (☎ 011-436-1455). Admission: 6.50€ (£4.35). Tues–Sun 8:30am–7:30pm (to 11pm Sat in summer). Bus: 6, 11, 12, 27, 56 or 57.

Pinacoteca Agnelli

AGES 6 AND UP You'll probably recognise the iconic Fiat Lingotto test track from *The Italian Job*. Inside, adults will enjoy the 25 gems of ancient and modern art, including works by Canova, Tiepolo, Manet, Renoir, Matisse, Picasso, Balla and Severini. For scholars of the motor industry there are exhibits relating to the halcyon days of the Agnellis' Fiat company. Temporary exhibitions and an excellent shop are found on the five lower floors.

230/103 Via Nizza, Lingotto. (☎ 011-006-2713). Admission to permanent exhibition: 4€ (£2.70) adults, 2.50€ (£1.68) under 16s; temporary exhibitions: 6€ (£4) adults, 4€ (£2.70) under 16s. Tue–Sun 10am–7pm. Bus/Tram: 35/1, 18 or 34.

Activities, Attractions, Parks & Boat Trips by the Po

The **Parco Valentino** offers lots of green space for children to run around, playgrounds and riverside cafés.

☎ 011-669-9372; ***www.comune.torino.it/verdepubblico****. 8am–8pm.*

The modest **Orto Botanico** AGES 3 AND UP founded in 1729 is worth a look for its orangery, lily ponds and serene, shady paths.

Viale Matteotti 25. (☎ 011-670-5985; ***www.bioveg.unito.it****).*

Children will like the **Borgo e Rocca Medievale** ALL AGES which houses a mock medieval village with artisan workshops, churches, dwellings and shops. It was created in 1884 to raise public awareness about the past.

Viale Virgilio, Parco del Valentino. (☎ 011-443-1701). Free entry to Borgo. Admission to Rocca: 5€ (£3.35) adults, 2.50€ (£1.68) under 16s. March to November: Tue–Sun 9am–7pm.

Along the waterfront you'll come across the handsome red-brick façade of the **Castello Valentino** (Viale Mattioli 39), built in the

Rare Fiat Car

17th century as a summer French-style château residence for Maria Cristina. Unfortunately, visitors are seldom allowed a proper look inside, as it's now used by the university and is undergoing restoration.

If you fancy gliding down the Po, hop on the **Valentino or Valentina boats** ★ AGES 3 AND UP run by ATM at the Murazzi or Borgo Medievale jetties.

(011-576-4733). 3.10 € (£2.08). Winter: public holidays only 3pm, 4:15 and 5:45pm; spring/autumn: Saturday and holidays 3pm, 4:15 and 5:45pm; summer: 3pm, 4:15 and 5:45pm daily plus 7pm, 9:30pm and 10:45pm on public holidays.

Short Trips Out Of Town

Castello di Rivoli: Museo di Arte Contemporanea

AGES 4 AND UP ★★This former Savoy hunting lodge designed by Juvarra, in the Susa valley 20 km west of the city centre, was left to fall into ruin after the French pummelled it in 1690. Architect Andrea Bruno imaginatively transformed the skeletal remains into Italy's most bizarre contemporary art gallery. The restored interiors of the main palace house the permanent collection, which includes works by Richard Long, Bruce Nauman, Rebecca Horn and notoriously mischievous local artist Maurizio Cattelan (who made a sculpture of Pope John Paul II being struck by a meteorite). Temporary exhibitions, a café-restaurant, a multimedia lab (great for older children) and shop are housed in the Manica Lunga annexe. On Saturdays and Sundays a shuttle bus (3€ (£2) return, free for under 11s) serves the castle: departing from the corner of Piazza di Castello and Via Po (by the newsstand) and at Piazza Carlo Felice (in front of Hotel Roma).

*Piazza Malfalda di Savoia, 10098 Rivoli. (011-956-5222; **www.castellodirivoli.it**). 7 €, Free for under 11s.Tues–Thu 10am–5pm, Fri–Sun 10am–9pm. Bus: 36.*

Basilica di Superga and the **Sassi-Superga Tranvia** ★★ AGES 4 AND UP *Torinesi* families will tell you that a visit to this loftily-perched baroque basilica is best enjoyed by taking the verdant Funivia railway route. Vittorio Amedeo II commissioned Sicilian Filippo Juvarra to build the church in 1715 as a votive offering to the Virgin Mary for Turin's deliverance from the French siege of 1706. The light pastel-coloured exterior contrasts with the vast gloomy chamber and chapels inside. Its symbolic significance may be lost on us, but the 360-degree views of the city and Alpine silhouette from the terrace definitely strike a chord. Footie fans should make the pilgrimage to the small museum here dedicated to *Il Grande Torino*: the members of the great Torino side who died when their plane crashed into the hill at Superga in 1949.

Strada della Basilica di Superga 73, about 6.5 km (4 miles) north-east of the town centre in Parco Naturale *della Collina di Superga. (☎ 011-898-0083. **www.basilicadisuperga.com**). Free admission. Grande Torino Museum: 2€ (£1.34). Daily 9am–noon and 3–6pm (until 5pm November to March). Reached by funivia railway at Stazione Sassi on Piazza Gustavo Modena (follow Corso Casale on east side of the River Po). Tram: 15 from Via XX Settembre to Stazione Sassi.*

Shopping

The Torinesi have a passion for fashion, football and chocolate. Being a university town, it also has its fair share of bookshops. Dedicated clothes pegs flock to the sales on Via Roma in January and July. Shopaholics should find something to tempt them among the wide range of shops on Via Garibaldi (Europe's longest pedestrianised street), whilst Via Mercanti, Via Barbaroux and Via San Tommaso have a compelling mix of artigiani workshops, boutiques, delis and various curiosities.

Fashion

For Dolce e Gabbana, Miu Miu, Prada, Gucci, Fendi and other designer labels, visit **San Carlo** at Via Roma 53 (☎ *011-516-3201*). If bling is still your thing you might want a look at **Versace Galleria** (San Federico 60 ☎ *011-547-002*).

Football

Juventini should check out **Juventus Store** (Via Garibaldi 4 ☎ *011-433-870*). **Olympic Store** next door (Via Garibaldi 6 ☎ *011-52-17371*) has a wide selection of sportswear.

Books

The sturdy old bookstands under arcaded Via Po are filled with intriguing titles. Look out for some beautifully illustrated guides to botany and architecture. **Materiale Resistente** (Via Po 25 ☎ *011-812-669*) is a technicolour dream of posters, CDs, vinyl and second-hand books. As you head off Via Po and towards the Mole: **Little Nemo** ★★ FIND will thrill movie memorabilia and comic collectors. *Via Montebello 2, (☎ 011-812-7089, **www.littlenemo.it**).*

Chocolate

Come to Turin and make like the *Torinesi*. Happily, this means having a daily dose of *cioccolato*. Unlike some kinds of gourmet chocolate, the smoothness of *gianduja* means that children will like it – and unlike most of the mainstream chocolate brands available back home, these are free of E-numbers, chemical stabilisers and frightening trans-fats. So, a little bit will do them no harm. Two terms you need to become familiar with: a **gianduja** is the result of lovingly pulverised and pasted sugar, mashed cocoa nibs and ground hazelnuts. A **gianduiotto** is a gianduja moulded into a distinctive shape and wrapped in foil.

If you're serious about tasting what the too-many-to-mention chocolate shops and cafés offer, a

ChocoPass buys you 10 temple-aching tasting sessions in 24 hours for 10€ (£6.70); 15 sessions in 48 hours costs 15€ (£10); or 20 in five days, 20€ (£13.40). Contact Turismo Torino information points. And if you're truly hardcore, arrange to be in the city in March for **La Grande Festa dei Cioccolato Torino e in Piemonte** – a festival of chocolate with tasting trails, stands, samplings and live demonstrations. See ***www.cioccola-to.com***

Here's a small taster of Turin's chocolate outlets to visit:

Peyrano ★★ Since 1915 Peyrano's have conched wood-toasted cocoa nibs to make a velvety gianduja that weakens even the steadiest knees.

*Via Andrea Doria 4 (011-517-1641); Corso Moncalieri 47 (011-660-2202; **http://www.peyrano.com/**)*

Confetteria Avvignano You'll find hand-made giandujas for those who appreciate size as much as quality. Children will love the chocolate fashioned into fun shapes, including spoons, tools, football boots and cups.

*Piazza Carlo Felice 50 (011-541-992; **http://www.confetteria-avvignano.it**)*

Confetteria Stratta ★ Stratta's speciality is plain chocolate flavoured with spices like cardamom, cinnamon and pink pepper. They also sell crystallised rose petals and mint leaves – a great gift for gran.

*Piazza San Carlo 191 (011-547-920; **http://www.stratta1836.it/**)*

Gelateria Pepino ★ Opened by a Neapolitan in the late 1800s, Pepino is a *gelato* glutton's dream, and home of the legendary *pinguino* – white ice cream covered in chocolate.

Piazza Carignano 8 (011-542-009).

Guido Gobino The original makers of the *Tourinot* – a small gianduiotto containing their own roasted hazelnuts made according to an old Piedmontese recipe.

*Via Cagliari 15/b (011-247-6245; **http://www.guidogobino.it**)*

Caffè Platti Pop in for an array of inventive confectionery recipes, but you can't go wrong with their arresting bits of ginger and orange enrobed in the smoothest dark chocolate.

*Corso V. Emanuele II 72 (011-506-9056; **http://www.platti.it/**)*

Cafés, Snacks & Family-Friendly Dining

Turin is famed for its elegant and ornate cafés, many of which sell their own chocolate creations, including **Caffè Roma già Talmone** (Piazza Carlo Felice 36. *011-506-9215*. ***www.romagiatalmone.it***. 7am–1am daily), which has wonderful interiors (a 1912 cash register and a 1930s bar) and tempting pastries. For a taste of the heady Bicerin concoction of coffee, chocolate and cream, pop into Turin's oldest caffè, **Al Bicerin**, at Via Po 8 (*011-817-3225*), once a haunt of Dumas and Nietzsche. **Caffè Torino** (Piazza San Carlo 204.

Wine Cellar

☎ *011-547-356*) is full of neo-baroque refinement and presents patrons with tasty nibbles to accompany a drinks order. Another old favourite, **Caffè Fiorio** (Via Po 8. ☎ *011-817-3225*) serves the most delicious gianduja ice-cream in town, as well as tasty panini and tramezzini (sandwiches). For picnic produce, look no further than the massive **Porta Palazza market** on Piazza della Repubblica. Nearby **Pastis** (Piazza Emanuele Filiberto 9. ☎ *01-521-1085*), an arty hangout, serves Torino's famous *aperitivo*, Vermouth, from the original Carpano bottle, as well as the ubiquitous Cinzano. Similarly, **Caffè degli Stemmi** ★★ FIND (Via Po 35. ☎ *011-817-2260*) has bags of character as well as a cornucopia of enthralling movie memorabilia that children will love. Italy's first cinema was opened here. Order a drink (the soft drinks, *aperitivi*, wines and *birra artiginiale* are superb), and ask for the huge platter of *salumi piemontesi*: cold cuts, cheeses, pickles and grissini.

La Cucina Torinese shows some Gallic influences: look out for the fondue-like *bagna caoda* (hot bath), a garlic, anchovy, milk, olive oil and

Caffè degli Stemmi

butter dipping sauce for vegetables. If your children are adventurous eaters they'll love it. *Agnolotti*, ravioli-like pasta pockets, are traditionally filled with meat, but you'll also find them with cheese, fish or even vegetarian-friendly fillings. Children are unlikely to complain about Turin's dolci (desserts), which include *panna cotta*, a smooth cooked cream, *zabaglione*, a whipped custard, and light pastries like *lingue di gatto* (cat's tongues). Remember that many eateries in the city centre are closed on Sunday night.

Fratelli La Cozza ★★

NEAPOLITAN For a mozzarella-melting slice of *la vera* pizza washed down with a good measure of Neapolitan humour, head for the double clam logo of La Cozza. Vivid colours and tastes will excite the senses of all ages here. Seafood devourers should try the ubiquitous *cozze* (mussels), which feature in over a dozen *deliziosi* dishes. The Margherita will win over the fussiest of palates: the *pizzaiolo* here is a direct descendant of the famous Raffaele Esposito Brandi, who invented the *trecolore* combination of pomodoro, mozzarella and basilico in honour of the Queen of Italy, La Regina Margherita di Savoia.

*Corso Regio Parco 39. (☎ 011-859-900. **www.lacozza.com**). Primi 7€–11€ (£4.70–7.40); secondi 9€–16€ (£6–10.70); AE, DC, MC, V. 12:30–2:30pm and 8–11:30pm. Closed Sun. Bus: 19 or 68.*

Kirkuk Kaffé ★ KURDISH VALUE

The Kurdish–Piedmontese partnership of Fuad and Giulia have created a relaxing eatery with a near-Eastern ambience of comfy cushions and ornamental hubbly-bubbly pipes at the back. The great-value dishes include kebabs, falafel and some veggie-friendly mezze and salads.

Via Carlo Alberto 18/16 Bis. (☎ 011-530-657). Primi 5€–10€ (£3.35–6.70); secondi 7€–13€ (£4.70–8.70); MC, V. 12:30–2:30pm and 8–11:30pm. Closed Sun. Bus: 18, 61 or 68.

Tre Galline PIEDMONTESE Turin's oldest restaurant is a great place to sample hearty regional classics. The cheery wood-panelled interior and friendly service make for an atmospheric backdrop and child-friendly dining experience. For the older palate, check out the Piedmont standard, *il bollito misto* (a meat and vegetable stew), in a *bagnetto verde* (green sauce of garlic, parsley, egg and anchovy) or *rosso* (fiery red sauce of chillis and tomatoes). Younger diners will love the *agnolotti* (meat-filled pasta pockets).

Via Gian Francesco Bellezia 37. (☎ 011-436-6553). Reservations highly recommended. Primi 8€–11€ (£5.35–7.40); secondi 11€–16€ (£7.40–10.70); tasting menu 32€ (£21.50) AE, DC, MC, V. Tues–Sat 12:30–2:30pm and 7:30–10:30pm; Mon 7:30–10:30pm. Bus: 3, 4, 16 or 57.

Sotto La Mole PIEDMONTESE

'Under the Mole' is a cheery little place to eat after an early evening visit to the cinema museum nearby, and has a buzzing, family-friendly vibe. Expect Piedmontese classics and imaginative dishes with a lighter Mediterranean flavour. They are also renowned for their excellent selection of *formaggi* and a reasonably priced wine list.

Via Montebello 9. (☎ 011 817-9398). Reservations recommended. Primi 6€–11€ (£4–7.40); secondi 9€–15€ (£6–10); MC, V. 8pm–midnight; Closed Wed and August. Bus: 55, 56, 61 or 68. Tram: 13, 15 or 18.

Family-Friendly Accommodation

EXPENSIVE

Grand Hotel Sitea ★★ The classy Sitea has a good reputation for looking after guests with children. Public and guest rooms are plush and comfortable – marrying traditional furnishings with fresh, light decorative touches. Marbled bathrooms are luxurious, although many are a little cramped. There are variously sized doubles where under-12s can sleep in added beds at no extra cost. The suites consist of interconnecting rooms with garden views. Many rooms facing the atrium can become airless, so make sure the air conditioning is working before you go to bed at night. The fabulous breakfasts include lots of fresh fruit and savoury food, although the service can be a little haphazard.

*Via Carlo Alberto 35, 10123 Torino. (☎ 011- 517-0171. [Fax] 011-548-090) 10132 Torino. (**www.thi.it.**). 120 units. 305€ (£204) double; 329€–590€ (£220–395) suite. Buffet breakfast included. AE, DC, MC, V. Free parking. Amenities: Piedmontese restaurant with high-chairs; bar; concierge; tour desk; car-rental desk; 24-hr. room service; fitness centre, laundry service; dry cleaning. In room: A/C, TV, dataport, Internet, minibar, hairdryer, safe.*

EXPENSIVE

Hotel Victoria A pleasant garden and recently refurbished rooms in varying sizes make this a great choice for families: there are four junior suites and four spacious duplex suites. Children and adults can take advantage of the excellent facilities, which include an indoor pool, gym, free wireless Internet and free bike hire. Under-16s can sleep on sofa beds at no extra charge in the double rooms. Room 511 is a two-level junior suite, ideal for larger family groups.

*Via Nino Costa 4, 10123 Torino. (☎ 011-561-1909. [Fax] 011-561-1806. **www.hotelvictoria-torino.com**). 100 units. 190€ (£127) standard double; 210€ (£140) deluxe double; 300 € (£200) junior. suite. Rates include breakfast. AE, DC, MC, V. Parking 20€ (£13.40) Amenities: bar; free bikes; concierge; limited room service; laundry service; dry cleaning; Internet point. In room: A/C (in some rooms), TV, dataport, minibar, hairdryer, safe.*

MODERATE

Best Western Hotel Genova ★ VALUE Turin has a few Best Western hotels, but the recently refurbished (in 2005) Genova is the best for location and facilities. Being opposite Porta Nuova station makes it really convenient for the airport and trains, and it's close to Via Roma and Piazza Carlo Felice. Public areas are bright and homely with elegant *Novecento* furnishings. There's a good choice of differently sized guest rooms for families – they even have a kettle for making hot drinks. The only downside is the lack of choice at the buffet breakfast.

*Via Sacchi 14/b, 10128 Torino. (☎ 011-562-9400 [fax]: 011-562-9896. **www.albergogenova.it**). 78 units. 100€–200€ (£67–134) standard double; 120€–270€ (£80–180) deluxe double/triple; one child under 12 free with two adults.Rates include breakfast. AE, DC, MC, V. Parking 21€ (£14). Amenities: limited room service; bar; laundry service; dry cleaning; tour desk; spa and gym available nearby. In room: A/C, satellite TV, Wi-Fi, minibar, hairdryer, kettle, safe.*

MODERATE

Le Petit Hotel The centrally located Le Petit offers good value family accommodation and a handy restaurant next door. The décor is a little dated and uninspiring but overall it's comfortable and clean. Book a room facing the inner courtyard, as street-side options can be noisy. Check out the last minute family deals on their website, which often include Torino Cards. They also have small apartments available for a one-week minimum stay.

*Via San Francesco d'Assisi 21, 10121 Torino. (☎ 011-561-2626. [fax] 011-562-2807. **www.lepetithotel.it**). 100 units. 165€ (£111) double; 260€ (£174) triple.Rates include breakfast. AE, DC, MC, V. Parking 20€ (£13.40). Amenities: bar-restaurant; laundry service. In room: A/C, TV, dataport, minibar, hairdryer, safe.*

MONFERRATO & LE LANGHE: WINE COUNTRY

Asti: 60 km (37 miles) SE of Turin, 127 km (79 miles) SW of Milan; Alba: 60 km (37 miles) S of Turin, 155 km (96 miles) SW of Milan.

South of Turin, the flat Po valley becomes the sweetly undulating hills of Le Langhe and Roero, a territory bisected by the River Tanaro. Vineyards stretch as far as the eye can see: their grapes, among them Moscato and Nebbiolo, produce the famous **Asti Spumante, Barbaresco** and **Barolo** wines. It's a relaxing area to visit after a trawl around Turin, Milan or Genoa; a place for tasting the venerated fruits of the land: the wine, truffles, cheeses, meats. For children, there are step-back-in-time hilltop villages like Cherasco and Renaissance towns such as Asti to explore. Not surprisingly, Le Langhe and Monferrato are popular with Swiss and French foodies, and not the natural choice for a family holiday in Northern Italy. However, the region is definitely worth dipping into – the best times being spring, when poppies and other wild flowers cluster around the gnarled vines, and the autumn, when oak, chestnut and poplar fire the landscape with colour, the grape harvest is cause for communal celebration and truffle fever hits the wooded valleys and bustling markets.

Poppies in Le Langhe

Essentials

Getting There

By Train There are frequent trains linking Asti with **Turin** (35–60 min.). To reach Alba (1½ hr) from Turin you need to change at Brà or Cavallermaggiore. Most trains from Turin to Brà (1 hr) require a change at Cavallarmaggiore.

By Car Asti, 60 km (37 miles) south-east of Turin, can be reached from Turin in about an hour via the A21. To reach Brà take the A6 for 35 km (22 miles) south and exit; to carry on to Alba, exit at the S231 and drive 24 km (15 miles).

Visitor Information

The Asti **APT tourist office** is near the train station at Piazza Alfieri 29 (☎ *0141-530-357;* fax: *0141-538-300*; ***www.terredasti.it***). Alba has two tourist offices: at Corso Vittorio Emanuele 19 (☎/fax: *0173-362-562;* ***www.comune.alba.cn.it***), and a regional office at Piazza Medford 3, opposite the bus station (☎ *0173-35-833* or *0173-362-807*; fax: *0173-363-878*; ***www.langheroero.it***). The **Ufficio Turismo** in Brà is at Via Moffa di Lisio 14 (☎ *0172-430-185*; ***www.comune.bra.cn.it***). You can pick up a *Carta dei Vini* and *Le Cattedrali del Vino* from these offices: an annotated map and detailed booklet showing wine tasting outlets (*enoteche*) in the region.

Festivals & Markets

Asti

Late June and early July sees the **Astiteatro** (☎ *0141-399-111*; ***www.astiteatro.it***), a festival of theatre, music and dance. The third Sunday of September hosts the **Palio,** a famous bareback horse race full of medieval pageantry, similar to the one in Siena. It coincides with the **Douja d'Or** (***www.doujador.it***), a week-long celebration of the *vendemmia* (grape harvest), an excuse for dancing, drinking, eating and general revelry. There are food and drink-related festivals throughout the year in the surrounding villages: check ***www.terredasti.it*** for a complete list.

Asti has two **food markets** heaving with agricultural bounty. The **Campo del Palio** (Wed and Sat 7:30am–1pm) has stalls selling all manner of produce, flowers and even farm machinery; there's also the covered food market, the **Mercato Coperto** (Piazza della Liberta. Mon–Wed and Fri 8am–1pm and 3:30–7:30pm, Thu 8:30am–1pm, and Sat 8am–7:30pm). An **antiques fair** is held here on the fourth Sunday of every month, except during August.

Alba

The annual **Fiera del Tartufo Bianco** (white truffle festival) takes place in the first week of October, climaxing in the **Palio degli Asini** (**Race of the Asses**; ☎ *0173-362-806*), a spoof version of Asti's equine extravaganza. It is a fun event that children and adults will never forget. From the second weekend in October to December, on weekend Sunday mornings, Alba hosts a **truffle market** where fragrant soil-speckled specimens fetch big sums. In late August, the humble hazelnut variety *Tonda Gentile* is given star status at the **Sagra della Nocciola** festival in nearby Cortemilia. The Alba calendar is awash with gastronomic extravaganzas: check ***www.comune.alba.cn.it*** or contact the tourist office for an up-to-date list of events.

Brà

You'll see lots of oversized veg at the annual **Fiera di Pasquetta**, an Easter fair with agricultural allure, including growers' prizes up for grabs and local produce to taste. The general **Friday market** (7am–1pm) covers a wide area from Piazza XX Settembre and Via Garibaldi to the Mercato Coperto and Via Carlo Alberto.

Planning Your Outings

Exploring Monferrato and Le Langhe requires a car: public transport services are unreliable and infrequent (see Fast Facts: car hire). Arm yourself with a decent road map: an easy-to-use map book will cost you 11–15€ (£7.40–10), the cheaper but more cumbersome, fold-out Istituto Geografico De Agostino 1:500,000 *Carta Stradale* just 7€ (£4.70). **Libreria Feltrinelli** (Piazza Castello 19) and the Autogrill motorway service station shops usually stock both.

If you want to visit vineyards and smaller towns, like the **Negro estate** and **Ellio Grasso** in Monforte D'Alba, the tourist offices have detailed leaflets. For sports activities near to where you are staying, your hosts will no doubt have excellent tips and recommendations – failing that, the tourist office has plenty of advice and leaflets.

Asti

Asti is a busy town with enough charm to warrant a few hours' gazing up at its 120 towers (it was known as the 'city of a hundred towers' by medieval types, who obviously didn't realise the future held 20 more), admiring

Battistero di San Pietro, Asti

its Renaissance *palazzi* and quaffing a glass or two of its *Spumante*, the sweetish, sparkling white wine that carries Asti's name all over the world. Just north of the train station and parking zones lies the town's focal point and market area: **Campo del Palio**, scene of the frenzied annual horse race; Piazza Libertà and Piazza Alfieri, where you'll find the tourist office; and Corso Alfieri, where handsome Renaissance palaces attest to the town's wealth. You can visit the home and a museum dedicated to Asti's famous son, the 18th century poet Vittorio Alfieri, at no. 375. The town's patron San Secondo was imprisoned in the **Torre Rossa**, the pink-bricked tower at the western end of Corso Alfieri. He was beheaded where the Romanesque-Gothic **Church of San Secondo** stands today, and his remains are kept in a creepy crypt inside. Also worth a gander is the 14th century **Duomo**, whose architectural features beckon you to look up and gape – the vast space inside, festooned with frescoes, is equally jaw-dropping. At the eastern end of the Corso Alfieri, next to the **Battistero San Pietro**, a rotund Romanesque baptistery is the 15th century **Church of San Consavia**, which houses an interesting:

Museum of Archaeology and Paleontology ★ ALL AGES

Children will love the Egyptian mummies and prehistoric mammals.

Museo Archeologico e Paleontologico. Corso Alfieri 2. Free admission. Tue–Sat 9am–noon, 3–6pm and Sun 10am–noon.

Alba

Alba is hemmed in by the rivers Tanaro and Cherasca, its compact, polygonal-shaped core studded with Gothic *palazzi* and medieval *torre*, giving it a magical atmosphere. The narrow streets are filled with fantastic little shops displaying the town's gastronomic gems: wines, truffles, cheeses, meats and hazelnut-chocolate treats. Take a leisurely stroll around the market and visit its principal sight, the **Duomo**, at the north end of the

Outdoor Pursuits: Getting Active in Piedmont's Wine Country

Many hotels provide bicycles, but if you are after a decent mountain bike try **Cicli Gagliardini** (Via Ospedale 7, Alba. ✆ *0173-440-726*) or **Cicli Chiesa** (Via Barbacana 10, Brà. ✆ *0172-412-465*). Keen outdoorsy families should check out **Fuoritraccia** (Rifugio Ristorante La Pavoncella, Loc. S. Giovanni Belbo 1, 12072 Camerana; ✆/[fax] 0174-906-414. ***www.fuoritraccia.com***), off the beaten track in the wilder Alta Langhe hills about 20 miles south of Alba. They organise themed tours and adventure sports throughout the year, including climbing, mountain-biking, skiing, rafting, horse-riding and even dog-sleighing.

main thoroughfare, Corso Vittorio Emmanuele. The 14th century interior was somewhat over-restored in the 19th century, but it retains the intricately carved and inlaid early stalls by Bernardino da Fossato from the 1500s.

Barolo

Amid the wine-producing vineyards of Alba's hinterland, there are hilltop villages with enticingly higgledy-piggledy historic centres. Here you'll invariably find *enoteche*: wine shops that allow you to taste before you buy. Barolo is one such charming place, crammed with fairytale dwellings and dominated by a 12th century castle:

Castello Faletti Children will love a nose around the grand rooms and the folk museum, which has a detailed model of medieval Barolo with hundreds of figurines going about their

Barolo

daily tasks of slaying pigs and baking bread.

Piazza Falletti. (☎ 0173-56277). 4€ (£2.70) adults, 2.50€ (£1.68) 6–18 years; 10am–12:30pm, 3–6:30pm; November, December and March reduced hours, please phone. Closed January.

Adults can have a sip or two of the town's rich and powerful vintages in the adjoining *enoteca* and find out more about the Nebbiolo grape, Dolcetto (a fruity number), Barbera d'Alba, Barbaresco, and the 'King of the Reds', Barolo itself.

*(☎ 0173-56277. **www.baroloworld.it**). Open 10am–12:30pm, 3–6:30pm. November, December and March reduced hours, please phone. Closed January.*

Brà

The twin charms of Brà are its bountiful markets and baroque beauty: you could easily enjoy half a day or more exploring the broad streets and hilly environs around the **Parco Zazzola**, where you can hear the town's distant bell chimes whilst picnicking and playing. Begin your tour in the historic centre, Piazza Caduti per la Libertà, known as 'della Rocca', with its elegant *palazzi* and churches: **Palazzo Mathis, Palazzo Comunale, Palazzo Garrone** and the 17th Century **Chiesa di Sant'Andrea,** which has an altar dedicated to the town's patron San Sebastiano. Corso Garibaldi connects the central square with Piazza XX

FUN FACT A Brimful of Brà Facts

'Brà' is said to come from the word *Braida*: a term describing the vines planted in wide rows, allowing the sowing of seeds in-between.

La Zizzola sits 365 metres above sea level on the site of the ancient Roman fortress, Rocca Fonteria.

Palazzo Rosso on Corso Garibaldi was owned by a wealthy noble who fought in the Napoleonic Wars in Russia: the palace is renowned for its vast *cantine* (cellars), nicknamed *I russi* ('the Russians'), carved out of the tufo rock by the engineer, Quaglia. They once contained nearly half a million bottles of wine.

The Slow Food Movement was born here in 1986, and Brà continues to have some of the bolder upholders of the Movement's mantra: 'to defend biodiversity in our food supply... spread the education of taste... and link quality producers with consumers'.

Brà's gourmet shops are filled with 30—40 cm diameter wheels of its locally matured cheese. Ask for a sliver (*posso assaggiare questi formaggi, per favore?*) of the Brà Tenero (soft type which is white), Brà Duro (harder type with a tangy taste), Brà Stravecchio (super-aged), and Brà Ciucco (rubbed in wine).

Nearby Pollenzo is the home of the Università di Scienze Gastronomiche, the only university of gastronomy in the world. Pollenzo is also the site of Roman baths, an amphitheatre which once held nearly 20,000 people and a bloody 5th century battle.

Settembre, epicentre of market day. Above the arcaded Portico dell'Ala is pedestrianised Corso Cottolengo, accessed via a set of steps, where you can peek through the wrought iron at lush private gardens. Along Corso Garibaldi you'll pass some grand bourgeois and aristocratic edifices, including the **Palazzo Rosso** (see 'A Brimful of Brà Facts', below), as well as the **Trinità church** ★★ before reaching Piazza XX Septembre and the 18th century **Chiesa di Santa Maria**.

Back at Piazza Caduti Libertà, there is the option of climbing Via Barbacana, toward Monte Guglielmo and the Parco Zazzola, where a curious octagonal building, Villa Zizzola stands, built in 1840 and, according to local legend, has hosted many a black magic ritual. This lofty spot commands sweeping views, and is perfect for picnics and play. On the way you can visit the Rococo church of **Santa Chiara** and **Palazzo Traversa** (Via Parpera 4. *0172-423-880*. Free admission. Tue and Thu 3–6pm; third and fourth Sat and Sun 10am–12pm and 3–6pm; other times by appointment only) with its Ghibelline-style medieval battlements and museum of archaeology and art. From the palace balcony, admire Bràs wonderful *tetti di terra cotta* (terracotta tiled roofs). A must for children with an interest in animals is the:

Museo Civico Craveri ★★

FIND ALL AGES which has exotic birds, a weather station, fossils and prehistoric finds from the Sahara.

Via Craveri 15. (0172-412-010). Free admission. Tue–Sun 3–6pm.

Cherasco

Compact Cherasco, 5 km south of Brà, is a pleasant little town to explore for a couple of hours. The austere **Castle Visconteo** was built by Luchino Visconti in 1348 and acquired by the Savoys in the 1500s: although the castle is seldom open to the public, children can re-enact medieval jousts in and around striking fortifications. There is a wonderful walk amidst plane trees here and stunning views of the surrounding hills, Novello, La Morra and Vergne. Visitors are welcome to wander the ornate *saloni* at 17th century **Palazzo Salmatoris** (Free admission. 9:30am–12:30pm and 3–6pm) where Napoleon signed the *armistizio di Cherasco* in 1796 and the Turin Shroud was exhibited in the *saletta del silenzio* in 1706. Temporary art exhibitions are held in the less flamboyant salons. Also worth a look is the beautiful 13th–14th century **church of San Pietro**, with its Romanesque-Gothic red-brick façade, campanile and frescoed interiors. A photo opportunity awaits at the **Madonna del Rosario triumphal arch** and archaeological finds fill sumptuously decorated rooms at the:

Museo Civico GB Adriani AGES 4 AND UP Palazzo Gotti di Salerano (*0172-427-050*). Free admission. March to December: 9:30am–12.30pm and 3–6:30pm.

The town has some enticing food emporia perfect for filling the picnic hamper: unless you're a fan of plump *lumache* (Cherasco is the Italian capital of snail production), the sight of these gastronomic gastropods might elicit a few yelps or guffaws from your group.

Parco Safari delle Langhe ★★ FIND ALL AGES Set in lush parkland, this has been delighting families for over 30 years with its 40 species of animals, including hippos, lions, tigers, panthers, bears, emus, camels, buffalos, ponies, monkeys, yaks, zebras, wolves and ostriches. Children will love the reptile house, aquarium and hilarious tortoise-shaped snack bar.

Frazione Rea, 12060 Murazzano. (Exit A6 at Carrù and follow signs for Farigliano-Belvedere-Murazzano; around 40 km from Alba; 0173-791-142. ***www.parcosafari.com****). Admission: 12€ (£8) adults, 8€ (£5. 2–12 years, Free 2 and under. March to October: Wed–Mon 10am–noon, 2–6pm, November to February limited opening times.*

Family-Friendly Dining

Le Langhe is renowned for its fabulous food – alongside the rich, complex tastes of veal *carpaccio* and grated truffle, most trattorias will serve tasty pasta, meat and fish dishes as well as veggie-friendly *contorni* (side dishes) suitable for children. Be extra careful when taking up dining recommendations from hoteliers – you might find yourself in the kind of gastronomic restaurant where hushed reverence for the food is a given. Children will feel uncomfortable in such a stuffy atmosphere, and although the food can be sublime, you'll pay a pretty penny for a soulless family dining experience. You'll know you've found the place when a young besuited Swiss or German walks in and informs the waiter that he too comes from a wine family.

Asti

Osteria del Diavolo ★★

PIEDMONTESE FIND A youthful, amiable atmosphere awaits here. Relaxed dining takes place in three rooms that once belonged to the San Michele church next door, or on the central Asti piazza outside. Don't worry because it's not all hushed culinary snobbery here – it's more family-friendly and has fantastic food, like *pasta e fagioli* (hearty pasta and beans) and an unbelievable cheese board.

Piazza San Martino 6, 14100 Asti. (0141-302-21. ***www.osteriadel diavolo.it.****) Primi 6€–8€ (£4–5.35); secondi 8€–12€ (£5.35–8); MC, V. 12:30–2:30pm and 7:30–11:30pm. Closed Mon, Tue and for two weeks in August.*

Alba

Vincafé PIEDMONTESE This popular local is an informal place for a family education in Le Langhe food and wine. Its brunch menu includes classic dishes like the meaty *ravioli al plin*, braised meats and rabbit dishes. Child-pleasing bites are also available, and the cheese and salami platters served throughout the day are sublime. To accompany the mouth watering fayre, ask one of the staff for a suitable bottle of plonk from the list of 400.

Via V. Emanuele 1 12051 Alba. ☏ 0173-364-603 Primi 7€–9€ (£4.70–6); secondi 8€–12€ (£5.35–8); MC, V. Noon–3pm lunch and 3–9pm salami and cheese platters and other finger foods. Closed Mon in January to March.

Cherasco

La Lumaca PIEDMONTESE This great osteria-cum-vineria with brick-vaulted ceilings, on the corner of Via Cavour, is the place in Italy to try snails; Cherasco is the *capitale delle lumache* after all. Even if you don't much like the idea of munching on a mollusc, it's a fun thing to try and a family story you can all regurgitate for years to come. For adults they do a rich *risotto al Barolo*, while children should like the tagliatelle-like *tajarin* pasta served with various sauces.

Via S.Pietro (Corner of Via Cavour), 12062 Cherasco. (☏ 0172 489-421). Primi 7€–10€ (£4.70–6.70); secondi 8€–14€ (£5.35–9.40); AE, DC, MC, V. 12:30–2:30pm and 8–11:30pm. Closed Mon and Tue, January and August.

Brà

Bocchondivino PIEDMONTESE This informal eatery run by Maria Pagliasso is the home of Slow Food – that is, it was the first establishment (in 1984) to join the Movement. Families are made to feel at home in jolly dining areas facing a small courtyard. Expect classic home-made food from the *Cucina Piemontese* recipe book: *zuppa di ceci* (chickpea soup), gnocchi, veal, and tempting *dolci* to please the youngsters. They even do a gastronomic breakfast of meats, cheeses and the freshest bread. Keep your eyes peeled for their regular cheese and white truffle events.

Via Mendicità Istruita 141 2042 Bra. (☏ 0172-425-674). Primi 8€–11€ (£5.35–7.40); secondi 8€–15€ (£5.35–10); AE, DC, MC, V. 10am–8pm. Closed Sun and Mon.

Family-Friendly Accommodation

A great way to enjoy the gorgeous countryside in Il Monferrato and Le Langhe is to stay at an *agriturismo*. Most of these establishments have restaurants serving delicious dishes. Some have superb sports facilities and pools. Others are quieter retreats more suited to families who just fancy luxury for a night or two. The few campsites in

Le Langhe are a world away from the brash, noisy ones: for a mixture of camping pitches, comfy guest rooms and family apartments, check out:

Alba Village Their excellent sporting facilities include two pools, tennis courts, mountain and quad bike hire, and an athletics track.

Corso Piave 219, 12051 Alba. (✆ 0173-280-972; fax: 0172-288-621; ***www.albavillagehotel.it****).*

Asti

La Violina ★★ Just north of Asti in the Monferrato hills is the verdant 11-acre Violina estate run by the Palazzettis. This is an ideal base for active families. As well as cultivating their own produce and Barbera wine, which is served in the restaurant, they provide lots of sporting distractions for children and adults with a heated pool, tennis court, sauna, gym, five-a-side football pitch, music room and billiard table. Ask for extra beds in the larger historic farmhouse guest rooms, at no extra cost.

Fraz. Mombarone 115, 14100 Asti. (✆ 014-129-4173 ***www.laviolina.it****) 7 units. 130€ (£87) double; 95€/120€ (£63.50/80) half-board/full-board per person; Children: free for under 3s and 50% discount for under 12s.Rates include breakfast. AE, DC, MC, V. Amenities: bar; free bikes; concierge; limited room service; laundry service; dry cleaning; Internet point. In room: A/C (in some rooms), TV, dataport, minibar, hairdryer, safe.*

Alba

Villa La Meridiana/Az. Agrituristica Reine ★★ This hillside villa, set in the idyllic *campagna delle Langhe,* is the home of the Pionzos, who have created a fabulous family retreat. Children will be kept busy in the swimming pool, billiard room and riding the bikes around the sweet-scented country lanes. Adults can relax on the flowery terrace, with stunning views, explore the Barbera vineyards and apricot orchard, or work up a sweat in the gym or around the barbecue/ wood-fired oven (perfect for pizza experimentation). There's a great choice of accommodation: all rooms have a comfy, rustic ambience. Numbers 3 and 4, or 5 and 6, can be combined to create large family suites, and there are a few mini-apartments.

Località Altavilla 9, 12051 Alba Follow signs to Barbaresco and you'll see a sign to the villa about a mile outside Alba. (✆/[fax] 0173-440-112). 9 units. 85€ (£57) double; 110€ (£74) mini-apartments. Rates include breakfast. MC, V. Parking free. Amenities: concierge; outdoor pool; gym; bike rental; tour desk; limited room service. In room: TV; kitchenette. In apartments: hairdryer.

Brà

Carpe Noctem et Diem

Located at Pollenzo, just outside Brà, this small *enoteca*/restaurant/hotel provides cosy accommodation at an affordable price. The six pastel-coloured rooms are roomy enough to add an extra bed. There's plenty of space to relax and play in the immaculately kept grounds. Fabulous food is served in the converted stables, under stunning vaulted ceilings.

*Via Amedeo di Savoia 5, 12042 Pollenzo. (☎/[fax] 0172-458-282. **www.carpenoctemetdiem.it**). 6 units. 85€ (£57) double; 110€ (£74) triple. Rates include breakfast. AE, DC, MC, V. Parking free. Amenities: limited room service; children's play area. In room: TV.*

8 Liguria: Genoa & the Italian Riviera

LIGURIA

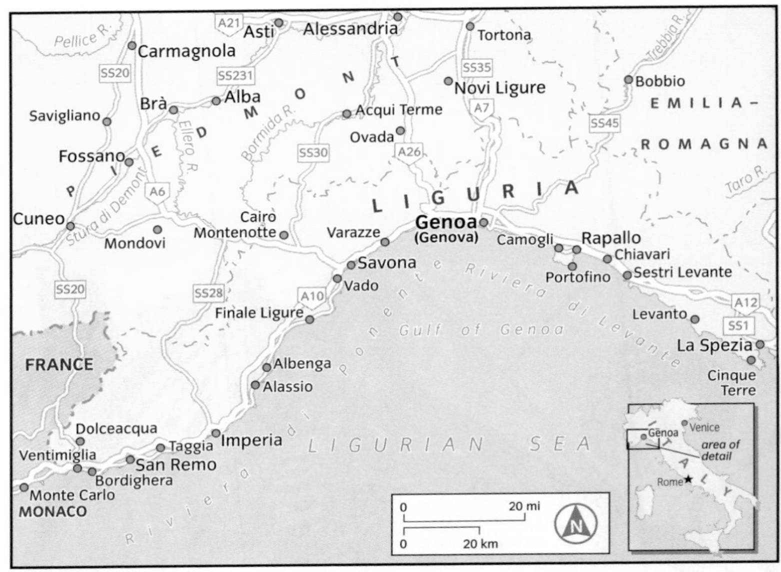

Liguria covers the crescent-shaped coast in the north-west, a region sheltered by the Alps and hemmed in by lush mountains, looking out to the turquoise Mar Ligure. The capital, Genoa, profited from this position, its industrious seafaring inhabitants creating a pre-eminent maritime power between the 13th and 17th centuries. Today, Genoa offers travellers with children quayside attractions including a fantastic aquarium, boat trips, thrilling airborne vistas, grand *palazzi* treasures, exotic gardens and eclectic entertainments. In the 19th and early 20th centuries, Liguria's genteel resorts and evocative fishing villages attracted British gentry and adventurous poets. For families with younger children, take your pick of the resorts along the Riviera di Ponente with their long sandy beaches and palm-fringed *lungomari*. San Remo and Bordighera both offer a mix of beach, dilapidated grandeur and day trips to hilltop towns. The Riviera di Levante to the east, with its charming fishing villages, intimate pebbly beaches and more rugged terrain, is less suited to tottering toddlers, but mums will love a visit to super-chic Portofino.

GENOA (GENOVA)

142 km (88 miles) S of Milan, 501 km (311 miles) N of Rome, 194 km (120 miles) E of Nice

If, like its favourite son Cristoforo Colombo, you have an inquisitive explorer's nose for seafaring empires and the oceans, Genoa is well worth dipping into. Although you might still sniff out a rat or two in the atrocious post-war rebuilding and distinctly seedy areas, an exploration of the old city with its historic buildings, characteristic *caruggi* alleys and the impressive waterfront developments will reap rewards. There are a number of child-friendly attractions in and around the revamped Old Port, including the **Acquario di Genova**, the biggest aquarium in Europe. You can scale dizzying heights in lifts, trains and funiculars, and explore lush parks, beguiling villas and spectacular shoreline *passeggiate.*

Trade links with the Phoenicians and Greeks in the centuries before Christ gave the locals here the know-how to conquer Corsica and Sardinia. In 1284, the defeat of its maritime rival Pisa heralded the start of Genoa's golden colonial period: at the height of its power it had commercial links throughout North Africa and the Middle East. It was not all plain sailing though: frequent disputes with Venice and tiffs between its patrician families (the Doria, Fieschi and Spinola) made it vulnerable to foreign influence, leading to decline in the 17th and 18th centuries. After French rule under Napoleon and his subsequent defeat, the statesmen at the Vienna Congress in 1815 decided to join Genoa with Piedmont under the rule of the King of Sardinia. In the subsequent 50 years, a resurgence of feeling against foreign rule and the kindling of Italian nationalism (*Il Risorgimento*) by heroic figures like Genoa-born Giuseppe Mazzini, made the city a leading player in the unification of Italy. In 1860, Garibaldi led his red-shirted *i mille* (the thousand) from here to Marsala in Sicily, a defining moment in the destiny of an emerging Italy.

The scars of World War II bombing can be seen in the proliferation of modern high-rise buildings. Indeed, the view from the raised motorway that passes through the endless urban sprawl, with glimpses of a large modern port through the smog, is hardly enticing. In 1992, on the 500th anniversary of the discovery of the Americas by its most famous son, the city attempted a regeneration, which was only partly successful. Despite the attempts to clean up the port area and ambitious developments such as the **Bigo lift**, the city has yet to rediscover its glory years or fulfil its potential. The chaos and violence surrounding the G8 summit in 2001, when rioting broke out, didn't help either. However, a year as European Capital of Culture in 2004 gave the city fresh impetus, and saw the opening of the **Galata Museum of the Sea**. Don't let Genoa's slightly tarnished image and poor first impression put you off coming. A visit to the city's old port, historic centre and abundant parks will host some memorable family fun and build an enduring bond with a flawed but fabulous city.

Essentials

Getting There

By Plane Flights to and from Britain and Ireland serve **Aeroporto Internazionale di Genova Cristoforo Colombo,** just 6.4 km (4 miles) west of the city centre (☎ *010-601-5410* for information; ***www.airport.genova.it***). **Volabus no. 100** (☎ *010-558-2414*) connects the airport with Stazione Principe and Stazione Brignole, with buses running every 20 minutes from 6:15am–11:20pm; buy tickets (3€ (£2)) on the bus.

By Train Genoa has two major train stations, **Stazione Principe** (designated on timetables as Genova PP), near the old city on Piazza Acqua Verde, and **Stazione Brignole** (designated on timetables as Genova BR.) in the modern city on Piazza Verdi. Many trains serve both stations; however, some trains stop at only one, making it essential that you know the station at which your train is scheduled to arrive and from which it will depart. Trains connect the two stations in just 5 minutes and run about every 15 minutes. City bus nos. 40 and 37 also run between them, leaving from the front of each station about every 10 minutes; allow at least 20 minutes for the connection on Genoa's crowded streets.

Genoa is the hub for trains serving the Italian Riviera: trains to and from Ventimiglia on the French border pass through every half-hour, while those to **La Spezia,** on the eastern fringes of Liguria, are even more frequent (regional: 1¾ hr; high-speed: 1 hr). Most trains make local stops at the coastal resorts. Genoa has excellent rail links with major Italian cities: **Milan** (one to three per hour; regional: 1¾ hr; high-speed: 1½ hr), **Rome** (hourly; 4½–5½ hr), **Turin** (one to two per hour; regional: 1 hr 50 min; high-speed: 1½ hr), **Florence** (hourly but always with a change, usually at Pisa; 3 hr), **Pisa** (hourly; regional: 3 hr; high-speed: 1½–2 hr).

By Bus Buses to all parts of Liguria, as well as to other Italian and European cities, depart and arrive from the main bus station next to Stazione Principe. Seaside resorts are best reached by train. The many small towns in the region's hilly hinterlands can be reached by bus. For tickets and information, contact **PESCI,** Piazza della Vittoria 94r (☎ *010-564-936*).

By Car Genoa is linked to other parts of Italy and to France by an excellent network of roads. The A10/A12 follows the coast and passes through dozens of tunnels to link Genoa with France to the west (Nice is about 2 hr away) and Pisa, about 1½ hours to the south-east. The A7 links Genoa with Milan, just over an hour north.

By Ferry As a major port town, Genoa is linked to several other Mediterranean ports, including Barcelona, Palermo and Tunis, by ferry service (*www.traghetti genova.it*). Most boats leave and depart from the Stazione Marittima (✆ *010-256-682*), which is on a waterfront roadway, Via Marina d'Italia, about a 5-minute walk south of Stazione Principe. For services to and from the **Riviera Levante,** check with **Tigullio** (✆ *800-014-808; www.traghettiportofino.it*); there's a once-daily service from early July to late September.

Visitor Information

The **main tourist office** is near the aquarium on Via al Porto Antico (✆ *010-253-0671* or *010-248-711*; fax: *010-246-7658*; *www.apt.genova.it*), open daily 9am–1pm and 2–6pm. There are branches at **Stazione Principe** (✆ *010-246-2633*), open Monday–Saturday 9:30am–1pm and 2:30–6pm; **Cristoforo Colombo airport** (✆ *010-610-5247*), open Monday–Saturday 9:30am–12:30pm and 1:30–5:30pm; and a seasonal one at the cruise terminal (✆ *010-246-3686*), whose hours vary year to year.

City Layout

Genoa extends for miles along the coast, with suburbs tucked into valleys and clinging to the city's many hills. Most sights are in the **Old Town,** an alluring mishmash of intimate squares, colourful tenements, old *palazzi* and narrow alleyways (known as *caruggi* in dialect) around the eastern side of the old port. Some of the small streets around here are quite steep, so may prove tricky if you have a pram or small children. The city's two train stations are on either side of the Old Town: **Stazione Principe** is the closest, just to the west; from **Piazza Aquaverde** in front of the station, follow **Via Balbi** through **Piazza della Nunziata** to **Via Cairoli,** which runs into Via Garibaldi (about a 15-min. stroll). Many of the city's museums and monuments are in or around **Via Garibaldi**: from here you can descend into the warren of atmospheric lanes that lead down to the port.

From **Stazione Brignole,** walk straight across the open space to Piazza della Vittoria and Via Luigi Cadorna, turn right to follow **Via XX Settembre,** a broad shopping avenue, then due west for about 20 minutes to **Piazza de Ferrari,** on the eastern edge of the Old Town. **Via San Lorenzo** passes by the cathedral and leads you on to the port. Otherwise, if proceeding north from the piazza on **Via XXV Aprile** to **Piazza delle Fontane Marose,** you'll hit the eastern end of Via Garibaldi.

Getting Around

Given Genoa's labyrinthine layout (many of the small streets are out of bounds to taxis or buses), the best way of getting around is **on foot.** You'll need a good map, mind: pick up a basic one at the tourist office for free, or a more detailed map with a good street index at an *edicola* (newsstand). Genoa's unusual street numbering system doesn't help: addresses in red (marked with an 'r') generally indicate a commercial establishment, while those in black are residences or offices. This means that two buildings on the same street may share the same number: one in black, one in red.

By Bus Bus tickets (1€ (£0.67)) lasting 90 minutes are available at newsstands and at ticket booths, *tabacchi* (tobacconists, marked by a brown and white 'T' sign), and the train stations; look for the symbol **AMT** (*010-254-3431; **www.amt.genova.it***). You must validate your ticket by stamping it when you board a bus. Bus tickets can also be used on most of the funiculars and public lifts that climb the city's steep hills. Day tickets cost 3€ (£2).

By Taxi Metered taxis, found at cab stands (Piazza Fontane Marose, Piazza della Nunziata and Piazza de Ferrari are useful for the Old Town), are the safest way to get around Genoa – especially at night. Alternatively, call a **radio taxi** *010-5966.*

By Subway In 2004, the city opened its embryonic underground system: just six stops on a single line stretching from just south of the aquarium to a little beyond Principe train station. You can use the same tickets as for the buses.

Child-Friendly Festivals, Sports, Entertainment & Markets

On 2nd June 2008, it's Genoa's turn to host the **Regata delle Antiche Repubbliche Marinare,** when its chosen crew competes against old maritime rivals, Amalfi, Pisa, and Venice. Each April, Genoa's bay is awash with sailing boats from around the world for the **Millevele**, or 'thousand sails'. The **Fiera** has many trade fairs and exhibitions throughout the year, including the **Euroflora** flower show in April, **Disco Fumetto Usato** (a second-hand comic, CD and record fair) in September, various art and antique events and the **Salone Nautico Internazionale**, an impressive boat show in September, which should make a splash with children.

Salone Nautico Internazionale

*Piazzale J. F. Kennedy 1. (010-53911; **www.fiera.ge.it**). Boat show admission: 13€ (£8.70). Free for under 6s; Bus: 19, 31 or 48.*

Music fans should check out the **Goa-Boa festival** (***www.goaboa.net***) that takes place in July and often has an alternatively eclectic line-up. Although currently only in Italian, ***www.centrostoricogenova.com*** is a navigable source for upcoming events.

Antico Porto Sports Centre

Young and old sports addicts should find something to do at the Antico Porto sports centre, whether it's swimming, inline skating or the more sedate *bocce* (boules).

Palazzina San Giobatta. (☎ 010-248-5711). Bus: 1, 2, 3, 4, 7, 8, 12, 15 or 32.

Stadio Luigi Ferraris

The city's two prestigious football clubs, Sampdoria and Genoa (currently in Serie A and Serie B, respectively) may be trophy-less of late, but their compact and atmospheric British-style stadium, the Stadio Luigi Ferraris is worth a matchday visit.

Via del Piano 9. Bus: 37 or 47. Tickets are available in advance at Sampdoria Point (Via Cesarea 107 R. ☎ 010 860-2722) near Piazza della Vittoria, and Genoa Store (☎ 010-2511-049) in Piazza Portello.

The Mercato Orientale

This is an indoor food market where local banter and a flurry of sights and smells make it a fun and stimulating place to wander: grab yourself some *frutta e verdura* (fruit and veg) for a picnic and then view the bountiful catch in the seafood section.

Via XX Settembre/Via Galata. Mon–Sat 7am–1pm and 3:30–7:30pm; closed Wed afternoon.

Frutta e verdura

Planning Your Outings

The dense topography of Genoa's street layout can make days out in stiflingly hot summer weather into tear-strewn affairs, so make sure you bring all the essentials and don't plan too much. The narrow *caruggi* and hills mean that you're best armed with a detailed map to minimise frustration: getting around with a pushchair is particularly tricky, so plan your route. A word of warning about street crime: some areas near the Old Port are frequented by dodgy characters, so keep your credit cards, cash and valuables in a safe place – preferably in a concealed money-belt. Organise your days so as to visit galleries, museums or the leisure facilities around the Old Port during the time when only mad dogs and Englishmen venture out into the pavement-splitting sunshine. The **Magazzini del Cottone** here is a good place to go if the weather is inclement. All the main attractions listed have decent toilets and changing facilities, but a spare roll of toilet paper in your bag never goes amiss.

FAST FACTS: GENOA

Bookstores For English-language and children's books visit **Feltrinelli,** Via XX Settembre 231–233r (☎ *010-570-4818; www.lafeltrinelli.it*).

Chemists Pharmacies have extended hours on a rotating basis; dial ☎ *192* to learn which ones are open late in a particular week. Usually open overnight are **Europa,** Corso Europa 676 (☎ *010-397-615*), **Ghersi,** Corte Lambruschini 16 (☎ *010-541-661*) and **Pescetto** on Via Balbi 185r (☎ *010-246-2697*), near Stazione Principe.

Crime Be wary of pickpockets, especially around the Old Port.

Emergencies The general emergency number is ☎ *113.* For police assistance, call ☎ *118.* If you have car trouble, call **ACI,** Soccorso Stradale ☎ *116.* These calls are all free.

Hospitals The **Ospedale San Martino,** Largo Rosanna Benzi 10 (☎ *010-5551*).

Internet Nondove Internet Point, Corso Buenos Aires 2 (☎ *010-589-990*), charges 5.50€ (£3.70) per hour and is open daily from 9:30am–7:30pm.

Genoa with a Pram: An Itinerary

With its cobbled streets, claustrophobic lanes and steep hills, Genoa is as difficult a city for the pram-pusher as any in Italy. Fortunately all hills lead to the sea and the revamped ancient harbour is the best place to start as its full of child-friendly attractions. Start at the aquarium – hop in the lift, drop the pram at the luggage deposit window and enter a watery world of entertainment. Older children will love the 3D cinema and the shark tanks, while younger ones can try to spot movie star Nemo, stroke skates' backs and go nose-to-beak with the penguins.

Next stop is the Neptune, a life-size 17th century pirate galleon. Watch out for the skeletons. Across the marina, a converted cotton warehouse is home to Città dei Bambini (Children's City), a hidden gem that brings science and play together for children aged three to 14.

Now the hard bit: leave the harbour and drag the pushchair 200 yards or so up Via San Lorenzo, stopping for pictures of the cathedral half-way up, then exit into the wide-open space of Piazza de Ferrari, the hub of central Genoa. The bustling square is the perfect spot for parents to catch their breath and down an espresso while screaming youngsters drench themselves in the ground-level fountains. Stretching east from the piazza is the modern and elegant Via XX Settembre, one of the two principal shopping areas in Genoa. With its covered galleries and smooth pavements, it's far easier to negotiate with a pram than the hawker-filled cobbled alleys around the harbour.

Piazza de Ferrari

There's a Wi-Fi hotspot at the Ferry terminal bookstore (Librerie del Centro - Genova2, Via Milano 101/r).

Lost Property Contact L'Ufficio Oggetti Rinvenuti della Polizia Municipale del Comune di Genova at Via Oristano 12 off Corso Sardegna (☎ *010-500-519*. Mon-Fri 8:30am-12:30pm).

Laundry The **Ondablu** self-service Laundromat, at Via Gramsci 181r, is open daily from 8am–10pm.

Post Offices Genoa's main post office is at **Piazza Dante 4** (☎ *010-591-762*). There are two at the main train stations and one at the airport – open Monday–Saturday 8:10am–7:40pm.

Taxis See 'City Layout', above.

Family-Friendly Sights

Acquario di Genova (Aquarium of Genoa) ★★★
Genoa's best attraction for children is Europe's largest aquarium. Visitors can view the 50 massive tanks containing 20,000 creatures from above and below the water, and even delicately touch some species including small rays and black sea bass (only their backs). Amid the coral in the 18-metre (49 ft) long Caribbean Sea tank swim tortoises, clown fish (if your children are *Finding Nemo* fans, they'll spot them), barracudas and sharks. Other popular residents include dolphins, seals and penguins, whose antics are very entertaining. A 3-D film depicting life in the oceans will captivate children (the English narrative is available on a sheet). You'll need a half-day to explore the marine habitats recreated here.

GENOA

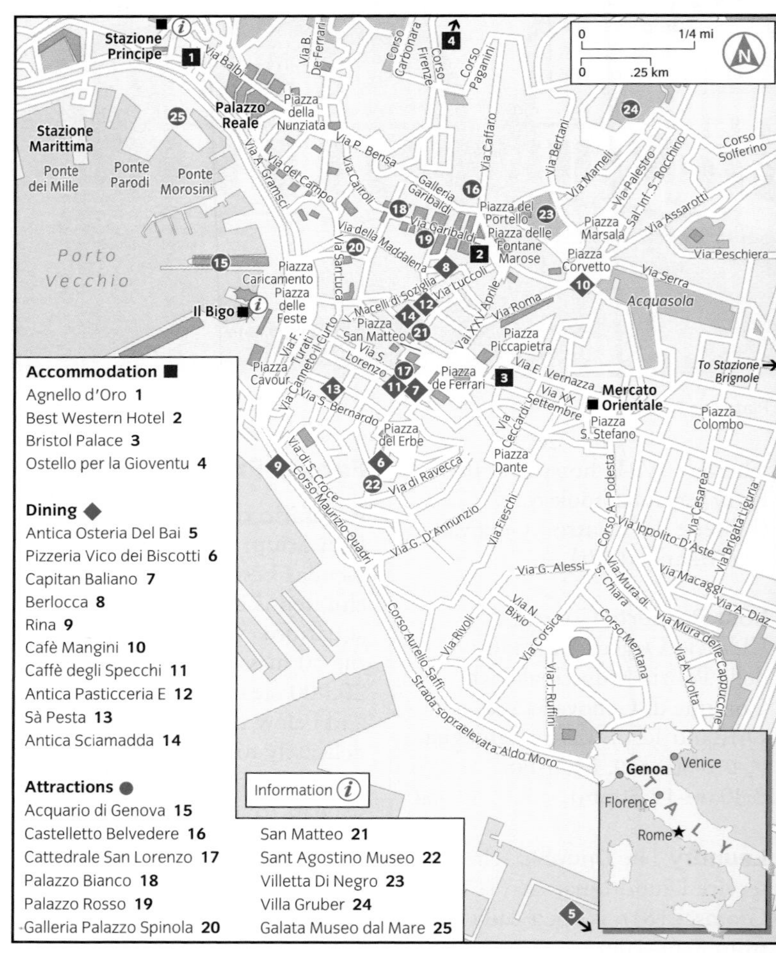

*Ponte Spinola. (☎ 010-234-5678; **www.acquario.ge.it**). Admission: 14€ (£9.40) adults, 8.50€ (£5.70) ages 4–12. Mon–Fri 9:30am–7:30pm; Sat–Sun 9:30am–8:30pm; July, August and public holidays 9am–9:30pm. Bus: 1, 2, 3, 4, 5, 6, 7, 8, 12, 13, 14 or 15.*

Attractions at nearby Molo Vecchio There is a mélange of ancient and modern attractions by the Old Port, many of which are nautical but nice, as well as fun and informative for children. On **Piazza Caricamento**, the 13th century Gothic **Palazzo di San Giorgio**, with its frescoed façade, was once the source of the city's prosperity: the San Giorgio bank opened here in 1408 introduced the world to the idea of cheques. Bounce across the piazza under the incongruously ugly Strada Aldo Moro flyover toward the waterfront for more stimulating sights for children. Beyond the quay, whose foundations were laid by Cistercian friars in the 13th century, is the large area revamped in the early 1990s. Take a walk beside the aquarium to see the tropical biosphere and then follow the narrow strip with moored yachts to the floating jetty. On the next quayside protrusion stands an armadillo-like covered square, the **Piazza delle Feste**, which hosts events and is transformed into an ice-rink between November and March. The white outstretched arms of the modernist **Bigo** structure and panoramic crane-lift (see 'Vistas & Cruises', below) burst from the water here.

Museo dell'Antardide

AGES 3 AND UP Set further back is the Museo dell' Antardide. It lets you experience the harsh climate and delve into the archive of Italian Antarctic expeditions.

(☎ 010-254-3690). Admission: 6€ (£4), family ticket 12€ (£8), free for under 6s. June to September 10:30am–6:30pm. October to May 9:45–5:30pm; closed Mon.

The nearby **Mandraccio** is an area crammed with playgrounds, a gym, public baths and bars.

Galata Museo dal Mare ★★

AGES 3 AND UP North of the aquarium is the Galata Museo dal Mare, housed in the old arsenal shipyards. Genoa's seafaring past is brought to life through spectacular reconstructions and displays on themed floors: Transatlantic Voyages, Age of the Sail and Age of the Oar.

*Calata di Mari 1, Darsena. (☎ 010-234-5655; **www.galatamuseodelmare.it**). Admission: 10€ (£6.70) adults, 5€ (£3.35) ages 4–12; various cumulative ticket options. March to October 10am–7:30pm; November to February Tue–Fri*

Old Port, Genoa

HISTORY The Life of Christopher Columbus 

c1451 Cristoforo Colombo (Christopher Columbus) allegedly born in Genoa. City registers mention his weaver father and family residences around Genoa. A small house (still standing today) next to Porta Soprana may have been his home.

August 1492 Sponsored by Spanish *Castile* royalty, his three-ship fleet set sail from Palos in Spain for what he believed to be the Indies, looking for spices like black pepper, ginger and nutmeg. Instead, he came across the Bahamas (that he named San Salvador), Cuba and Hispaniola (now called Haiti and the Dominican Republic), encountering the friendly indigenous people, the Taíno.

March 1493 He returned as a hero to Spain via Portugal, after surviving a savage storm, with a world-changing swag of tobacco, pineapples and turkeys.

September 1493 Admiral Colombus's 17-ship fleet and 1000-strong crew set sail on a second voyage, to conquer the Taíno people and establish a Spanish colony. He sighted, explored and named many islands in the Caribbean on the way: Dominica, Galante, Guadalupe, Montserrat, Antigua, Nevis, St Kitts, St Eustasius, Saba, St Martin, St Cruz and the Virgin Islands. Contrary to his Spanish patrons' wishes, he brutally enslaved native tribes in pursuit of gold and prostitution on Haiti and Hispaniola.

May 1498 Set off with a fleet of six to Porto Santo and via the Canary Islands and Cape Verde, set anchor at Trinidad, thereupon exploring the coast off Venezuela and the South American mainland. Tobago and Grenada were next. He noted in his log that he thought he'd found a new continent, believing it to be hanging off the end of China.

August 1498 Columbus was brought back to Spain in shackles having clashed with unhappy Hispaniola colonists, who accused him of mistreatment and mismanagement. He lost prestige and privileges. Meanwhile, the Portuguese explorer Vasco Da Gama had won the race to the Indies.

May 1502 Set sail from Cádiz with his brother and 13-year-old son seeking to further explore the 'Indian Ocean', in reality the Americas. First stop was Morocco, where he went to aid Portuguese troops under siege. He went on to Martinique and attempted to land at Hispaniola while a hurricane was brewing. However, the island governor refused him port and laughed off Columbus's warnings of an almighty storm, sending a Spanish fleet and crew to a deadly shipwrecked fate. As usual, it fell jammy side up for Columbus: the only ship that reached Spain intact was the one containing Columbus's money and belongings.

August 1502 Colombus's adventures continued toward South America via Jamaica. He landed at Honduras on the mainland. A two-month exploration of Nicaragua, Costa Rica and Panama elicited more daring tales and discoveries in his log. Panama natives led him to gold but thereafter his luck turned: his ships were damaged and his garrison was attacked before fleeing. After sustaining storm damage off the coast of Cuba, he ran aground at St Ann's Bay,

Jamaica, where he was stranded for a year. A reconnaissance crew of Spaniards and natives set off from Hispaniola in a canoe. Meanwhile, his more astute navigational and astronomical skills (if you ignore his belief that he was near China) saved his bacon with the locals: his successful prediction of a lunar eclipse impressed the natives enough to keep him and his men adequately fed.

June 1504 A rescue fleet arrived. Columbus and his men returned to Sanlúcar, Spain, in November.

May 1506 Columbus died in Valladolid, still believing that his voyages had been to Eastern Asia. His journeys marked the beginning of European colonisation of the Americas.

10am–6pm, Sat, Sun and public holidays 10am–7:30pm; closed Mon.

The Neptune ★ For swashbuckling shenanigans hop onboard this imposing galleon, a docked film-set which starred in the action flick *Pirates*. It's a few planks' lengths from the aquarium.

Mol Vecchio. ☎ 010-247-6608 5€, 3€ 4–12 years, free 0–3 years. Daily Winter 10am-6pm; Summer 9am–7pm).

In front of the imposing 16th century **Porta Siberia** is an outdoor space used for events: a children's carnival, summer concerts and a Christmas circus/theatre festival. A huge Renzo Piano-designed **exhibition complex** housed in former cotton warehouses has much to offer, especially on rainy days – here you'll find shops, bars, an outdoor pool, entertainment centre with cinema and computer games, and the:

Città dei Bambini ★ AGES 4–14 which contains nine themed islands with over 90 fun, educational and interactive games for children aged 3–14: visit on a weekend or holiday for additional live attractions.

*First Floor of Magazzini del Cottone, Porto Antico. (☎ 010-247-5702; **www.cittadeibambini.net**). Admission: 7€ (£4.70) adults, 5€ (£3.35) ages 3–14, under 3s free.*

Cattedrale San Lorenzo and Palazzo Ducale AGES 4 AND UP Behind the black-and-white striped façade of this spooky Romanesque-Gothic cathedral

Christopher Columbus

Cattedrale San Lorenzo

(consecrated in 1158 and modified two centuries later) are many frescoes, dark Corinthian columns, a sumptuous chapel dedicated to St John the Baptist and a green dish reputedly used at the Last Supper. Entrance to the adjoining treasury, filled with fabled tableware and bejewelled objects, is by guided tour.

Piazza San Lorenzo. (010-311-269). Admission to cathedral free. Treasury: 5.50€ (£3.70) adults, 4.50€ (£3) students, 11€ (£7.40) family ticket for two adults and two children. Cathedral: Mon–Sat 9am–noon and 3–6pm. Treasury: by half-hour guided tour only (ask when you get there) Mon–Sat 9am–noon and 3–6pm. Bus: 1, 7, 8, 17, 18, 19 or 20.

Palazzo Ducale FIND With its elegant courtyards, art exhibitions (including contemporary, modern and photographic) and cultural events, this is well worth a visit. The best bits are the tower and dungeons, but reservations are necessary.

*Piazza Matteotti 9. (010-557-4000; **www.palazzoducale.genova.it**). Admission charges change for various exhibitions and events..*

Galleria Nazionale di Palazzo Spinola ★ AGES 5 AND UP
Children may turn their noses up at the lavish art here, but they'll lap up the views from the roof. The Spinola family bequeathed the city this 16th century mansion, with its 17th–18th century interiors and a magnificent art collection, in 1958. You get a real feeling of their wealth and tastes by walking around the lavish *saloni*. The first two floors have been restored to their original layout, while the third contains

DID YOU KNOW? Investigations at San Lorenzo

Keep your eyes peeled for:

- Outside: two *leoni*, and less obviously on the campanile, a sundial nicknamed *L'Arrotino* (the knife grinder).
- Inside: there are some marks left by an unexploded British naval shell (clue: it's in the South Aisle) – the shell is on display beside a marble relief called *The Crucifixion*.
- Opposite the church: find the two houses where Andrea Doria lived – he was the city's admiral in the 16th century, and waged war on pirates and Turks. Just one more thing... it's the tricky one: can you find out what he famously discovered that changed sailing techniques forever?

Answer: He devised a method for sailing against the wind.

TIP Cumulative Tickets

Admission to Palazzo Bianco, Palazzo Rosso and Palazzo Tursi is grouped together in a 7€ (£4.70) cumulative ticket. The excellent Card Musei (16 € (£10.70) for 48 hours or 20€ (£13.40) including unlimited use of public transport), allows entrance to Palazzo Spinola, the Museo Sant'Agostino, San Lorenzo and the Museo di Palazzo Reale, as well as discounted admission to the: Acquario di Genova, Palazzo Ducale, Museo Luzzati at Porta Siberia, Parco Pallavicini di Pegli, Villa Durazzo at S. Margherita Ligure, Palazzo Imperiale, Teatro Carlo Felice, Teatro Stabile di Genova, Teatro dell'Archivolto, Teatro della Tosse and Teatro Cargo.

the **Galleria Nazionale della Liguria**: highlights include *Carlo Doria* by Rubens and Van Dyck's *Portrait of a Lady with a Child*. After seeing the porcelain and textile collection on the fourth floor, you can access the roof terrace via the Mirador walkway.

*Piazza Pellicceria 1. (☎ 010-270-5300; **www.palazzospinola.it**). Admission: 4€ (£2.70) adults, free for under-18s; or 6.50€ (£4.35) Cumalitivo Ticket for Palazzo Spinola and Palazzo Reale. Tues–Sat 8:30am–7:30pm; Sun and Public Holidays 1:30–7:30pm. Bus: 1, 3, 7, 8, 18, 20 or 34.*

Patrician Palaces on Via Garibaldi ★ AGES 5 AND UP There are a number of impressive *palazzi* on Via Garibaldi, where wealthy Genovese families swanned around in fancy garb admiring their artistic purchases.

Palazzo Bianco Perhaps the finest is Palazzo Bianco, built for the Grimaldis in the 16th century and containing beautiful Flemish and Dutch paintings.

*Via Garibaldi 11. (☎ 010-557-2057; **www.museopalazzobianco.it**).*

Palazzo Rosso 17th century Palazzo Rosso has portraits of the Brignole family by Van Dyck and fine examples by Genoese masters Strozzi and Giordano.

*Via Garibaldi 18. (☎ 010-247-6351; **www.museopalazzorosso.it**).*

Palazzo Podesta The Palazzo Podesta at no. 7 has wonderful courtyard fountains.

Palazzo Doria Tursi houses the town hall and letters written by Columbus.

Via Garibaldi 10. ☎ 010-557-111. Admission 7€ includes entrance to Palazzo Rosso and Palazzo Tursi. Open Tues–Sat 9am–7pm; Sun 10am–7pm. Bus: 18, 19, 20, 30, 35, 37, 39, 40, 41, 42, or Volabus 100.

Palazzo Balbi-Durazzo Next door Palazzo Balbi-Durazzo is a former royal seat.

Museo di Palazzo Reale was once the residence of the Royal House of Savoy. It now houses an art collection displayed in a series of ostentatious rooms, replete with stuccowork, gilded mirrors and dandy crushed velvet.

*Via Balbi 10. (☎ 010-27-101. 101; **www.palazzorealegenova.it**). Admission: 4€ (£2.70) adults, under-18s free. Tues–Wed 9am–1:30pm; Thurs–Sun 9am–7pm. Bus: 20.*

Museo di Architettura e Scultura Ligure di Sant'Agostino AGES 5 AND UP Older children with an interest in art should enjoy the walk within the pink walls of these 13th century cloisters. Bombed in World War II, the St Augustine Museum of Ligurian Architecture and Sculpture has an eclectic collection of building fragments from Roman times and Genoa's churches, strewn over the lawns and a few inside spaces.

Piazza Sarzanno 35r. (☎ 010-251-1263 or 010-557-2057). Admission: 4€ (£2.70) or pay 9€ (£6) for a Card Musei. Free for under 18s and over 60s and for all on Sun. Tues–Fri 9am–7pm; Sat–Sun 10am–7pm. Bus: 17, 18, 19, 20, 30, 32, 33, 35, 37, 40, 41, 100, 605, 606 or 607.

Vistas & Cruises

For a scenic bus ride around the **Circonvallazione a Monte** take no. 33 from Stazione Brignole or Stazione Principe.

At Piazza del Portello (at the eastern end of Via Garibaldi) a lift takes passengers up to the cooler heights of **Castelletto Belvedere** (40¢ (£0.27) each way, daily 6:40am to midnight).

You can also take the:

Granarolo ★★ funicular from Piazza del Principe, just behind the railway station, to Porto Granarolo (300 m or 1000 ft), one of the 17th century city gates. There's plenty of space to relax, have a picnic and soak up the views.

1€ (£0.67) each way or you can use a bus ticket; daily every 15 min. 6am–11:45pm.

Il Bigo ★ An unusual crane lift carries visitors to the top of this striking structure.

*(**www.acquariodigenova.it/chi_bigo.asp**). 3.30€ (£2.20) adults, 2€ (£1.34) children aged 3–12. Tue–Sun 10am–5pm; March to May and September until 6pm; June to August until 8pm.*

Harbour Cruises ★★ These hour-long cruises allow glimpses of the busy port and the 1544 **Lanterna** lighthouse, which at 108 m (354 ft) is the tallest in Europe. They also do trips to Camogli, Portofino and the Cinque Terre.

Il Bigo

*Cooperativa Battellieri dei Porto di Genova, Stazione Marittima (☎ 010-265-712; **www.battellierigenova.it**); 7€ (£4.70); free for under 4s.*

The waters around Genoa and the Ligurian coast are home to many species of whales and dolphins, which are protected by a WWF sanctuary.

Whale Watch Liguria Boat Excursions ★★ Children will love these boat trips that run from July to the end of September, accompanied by a specialist whale watcher/biologist, allowing spectacular close encounters with these marine mammals. Book well in advance to avoid disappointment and remember the seasickness pills if small boats leave you feeling queasy.

*Depart from aquarium. (☎010-265-712; **www.whalewatchliguria.it**). 35€ (£23.50) adults, 18 € (£12) 5–14 years.*

The **Ferrovia Genova-Casella Railway** ★ snakes its way through the valleys of Valbisagno, Valpolcevera and Valle Scrivia for about an hour, taking in fantastic views of hills and forts. Stazione Piazza Manin. *(**www.ferroviagenovacasella.it**). Round-trip: 4€ (£2.70) weekdays, 6€ (£4) weekends and public holidays. Check website for seasonal timetables. Bus: 34.*

Villas, Gardens & Rocky Shores

There may not be any large parks or natural shoreline terrain in the *centro storico,* but venture further out to find some wonderful spaces to run around and relax in.

Orto Botanico AGES 3 AND UP In the city, the modestly sized university botanical gardens offer a tranquil wander amongst the exotic species and seaward views.

Corso Dogali, 1. (☎ 010-209-9392). Free admission. 8:30am–12, 3–6pm.

Villetta di Negro AGES 3 AND UP at the eastern end of Via Garibaldi, houses the **Oriental Art Museum** and is surrounded by grand parkland, lakes, a waterfall and plenty of bird life.

Mueso d'Arte Orientale, Piazzale Mazzini 4. (☎ 010-542-285). 4€ (£2.70), free for under 18s. Tues–Fri 9am–1pm; Sat and Sun 10am–7pm; closed Mon.

Villa Gruber ALL AGES A little further north and set in lush grounds is the home to a colony of parrots and a museum of Americana.

Corso Solferino 29. (☎ 010-814-737). Free admission. 8am–6pm.

Villa Serra ALL AGES North-west of Genoa and set in verdant English landscape gardens complete with lakes, playgrounds and picnic areas.

*Via Carlo Levi 2, Comago. (☎ 010-715-577; **www.villaserra.it**). Admission: 2€ (£1.34); free for under 12s. November to March 10am–5pm; March to May 10am–7pm; June to September 9am–8pm; Open Mon from 2pm. Train: Bolzaneto. By Car: A7 Genova – Milano, exit Bolzaneto.*

For a similar dose of tranquility and even grander gardens, head 6.5 km (4 miles) west of the city centre to **Pegli**, famed for its 16th century **Villa Doria** and 19th century **Villa Durazzo-Pallavcini.**

Villa Doria ALL AGES houses a fine naval museum.

*Piazza Bonavino 7. (☎ 010-696-9885; **www.museonavale.it**). Admission: 4€ (£2.70), free for under 18s.*

Villa Durazzo-Pallavcini ALL AGES has a captivating archaeological museum and Romantic-style botanical gardens.

Via Ignazio Pallavicini 13. (☎ 010-666-864). Admission: 6€ (£4), 4€ (£2.70) under 18s. Park open winter). 9am–5pm; spring/summer 9am–7pm; Botanical Gardens 9am–12:30pm.

A few miles from the city centre, **Boccadasse** retains some rustic fishing village charm with its colourful houses and rocky beach. A couple of miles further east is **Nervi** – a beguiling former resort town renowned for its gorgeous **Passeggiata Anita Garibaldi** (a promenade along the rocky foreshore), lush **Parco Municipale** and magnificent villas (***www.parchidinervi.it***), including:

Villa Saluzzo Serra home of an excellent modern art museum.

*Via Capolungo 3. (☎ 010-372-6025; **www.gamgenova.it**). Admission: 7 € (£4.70). Metropolitana train from Brignole or Piazza Principe. Bus: 15 or 17.*

A word of warning: think twice before swimming in Genoese waters, as they are polluted.

Shopping

There's an excellent range of shops here, from kitsch tourist tat to high-end fashion. *Artiginato* handicrafts are aplenty on Via Soziglia, where small shops display carved wooden items, lace, ceramics and jewellery. Don't miss the fabulous Pietro Romanengo Fu Stefano at 74r, which has been selling its sweet specialities from here since 1814. Head for the 12th century porticos of Via Sottoripa for exotic market goods and bargains. For designer labels, like Zara, Max Mara and Sisley, head to Via XX Settembre and Via Luccoli. Peter Pan at 11r Via XX Settembre has classic and funky children's shoes while further along this shopping drag is the bustling Mercato Orientale, which has fresh produce and tempting foods aplenty. Via San Luca attracts a younger crowd looking for more affordable rags and accessories. For jeanswear try the long-established Box 86 at Piazza della Vittoria 86r. Outlet addicts and bargain hunters should head to Via Caffa.

Family-Friendly Accommodation

Decent inexpensive accommodation is scarce in Genoa, as hotels are very much geared to the business traveller. There are some decent mid-range hotels in the *centro storico* but avoid ones near the Old Port, as many streets here are seedy and unsafe.

VERY EXPENSIVE

Bristol Palace If you expect a little tranquil luxury amidst grand public areas with designer-label shopping on your doorstep, then the Bristol is for you. Children will marvel at the grand staircase (take care, though, as there's lots of exposed marble) and the stained-glass dome. The mammoth breakfasts should keep everyone going until mid-afternoon. Most rooms are modest in size but there are some cavernous spaces on the upper floors if you're feeling flush and have a large entourage.

*Via XX Settembre 35, 16121 Genova. (☎ 010-592-541; fax: 010-561-756; **www.hotelbristolpalace.com**). 133 units. 170€–420€ (£114–282) double; 450€–650€ (£301–435) junior. suite. Suitable for families. Buffet breakfast included. AE, DC, MC, V. Parking in garage 22€ (£14.75). Amenities: babysitting; bar; bike rental; car-rental desk; concierge; courtesy car (for a fee); Italian restaurant; limited room service; massage (in room); laundry service; dry cleaning. In room: A/C, dataport, hairdryer, minibar, TV w/pay movies.*

EXPENSIVE

Best Western Hotel Metropoli This reliable chain-hotel option is in a fabulous location for seeing Genoa's sights. The area is largely pedestrianised, so it's comparatively quiet and less dangerous for children. It is near the Palazzo Ducale, the Porto Antico and Via Garibaldi, and faces a beguiling square. For added convenience, the airport bus stops close by. The atmosphere is friendly and the breakfast buffet excellent, including a refreshing fruit salad. Guest rooms have a functional contemporary style. There is no charge for children under 12 with two paying adults.

*Piazza delle Fontane Marose, 16123 Genova. (☎ 010-246-8888; fax: 010-246-8686; **www.bestwestern.it/metropoli_ge**). 48 units. 110€–200€ (£74–134) double; 125€–215€ (£84–144) triple. Rates include buffet breakfast. AE, DC, MC, V. Parking 20€ (£13.40) in nearby garage. Amenities: bar; bike rental; car-rental desk; concierge; dry cleaning; laundry service; limited room service; Wi-Fi. In room: A/C, dataport, hairdryer, kettle minibar, TV.*

MODERATE

Agnello d'Oro VALUE This ever-friendly establishment offers reasonably priced accommodation in a quiet, converted convent setting near Stazione Principe. Some of the original 16th century features remain downstairs, while the upstairs rooms have been renovated to a decent standard. If you feel the heat and crave views of the Old Port, ask for one of the rooms with air-conditioning and balconies.

Via Monachette 6 (off Via Balbi), 16126 Genova. (☎ 010-246-2084;

fax: 010-246-2327; ***www.hotel agnellodoro.it****). 25 units. 90€ (£60) double; 100€ (£67) triple. Ask about lower rates on weekends and January to March. Breakfast 7€ (£4.70) . AE, DC, MC, V. Private parking 13€ (£8.70). Amenities: restaurant (local cuisine); bar; concierge; 24-hr room service; laundry service; non-smoking rooms. In room: A/C (5th floor only), TV, hairdryer (in some rooms).*

INEXPENSIVE

Ostello per la Gioventu VALUE

The thought of hostelling might send shivers down your spine, but this newish hillside place is worth considering for families on a budget: stay here and you can splurge elsewhere. The family accommodation is functional and pretty clean. Facilities are great for the money and there are lots of opportunities for children to make friends.

Via Costanzi 120, 16136 Genova. (✆/fax: 010-242-2457; ***www.geocities.com/hostelge*** *or* ***www.ostellionline.com****). 213 beds. 15€ (£10) per person in family rooms with private bathroom for 3–5; 17€ (£11.40) per person in family double with private bathroom. IYH card required, or pay extra 3€ (£2) per person. Rates include breakfast. No credit cards. Closed late December to January. Check-in 3:30pm–midnight. Curfew 12:30am. Bus: 40. Amenities: restaurant; bar; games room; laundry service. In room: no phone.*

Cafés, Snacks & Family-Friendly Dining

You'll find lots of tasty *focaccia*, as it was raised in these parts – this salty, soft white bread can be bought plain or stuffed with various fillings. To build a picnic feast go to Piazza Caricamento and Via Sottoripa, which have many great little food outlets, where you can buy meats, cheeses, fried seafood and breaded snacks like *fugassa* and the *pandolce*. **Sà Pesta** ★ (Via Giustiniani 16) and **Antica Sciamadda** ★ VALUE at (Via Ravecca 19) have some of the best *farinata*, a pizza-like snack made with chickpea flour and served with the indigenous pesto sauce. *Pesto alla Genovese* combines the area's legendary basil leaf, extra virgin olive oil, garlic, pine nuts and grated *pecorino* or *parmigiano* cheese. Once tasted your children will eschew the supermarket version, so here's hoping you can work a pestle and mortar.

The best pastry creations and ice cream are found at:

Antica Pasticceria Gelateria Klainguti ★★, Genoa's oldest bakery, whose baroque interiors and nutty *cornetti,* called a *Falstaff,* were once savoured by the composer Verdi.

Piazza Soziglia 98r.

For more refreshments, *aperitivi*, pastries and light meals in historic surroundings visit **Café Mangini** (Piazza Corvetto 3r) and Art Deco gem **Caffè degli Specchi** (Salita Pollaiuoli 43r). Remember the old Ligurian

Spaghetti allo scoglio

proverb while you're drinking: *Sciûsciâ e sciorbî no se peu,* 'you cannot sip and breathe at the same time'.

In and around the Old Port there's a host of seafood choices, many with outdoor seating perfect for lounging-about feasts.

Berlocca ★ Near the aquarium and named after the drum roll that signalled lunch in the shipyards. It serves the freshest *piatti di mare,* delicious ravioli, juicy *Chianina* steaks cooked in the wood-burning oven and the cure for all of life's disappointments, *gnocchetti (little potato dumplings)* with a simple sauce made with seasonal produce.

Via dei Macelli di Soziglia 45r. (☎ 010-247-4612). Reservations recommended. Primi 8–13€ (£5.35–8.70). Secondi 7–16€ (£4.70–10.70). AE, DC, MC, V. Closed Sat and Sun lunch and Mon.

Rina A little pricier and equally blessed with a relaxed air is **Rina,** which displays its catch as you enter. As well as marine treats like *polpi, triglie, branzini, acciughe* and *gamberi*, they do some fine pasta and meat dishes. It's also a great place to try some Ligurian wine like Pigato and Cinque Terre.

Via Mura delle Grazie 3. (☎ 010-246-6475). Reservations recommended. Primi 8–14€ (£5.35–9.40). Secondi 11–18€ (£7.40–12). AE, DC, MC, V. Closed Mon.

Capitan Baliano GENOVESE Near Palazzo Matteoti, this popular eatery has a daily menu, which often features seafood including tuna, clams and oysters, as well as flavoursome *ravioli* and Genovese standards like *trenette al pesto.*

Piazza Matteoti 11r. (☎ 010-265-299). Reservations recommended. Primi 8–13€ (£5.35–8.70). Secondi 13–18€ (£8.70–12) 7pm–midnight. Closed Sun and August.

Pizzeria Vico dei Biscotti PIZZERIA It may not be the most intimate of restaurants, but this large locale on Piazza delle Erbe has a warm, family atmosphere. Footie fans and adults will enjoy the large screen showing live Italian football and other big events. As well as pizza classics they raise their game with equally yeasty *specialità genovese*, cheesy *focaccia* and *farinata*. Don't forget to try an *aperitivo* in one of the many bars on the piazza.

Vico dei Biscotti. (☎ 010-251-8990). Pizzas 6–9€ (£4–6). AE, DC, MC, V. Mon–Fri 11–midnight. Closed Sat and Sun lunch.

Antica Osteria Del Bai LIGURIAN It's well worth a taxi ride to this old beachside Quarto eatery, where Robert de Niro may be waiting – talking Italian with one of the waiting staff. Apparently, Bob always pops in when he's in the area, as have Garibaldi and Pope Pio VII. Highlights include *seppie al Zemin*, a Ligurian cuttlefish dish, and gooey roast figs with caramel ice-cream. Choose the *menu degustazione* for a number of dishes that everyone can try. For a special dining occasion, dress up smartly, reserve a table and make it a day out east of the city.

Via Quarto 12. (☎ 010-387-478). Reservations required. Primi 10–17€ (£6.70–11.40). Secondi 13–23€ (£8.70–15.40). Menu degustazione from 50€ AE, DC, MC, V. Closed Mon in January and August.

THE RIVIERA DI PONENTE: FINALE LIGURE, SAN REMO & MORE

Finale Ligure: 72 km (44 miles) W of Genoa; San Remo: 140 km (87 miles) W of Genoa, 59 km (37 miles) E of Nice; Bordighera: 155 km (96 miles) W of Genoa, 15 km (9⅓ miles) W of San Remo, 45 km (28 miles) E of Nice

The Riviera di Ponente (setting sun) has a mixture of family-orientated beach resorts like Finale Ligure, the grand dame San Remo, and some alluring attractions like the **Toirano caves** and **Villa Hanbury gardens**. The stretch of coast west of Genoa as far as the largely uninspiring port of Savona is lined with identikit resorts: apart from Pegli's gardens and Verazze, with its medieval ramparts, Romanesque church and attractive promenade, the coastline holds little interest. Finale Ligure has child-friendly attractions aplenty including beaches, dramatic terrain, prehistoric caves, castle ruins, holiday shopping and *gelaterie.* San Remo, with its slightly faded grandeur, may be known for its chiuahua-wielding casino players but it also has lots to offer as a family base. A word of warning: the whole coast is best avoided in late July and August when roads are clogged and beaches crammed.

Playing on the Beach

Finale Ligure

Apart from in high season when the place is mobbed, this resort and the quieter Varigotti, Spotorno and Noli along the coast (the latter being an alluring medieval gem 9 km, or 5.6 miles, away) are probably the best bets for families seeking a beach holiday on the Riviera di Ponente. The beaches are good and generally clean, with outdoor activities aplenty by the sea or in the inland *alpi liguri*, and there are charming towns, historic buildings, interesting shops and tasty restaurants in which to spend your time and money.

Around Town

Finale Ligure consists of three villages: Finalborgo, Finalmarina and Finalpia. **Finalborgo** has the soul and medieval charm with its impressive **Castel Gavone**, baroque **San Biagio** church and Dominican convent of:

Santa Caterina AGES 3 AND UP with an archaeological museum and shaded courtyards.

*Chiostri di Santa Caterina. (☎ 019-690-020; **www.museoarcheofinale.it**). Admission: 3.50€ (£2.35) adults, 2 € (£1.34) under 16s. July to August: 10am–12pm, 4pm–7pm; September to June: 9:30am–12pm, 2:30–5pm; closed Mon.*

There are attractive craft shops and cafés to explore in the town's intimate *piazze* and narrow streets. **Finalmarina** is the hub of the town's eating, drinking and shopping activity. It has a pebbly beach and promenade, which is the focus of posing and play for much of the day. The area around Piazza di Spagna and Piazza Vittorio Emanuele II is full of bars and restaurants. A short distance east on the far side of the River Sciusa, small but perfectly formed **Finalpia** has fine sandy beaches and the twin charms of the 12th century church of Santa Maria di Pia and a cloistered abbey.

Attractions & Activities

Outdoor Sports For Active Families AGES 6 AND UP Finale Ligure has some of the best rock-climbing in Italy and is a mecca for outdoor enthusiasts. There are over 1500 climbing routes within 10 square miles of the town. If you fancy a go at **climbing, canyoning, mountain-biking, skiing** or any other adventure sport, get in touch with the experienced instructors at **Blu Mountain** (✆ *019-681-6276; **www.blumountain.it***). If you ever fancied **windsurfing** and your children are over 7, head to the:

Bagni Mariella di Varigotti

where experts Daniela and Fabrizio will let you have a go for free to see if you like it. They also hire out mountain bikes, give swimming lessons, organise children's games and concerts on the beach, and their funky little bar has a children's menu.

*Via Aurelia 68, 17029 Varigotti. (✆ 019-698-760; **www.bagnimariella.it**).*

The **Società Ippica Finalese** has been organising **horse-riding** courses for anyone over the age of 6 since the 1960s (✆ *019-695-640*; lorenzo_sif@libero.it). If you yearn for a trek along signposted inland paths ask about the **Sentieri Parlanti**: you can pick up detailed maps and information at the **tourist office** at Via San Pietro 14 (✆ *019-681-019*; ***www. italianriviera.com***).

Grotte di Toirano ★★

AGES 5 AND UP In the verdant Varatella valley, near the medieval village of Toirano, is a series of extraordinary caves. There are three main complexes to be explored (70 mins): the *Grotta della Basura* ('The Witch's Cave' in local dialect) was the home of troglodyte people who shared their primitive home with bears; you then visit the *Grotta di Santa Lucia*, which contains stalactite and stalagmite formations and a natural spring dedicated to Santa Lucia, patron saint of eyesight, having miraculously restored the vision of many eyes in the Middle Ages. The last set of caverns lie in the *Grotta del Colombo*, which is full of more weird and wonderful shapes made of fragile limestone crystals.

(✆ 0182-98062). Admission: 9€ (£6) adults, 5€ (£3.35) ages 5–14. 9:30am–12:30pm; 2–5pm. By car: Borghetto S.Spirito exit on A10 autostrada. Bus or train to Borghetto S.Spirito and local shuttle bus.

Family-Friendly Accommodation

Hotel Medusa ★★ FIND

Beloved of Scandinavian families and located right on the beach, the Medusa offers bewitching value for money. Much thought has gone into catering for families, including a Mini Club for youngsters and a children's menu in the restaurant. The spacious family rooms have all you need for guests with babies, including a videophone, cot and baby bath. Breakfast is taken on the wonderful covered terrace. The staff have lots of information on sports and activities in the area, including mountain-biking (they have their own bike workshop), climbing, horse-riding, diving and even paragliding.

Lungomare di Via Concezione, Finale Ligure 17024. (☎ 019-692-545; fax: 019-695-679; ***www.medusahotel.it****). 32 units. 120€–160€ (£80–107) family room, half-board. Rates include continental buffet breakfast. AE, DC, MC, V. Amenities: restaurant (international cuisine); children's club and games; bike hire; parking. In room: A/C, minibar, TV.*

Hotel Albatross. ★ If you love being by the sea, this superb little hotel just up the coast at Varigotti is a must. It's right on the beach, which makes it great for children. Many of the recently renovated rooms have large balconies, and the public terrace is the perfect place to relax with a drink and watch the sun go down. There are lots of sporting activities to do in the area, including trekking, windsurfing, sailing, diving and tennis. Book well in advance.

Via Aurelia, 58 Varigotti, Finale Ligure 17029. (☎ 019-698-039; fax: 019-698-8268; ***www.hotelalbatros varigotti.it****). 16 units. 80€–180€ (£54–120) double. 130€–200€ (£87–134) triple, 200€–300€ (£134–200) suite sleeping four. Rates include continental buffet breakfast. AE, DC, MC, V. Amenities: discounts at local restaurants; parking. In room: A/C, hairdryer, minibar, safe, TV.*

Family-Friendly Dining

There's no shortage of eateries along the seafront, but alas many of them are overpriced and charmless. For a reasonably priced meal try **Gnabbri**, near the San Giovanni Battisti church (Via Pollupice 1. ☎ *019-693-289*), a welcoming trattoria with a decent selection of fish, meat and vegetarian *antipasti* options. For affordable pizza and seafood head to **La Caprazoppa** (Via Concezione 57. ☎ *019 690-415*).

Ai Torchi ★ It may be pricier than many of its neighbours, but this perennial favourite in Finalborgo is worth considering if you're after a superb family-dining outing. The choice of *antipasti* should be enough to satisfy children, as will the *trenette* pasta with pesto. Crustacean creations and various seafood combinations dominate the menu. Sublime desserts, fruit, cheese platters, a quality wine list and the ancient olive oil refinery setting complete the epicurean experience.

Via dell'Annunziata 12.(☎ 019-690-0531). Reservations recommended. Primi 9€–14€ (£6–9.40), secondi 11€–20€ (£7.40–13.40). AE, DC, MC, V. 12–2:30pm and 7–10:30pm. Closed January and February and Tue September to July.

Lilliput Combine a fantastic meal with a game of mini-golf at this quality restaurant near the medieval village of Noli up the coast. The setting up on the hill above the coastal crowds is truly special. The food is equally sublime: children will love the pesto and maybe even the *risotto alla marinara*, made with freshly caught seafood. If you pine for a prawn, grab a plate of *gamberi* here and you'll be in crustacean heaven. Their fantastic *gelati* and

Gelati

sorbetti flavours will melt on the tongue of the fussiest eater. It's a little formal, but an enjoyable dining experience nonetheless.

Regione Zuglieno 49, Voze – Noli. (✆ 019-748-009). Reservations recommended. Primi 9€–14€ (£6–9.40), secondi 12€–21€ (£8–14). AE, DC, MC, V. 12:30–2:30pm and 7:30–11pm. Closed for three weeks in January and February and Mon lunch.

San Remo

The Riviera di Ponente's most illustrious resort retains some of the glamour of its pre-World War II heyday when its handsome hotels, promenades, decadent casinos and exotic gardens were the haunt of composers, Russian royalty and the British well-to-do. As well as beachside pursuits, there's lots to see around town, and it makes a good base for trips to **Villa Hanbury**, the **Balzi Rossi caves**, **Dolceacqua** and forays into the cooler inland valleys.

Around Town

San Remo's two main streets, Corso Giacomo and Corso Roma, contain a busy shopping district: the former leads to the imposing Art Nouveau Casino

La Pigna, San Remo

Volare (Nel Blu, Dipinto Di Blu)

Volare, oh oh, cantare, oh oh oh oh
Nel blu, dipinto di blu, felice di stare lassù
E volavo, volavo felice più in alto del sole ed ancora piu su
Mentre il mondo pian piano spariva lontano laggiù
Una musica dolce suonava soltanto per me
Volare, oh oh, cantare, oh oh oh oh
No wonder my happy heart sings, your love has given me wings
Nel blu, dipinto di blu, felice di stare lassù

Excerpt of chorus from 1958 San Remo song with words added in English and famously sung by Dean Martin and also covered by Frank Sinatra: original song by Domenico Modugno and Franco Migliacci.

building on Corso Inglesi. The palm tree-lined **Corso dell'Imperatrice** contains the flamboyant onion-domed **San Basilio** Russian Orthodox Church, the verdant **Parco Marsaglia** and numerous stuccoed palazzi where the likes of Tchaikovsky and Alfred Nobel resided. Beyond the huge Piazza degli Eroi Sanremesi, with its fabulous daily market and gothic **San Siro Cathedral**, Via Monte leads to *La Pigna* (meaning the pine cone), an evocative district of medieval alleyways. It may be an effort with small children, but it's well worth heading up to **Piazza Castello**, where ruins within a park and fabulous views of rooftops and the ocean beyond await.

Essentials

Getting There

By Train There are regular trains from **Genoa to Finale Ligure** (1 hr approximately) and to **San Remo** (1¾ hr and 2½ hr.) **Ventimiglia** on the French border is another 20 minutes' ride and **Nice** is an additional 40 minutes further west.

By Bus **Riviera Trasporti** buses (☎ *0184-592-706; **www.rivieratrasporti.it***) run various services along the coast and inland. Check ***www.orariotrasporti.regione.liguria.it*** for specific journey times.

By Car Take the Autostrada A10 for fast transit in and out of San Remo: Genoa is about 45 min. away. The slower S1coastal road bisects the town centre.

Visitor Information

The **APT tourist board** is at Largo Nuvoloni 1 (☎ *0184-571-571;* fax: *0184-567-649*; ***www.apt.rivieradeifiori.it*** or ***www.sanremonet.com***), at the corner with

Corso Matteotti/Corso Imperatrice. It's open Monday–Saturday 8am–7pm and Sunday 9am–1pm. This is a good stop to gather information on the entire Riviera dei Fiori area.

Festivals & Markets

The **Feast of the Assumption (on 15th August)**, is celebrated with much gusto in San Remo, with the **festival of Nostra Signora della Costa** (Our Lady of the Coast). The Virgin Mary is honoured with fireworks and a kitsch procession to a hillside shrine.

The **Sanremo Festival** (late February to early March) has been Italy's premier festival of *La Canzone Italiana* (Italian song) since the 1950s. For lovers of Italian pop classics like *Volare* and *Parole, Parole, Parole* this is the place to catch legendary acts and emerging talent.

The **Mercato dei Fiori di Valle Armea**, Italy's most important wholesale flower market, is worth an early rise (Monday–Friday, 4am–8am) to witness the bustling and colourful spectacle. Take the SS1 towards Aurelia and follow directions to **Mercato dei Fiori** (Via Quinto Mansuino 12. ☎ *0184-510-309*. ***www.sanremoflowermarket.it***).

There is a daily fish and general food market and a larger general market on Tuesdays and Saturdays at **Piazza Eroi Sanremesi**, which is a great place to buy picnic provisions.

Beach Essentials

The pebbly beach below the Passeggiata dell'Impetrice is accessed via private beach stations, which provide showering and changing facilities, bars and beach paraphernalia. Expect to pay at least 6€ (£4) for a basic sunlounger. Ask at your hotel for good family beach deals.

Family-Friendly Accommodation

In high season, at the end of July and throughout August, Italian families book up most hotels and you may be required to take the half-board option.

MODERATE

Hotel Eletto VALUE This is a good bet in the centre of town and makes a good base for a short stay, if the kids aren't clamouring for a pool – the beach is just down the road. The rooms are hardly luxurious, but are functional and offer excellent value, especially the triples which are great for small families. For those with little Italian there is a bonus in that the staff are not only friendly but also geared to English-speaking guests. The onsite restaurant has sea views and offers superb value.

Corso Matteotti 44, 18038 San Remo. (☎ 0184-531-548; fax: 0184-531-506) 29 units. 100€–120€ (£67–80) double. 130€–150€ (£87–100) triple. Half-board 75€ (£50) per person. Rates include buffet breakfast . AE, DC, MC, V. Free parking in Via Roma. Amenities: restaurant (Italian); bar. In room: TV, minibar.

Paradiso This former private villa run by the third generation of the Gaiani family is set in lush, tranquil gardens near the promenade. The rooms are a little on the small side but the bathrooms are well kitted out and there are flower-filled balconies with sea views. The old-fashioned elegance throughout is very relaxing, and dining in the recently refreshed Liberty-style dining room is a grand event for young and old. Children will love the recent addition of a pool and the sandy beach just a short walk away. The air-conditioning is a godsend in the summer months.

*Via Roccasterone 12, 18038 San Remo. (☎ 0184-571-211; [fax] 0184-578-176; **www.paradisohotel.it**). 41 units. 110€–175€ (£74–117.25) double. Half-board 75€–105€ (£50–70.35) per person. Rates include buffet breakfast. AE, DC, MC, V. Parking 9€ (£6) in hotel garage. Amenities: restaurant (Italian cuisine); bar; outdoor pool; bike rental; concierge; tour desk; car-rental desk; courtesy car; 24-hr room service; babysitting; laundry service. In room: A/C, TV, dataport, minibar, hairdryer.*

INEXPENSIVE

Ca du Rampillu ★★ VALUE FIND
If you have your own transport and fancy a quieter retreat amidst orange and lemon groves, try this *agriturismo* 2 km (1.25 miles) to the north. Some of the simply furnished rooms here have pretty terraces with beautiful views of the countryside and sea. The accommodation offers great value for families and its small restaurant serves tasty fare using organic produce.

*Via G. d'Annunzio 49, 18038 San Remo. (☎ 0184-535-211; **www.biosanremo.it**). 6 units. 70€–90€ (£47–60) double. Extra bed 15€ (£10). Under 12s 5€ (£3.35). Tourist menu 15€ (£10). Rates include buffet breakfast. AE, DC, MC, V. Free parking. Amenities: restaurant (Italian); bar. In room: A/C, TV.*

Family-Friendly Dining

San Remo has many eateries and cafés, many serving the local speciality, *sardenaira*, a pizza-like creation topped with tomatoes, olives, garlic, capers and oregano. For a quick bite try the centrally located **Cantine Sanremesi** (Via Palzazzo 7) or the pizzeria **Graziella** (Piazza Eroi Sanremesi 49). The market here is a great place to pick up picnic supplies.

Bagatto ★★★ FIND LIGURIAN
Bagatto is an award-winning eatery and reasonably priced to boot. The attentive service and fulsome choice of delicious dishes make this a great holiday find. Perennial favourites include minestrone with pesto and a long list of homemade pasta shapes accompanied by delicious sauces. They even do small vegetarian *ravioli.*

Via Matteoti 145. (☎ 0184-531-925). Reservations recommended. Primi 9–14€ (£6–9.40); secondi 11–22€ (£7.40–14.75). MC, V. Mon–Sun 12:30–2pm and 7:30–11:30pm.

Nuovo Piccolo Mondo ★ VALUE LIGURIAN This intimate family-run *trattoria* retains much of the charm and some of its furnishings from the 1920s, when it opened. Local characters and families flock here for the Ligurian treats like *polpo e patate* (octopus and potatoes) and *verdura ripiena* (stuffed vegetables). They have a great selection of seafood and meat dishes, and will even rustle up a veggie-friendly creation or two on request.

Via Piave 7. (☎ 0184-509-012). Reservations recommended. Primi 6€–9.50€ (£4–6.35); secondi 7€–16€ (£4.70–10.70) No credit cards. Tues–Sat 12:30–1:50pm and 7:30–9:30pm.

SIDE TRIPS FROM SAN REMO

Bordighera Famed for its palm trees and the genteel English colony that settled here in the late 19th century, Bordighera is a civilised and peaceful place to stop on the way down the coast. The self-styled Queen of the Palms was the first town in Europe to grow date palms – some claim that seeds were carried here from Egypt by sea. It has the honour of providing the palm fronds for the Vatican's Easter festivities. Follow in the footsteps of Claude Monet who fell in love with the place, by walking along the Lungomare Argentina, a handsome promenade with westward views of the Côte d'Azur. Monet arrived in 1884, painting many palms in the 40 works with Bordighera scenes. There is a wide pebbly beach with public areas for an afternoon's messing about, as well as private lidos offering loungers and parasols. If you can muster the energy, wander among the palms and pastel-hued villas up to the Old Town with its beguiling atmosphere and elegant architecture. The publication of the novel *Doctor Antonio* (1855) by Italian exile Giovanni Ruffini, in Edinburgh brought the area to the attention of the British, who thought it rather spiffing and began flocking here thereafter, opening Italy's first tennis club in 1878.

Villa Hanbury ★ ALL AGES 23 km (14.3 miles) west of San Remo, just north of Ventimiglia at La Mortola, is this wonderful botanical garden founded by Sir Thomas Hanbury in 1867. The London merchant made his fortune in Shanghai and settled here, creating terraced gardens filled with 6000 species of exotic plants from all five continents, now looked after by the University of Genoa. While strolling around the lush grounds you'll come across a plaque marking the site of the famous **Roman Via Aurelia**. Concerts are held here throughout the summer.

Corso Montecarlo 43, La Mortola. (☎ 0184-229-507; ***www.amici hanbury.com****). Admission: 8€ (£5.35). 20€ (£13.40) family ticket. Autumn/spring: 10am–5pm; summer: 9am–6pm; winter: 10am–4pm. Closed Wed.*

Calzi Rossi Caves and Museum ★★ **AGES 4 AND UP** A mile west of Villa Hanbury, below the village of Grimaldi, are rugged red rock caves, which 200,000 years ago were the home of our ancestor *Homo erectus* and, further back, various Paleolithic and Neanderthal groups. The fascinating artefacts found here are housed in the **National Museum of Prehistory**, founded by Sir Thomas Hanbury. As well as rather complicated tools and stone-etched female figurines, the museum has a collection of wonderful hippopotami, elephants, rhinoceroses, marmots and reindeer fossils, demonstrating how the climate has altered dramatically here.

Via Balzi Rossi 9. (☎ 0184-38113). Admission: 3€ (£2). 8:30am–5:30pm Tue–Sun.

The Nervia Valley ★★★ **ALL AGES** The *Alpi Liguri* mountains along the coast are well worth exploring for their rugged terrain and captivating hilltop villages. One of the most attractive trails is along the Nervia valley, which threads inland to the east of Ventimiglia. Set aside at least four hours for the drive and numerous stops at picturesque spots. For active groups wanting to explore the area on foot, the Bordighera tourist office (Via Vittorio Emanuele 172. ☎ *0184-262-322*) has detailed information and maps. Beyond the wetland areas near the coast, where the River Nervia's abundant waters are home to migrant birds, you reach Camporosso, (a 20 minute drive) famed for its procession each 20th January to commemorate the feast day of its patron, Saint Sebastian. Leaving the town, the church of **Santi Pietro e Paolo** is worth visiting for its bell tower and Roman apse. Further up the flower-strewn valley driving leisurely for another 20 minutes, the ancient village of **Dolceacqua** (9 km from Bordighera) rewards a couple of hours' lingering to explore the beautiful Téra area with its historic buildings, ruined 16th century castle and baroque church of **Sant'Antonio Abate**, painted several times by Claude Monet. Children will enjoy the activity surrounding the many craft workshops, and adults can sample the famous *Rossese* wine produced from grapes grown on the terraced vineyards. Carry on to the equally beguiling villages of Isoblana, Apricale and Pigna (10 km from Bordighera) if you have time – you'll need at least an hour to see these – you can snake your way back to San Remo using the mountain roads. Just make sure the map-reader has a decent map and the driver's gear-changing skills are at the ready.

THE RIVIERA DI LEVANTE: CAMOGLI, SANTA MARGHERITA LIGURE, PORTOFINO, RAPALLO, SESTRI LEVANTE & THE CINQUE TERRE

Camogli: 26 km (16 miles) E of Genoa; Santa Margherita Ligure: 31 km (19 miles) E of Genoa; Portofino: 38 km (24 miles) E of Genoa; Rapallo: 37 km (23 miles) E of Genoa; Sestri Levante 50 km (31 miles) E of Genoa; Monterosso 80 km (50 miles) E of Genoa.

The coastline east of Genoa, the *Riviera di Levante* (Riviera of the Rising Sun), has less generic beach-holiday tourist development, partly due to its rugged mountains that plunge straight into the ocean. Indeed the hilly terrain of the picturesque towns of the Monte Portofino Promontory just east of Genoa (Camogli, Santa Margherita Ligure, Rapallo and Portofino) and the hiker's paradise of the Cinque Terre near La Spezia can turn travelling with younger children and toddlers in prams into an SAS sortie. Be warned as well that in July and August the towns and narrow roads are chocker and hotel prices soar. Despite the drawbacks, these are magical places to spend family time. An overlooked alternative base for a beach holiday is Sestri Levante, lying between these two outstandingly beautiful stretches of coast: it also has two sandy beaches, whereas most of the shoreline on the Riviera Levante is rocky or has pebbles.

Essentials

Getting There

By Train One to three trains per hour connect **Camogli** with **Genoa** (30–45 min.) and **Santa Margherita** (5 min.), **Rapallo** (10 min.), **Sestri Levante** (30 min.) **Monterosso** (50–60 min.) and other Cinque Terre towns. For **Portofino**, get off at **Santa Margherita** and take the local bus.

By Bus A **Tigullio** bus (☎ *0185-288-835; www.tigulliotrasporti.it*) leaves from the train station at **Santa Margherita** every half-hour for **Portofino**. There is a bus service from here to **Rapallo**.

By Boat In summer, boats operated by **Golfo Paradiso** (☎ *0185-772-091; www.golfoparadiso.it*) sail from Camogli to **Portofino. Tigullio ferries** (*www.traghetti portofino.it*) have six routes connecting the towns along the coastline between Genoa and Portovenere.

By Car The swiftest route into the region is via the A12 Autostrada from Genoa; exit at Recco for **Camogli.** For **Monterosso,** exit at Corrodano. For a more scenic but slower journey, take the S1 along the coast. A word of warning when visiting Portofino: summer traffic is horrific and the prices to park

Somersaults

in the garage are exorbitant – 4.50€ (£3) for an hour and 12€ (£8) for four hours.

Visitor Information

The **Camogli tourist office** is opposite the train station at Via XX Settembre 33 (☎/fax: *0185-771-066; www.camogli.it* or *www.portofinocoast.it*). The one at **Santa Margherita Ligure** lies near the harbour at Via XXV Aprile 2B (☎ *0185-287-485*; fax: *0185-283-034*; *www.apttigullio.liguria.it*). **Portofino's tourist information** is at Via Roma 35 (☎/fax: *0185-269-024*; *www.apttigullio.liguria.it*). The **Rapallo** office is at Lungomare Vittorio Veneto 7 (☎ *0185-230-346*; fax: *0185-63-051*). **Sestri Levante's** office is at Via Verdi 1 (☎ *0185-44238*). The Cinque Terre APT office is at **Monterosso** train station (Via Fegina 38 ☎ *0187-817-506;* fax: *0187-817-825*).

Santa Margherita Ligure

Festivals & Markets

Camogli

The ever-popular **Sagra del Pesce** ★★★ (second Sunday in May) sees thousands of sardines fried in a 3.65-metre (12-ft) wide pan to the delight of hungry hordes. The **Festa della Stella Maris** (first Sunday in August) involves the release of 10,000 burning candles from Punta Chiappaone a mile down the coast and the same distance from the beach – if currents are favourable, the candles mingle at sea, signifying a year of unity for watching couples.

Santa Margherita Ligure

The **Festa di Primavera** (changing date in February) heralds the onset of spring with a feast around roaring bonfires. Don't miss the daily fish market **on Lungomare Marconi** (8am–12:30pm), which becomes a full-blown food market on Fridays.

Portofino

The **Processione di San Giorgio** (30th April) sees pyrotechnic displays and a procession in honour of the saint.

Rapallo

An icon of the *Madonna di Montallegro* is carried through the streets (1st to 3rd July) and an impressive firework display culminates in the mock burning of the castle.

Chiavari

The **Festa della Madonna dell'Orto** (1st to –3rd July) involves processions, pyrotechnics and events along the promenade. Piazza Mazzini hosts a thriving daily market, and there is an antiques market in and around Via Martiri della Liberazione (second Saturday and Sunday).

Portofino Jaunts For Active Families

If you fancy a walk and the group is feeling reasonably nimble, grab a free map at the tourist office and head south towards **Castello Brown**, a castle with medieval relics and attractive grounds bought by English consul Sir Montague Yeats Brown in 1870. The nearby **San Giorgio church** reputedly contains the relics of its namesake, brought here by crusaders from the Holy Land. Further on, you can buy refreshments and ice cream near the lighthouse at the **Punta del Capo**, which affords sweeping views of the bay and beyond. For the adventurous with older children, there is the option of going on to San Fruttuoso. Heading in the other direction toward Santa Margherita, you'll find the nearest sandy beach in a cove named Paraggi.

Sestri Levante

The **Hans Christian Anderson Bay of Fables Festival** ★★ (late May) showcases storytelling and street theatre. Regional dishes, fireworks and music make up the lively **Festa Patronale di Santo Stefano del Ponte** at the start of August.

Monterosso

Taste the fruits of the area at the **Festa del Limone** (end of May).

Monte Portofino Promontory

Camogli

The first stop on the promontory is this unspoiled fishing harbour. The tall ochre-painted houses adorned with seashells that encircle the pebbly beach, and the seafood aromas in the air, create an enchanting atmosphere. Its fine eateries and restful ambience will appeal to many families. Children can enjoy

Portofino

FUN FACT

Home Guard

Camogli is an abbreviation of 'Casa dei Mogli' – Home of the Wives – in praise of the women who held the fort while their fishermen husbands went on long sea voyages.

re-enacting swashbuckling raids of Saracen pirates in and around the medieval **Castello Dragone** before unearthing the treasure trove of maritime paraphernalia and model boats in the:

Museo Marinario AGES 4 AND UP Escape the summer heat in the flamboyant 12th century **Basilica di Santa Maria Assunta**.

Via Gio Bono Ferrari 41. (0185-729-049). Mon, Thu and Fri 9am–12pm, Wed, Sat and Sun 9am–12pm and 3–6pm.

Agile walkers should visit one or all of the westerly hamlets: San Rocco for its Romanesque **San Niccolo church**, where sailors who have survived deadly scenarios at sea come to offer thanks; the fishing village **Punta Chiappa,** blessed with sublime views; and the:

Benedictine Abbey of San Fruttuoso AGES 4 AND UP There are lots of boats that will also take you along this wonderfully unspoiled coast from most harbours in the vicinity. If you can scuba you could make the watery pilgrimage to see Christ of the Depths, a bronze statue 50 feet beneath the surface erected in honour of divers who died in these waters during World War II.

(0185-772-703).Admission: 4€ (£2.70) adults, 2.50 € (£1.68) 4–12-year olds. December to February public holidays only: 1am–4pm; March to May and October: Tue–Sun 10am–4pm; Jun–Sep: daily 10am-6pm.

Golfo Paradiso ★★★ AGES 4 AND UP Make the round trip, and Tigullio (see 'Essentials', above) make the round trip from Santa Margherita, Portofino and Rapallo.

*(0185-772-091; **www.golfoparadiso.it**) Admission for round-trip Camogli–San Fruttuoso: 9€ (£6) adults, 7€ (£4.70) ages 5–10, under 5s free*

Santa Margherita Ligure

This is another fabulous base on the Golfo di Tigullio. It's a fishing village turned resort beloved of Italian families who flock in summer to its palm-fringed waterfront, pebbly beaches and yacht-filled marinas. Cafés and *gelaterie* fill the main squares, Piazza Vittorio Veneto and Piazza della Libertà. There's culture too, at the 16th century **Villa Durazzo** on Piazzale San Giacomo whose grand *saloni* and splendid gardens are open during the summer months. It also hosts concerts and events. Young children will enjoy the fantastical playgrounds at the **Parco**

Carmagnola (Viale Rainusso ☎ *0185-205-423*. Free. 9am-5pm Winter, 9am-7pm summer) inspired by Mozart's *Magic Flute.* Special shows for children are held at the small amphitheatre by the seafront and on the Spiaggia La Valletta beach throughout the summer.

Portofino

This is the quintessential jet-set retreat – a picturesque village turned affluent resort nestled in a sheltered inlet, worth a gander for a couple of hours at least. It's come a long way since Pliny the Elder dubbed it *Portus Delphini* (Dolphin's Harbour) because of the many dolphins that lived in its surrounding waters. Unless your wallet allows you to check into one of the luxury hotels, be prepared to join the day-tripping throng that queue for a parking space (very efficiently policed by traffic cops), then wander the cobbled quayside, dipping into the boutiques, before reclining and sipping a 4€ (£2.70) *caffè* whilst trying to out-pose the poseurs at the neighbouring tables. Apart from hanging around trying to look cool, taking a languid 15-minute stroll around the harbour or going for a jaunt up towards Punta del Capo, there's not much else to do.

Rapallo

Although spoiled by modern developments in the 1960s and 1970s, Rapallo retains some of the grace and charm that attracted English grand-tourists, poets and artists, including D. H. Lawrence. You could easily spend a day here admiring the grand villas, the 16th century castle, the **Cathedral of Santi Gervasio e Protasio** and taking the *funivia* (aerial cableway) to the fairytale-like:

Santuario di Montallegro ★★ **AGES 5 AND UP** for sweeping views of the coastline (☎ *0185-239-000*).

The *funivia* (☎ *0185-239-000*) runs from 8am to sunset and costs 8€ (£5.35) for a round-trip. The 16th century church contains lavish frescoes and a Byzantine icon of the Virgin that apparently made a solo flight to these shores from Dalmatia. For

DID YOU KNOW?

Marconi: A Wave of Communication

In 1934 Guglielmo Marconi carried out the first experiments in short-wave radio transmission at Sestri Levante's *Torretta*, in the fabulous grounds of the present-day Grand Hotel Dei Castelli. In the presence of British and Italian naval officers, and the press, he carried out a blind navigation, by radio beacon, guiding the boat *Elettra* from Santa Margherita to Sestri Levante. This was a precursor of the radar technology that played such a significant role in the Allies' World War II victory.

even more spectacular vistas, head to **Monte Rosa**, a short walk uphill.

Sestri Levante, Chiavari & Lavagna

In terms of value-for-money for those travelling with children, **Sestri Levante** (down the coast at the base of the Isola peninsula) is well worth considering as a holiday resort. It may not have the sheer cliffs of the more celebrated hamlets, but its flatter terrain and excellent facilities make it especially suited to younger families. This so-called 'town of the two seas' has two alluring bays: the lively **Bay of Fables** with ample beach space to play, and the more intimate **Bay of Silence**, a beach backed by colourful fishermen's houses. The recently revamped waterfront and city centre have some decent eateries, bars and cafés, and there are interesting sites to visit, including the:

Galleria Rizzi AGES 6 AND UP on the Bay of Silence, which has a fine collection of paintings, sculpture and other works (*0185-41300*).

On the edge of town, the colossal cranes looming over huge vessels in the shipbuilding docks are worth a look. The grander shipbuilding town **Chiavari,** a few miles up the coast, has arcaded streets and handsome *piazze* filled with colourful houses and trompe l'oeil architectural flourishes.

The **Civica Galleria di Palazzo Rocca** AGES 6 AND UP displays artwork by Genoese masters.

Via Costaguta 2 (0185-314-781). Free admission. Sat, Sun and public holidays 10am–noon, 4–7pm.

The **Museo Archaeologico** AGES 5 AND UP next door has artefacts from a nearby 7th century necropolis.

Via Costaguta 4. (0185-320-829). Tue–Sat 9am–1:30pm.

Across the Entella bridge, the resort of **Lavagna** is worth visiting for its long sandy beach, Gothic **Basilica dei Fieschi** and the '**Via della Pietra Nera**' trail (hilly sections not suitable for young children) that links the slate quarries. Indeed, 'Lavania' is the Roman word for slate; the stone brought wealth to the city and gave the town notoriety, not least through the slate boards quarried here and used by schoolchildren around the world. The large marina is worth a stroll around for its fabulous yachts.

Sports & Activities

To hire **bikes** in Sestri Levante contact **Cicli Enrico** at Via Nazionale 415 (*0185-44725*). There are tennis courts, a squash court and *calcetto* five–a-side footie pitches at **Centro Sportive Le Mimose** (Via Lombardia 26. *0185-482-937).*

Indian Forest Adventure Park. AGES 8 AND UP If you fancy swinging from the trees like Tarzan with a safety harness on, and you have your own transport, take the road inland from Lavagna to Carasco (or the bus from Chiavari station). The obstacle courses in the trees are fun for all ages and abilities.

Belpiano, Borzonasca. (☎ 0185-340-366). From 8€ for a half day session. Fri-Sun 10am–7pm and by appointment during the week.

The **European Diving Centre** based at Santa Margherita offers 'Bubblemaker' diving courses with an emphasis on fun for children over the age of 8.

*La Valletta. (☎ 0185-293 017; **www.europeandc.com**). 40 € (£27) per child.*

B&B Diving Centre in Camogli runs guided dives and also hires out small boats, canoes and snorkelling equipment.

*Via San Fortunato 11–13. (☎ 0185-772-751; **www.bbdiving.it**). 40€ (£27).*

The Cinque Terre

This protected stretch of rocky coast consists of five villages that cling to vertiginous cliffs: Monterosso, Vernazza, Corniglia, Manarola and Riomaggiore. These remote fishing villages were only accessible by sea until a railway line was built that forged a path through the craggy terrain. Cars have to negotiate steep and winding roads. It's not an ideal area to visit for those with small children, but if you adore dramatic scenery and stunning walking territory, make sure you pack sturdy boots and your best outdoor kit. The northernmost and largest of the villages, **Monterosso**, has retained much of its higgledy-piggledy charm, despite the appearance of some incongruously modern buildings amid its narrow alleys and stairways. Most of Cinque Terre's

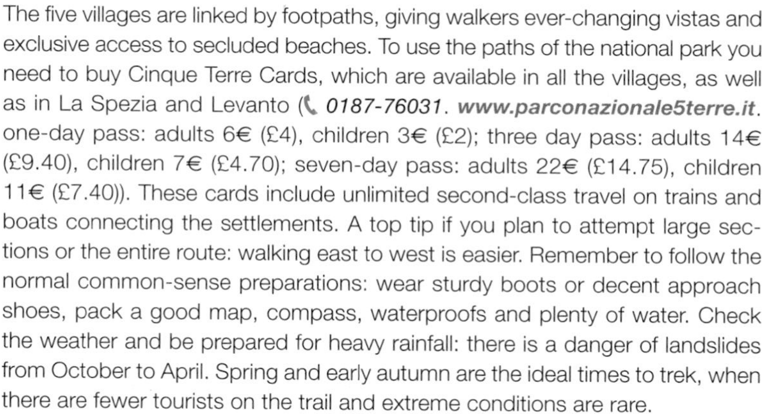

TIP

Walking in the Cinque Terre

The five villages are linked by footpaths, giving walkers ever-changing vistas and exclusive access to secluded beaches. To use the paths of the national park you need to buy Cinque Terre Cards, which are available in all the villages, as well as in La Spezia and Levanto (☎ *0187-76031*. ***www.parconazionale5terre.it***. one-day pass: adults 6€ (£4), children 3€ (£2); three day pass: adults 14€ (£9.40), children 7€ (£4.70); seven-day pass: adults 22€ (£14.75), children 11€ (£7.40)). These cards include unlimited second-class travel on trains and boats connecting the settlements. A top tip if you plan to attempt large sections or the entire route: walking east to west is easier. Remember to follow the normal common-sense preparations: wear sturdy boots or decent approach shoes, pack a good map, compass, waterproofs and plenty of water. Check the weather and be prepared for heavy rainfall: there is a danger of landslides from October to April. Spring and early autumn are the ideal times to trek, when there are fewer tourists on the trail and extreme conditions are rare.

Vernazza

restaurants and hotels are here, and you'll also find the area's largest beach – whose every grain of precious sand seems to be covered in August. The **church of San Francesco** is worth a look for its *Crucifixion*, attributed to Van Dyck. **Vernazza** has the largest harbour, a cylindrical tower and the beguiling **Piazza Marconi** crammed with café tables and gossiping clientele. **Corniglia**'s colourful houses cling limpet-like to crags high above the sea. It has a stunning backdrop of terraced vineyards that have been producing excellent wine since Roman times. It's the quietest enclave due to its isolated location, and the least touched by tourism. Visitors have to climb more than 300 steps to reach the village – a definite no-no for pram or stroller-wielding parents. **Manarola** has a cluster of elongated dwellings and is home to the region's major wine concern, the *Cooperativa Agricoltura Cinque Terre*, made up of 300 local producers. You can tour its facilities (📞 0187-920-435; **www.cantinacinqueterre.com**). Prosperous **Riomaggiore** has more intimate flowery *piazze* and charming architecture, but is less isolated than its neighbours, being closer to bustling La Spezia. Its narrow lanes lead to belvederes and a staircase opens out into a small port and pebbly beach. Here you can watch local fishermen heave their boats on to the shore and unload their catches.

Family-Friendly Accommodation

On the Monte Portofino promontory, the best balance of value and location for those with children is found at Camogli and Santa Margherita. The former offers the intimacy of Portofino without the emphasis on overpriced 'luxury' and supposed hipness. There's also a proper beach at livelier Santa Margherita – and you can always don your best billionaire's sailing leisurewear and saunter into Portofino for a look around. Down the coast, Sestri Levante sits on flatter terrain, making it easier to walk around with toddlers. The Cinque Terre is difficult to get around, and its rugged charms are more suited to travel with older children: you're better off using the scenic train service here. If you are on a budget or just fancy taking the children **camping**, there are a number of campsites along the coast. If you prefer a quieter stay under canvas, avoid the large sprawling sites and seek out smaller ones like Camping Acqua Dolce at Levanto (Via Guido Semenza. *0187-808-465.* ***www.campingacquadolce.it.*** From 45€ per night for two adults, two kids, a vehicle and pitch.) (see Chapter 2: Planning a Trip to Northern Italy).

Camogli

Cenobio dei Dogi. ★ This former residence of Genoa's patrician families is perched high above Camogli, giving many rooms fabulous seaside views. Children will love the pools and the grounds, which hold a tennis court, and the pebbly beach, giving access to the limpid waters. Rooms vary in size, so insist on a spacious one. There are three suites suitable for larger families – ask for one with a large terrace and views.

Via Cuneo 34, 16032 Camogli. (0185-7241; fax: 0185-772-796; ***www.cenobio.it****). 106 units. 150€–285€ (£100–191) standard double;175€–315€ (£117–211) superior double; 260€–425€ suite (£174–285). 31€–41€ (£21–28) third bed supplement. Rates include continental breakfast. Half-board 35€ (£23.50), full-board 70€ (£47). AE, DC, MC, V. Amenities: two*

Riomaggiore

restaurants (one on the beach); two bars; two pools (indoor and outdoor saltwater pool); nearby golf course; tennis courts; gym and sauna across the street; water sports equipment/rentals; bike rental; concierge; tour desk; car-rental desk; salon; limited room service; massage; babysitting; laundry service; dry cleaning. In room: A/C, TV, dataport, hairdryer, minibar, safe.

Santa Margherita Ligure

Fasce Aristide and his British wife Jane run this pleasant little hotel, which has three triples and a quad ideal for families. If you fancy a trip to the shops you can borrow one of their bikes. For those staying three nights or more they'll provide you with return tickets to Riomaggiore, so you can sample the delights of the Cinque Terre villages. The intimate roof terrace is a great place to wind down with a beverage and drink in the sea views.

*Via Luigi Bozzo 3, 16038 Santa Margherita Ligure. (☎ 0185-286-435; fax: 0185-283-580; **www.hotelfasce.it**). 16 units. 100€ (£67) double; 130€ (£87) triple; 150€ (£100) quad. 160€ (£107) family room. Rates include breakfast. Parking 16€ (£10.70). AE, DC, MC, V. Closed 12th December to 15th March. Amenities: bar; free bikes; tour desk; limited room service; laundry service. In room: TV, dataport, hairdryer, minibar, safe.*

Sestri Levante

Vis-à-vis ★ Fabulous views, a pool and excellent all-round facilities make Vis-à-vis the best family-orientated address in Sestri Levante. Its elevated position means you have to take a lift, via a curious green-lit, red-carpeted tunnel. Many of the rooms have their own small balconies and a glimpse of the sea. The real winner is the terrace, where you can relax in the comfy cane chairs with a view of the nearby pool and the twin bays below. You can dine at the excellent glass-encased Olimpico restaurant, where the top-notch breakfast is served – in summer you'll want to eat on the cooler terrace. Weddings often take place here, so be prepared to be a background star in cheesy photos.

*Via della Chiusa, 28 16039 Sestri Levante. (☎ 0185-42661; fax: 0185-480-853; **www.hotelvisavis.com**). 46 units. 170–240€ (£114–161) double; discounts: 0–6 years 50%; 7–10 30%; 11–14 20%. 20€ (£13.40) per day to add an extra bed. Rates include breakfast. AE, DC, MC, V. Amenities: bar; Ligurian restaurant with children's menu; room service; laundry service; children's miniclub May to October. In room: A/C, TV, dataport, minibar, safe.*

Monterosso

Hotel Pasquale/Villa Steno ★★ VALUE have created a wonderful atmosphere at this hotel overlooking the beach, *la spiaggia dei pescatori*. Many of the rooms and bathrooms are a little cramped, and fittings a bit dated, so ask for the roomier quad, which has adjoining bedrooms. La Famiglia Pasini also have another place, Villa Steno, further up the *borgo antico*, which has room arrangements suited to families, many of which have small outdoor spaces with sea views.

*Via Fegina, 19016 Monterosso al Mare. (0187-817-550; [fax] 0187-817-056; **www.pasini.com**). 15 units. 120–185€ (£80–124) double; 160–220€ (£107–148) triple; 180–260€ (£120–174) quad. Rates include breakfast. AE, MC, V. Closed December. Amenities: bar; babysitting; limited room service; laundry service. In room: A/C, TV, dataport, hairdryer, safe.*

Cafés, Snacks & Family-Friendly Dining

Portofino

The main pastime at this archetypal picturesque harbour is to savour *dolce vita* moments seated at one of the expensive café-restaurants like Delfino and Stella.

Da Puny ★ LIGURIAN For the best value, service and atmosphere, book a table here.

Piazza Martiri dell'Olivetta 5. (0185-269-037). Primi 9€–16€ (£6–10.70); secondi 11€–22€ (£7.40–14.75). No credit cards. Wed–Fri noon–3pm and 7–11pm.

Or the more refined **Chuflay Bar** LIGURIAN Remember, a mere espresso will set you back 4€ (£2.70) if seated.

Via Roma 2. (0185-26037). Primi 9€–18€ (£6–12); secondi 12€–24€ (£8–16). AE, DC, MC, V. 7am–midnight.

As you enter this amphitheatre-of-a-harbour, you'll find **Pasticceria Canale** on Via Roma, which has been producing Ligurian specialities, savoury snacks and sweet treats like *Focaccia Genovese*, *pizza cipolle* and meringues since 1911. *Gelati* gluttons should visit **Gelateria San Giorgio** on Piazza Olivetta.

Camogli

Dining is a less self-consciously laid-back affair here and you don't have to be a VIP (pronounced 'Veep' in Italian) to get a table.

Nonna Nina has the homely atmosphere of eating *da nonna* (at grandma's place) with serene San Rocco laid before your eyes. Alongside seafood dishes and rabbit, they do some veggie-friendly creations like *polpettone di verdura*.

Via Molfino 126, San Rocco. (0185-773-835). Primi 7€–15€ (£4.70–10); secondi 9€–19€ (£6–12.75). AE, DC, MC, V. Noon–2:30pm, 7:30–10:30pm. Closed Wed.

For sublimely sweet *paste* and salty *focaccia* snacks check out **Revello** FIND at Via Garibaldi 183.

Santa Margherita Ligure

There are plenty of eateries with sea views, including the excellent:

Trattoria Baicin which serves a fine *fritto misto* (lightly fried seafood) that is finger-licking fun to share.

Via Algeria 9. (☎ 0185-286-763). Primi 4€–8€ (£2.70–5.35); secondi 9€–18€ (£6–12); fixed-price menus 20€–23€ (£13.40–15.40). AE, DC, MC, V. Tues–Sun noon–3pm and 7–10:30pm. Closed January.

Santa Lucia For a proper Neapolitan pizza made in a *forno a legna*.

Piazza Martiri Libertà 42. (☎ 0185-287-163). Primi 5€–8€ (£3.35–5.35); secondi 8€–18€ (£5.35–12). AE, DC, MC, V. Tues–Sun noon–3pm and 7–10:30pm.

There are a number of *caffè-gelaterias* on Piazza Martiri Libertà including **Il Portico Di Simonetti**.

Sestri Levante

You'll discover some great shops for picnics and snacks here, where you and the children can practice some Italian (see the appendices): for fantastic *frutta e verdura*, much of it organic, pop into **Di Segarini Cristina** at Corso Colombo 73.

Balin Bar Order an *aperitivo* and soft drinks for the children at this funky bar and they'll present you with a wooden platter heaped with *crocanti*, cheeses, pickles and prosciutto.

Viale Rimembranza 34 (☎ 0185-458-025).

Nearby **Il Cocodrillo** at no.27 (☎ *0185-480-747*) offers great value, serving tasty *insalate di mare* (seafood salad) and *pizze*, including the sublimely simple Margherita and their ridiculously named Rustica, topped with processed cheese – hardly Neapolitan DOC, but some children will love it.

Monterosso

For genuinely rustic fast food try **Il Frontoio** ★★, which serves some of the best *focaccia* in these parts. There are a couple of superb eateries with outside spaces, but ensure you book in advance.

Il Gigante is a welcoming *trattoria* with a beguiling garden, serving freshly caught seafood dishes.

Via IV Novembre 9. (☎ 0187-817-401). Reservations recommended. Primi 6€–14€ (£4–9.40); secondi 9€–19€ (£6–12.75). AE, DC, MC, V. Daily noon–3pm and 6:30–10pm. Closed November and Tues in winter.

Il Pirata It's kitsch and cute and famed for its adventurous *acciughe* (anchovies) creations and tasty ravioli filled with prawns and courgettes, making it a great place to expand the palates of the young and impressionable.

Via Molinelli 6. (☎ 0187-817-536). Reservations recommended. Primi 8€–16€ (£5.35–10.70); secondi 10€–21€ (£6.70–14). AE, DC, MC, V. Daily noon–3pm and 6:30–10pm.

Appendix: Useful Terms and Websites

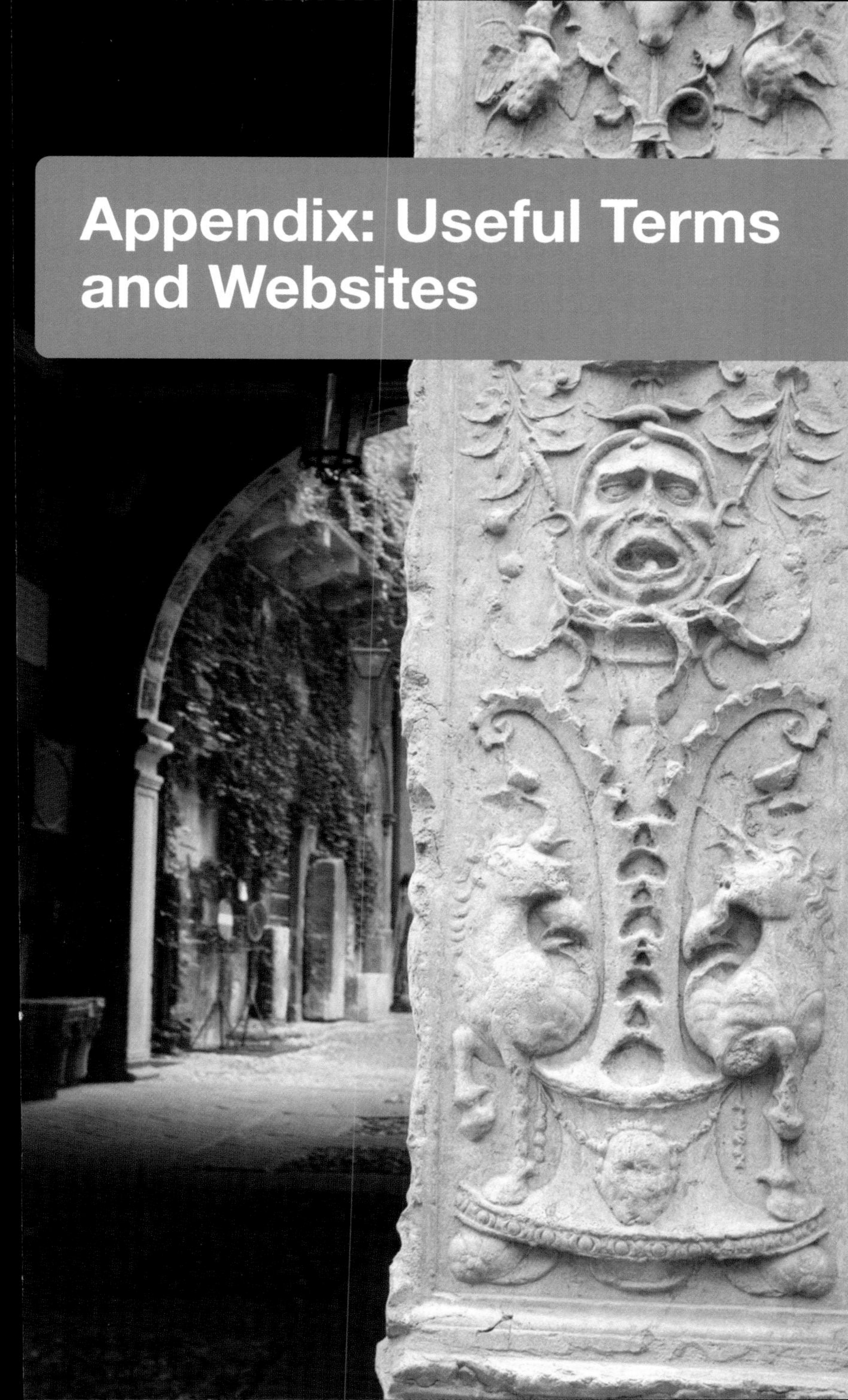

This section has an essential English–Italian vocabulary with some pronunciation guidance.

For those keen on learning some Italian get hold of a copy of *Italian for Children* (Contemporary Books), which is a fun CD/book course for children and adults wanting to learn the basics. *Teach Yourself* do some well-thought out introductory language books including a good vocabulary for beginners. The free BBC Italian language pages at ***http://www.bbc.co.uk/languages/italian*** are well worth delving into. For details about Italian language courses and cultural events contact your nearest Italian Cultural Institute: in London (39 Belgrave Square SW1X 8NX. ☎ *020 –7235-1461*. ***www.icilondon.esteri.it***); Dublin (11 Fitzwilliam Square East, Dublin 2. ☎ *00-353 (1)-662-0509*) or Edinburgh (82 Nicolson Street, Edinburgh EH8 9EW ☎ *0131-668-2232*).

Greetings & Pleasantries

Thank you	**Grazie**	graht-tzee-yey
You're welcome	**Prego**	prey-go
Please	**Per favore**	pehr fah-vohr-eh
Good morning or Good day	**Buongiorno**	bwohn-djor-noh
Good evening	**Buona sera**	Bwohn-ah say-rah
Good night	**Buona notte**	Bwohn-ah noht-tay
Hi/bye	**Ciao**	Chow
How are you?	**Come sta?**	koh-may stah
Very well	**Molto bene**	mohl-toh behn-ney
Good-bye	**Arrivederci**	ahr-ree-vah-dehr-chee
What's your name?	**Come si chiama?**	Ko-may see kee-ah-mo
My name is...	**Mi chiamo...**	mee kee-ah-mo
Excuse me (to get attention)	**Scusi**	skoo-zee
Excuse me (to get past someone)	**Permesso**	pehr-mehs-soh
I don't understand	**Non capisco**	nohn ka-pee-sco
I don't speak Italian	**Non parlo italiano**	non par-lo ee-tal-yah-no
Correct	**Giusto**	jew-stoh
No, I don't want . . .	**No, non voglio . . .**	no, non vohl-yo

Nationalities

I'm . . .	**Sono** . . .	*so*-no . . .
English	**Inglese**	een-*glaze*-eh

Irish	**Irlandese**	ear-lahn-*dayz*-eh
Scottish	**Scozzese**	scot-*tzeh*-zeh
Welsh	**Gallese**	gah-lah-zeh
Australian	**Australiano**	a'ws-tra-lee-*ah*-no
New Zealander	**Dalla nuova zelanda**	dah-la nu-*wo*-va zee-*lahn*-dee-yah
American	**Americano**	ah-mehr-ee-*kahn*-oh
Canadian	**Canadese**	kahn-ah-*dayz*-eh

Family & Friends

Mother	**la madre**	la mah-dreh
Father	**il padre**	eel pah-dreh
Dad	**il papà, il babbo**	ell paa-pa, eel bah-bbo
Mum	**la mamma**	lah-mah-mah
Children	**i figli**	ee fee-ylee
Baby (boy/girl)	**un/una bambino/a**	oo/oona bam-bee-nah
Son/Daughter	**il/la figlio/a**	eel/lah fee-yl-eeo/fee-yl-ah
Brother	**il fratello**	eel frah-teh-llo
Sister	**la sorella**	la so-reh-lla
Husband	**il marito**	eel mah-ree-toh
Wife	**la moglie**	la mo-yl-ee-eh
Grandparents	**i nonni**	ee noh-nnee
Friend	**un/una amico/a**	oon/oonah a-mee-koh / a-mee-kah
Friends	**gli amici**	ylee a-mee-chee
Boy	**un ragazzo**	oon ra-gah-dzz-oh
Girl	**una ragazza**	oo-nah ra-gah-dzz-ah

Directions

Where is . . .?	**Dovè . . .?**	doh-*vey*
the station	**la stazione**	lah stat-tzee-*oh*-neh
a hotel	**un albergo**	oon ahl-*behr*-goh
a restaurant	**un ristorante**	oon reest-ohr-*ahnt*-eh
the bathroom	**il bagno**	eel *bahn*-nyoh
To the right	**A destra**	ah *dehy*-stra
To the left	**A sinistra**	ah see-*nees*-tra
Straight ahead	**Avanti (or sempre diritto)**	ahv-vahn-tee (*sehm*-pray de*reet*-toh)

Shopping & Transactions

I would like . . .	**Vorrei** . . .	vohr-*ray*
Do you have . . .?	**Ce l'hai** . . .?	cheh lie
How much is it?	**Quanto costa?**	*kwan*-toh *coh*-sta?
This one	**Questo**	*kway*-sto
That one	**Quello**	*kwel*-loh
Too expensive	**Troppo costoso**	*troh*-poh koh-*sto*-zoh
I would like to change . . .	**Vorrei cambiare** . . .	vohr-*ray* kahm-bee-*yar*-eh
cash	**contanti**	cone-*tahn*-tee
credit card	**carta di credito**	*kar*-tah dee *creh*-dee-toh
Deposit	**Deposito**	deh-*po*-zee-toh
Market	**Mercato**	mehr-*kah*-toh
Supermarket	**Supermercato**	*su*-pehr-mehr-kah-toh
I want to buy . . .	**Vorrei comprare** . . .	vohr-*ray* com-*prar*-eh

Numbers

1	**uno** (oo-noh)
2	**due** (doo-ay)
3	**tre** (tray)
4	**quattro** (kwah-troh)
5	**cinque** (cheen-kway)
6	**sei** (say)
7	**sette** (set-tay)
8	**otto** (oh-toh)
9	**nove** (noh-vay)
10	**dieci** (dee-ay-chee)
11	**undici** (oon-dee-chee)
20	**venti** (vehn-tee)
21	**ventuno** (vehn-toon-oh)
22	**venti due** (vehn-tee doo-ay)
30	**trenta** (trayn-tah)
40	**quaranta** (kwah-rahn-tah)
50	**cinquanta** (cheen-kwan-tah)
60	**sessanta** (sehs-*sahn*-tah)
70	**settanta** (seht-*tahn*-tah)
80	**ottanta** (oht-*tahn*-tah)
90	**novanta** (noh-*vahnt*-tah)
100	**cento** (*chen*-toh)
1000	**mille** (*mee*-lay)
5000	**cinque mila** (*cheen*-kway *mee*-lah)
10,000	**dieci mila** (dee-*ay*-chee *mee*-lah)

Time

When?	**Quando?**	*kwan*-doh
Yesterday	**Ieri**	ee-*yehr*-ree
Today	**Oggi**	*oh*-jee
Tomorrow	**Domani**	doh-*mah*-nee
Morning	**Mattina**	mah-*tee*-nah
Afternoon	**Pomeriggio**	pohm-mehr-*ree*-joe
Evening	**Sera**	*seh*-rah

1 hour	**Un ora**	oon-*or*-rah
7 hours	**Sette ore**	set-tay *or*-reh
What time is it?	**Che ore sono?**	kay *or*-ay *soh*-noh

Days Of The Week & Months Of The Year

Monday	**Lunedì**	loo-nay-*dee*
Tuesday	**Martedì**	mart-ay-*dee*
Wednesday	**Mercoledì**	mehr-cohl-ay-*dee*
Thursday	**Giovedì**	joh-vay-*dee*
Friday	**Venerdì**	ven-nehr-*dee*
Saturday	**Sabato**	*sah*-bah-toh
Sunday	**Domenica**	doh-*mehn*-nee-kah
January	**Gennaio**	Jeh-*nneye*-oh
February	**Febbraio**	Feh-*breye*-oh
March	**Marzo**	*Martz*-oh
April	**Aprile**	A-*pree*-lay
May	**Maggio**	Mah-*jee*-oh
June	**Giugno**	*Jew*-ny-oh
July	**Luglio**	*Loo*-lee-oh
August	**Agosto**	A-*gos*-toh
September	**Settembre**	Se-*ttem*-breh
October	**Ottobre**	O-*ttoh*-breh
November	**Novembre**	No-*vem*-breh
December	**Dicembre**	Dee-*chem*-breh

Travel

What time does . . . leave?	**à che ora parte**	ah kay *or*-ah *par*-the
the train	**il treno**	eel *tray*-no
the intercity bus	**il Pullman**	eel *pool*-mahn
the city bus	**l'autobus**	*lout*-toe-boos
the ferry	**il traghetto**	eel tra-*get*-toh
the ship	**la nave**	lah *nah*-vey
I want to go to . . .	**Voglio andare . . .**	*vohl*-yo ahn-*dar*-eh
Stop or station (bus or train)	**Fermata**	fehr-*mat*-tah
Ticket	**Biglietto**	beel-*yeh*-toh
Passport	**Passaporto**	pahs-sah-*por*-toh
What time do you open/ close?	**à che ora aprite/ chiudete?**	ah kay *or*-ah ah-*pree*-teh/ kee-you-*deh*-the

Useful Terms At The Chemist With Children

Chemist	**farmacia**	farr-mah-*chee*-ah
Cold	**raffreddore**	a-frreh-*ddoh*-reh
Sore throat	**mal di gola**	mal dee *goh*-lah
Headache	**mal di testa**	mal dee *teh*-sta
Stomach ache	**mal di stomaco**	mal dee *sto*-mah-koh
A children's painkiller containing paracetamol	**Tachipirina**	tah-key-pee-*ree*-nah
Vomit	**Vomito**	*vo*-mee-tto
Diarrhoea	**Diarrea**	Dee-ah-*rreh*-ah

Baby Stuff

Dummy	**ciuccio**	*choo*-chee-o
Nappies	**pannolini**	pah-nno-*lee*-nee
Baby-changing table	**fasciatoio**	fash-ee-a-*toy*-o
Baby chair	**seggiolino**	se-gee-o-*lee*-noh

Hotel Booking

A single room	**Una singola**	oo-nah *seen*-goh-lah
A double with one big bed and a cot	**Una doppia matrimoniale e una culla**	oo-nah *doh*-pee-yah ma-tree-moan-ee-*y'all*-eh eh oo-nah *koo*-lah
A double with two beds	**Una doppia con due letti**	oo-nah *doh*-pee-yah con *doo*-ay let-tee
with a private bathroom	**con bagno**	con *bahn*-yoh
Half-board	**Mezza pensione**	meh-dzz-ah pehn-see-*oh*-neh
Full-board	**Pensione completa**	Pehn-see-*oh*-neh com-*pleh*-ta

Eating

Breakfast	**Prima colazione**	*pree*-mah coh-laht-tzee-*ohn*-ay
Lunch	**Pranzo**	*prahn*-zoh
Dinner	**Cena**	*chay*-nah
Snack	**Merenda/spuntino**	meh-rehn-dah/ spoon-*tee*-noh
Have you got a table for four?	**Avete una tavola per quattro?**	Ah-*veh*-te *oo*-nah *tah*-voh-lah purr *kwah*-troh
I'd like to reserve a table	**Vorrei riservare una tavola**	vor-*ray* ree-sair-*vah*-reh *oo*-nah *tah*-voh-lah
The bill, please	**Il conto, per favore**	eel kon-toh *pehr* fah-*vohr*-eh
Vegetarian	**Vegetariano/a**	veh-jeh-tar-ee-*ah*-noh/nah

I'm allergic to . . .	**Sono allergico à . . .**	so-no ahl-*lair*-gee-koh ah
nuts	**noci**	*no*-chee
peanuts	**arachidi**	ah-*rah*-kee-dee
milk	**latte**	*la*-teh
shellfish	**molloschi**	*mohl*-loh-skee
I can't eat meat/pork	**Non posso mangiare carne/suino**	non po-so mahn-*giar*-eh *car*-neh/soo-*ee*-no
I can eat	**Posso mangiare**	poh-so mahn-*giar*-eh
fish	**pesce**	*peh*-shay
chicken	**pollo**	*pol*-loh
duck	**anatra**	*ah*-nah-tra
beef	**manzo**	*mahn*-zoh
steak	**bistecca**	bee-*steh*-kah
lamb	**agnello**	ahn-*yell*-oh
boar	**cinghiale**	cheen-*g'yah*-leh
venison	**cervo**	*chair*-voh
sausage	**salsicce**	sahl-*see*-chay
eggs	**uove**	*woh*-veh
salad	**insalata**	een-sah-*lah*-ta
vegetables	**verdure**	vair-*doo*-ray
eggplant	**melanzane**	meh-lahn-*zahn*-eh
zucchini	**zucchini**	zoo-*keen*-ee
bell peppers	**pepperoni**	pep-pair-*oh*-nee
fruit	**frutta**	*froo*-tah
Water	**acqua**	*ah*-kwah
Fizzy/still	**frizzante/naturale**	free-*zahn*-the/nah-too-*rah*-leh
Tap water	**acqua dal rubinetto**	*ah*-kwah dahl roo-bee-*net*-toh
Beer	**Birra**	*bee*-rah
Red wine	**Vino rosso**	*vee*-no *rohs*-so
White wine	**Vino bianco**	*vee*-no bee-*yahn*-koh
Bread	**Pane**	*pah*-neh
Butter	**Burro**	*boo*-roh
Ice	**Ghiaccio**	ghee-*yah*-cho
Bottle	**Bottiglia**	boh-*teel*-yah
Fork	**Forchetta**	for-*ket*-tah
Glass	**Bicchiere**	bee-key-*air*-eh
Spoon	**Cucchiaio**	koo-key-*yai*-oh
Knife	**Coltello**	kohl-*tell*-loh

Oil	**Olio**	*oh*-lee-oh
Pepper	**Pepe**	*peh*-pay
Plate	**Piatto**	pee-*yaht*-toh
Cream	**Crema**	*kray*-ma
Salt	**Sale**	*sah*-leh
Cup	**Tazza**	*taht*-zah
Sugar	**Zucchero**	*zoo*-cair-oh
Rare	**Al sangue**	ahl *sahn*-gway
Well done	**Ben cotto**	ben *koh*-toh
Baked	**Al forno**	ahl *fore*-noh
Fried	**Fritto**	*free*-toh
Grilled	**Alla griglia, alle brace**	ah-la *gree*-ylia, ah-lay *brah*-chay
Steamed	**Al vapore**	ahl vah-*pohr*-ay
Stuffed	**Ripieno**	ree-pee-*yay*-no
Boiled	**Bollito**	boh-*lee*-toh
Roasted	**Arrosto**	ah-*roh*-sto
The menu	**La carta**	lah *kar*-tah
Fixed-price menu	**Menu à prezzo fisso**	men-*you* ah *pret*-zoh *fees*-soh

Menu Terms

Abbacchio Roast shoulder or haunch of lamb baked and served in a casserole.

Agnolotti A crescent-shaped pasta shell with various fillings including the classic version with a mix of chopped meat, vegetables, spices and cheese; the rectangular version is **ravioli** (which contrasts with the cheap school dinner version and is filled with cheese or pumpkin).

Amaretti Sweet and crunchy, almond-flavoured macaroons.

Anguilla alla veneziana Eel cooked in a tangy sauce.

Antipasti Titbits served at the beginning of a meal (before the *primo piatto*) which might include cured meats, seafood, or cooked and seasoned vegetables.

Aragosta Lobster.

Arrosto Roasted meat (usually pork).

Baccalà Dried and salted codfish.

Bagna caoda A 'hot bath' for dipping raw vegetables: it's a well-seasoned piquant sauce, flavoured with anchovies.

Bistecca alla fiorentina Chunky steaks cooked Florentine-style over an open fire.

Bollito misto Assorted boiled meats.

Braciola A chop, steak or slice of meat.

Bresaola Air-dried seasoned beef.

Bruschetta Toasted bread, slathered with olive oil and garlic and normally topped with tomatoes.

Bucatini Hollow spaghetti originating from the South.

Busecca alla Milanese Flavoured tripe.

Cacciucco ali livornese Seafood stew.

Calzone Pizza dough rolled with the chef's choice of sausage, tomatoes, cheese, and so on, then baked into a kind of savoury turnover.

Cannelloni Tubular dough stuffed with meat, cheese or vegetables, then baked in a creamy white sauce.

Cappelletti Small ravioli ('little hats') filled with meat or cheese.

Carciofi Artichokes.

Carpaccio Thin slices of raw cured beef.

Cassatta alla siciliana A rich dessert combining layers of sponge cake, sweetened ricotta cheese and candied fruit, with chocolate butter-cream icing.

Cavallo or caval Horse meat, very popular in Veneto and Friuli, especially in Verona.

Cima alla genovese Baked roll of veal usually stuffed with eggs, mushrooms and sausage.

Cotoletta alla milanese Veal cutlet covered in breadcrumbs.

Cozze Mussels.

Fagioli White beans.

Fave Fava beans.

Fegato alla veneziana Thin slices of calf liver fried with salt, pepper and onions.

Focaccia A Genovese type of bread garnished with salt and olive oil, and sometimes with various toppings and additional seasonings.

Fontina Rich cow's-milk cheese from the Valle d'Aosta.

Fritto misto A medley of deep-fried goodies: usually small fish, squid and shellfish.

Fusilli Spiral-shaped pasta.

Gelato (produzione propria) Ice cream (homemade).

Gnocchi Dumplings usually made from potatoes *(gnocchi alla patate)*.

Gorgonzola A blue-veined cheese which is strong, creamy and a tad whiffy.

Granita Flavoured ice, usually with lemon *(limone)*: a healthy Slush Puppy.

Insalata di frutti di mare Seafood salad (usually including prawns, squid and octopus) often simply garnished with lemon and spices.

Involtini Thinly sliced beef, veal or pork, rolled around a stuffing or vegetables, then cooked.

Minestrone A rich vegetable soup usually studded with noodles and sprinkled with grated Parmesan.

Mortadella Mild-tasting pork sausage served as slices.

Nervetti Chewy calf tendons.

Osso buco Beef or veal knuckle slowly braised and served with a flavoursome sauce.

Pancetta Herb-flavoured pork, rolled into a cylinder, sliced and often cubed – the Italian bacon.

Panettone Sweet yellow-coloured bread – a Christmas favourite.

Panna Cream.

Pansotti Pasta pockets with vegetable , herb and cheese fillings, often served with a walnut sauce.

Pappardelle alle lepre Large pasta ribbons with rabbit sauce.

Patatine fritte Chips.

Peperoni Green, yellow or red sweet peppers.

Pesce al cartoccio Fish baked in a tinfoil or parchment envelope.

Pesto The Genovese green sauce made from basil leaves, garlic, Parmesan or pecorino cheese and pine nuts.

Piselli al prosciutto Peas with strips of ham.

Pizza Traditional Neapolitan pizza is cooked in a wood-fired stove and is topped with buffalo mozzarella. Classic varieties include *margherita* (with tomato sauce, cheese and fresh basil), *napoletana* (with tomatoes, mozzarella, ham, capers, oregano and anchovies) and *quattro stagioni* ('four seasons', topped with various vegetables as well as ham).

Polenta Cornmeal flour sometimes made into dense bricks lightly fried and often covered with toppings.

Polenta e coniglio Rabbit stew served with polenta.

Pollo alla cacciatore Chicken with mushrooms and tomatoes cooked in wine.

Pollo all diavola Spicy grilled chicken.

Ragù Meaty sauce (what we'd call 'Bolognese', essentially).

Ricotta A soft cheese made from cows' or sheep's milk.

Risotto Italian arborio or carnaroli rice boiled to be thick and sticky, usually studded with accompaniments like Parmesan cheese, vegetables or fish.

Risotto alla milanese Rice with saffron and wine.

Salsa verde 'Green sauce', made from capers, anchovies, parsley, lemon juice and/or vinegar.

Saltimbocca Veal escalope layered with *prosciutto* and sage; its name literally translates as 'jump in your mouth', a reference to its tart and savoury flavour.

Salvia Sage.

Scaloppine Thin slices of meat (usually veal) coated in flour and sautéed in butter.

Semifreddo A partially frozen dessert; usually ice cream with sponge cake.

Seppia Cuttlefish; its black ink (**nero di seppia**) is used for flavouring some pasta sauces and risotto dishes.

Sogliola Sole.

Spaghetti A long, round, thin pasta, served: *alla bolognese* (with meat and vegetables), *alla carbonara* (with *pancetta* bacon, eggs and black pepper), *al pomodoro* (with tomato sauce), *al sugo/ragù* (with meat sauce), *alle vongole* (with clam sauce), and *al nero di seppia* (with cuttlefish ink).

Spiedini Meat pieces grilled on a skewer over an open flame.

Stufato Meat stew (often beef).

Tagliatelle Long flat egg noodle pasta.

Tiramisù Rich 'pick-me-up' dessert containing layers of espresso- and rum-soaked lady fingers and sweetened mascarpone cheese, all dusted with cocoa powder.

Tonno Tuna.

Tortellini Ring-shaped pasta pockets stuffed with minced, seasoned meat and served covered with a sauce or in a *brodo* (broth).

Trenette Thin noodles served with pesto sauce and potatoes.

Trippe alla fiorentina Beef tripe (stomach lining).

Valpellinentze Hearty mountain soup from Valle d'Aosta, made with Fontina cheese and cabbage.

Vermicelli Very thin pasta resembling 'little worms'.

Vitello Veal (calf meat).

Zabaglione/zabaione Whipped egg yolks flavoured with Marsala wine, served warm as a dessert.

Zampone Stuffed Pigs' trotter.

Zuccotto A liqueur-soaked sponge cake, moulded into a dome with layers of chocolate, nuts and whipped cream.

Zuppa inglese An English-style trifle.

USEFUL WEBSITES & TELEPHONE NUMBERS

There are lots of handy resources and travel websites out there for families travelling to Northern Italy. Here are some you might find useful.

Airlines

The major airlines flying to Northern Italy are:

Alitalia (☎ UK *0870-544-8259*/ Ireland *01-677-5171*; **www.alitalia.co.uk**/ **www.alitalia.ie**); Aer Lingus (☎ Eire *0818 365000*/ UK *0870 876 5000* **www.flyaerlingus.com**); British Airways

(📞 *0870-850 –9850*; ***www.british airways.com***); Flybmi (📞 *0870-6070-555/ 01332-64 –8181* ***www.flybmi.com***); easyJet (📞 *0905-821- 0905*. ***www.easyjet.com***); Jet2 (📞 UK *0871-226-1737*/ Ireland *0818-200-017*; ***www.jet2.com***); Ryanair (📞 UK *0871-246-0000*/Ireland *0818-303-030*; ***www.ryanair.com***); For cheap flights check out LowFareFlights.co.uk which does price comparisons for you.

Tourist Boards: Information About Northern Italy's Regions

For advice about all aspects of travelling to Italy contact the Italian Tourist Board: ENIT (1 Princes Street, London W1B 2AY 📞 free from UK and Ireland *0800-0048-2542*. ***www.enit.it***). The APT regional tourism websites vary in quality; some have excellent content and even direct you to recommended hotels and local operators:

Piedmont: ***ww.regione.piemonte.it***; Liguria: ***www.turismoinliguria.it***; Lombardy: ***www.regione.lombardia.it***; Valle d'Aosta: ***www.regione.vda.it***; Trentino Alto Adige ***www.trentino.to***, ***www.suedtirol.info***; Veneto and the Friuli: ***www.turismo.regione.veneto.it***; ***www.turismo.fvg.it***.

For general info about Northern Italian regions go to ***www.frommers.com*** and ***www.discoveritalia.com.***

Independent Advice With Customer Feedback About Hotels etc

There are many interactive sights full of candid reviews, pictures, advice and even video clips from travellers – these are great for checking if sights, restaurants and hotels are all they are cracked up to be. The biggest resource is ***Tripadvisor.com*** followed by ***www.virtualtourist.com***. Other useful sites include ***HolidayWatchdog.com; Holidays-uncovered.com***; and the excellent ***www.slowtrav.com***, which has insightful entries from travellers who seek out the more obscure and interesting places.

Tour Operators and Specialist Travel Companies

Good places to start on the web are the big travel sites ***expedia.co.uk*** and ***opodo.co.uk***. For decent hotel rates, check out ***www.priceline.co.uk***. For all manner of speciality holidays, go to ***www.infohub.com*** and ***www.specialty travel.com***. Classy hotels and apartments can be found at ***www.andandoslowtravel.com***. Other operators worth investigating are ***www.directholidays.co.uk***; ***Thomsonfly.com***; ***Thomas Cook.com; lastminute.com***; ***www.teletextholidays.co.uk; www.travelcounsellors.com.*** Always check independent reviews of hotels before you book though, to avoid disappointment: the descriptions on many websites are often way off the mark.

For skiing holidays, igluski.com and ifyouski.com have easy to use booking engines. Other good websites for skiers include j2ski.com, ***www.crystalholidays.co.uk***; ***www.inntravel.co.uk***; ***www.waymarkholidays.com***: the last three also specialise in other active and sporty holidays. To save money on ski hire, go to ***snowrental.net***.

Footie-mad kids might like to attend a soccer school: the Milan Junior Camp (via Pastore, 44, 31029 Vittorio Veneto; *0438-941980* ***www.sporteventi.com***) is near Venice. Other sporty and adventure breaks for families can be found at ***www.activitybreaks.com; www.responsibletravel.com; www.exodus.co.uk***.

Villa Rental, Agriturismo, Camping & Hostelling

To rent a villa or appartment have a look at ***www.rentvillas.com***; ***www.homelidays.com***. Agriturismi vary in quality and rusticity, but you are almost always certain to get fab local food and superb value for families. These Italian websites are well worth a gander: ***www.agriturist.it***; ***www.agriturismo.net***; ***www.agriturismo.com***;

UK tour operators specializing in camping holidays include ***www.eurocamp.co.uk***; ***www.keycamp.co.uk.*** For details about all kinds of campsites go to these Italian webpages: ***www.federcampeggio.it***; ***www.easycamping.it***; ***www.camping.it***; ***www.campeggi.com.*** Youth hostelling is a budget option worth considering ***(www.ostellionline.org).***

An even cheaper way of finding suitable family accommodation is to swap your house with someone in Italy: check though the listings at ***Homeexchange.com*** and ***homelink.org.uk***.

Hotel Chains

For good value accommodation you might consider Ibis or Novotel: (***www.ibis.com***; *0801-606-606*) ***(www.novotel.com.*** *0870-609 –0962*). The huge Best Western chain ***(www.bestwestern.co.uk;*** *08457-737-373*) has lots of hotel options, from tired yet cheap to totally chic. Leading Italian hoteliers in the north include the stylish Star Hotels ***(www.starhotels.com;*** *0800-313-132*) and prestigious Turin Hotels International (***www.thi.it;*** *0039 011-5151-926*).

Medical Information

For medical information go to FCO.gov.uk; Ireland: ***www.foreignaffairs.gov.ie***

Train Travel

To plan train journeys go to Ferrovia Italiana ***(www.trenitalia.com)*** or the new site ***www.italiarail.co.uk*** where you can buy tickets. If you're planning to travel through France or other countries on the way to Italy check out ***www.raileurope.com***.

Driving & Car Rental in Italy

There are lots of resources on the web for car drivers. For details about the Italian motorway network and advice about driving on those crazy Italian roads check out ***www.autostrade.it*** and ***www.driving.drive-alive.co.uk***. Advice and Hire:. The leading car hire company websites and their phone numbers are: ***www.avis.co.uk*** (*0844-581-0147*; ***www.budget.co.uk*** (*0844-581-2231*); ***www2.hertz.co.uk*** (*08708-448-844*). For cheap car rental deals go through: ***www.carjet.co.uk*** (*08702-67-67-67*); ***www.easyautos.co.uk*** (*08700-540-205*); ***www.autoeurope.com*** (*0800-358-1229*); ***www.alltravelitaly.com*** UK *0800-018-6682*/Ireland *1800-200-115*).

Family Travel

Travelling as a family can be fun, exciting and create memories to savour, but a bit of preparation will go a long way in forging a smooth journey and holiday. Although there isn't a glut of sites dealing with family travel in Italy specifically, there are plenty of sites providing parents with essential holiday information and even sites popping up for youngsters, too. From what to pack and coping with flights to childcare and accessories, the sites below will help give you a headstart.

www.babygoes2.com: An innovative guide for parents travelling with babies and children with independent recommendations.

www.all4kidsuk.com: Links to tour companies offering family-friendly holidays, some of them in Croatia.

www.youngtravellersclub.co.uk: Currently in its early days, this is a site for children themselves, which deserves to succeed.

www.deabirkett.com: The website of *Guardian* journalist Dea Birkett, who specialises in travelling with children. It includes a very useful Travelling with Kids Forum.

www.babycentre.co.uk: The travel section throws up some interesting articles on family holidays.

www.mumsnet.com: Set up by a journalist, TV producer and radio producer. Product reviews, interviews and planning help.

www.travellingwithchildren.co.uk: Comprehensive site with lots of handy tips for travelling parents.

www.travelforkids.com: An American site that has some good information on different countries with 'what not to leave at home' type tips.

www.familytravelforum.com: Lots of useful stuff on family travel in general.

www.travelwithyourkids.com: Easy to navigate with advice you feel comes from real experience of things having gone wrong!

www.thefamilytravelfiles.com: Heavily American, but with a section on Europe.

www.family-travel.co.uk: Independent advice on travelling with children: Lots of sound general advice.

HolidayTravelWatch.com: Good for travel news and health information.

It may be in Italian but the website ***www.bambinopoli.it*** is worth trying to navigate as it has lots of valuable info about child-friendly hotels, museums and even has a list of babysitting agencies.

RESPONSIBLE TOURISM

Although one could argue any holiday including a flight can't be truly 'green', tourism can contribute positively to the environment and communities UK visitors travel to if investment is used wisely. Firstly, by offsetting carbon emissions from your flight, you can lessen the negative environmental impact of your journey. Secondly, by embracing responsible tourism practises you can choose forward looking companies who care about the resorts and countries we visit, preserving them for the future by working alongside local people. Below are a number of sustainable tourism initiatives and associations to help you plan a family trip and leave as small a 'footprint' as possible on the places you visit.

www.responsibletravel.com: A great source of sustainable travel ideas run by a spokesperson for responsible tourism in the travel industry.

www.tourismconcern.org.uk: Working to reduce social and environmental problems connected to tourism and find ways of improving tourism so that local benefits are increased.

www.climatecare.org.uk: Helping UK holidaymakers offset their carbon emissions through flying by funding sustainable energy projects.

www.thetravelfoundation.org.uk: Produces excellent material on how to care for the places we visit on holiday. It also produces a special guide for children aged 7–10 and parents incorporating 'Hatch the Hatchling Hawksbill' with a play and puzzle book. Highly recommended.

www.abtamembers.org/responsibletourism: The Association of British Travel Agents (ABTA) acts as a focal point for the UK travel industry and is one of the leading groups spearheading responsible tourism.

www.aito.co.uk: The Association of Independent Tour Operators (AITO) is a group of interesting specialist operators leading the field in making holidays sustainable.

Index

See also Accommodations and Restaurant indexes, below.

General

A

B

C

D

E

F

G

N

O

P

R

S

T

U

V

Accommodations

Restaurants

Frommer's®

with your Fami

TRAVEL GUIDES

Frommer's
Normandy With Your Family
ISBN 10: 0470319518
ISBN 13: 9780470319512
£12.99 • $18.99

Frommer's
Brittany With Your Family
ISBN 10: 0470055251
ISBN 13: 9780470055250
£12.99 • $18.99

Frommer's
The Algarve With Your Family
ISBN 10: 047005526X
ISBN 13: 9780470055267
£12.99 • $18.99

Frommer's
Croatia With Yo
Family
ISBN 10: 04700553
ISBN 13: 978047005
£12.99 • $18.99

Frommer's
Mediterranean Spain With Your Family
ISBN 10: 0470055286
ISBN 13: 9780470055281
£12.99 • $18.99

Frommer's
Northern Italy With Your Family
ISBN 10: 0470055278
ISBN 13: 9780470055274
£12.99 • $18.99

Frommer's
The Balearics With Your Family
ISBN 10: 0470055294
ISBN 13: 9780470055298
£12.99 • $18.99

Available from all good bookshops

Frommer's
A Branded Imprint of WI